NCTE Bibliography Series

Your Reading

A Booklist for Junior High
and Middle School Students

Eighth Edition

Alleen Pace Nilsen, Editor,
and the Committee on the Junior High
and Middle School Booklist
of the National Council of Teachers of English

National Council of Teachers of English
1111 Kenyon Road, Urbana, Illinois 61801

Staff Editors: Marya Ryan and Rona S. Smith

Cover Design: R. Maul

Interior Design: Tom Kovacs for TGK Design

NCTE Stock Number 59400-3050

Library of Congress Cataloging-in-Publication Data

Your reading: a booklist for junior high and middle school students/
    Aleen Pace Nilsen, editor, and the Committee on the Junior High and
    Middle School Booklist of the National Council of Teachers of
    English. — 8th ed.
        p.   cm. —(NCTE bibliography series, ISSN 1051-4740)
    Includes indexes.
        Summary: An annotated booklist of recently published fiction and
    nonfiction for middle school and junior high students, arranged
    alphabetically by author under broad topical categories.
        ISBN 0-8141-5940-0
        1. Children's literature—Bibliography.   2. Bibliography—Best
    books—Children's literature.   3. Junior high school students—Books
    and reading.   4. Junior high school libraries—Book lists.
    5. School children—Books and reading.   6. Middle school libraries—
    Book lists. [1. Bibliography—Best books.]   I. Nilsen, Aleen
    Pace.   II. National Council of Teachers of English. Committee on
    the Junior High and Middle School Booklist.   III. Series.
    Z1037.Y68   1991
    [PN1009.A1]
    011.62'5—dc20   91-23533
                                                                                 CIP
                                                                                 AC

Contents

15. Imagining Chills and Thrills: Mysteries and the Supernatural 174
16. Imaginings from Our Ancestors: Classics, Myths, Legends,
    and Folklore   193

    IV Contemporary Poetry and Short Stories   205

17. Books of Poetry   207
18. Collections of Short Stories   214

    V Books to Help with Schoolwork   223

19. Physical Sciences, Math, and Technology   225
20. Natural Sciences   232
21. Social Studies: Contemporary Lives and Issues   242
22. History   252
23. Language Arts, Drama, Music, Art, and Architecture   262

    VI Books Just for You   269

24. Managing Your Life: Physical and Emotional Health   271
25. How-to Books: Crafts, Hobbies, and Future Careers   282
26. Fun and Facts: Entertainment, Jokes, and Interesting
    Information   290

    Appendix for Teachers and Librarians   297
    Best Books for Young Teens 1990, 1989, and 1988   301
    Directory of Publishers   305
    Author Index   312
    Title Index   320
    Subject Index   333
    Contributors   341

Acknowledgments

Our first thanks must go to the publishers who over the course of the past three years provided us with so many review copies. Next are the readers and contributors, who range from committee members' colleagues to our students, our spouses, and our children. Anne Sherrill was especially persuasive in soliciting help from these book lovers in Tennessee: Anna Allred, Lisa A. Buchanan, Jean Roeder Darling, Carol Hitchcock, Mary D. Manning, Patti J. Patterson, Kim Salyer, and Charlotte M. Slagle. Susan Rakow's daughter, Rebecca Rakow, from Cleveland Heights, Ohio, both read and wrote for us, as did the following Arizonans: Karen Allen, Mary Beth Anderly, Nancy J. Baniszewski, Marsha Batterberry, Norma Beauchat, Lisa Bessoff, Paula E. Blackham, Robin D. Bridges, Eliza G. Brunner, Barbara Buchanan, Robyn A. Burnham, Angela R. Calhoun, Mina R. Calvert, Stephen Carter, Catherine Castor, Melissa L. Chaney, Isabel E. Chanley, Margaret Bird Christiansen, Liana Clarkson, Linda Copus, Mary S. Courtney, Alexa R. Cunningham, Karen Cunningham, Phyllis G. Clement, Karen Cure, Myra Dennis, Lisa C. Devine, Wilda Dick, Sally J. Dickman, Michelle Dittface, Mary Ann Eck, Christina Emmons, Faye Williams Fernando, Elaine Fisher, Karen Franevsky, David Gardner, Janice Gilbert, Kathleen M. Gilbert, Libbie Gilmore, Corlie Grenz, Letha K. Grosvenor, Emily Gullikson, Rosemary Hallquist, Jean Harris, Marion W. Hickman II, Kay Morris Holzwordt, Cassandra Horn, Debra Horton, Pamela Jewett, Barbara Jordan, Gerald Hankins Johnston, Linda Howell, Mary J. Kelly, Karen Kennedy, Jullee Ann Konomos, Elaine A. Kross, Dana R. Kyle, Margaret Lammers, H. Kathleen Lee, P. J. Linsley, Lorraine Little, Cathie Lowmiller, Susan Huegel Lundy, Linda L. Lye, Randy Magie, Robin McAllister, Larry Mann, Veronica Marshall, Annette Mickle, Donna Miller, Archie Milhollon, Mary Millhollon, Shiela M. Millhollon, Caron G. Moore, Brenda J. Napier, Nancy Newendyke, Debra O'Huallachain, Carol L. Pachek, Gayle R. Parent, Matt Parsons, Whitney Peterson, Donna R. Pyle, Marcy Reichenberger, Donna J. Reynolds, Maria Richards, Margaret Roberts, Dianne Ruderman, Ellen Marie Ruhlman, Catherine Rushing-Vontsolos, Eileen Sacks, Louise Sallquist, Michelle Schmitt, James A. Schmitz, Sandra K. Schultz, Lucee K. Seiter, Kirsten J. Shields, Heather Shumway,

Deborah Siegel, Janet Smith, Lois Dahlgren Snider, Joan L. Snyder, Jonah D. Spaulding, Betty Upchurch, Judith Van, Kathleen G. Victor, Carolyn Wagstaff, Susan Wedell, Romaine A. Westberg, Debra Wheelis, Amy Whetten, Nancie Whitaker, and Connie S. Young. California contributors include Anne C. Burns and Nicolette Nilsen Wickman.

A special thanks to our colleague Ken Donelson, who gave us encouragement and lent us his graduate students as reviewers, and to my husband Don Nilsen, who, for more months than he cares to remember, carried great heaps of book wrappings to the alley and in every room of his house stepped over and around piles of books. And another special thanks to NCTE staff members Miles Myers, Michael Spooner, and Rona Smith, who not only listened to interminable moanings about how impossible this task was, but pitched in to pull it all together when the rest of us were exhausted.

Alleen Pace Nilsen, for the Committee on the
Junior High and Middle School Booklist
Tempe, Arizona, March 1991

Foreword

The National Council of Teachers of English is proud to publish four different booklists, renewed on a regular rotation, in its bibliography series. The four are *Adventuring with Books* (pre-K through grade 6), *Your Reading* (middle school/junior high), *Books for You* (senior high), and *High Interest—Easy Reading* (junior/senior high reluctant readers). Conceived as resources for teachers and students alike, these volumes reference thousands of the most recent children's and young adults' trade books. The works listed cover a wide range of topics, from preschool ABC books to science fiction novels for high school seniors; from wordless picture books to nonfiction works on family stresses, computers, and mass media.

Each edition of an NCTE booklist is compiled by a group of teachers and librarians, under leadership appointed by the NCTE Executive Committee. Working for most of three or four years with new books submitted regularly by publishers, the committee members review, select, and annotate the hundreds of works to be listed in their new edition. The members of the committee that compiled this volume are listed on one of the first pages.

Of course, no single book is right for everyone or every purpose, so inclusion of a work in this booklist is not necessarily an endorsement from NCTE. However, it is an indication that, in the view of the professionals who make up the booklist committee, the work in question is worthy of teachers' and students' attention, perhaps for its informative, perhaps its aesthetic qualities. On the other hand, exclusion from an NCTE booklist is not necessarily a judgment on the quality of a given book or publisher. Many factors—space, time, availability of certain books, publisher participation—may influence the final shape of the list.

We hope that you will find this booklist useful and that you will collect the other booklists in the NCTE series. We feel that these volumes contribute substantially to our mission of helping to improve instruction in English and the language arts. We think you will agree.

Michael Spooner
NCTE Senior Editor for Publications

Introduction for Young Readers*

Many people read many books to prepare this list for your use. We hope it will help you find new books to enjoy in your free time as well as to help with school assignments. Here are answers to some of the questions we think you might have as you start to use this booklist.

What books are described?

Our job was to look at the books published for young readers in 1988, 1989, and 1990 and choose from those books the ones we think you would most like to read. However, there were more books published over the last three years than any one committee could possibly read, so we can't guarantee that we examined every book. Nevertheless, we have tried to include those we think you will find useful.

How is the list organized?

Within each chapter, most of the books are listed alphabetically according to the authors' last names. (The exception is series books, which are grouped at the back of each chapter in alphabetical order according to the series name.) After we had read and made notes on hundreds of books, we sat down and tried to figure out what these books might have in common from your standpoint and then grouped them in that way. But please realize that our categories overlap. For example, a book about war may also be about family relationships, and a book about family relationships may also be about a boy-girl relationship. Before you start looking at the specific descriptions of books, spend a few minutes with the table of contents: the first three sections, "Connections," "Understandings," and "Imaginings," are mostly fiction and biographies. After these sections come books of short stories and poetry, and then we go on to "Books to Help with Schoolwork," and "Books Just for You," which includes books dealing with physical and emotional health, followed by how-to books that talk about hobbies, crafts, and future careers. We end with a chapter

---

*The Appendix for Teachers and Librarians begins on p. 297.

on "Fun and Facts," or pleasure-time reading, which is what we hope this whole book is about.

Do you include books that come in series?

Yes, but we didn't try to list all the titles. Whether paperback or hardback, fiction or nonfiction, we listed the series by name, told a little about the series, and gave some of the titles as examples. We couldn't include all of the titles because many of the series are ongoing, and by the time you read this, there will already be new titles. Also, we didn't have enough space because some of the series, like *Sweet Dreams* and *Choose Your Own Adventure*, already have more than a hundred titles. These books are most often listed under the names of the series rather than under the authors' names because many of the series books are written by groups of people rather than individuals. With the paperback series books, you should realize that you may not be able to find the exact title you want. Bookstores carry series books for only a few months before they return unsold copies to the publisher. Publishers sometimes update books they think will sell well and send them out again with new covers.

What do the stars at the ends of the descriptions mean?

One of the ways we try to be sure we are doing our job is to look at what other people say about new books. Many groups of teachers, librarians, editors, and even some groups of young people review new books and make lists at the end of each year telling which books they think are the best ones published in that year. If one star is printed by a description of a book, it means that one group put this book on its "best book" list. A book that has two stars is on two "best book" lists, while three stars mean that the book is on three "best book" lists, and so forth. But please don't ignore the books that don't have any stars, because that doesn't mean they aren't good books. It simply means that they didn't come to the attention of prize givers. Besides, what makes a book good for one reader may not be the same as what makes it good for another reader. The important point is whether the author is writing about something—an idea, a hobby, a fear, or a hope—that matters to you as a reader.

At the ends of the chapters, there are lists called "Recommended Books Published before 1988." What are these lists for?

Our main purpose is to bring newly written books to your attention, and that's why we focus on books published within the last three years. However, we all know that many good books were published before 1988, and when you go to the library to find good books to read, we didn't think that you would want to have to refer to the seven previous editions of this booklist. So we made a list of titles from past "best book" lists that we know people have especially liked. The listings include the original year of publication, the author's name, and the name of the publisher for each book. Most of the books first appeared as hardbacks, and it's the hardback publisher whose name we've included, but by now you can also find many of them in paperback.

Why don't the last chapters of this book include lists of "Recommended Books Published before 1988"?

The last part of the book is mostly nonfiction, and nonfiction books are more likely to go out of date than fiction. For example, if you want a book on how to run a computer, you want the most recent one, not one that is four or five years old. With science and technology, and even with such social issues as ecology, criminal justice, or sex education, there are changes in information as well as in people's attitudes, and so you are better off looking for recent books.

How can I write to an author?

At the back of the book, there's a directory of publishers, which you can use if you wish to write a letter to an author. Address the letter to the author, in care of his or her publisher. To be on the safe side, write "Please Forward" on the outside of the envelope. Also, to improve your chances of getting an answer, enclose a stamped envelope addressed to yourself. And be sure to write your address on your letter, too, so that if the letter and the envelope get separated, the author will be able to get in touch with you. You can also use the publisher's address if you want to order a book.

Happy reading. We hope you enjoy these books as much as did the members of the committee and the many other teachers, librarians, college students, and young readers who examined over 5,000 books to prepare this list for you.

I Connections

Leaving childhood and moving into adulthood is one of the most traumatic changes that occurs in a person's lifetime, second only to the changes a baby goes through in its first two or three years of life. As people grow up, they have to get to know themselves—to "connect" with themselves—and that's what the books in this section are about. Rachel in Norma Fox Mazer's *After the Rain* writes to her brother, "There are times when I feel like I have this other thing, this something, that's living in me, messing around with me. I'm not trying to make excuses. It's there! Separate but united. Me and not me. D'ya know what I mean . . . ?" Richard Peck's Buck Mendenhall in *Remembering the Good Times* is also trying to connect with himself when he observes, "Every morning I woke up, I had to check me out to see who was there. Some mornings I was a kid. Some mornings I was a maniac."

With all these changes, teenagers sometimes surprise even themselves, not to mention their families and friends. Teens are suddenly different from the kids they were, and they treat the rest of their families differently and expect their families to treat them differently, too. They meet new friends and get to know a much more varied group of people. And on top of all this, boys and girls begin to relate to each other differently. In all these changes, authors find the ingredients for the fascinating stories that we have grouped into the four categories of connecting with ourselves, our families, our friends and foes, and our boyfriends and girlfriends.

1   Connecting with Ourselves: Accomplishments and Growing Up

1.1   Ames, Mildred. **Who Will Speak for the Lamb?** Harpercrest, 1989. 215 pp. ISBN 0-06-020112-6.

Seventeen-year-old Julie Peters is desperate to be out from under the pressure of the modeling career her mother has directed since Julie was nine. While she is still struggling with that problem, the family moves, and at her new school, Julie joins a demonstration against the slaughter of a lamb in a high school agriculture class. Julie's interest in the animal rights movement and in Jeff, who is one of its leaders, gives her the courage to speak up—not just for animals but for her own freedom as well.

1.2   Angell, Judie. **Leave the Cooking to Me.** Bantam Books, 1990. 185 pp. ISBN 0-533-05849-3.

Shirley makes a deal with her mother. She promises to have a productive summer if her mother won't ask any questions. Shirley develops a successful catering business, and the promise proves difficult for both of them. ★

1.3   Auch, Mary Jane. **Glass Slippers Give You Blisters.** Holiday House, 1989. 109 pp. ISBN 0-8234-0752-7.

Kelly wants a part in Riverton Junior High's production of *Cinderella*, but she gets assigned to the production team instead. Her artistic grandmother is behind her a hundred percent, but her overorganized, practical mother disapproves of anything to do with the theater. Through mishaps and good timing, Kelly helps salvage the show, wins her grandmother's gratitude, and opens a door to communicating with her mother.

1.4   Betancourt, Jeanne. **Not Just Party Girls.** Bantam Books, 1989. 165 pp. ISBN 0-553-28514-9.

Anne seems to have everything—money, friends, beauty, and a handsome boy who loves her. But then she spends time working with some nuns to help the children of California farm workers, and she sees a side of life that makes her feel uncomfortable about her own lifestyle. She learns a lot as she struggles with decisions about what she wants to do with her life.

1.5   Branscum, Robbie. **Cameo Rose.** Illustrated by Beth Peck. Harper and Row, 1989. 84 pp. ISBN 0-06-020559-8.

Cameo Rose is sure she's a girl, especially when Billy Joe is around. But since Grandma died, there has been no one in the Arkansas hills to teach Cam the finer points of being a girl and growing into a woman. Nevertheless, she is strong and smart and knows that she's Grandpa's right hand, both on the farm and in his job as sheriff. But when Cam takes it on herself to find out who murdered Homer Satterfield, she offends most of her neighbors and, to her sorrow, finds out more than she anticipated.

1.6   Caseley, Judith. **Kisses.** Alfred A. Knopf, 1990. 186 pp. ISBN 0-679-80166-9.

At the age of fifteen, Hannah Gold enters a competition as a violinist in the all-state orchestra. She earns a seat (eighteenth place out of forty-five chairs), but then troubles begin piling up. She can't get a date, her parents argue, her grandfather dies, and she worries about the abuse Deidre gets from her boyfriend. ★

1.7   Christiansen, C. B. **A Small Pleasure.** Avon/Flare Books, 1988. 116 pp. ISBN 0-380-70699-7.

Wray Jean Child has a "Three Year Plan" for becoming a popular, accepted, involved teenager, but her father's death changes her ideas about what's important. Only then does she begin to understand the small pleasures in life.

1.8   Cole, Brock. **Celine.** Farrar, Straus and Giroux, 1989. 216 pp. ISBN 0-374-31234-6.

Sixteen-year-old Celine is an artist trying to finish a painting for art class—while rewriting an essay on Holden Caulfield, babysitting for the weekend, and adjusting to life with a stepmother only six years older than she. Celine's father, in Europe on a lecture tour, left with orders that she "show a little maturity" before being allowed to spend the summer in Italy—a trip she doesn't plan to return from. ★★★★★

1.9   Coryell, Susan. **Eaglebait.** Harcourt Brace Jovanovich/Gulliver Books, 1989. 187 pp. ISBN 0-15-200442-4.

Wardy Spinks can be instantly spotted as a misfit, and bullies single him out for abuse. The attention of a demanding science teacher from Germany, a pretty girl, and Grandma Lou all help Wardy see how to take control and turn his life around.

1.10 Gerber, Merrill Joan. **Handsome as Anything.** Scholastic, 1990. 168 pp. ISBN 0-590-43019-X.

The summer before Rachel's senior year in high school is an exciting one. Everyone offers her advice, but no two people agree. Some tell her to marry. But if she does, who should she marry? Avram, the serious theology student? Jason, the Zen Buddhist who searches for enlightenment? Or Karl, the impish homebody? It's obvious that she can't please her parents or either of her sisters—the dedicated feminist Franny or the wedding-bound Erica. Will the full scholarship to go away to Mountainside School help her decide who she is? At least she'll be away from home and living in unique surroundings.

1.11 Glenn, Mel. **Squeeze Play.** Clarion Books, 1989. 135 pp. ISBN 0-89919-859-7.

Baseball player Jeremy is about to enter sixth grade when a wild pitch leaves him with a temporary patch over one eye, and he finds a permanent friend in Mr. Janowicz, an elderly Holocaust survivor. At school, Jeremy's teacher acts more as if he's running a boot camp than sixth grade, but with Mr. Janowicz's guidance and encouragement, Jeremy speaks out so that the whole class, including the teacher, learns something about oppression and respect for others' values.

1.12 Greene, Constance C. **Monday I Love You.** Harper and Row, 1988. 170 pp. ISBN 0-06-022205-0.

Fifteen-year-old Grace Schmidt wears a size 38D bra, and her classmates make sure she's miserable about it. She can't turn to her parents, since they barely pay attention to her. At school she feels alone except in her friendship with her gym teacher. But after a cruel trick from her classmates distresses her, a strange incident gives her the strength to take control of her life.

1.13 Johnston, Norma. **The Potter's Wheel.** William Morrow, 1988. 246 pp. ISBN 0-688-06463-9.

Sixteen-year-old Laura spends the summer of her parents' divorce with her eccentric Grandmother Van Zandt and many other relatives. The Van Zandt relatives are not your normal family, and Laura's summer is not your normal summer vacation. While Laura works through her problems, she must also help her relatives with theirs, and she comes to realize that she shouldn't feel so sorry for herself.

1.14   Jones, Janice. **Secrets of a Summer Spy.** Bradbury Press, 1990. 192 pp. ISBN 0-02-747861-0.

Ronnie Windslow has returned to Harbor Island for the summer, but this year things have changed. Her best friends, Amy and Jimmy, are now more concerned with each other than with her, and the old gang is breaking up. Feeling left out, Ronnie develops a friendship with the eccentric old Mrs. Peet and finds out that people are not always what they seem.

1.15   Katz, Welwyn Wilton. **False Face.** Margaret K. McElderry Books, 1988. 176 pp. ISBN 0-689-50419-5.

Laney is in the ninth grade, her parents are divorced, and she thinks her mother likes her older sister best. But when Laney finds some ancient Indian artifacts, her life takes an interesting turn. ★

1.16   Kirshenbaum, Binnie. **Short Subject.** Orchard Books, 1989. 193 pp. ISBN 0-531-08436-1.

Audrey bitterly resents having the figure of a ten year old at age fourteen. She is an avid fan of old movies, however, and escapes to the "big screen" almost every day. Trouble comes when she decides to become movie material herself by becoming a thief.

1.17   Koertge, Ron. **The Arizona Kid.** Little, Brown/Joy Street Books, 1988. 228 pp. ISBN 0-316-50101-8.

Billy, with his Izod shirts and sunblock, heads west to Arizona to spend the summer with his Uncle Wes and work at a racetrack. Things are certainly different there than in Missouri. The sun is hotter, the girls are cuter, and Uncle Wes is gay. In three months, Billy learns about himself and growing up. He finds his direction, experiences his first romance, defends the helpless, saves the day, and comes to understand his uncle. The frank language may offend some readers.

1.18   Little, Jean. **Hey World, Here I Am!** Illustrated by Sue Truesdell. Harper and Row, 1989. 88 pp. ISBN 0-06-024006-7.

Teenager Kate keeps a journal that includes drawings, poems, and funny and sincere stories. She tells all about her problems with her mother and her quarrels with her best friend—and makes all kinds of observations and funny remarks about them. ★★

1.19 Livingston, Alan W. **Ronnie Finkelhof, Superstar.** Fawcett Books, 1988. 184 pp. ISBN 0-449-70134-4.

According to his classmates, Ronnie Finkelhof is a nerd—he's tall, skinny, and awkward and gets good grades. But his secret passion for guitar playing and songwriting turns him into Spartacus, rock and roll superstar. How will he keep his two lives separate? You'll get a good look behind the glamor and flash of the music industry in this book.

1.20 Mazer, Norma Fox. **Babyface.** Morrow Junior Books, 1990. 165 pp. ISBN 0-688-08752-3.

Toni Chessmore's life suddenly changes when Julie, her best friend of fourteen years, has to move away because of her parents' separation. Timid and slight, Toni must overcome the loss of her bubbly, lively friend by developing more of her own friendships and spending time alone discovering herself. She also learns something from her older sister that changes her feelings toward her parents and makes her think about their relationship in a new way.

1.21 McHargue, Georgess. **See You Later, Crocodile.** Delacorte Press, 1988. 226 pp. ISBN 0-440-50052-4.

Johanna, a young teenager, takes on more responsibility than she'd bargained for when she agrees to help Aggie Pease with her cats. Aggie, an eccentric old lady who has spent a lifetime caring for stray cats, now has fourteen of them! When Aggie falls and breaks her hip, Johanna finds herself not only feeding the cats, but also handling all of Aggie's personal business—including keeping her house from being condemned by the Health Department.

1.22 Miklowitz, Gloria D. **Anything to Win.** Delacorte Press, 1989. 138 pp. ISBN 0-385-29750-5.

Cam Potter is going to fulfill dreams for himself, his father, and his coach by winning a college football scholarship. When the pressure is on to become bigger in order to compete, he agrees to take steroids. He gets results, including some he hadn't anticipated. ★

1.23 Paulsen, Gary. **The Voyage of the *Frog*.** Orchard Books, 1989. 141 pp. ISBN 0-531-05805-0.

The *Frog* is a beautiful, strong, old sailboat. But David doesn't want it—not this way, as a sudden inheritance from his dearly loved Uncle Owen. He takes the boat out to the ocean to fulfill his uncle's final request and unexpectedly finds himself faced not just with grief, but with a nine-day struggle to survive storms, sharks, and starvation. ★★★★

1.24 Paulsen, Gary. **The Winter Room.** Orchard/Richard Jackson Books, 1989. 103 pp. ISBN 0-531-08439-6.

Eldon tells what the year was like on the old northern Minnesota farm with his brother Wayne, his mother and father, and his uncles, Nels and David. You can smell, hear, and feel life on this farm through every season—the seasons of beginnings, of the slaughter of animals, and most important of all, of telling stories. Uncle David tells family stories in the winter—stories they all believe until he tells one that Wayne says could never be true. Eldon feels betrayed and calls Uncle David a liar, little realizing what his accusation will bring. ★★

1.25 Powell, Randy. **My Underrated Year.** Farrar, Straus and Giroux, 1988. 182 pp. ISBN 0-374-35109-0.

Roger Ottosen thinks his sophomore year in high school is going to be his best ever. He has a strong chance of making the varsity football team and of being "number one" on the tennis team. But all that changes when the Mountain family moves to town. Paul Mountain has a very good chance of beating Roger for the running back position, and Paul's sister, Mary Jo—whom Roger has a crush on—plans to challenge him for the top position on the tennis team. Roger grows a lot during the year, both physically and emotionally.

1.26 Ryan, Mary E. **I'd Rather Be Dancing.** Delacorte Press, 1989. 149 pp. ISBN 0-440-50121-0.

Katie Kusik is a seventeen year old coping with many changes. She has just moved to her stepfather's home in Manhattan, leaving her boyfriend in Brooklyn, and she has to adjust to the demands of the summer program at the prestigious but challenging American Dance Conservatory. Over the summer, she must decide how important her family, friends, romance, and dance are. This book is a sequel to *Dance a Step Closer*, but you do not need to have read the earlier book to enjoy this one.

1.27   Shettle, Andrea. **Flute Song Magic.** Avon Books, 1990. 217 pp. ISBN 0-380-76225-0.

Flutirr is called upon a quest that endangers his high position in his society's class structure. He is lured into this quest by his love of music as it is played by a member of the lower class: "This boy made the very stones sing, the very light on the waters tinkle, and the very grasses on the riverbank whisper poems of warmth." Music carries the sounds of nature and cannot, for Flutirr, be limited to a system. In his discovery of the poetic nature of music, Flutirr also discovers the value of all beings and the fallacy of his society's structure.

1.28   Springstubb, Tricia. **With a Name Like Lulu, Who Needs More Trouble?** Illustrated by Jill Kastner. Delacorte Press, 1989. 167 pp. ISBN 0-385-29823-4.

Lulu is a typical junior high kid, except that she's unusually shy. Despite her shyness, she's a good Little League catcher—a skill that comes in handy when she happens to be walking down the sidewalk at the very moment that a toddler climbs out of an apartment window three stories up. Lulu catches the baby and becomes an instant hero. Lulu learns to cope with the uncomfortable role of celebrity, and in the process, she learns some things about getting along with her mother and something about her own feelings.

1.29   Voigt, Cynthia. **Seventeen against the Dealer.** Atheneum, 1989. 189 pp. ISBN 0-689-31497-3.

If you've read Cynthia Voigt's other books about the Tillermans, such as *Homecoming* and *Dicey's Song*, you'll probably want to read this final volume, in which twenty-one-year-old Dicey starts her own boatyard business. She's determined to succeed, so much so that she almost forgets about the people she loves. ★★

1.30   Wersba, Barbara. **The Farewell Kid.** Harper and Row, 1989. 155 pp. ISBN 0-06-026379-2.

Heidi Rosenbloom is seventeen and a half, and this book starts with the year she realizes that her mission in life is to save all the stray dogs in New York. It is also the year that she says, "Goodbye to the male species," which has caused her "nothing but pain, and good-bye to adolescence—which had been like a long illness—and good-bye to living on Manhattan's Upper East Side." It's all these farewells that give the book its title, but by the end, Heidi's also ready to say hello to a few things in her life. She's the same Heidi Rosenbloom that readers liked in *Just Be Gorgeous* and *Wonderful Me.* ★

1.31   Wersba, Barbara. **Wonderful Me.** Harper and Row, 1989. 156 pp. ISBN 0-06-026361-X.

Heidi Rosenbloom is independent and lighthearted but lonely. Her mother wants her to be a glamour girl, while her father wants her to be an Einstein. Heidi wants neither and chooses to become a professional dog walker. She already has eight customers, along with a lot of daydreams and a collection of anonymous love letters. In this sequel to *Just Be Gorgeous*, Heidi learns much about herself, as well as about the emotional problems of others.

1.32   Wojciechowski, Susan. **Patty Dillman of Hot Dog Fame.** Orchard Books, 1989. 180 pp. ISBN 0-531-05810-7.

Patty met her best friend, Tracy, when they were in the same nursery school car pool, and Tracy taught Patty to stuff Hershey Kiss wrappers up her nose. They've been involved in dumb stunts ever since, and Saint Ignatius Junior High wouldn't be the same without them. In this continuation of their adventures, which started in *And the Other, Gold*, Patty begins to see that there's more to life than having a "hotdog" boyfriend.

1.33   Zable, Rona S. **An Almost Perfect Summer.** Bantam/Starfire Books, 1989. 201 pp. ISBN 0-553-27967-X.

Ellen creates exciting fantasies about her upcoming summer as a mother's helper on Cape Cod. Her romantic dreams show some potential of coming true, but her two charges—one, a spoiled ten year old, and the other a five year old who doesn't yet talk—are far from ideal.

Series

1.34   **The Portraits Collection.** Fawcett Books.

This new series focuses on a different girl in each story and shows how she overcomes a problem or takes a step toward maturity.

Titles include *Attitude* by Marilyn Kaye, *Summer Heat* by Janet Quin-Harkin, and *Stealing Josh* by Susan Blake.

Recommended Books about Accomplishments and Growing Up Published before 1988

Arrick, Fran. *God's Radar*. Bradbury Press, 1983.

Blume, Judy. *Are You There God? It's Me, Margaret*. Bradbury Press, 1970.

Blume, Judy. *Deenie*. Bradbury Press, 1973.

Blume, Judy. *Then Again, Maybe I Won't*. Bradbury Press, 1971.

Byars, Betsy. *The Cartoonist*. Viking, 1978.

Clements, Bruce. *Anywhere Else but Here*. Farrar, Straus and Giroux, 1980.

Cross, Gillian. *Chartbreaker*. Holiday House, 1987.

Danziger, Paula. *The Cat Ate My Gymsuit*. Delacorte Press, 1974.

Danziger, Paula. *The Pistachio Prescription*. Delacorte Press, 1978.

Davis, Jenny. *Good-bye and Keep Cool*. Orchard Books, 1987.

Gardam, Jane. *Bilgewater*. Greenwillow Books, 1977.

Hall, Lynn. *The Leaving*. Charles Scribner's Sons, 1980.

Hamilton, Virginia. *M. C. Higgins, the Great*. Macmillan, 1974.

Lipsyte, Robert. *The Contender*. Harper and Row, 1967.

Lipsyte, Robert. *One Fat Summer*. Harper and Row, 1977.

Lowry, Lois. *Autumn Street*. Houghton Mifflin, 1980.

Myers, Walter Dean. *Hoops*. Delacorte Press, 1981.

Naylor, Phyllis Reynolds. *A String of Chances*. Atheneum, 1982.

Oneal, Zibby. *In Summer Light*. Viking Penguin, 1985.

Oneal, Zibby. *The Language of Goldfish*. Viking Penguin, 1980.

Paterson, Katherine. *Come Sing, Jimmy Jo*. Lodestar Books, 1985.

Peck, Robert Newton. *A Day No Pigs Would Die*. Alfred A. Knopf, 1972.

Potok, Chaim. *The Chosen*. Simon and Schuster, 1967.

Rylant, Cynthia. *A Fine White Dust*. Bradbury Press, 1986.

Rylant, Cynthia. *Waiting to Waltz: A Childhood*. Bradbury Press, 1984.

Sachs, Marilyn. *The Fat Girl*. E. P. Dutton, 1984.

Sachs, Marilyn. *A Summer's Lease*. E. P. Dutton, 1979.

Savage, Deborah. *A Rumour of Otters*. Houghton Mifflin, 1986.

Slepian, Jan. *The Night of the Bozos*. E. P. Dutton, 1983.

Voigt, Cynthia. *The Runner*. Atheneum, 1985.

Walsh, Jill Paton. *Unleaving*. Farrar, Straus and Giroux, 1976.

2 Connecting with Families: Close Relationships

2.1   Adler, C. S. **Help, Pink Pig!** G. P. Putnam's Sons, 1990. 160 pp. ISBN 0-399-22183-2.

Eleven-year-old Amanda leaves her accepting grandmother, Pearlie, to start a new life with her critical mother in Los Angeles. A lonely latchkey child, Amanda creates a fantasy world around a gift from her grandmother, a rose quartz miniature pig. But Amanda's magical world is threatened by intruders, the "downstairs" children—scared Robbie and the bully, Angel. What will Amanda do?

2.2   Adler, C. S. **The Lump in the Middle.** Houghton Mifflin, 1989. 154 pp. ISBN 0-89919-869-4.

Ria is the oldest sister in the family, the pretty, athletic one. Sara is the baby, the favorite. Thirteen-year-old Kelsey is in the middle, the misfit. When their father loses his job, Kelsey and her family leave their home and friends to stay in a borrowed beach house. Kelsey feels angry, lonely, picked on, and unappreciated. Sometimes she runs off to the bay where the soothing sand and sun ease her hurt. There, she meets Gabe. Anxious to please him, she lies about her age, and to her surprise, he likes her. Between the raging battles with her mother and sisters, both Kelsey's relationship with Gabe and her self-confidence grow stronger.

2.3   Adler, C. S. **One Sister Too Many: A Sequel to *Split Sisters*.** Macmillan, 1989. 176 pp. ISBN 0-02-700271-3.

Case desperately wants people to think she's a good kid in spite of her "fast mouth." She's caught between her older sister, who's interested in boys, and a baby sister who isn't interested in anything except getting relief from a colicky stomach. This book continues the story of a likable family that first appeared in *Split Sisters*, but you don't need to have read the first book to enjoy this one.

2.4   Auch, Mary Jane. **Mom Is Dating Weird Wayne.** Holiday House, 1988. 146 pp. ISBN 0-8234-0720-9.

When Jenna's parents divorce, it's bad enough that her mother has to find a job, but then she also finds a boyfriend, television station WAKY's "Wacky Weatherman," who is as crazy as his title. Jenna resents him and hopes for her parents' reconciliation, despite her father's remarriage. Fortunately, Jenna finds some light moments amidst the turmoil.

2.5   Auch, Mary Jane. **A Sudden Change of Family.** Holiday House, 1990. 152 pp. ISBN 0-8234-0842-6.

Excitement overtakes Katy the summer before sixth grade as she and her mom plan a trip to the Connecticut seashore. All her mom's family, the Whitmarshes, lives there. It seems that nothing can keep Katy and her cousin Julie from having a great time. But then they discover that Katy's mother was adopted and Katy isn't really related to the Whitmarshes at all. Katy's mom leaves for Pennsylvania in the middle of the night in search of her "real" family—and Katy has to adjust to having *two* families.

2.6   Baehr, Patricia. **Louisa Eclipsed.** William Morrow, 1988. 140 pp. ISBN 0-688-07682-3.

Louisa is spending the summer with her grandfather, younger sister, and other relatives on the family farm. It is a summer of change. She must learn to turn around her self-centeredness when her grandfather becomes ill and her younger sister competes with her for a boy's attention.

2.7   Bawden, Nina. **The Outside Child.** Lothrop, Lee and Shepard Books, 1989. 160 pp. ISBN 0-688-08965-8.

Accompanied by her two eccentric aunts, thirteen-year-old Jane visits her seafaring father and accidentally discovers a family secret—a half-brother and half-sister. Hurt, angry, and wondering why she has never been allowed to meet her father's other children, Jane, with her best friend, Plato Jones, supersleuths her way to the truth while roaming around London during her summer vacation. ★★

2.8   Birdseye, Tom. **Tucker.** Holiday House, 1990. 112 pp. ISBN 0-8234-0813-2.

Sixth-grader Tucker lives with his divorced father in Idaho, and the most important thing on his mind is the upcoming hunting season when he thinks he will get to shoot his first deer. But then his little sister comes to stay, and life changes abruptly. He finally gets to kill his deer, but the experience isn't at all what he expected.

2.9		Brooks, Bruce. **Everywhere.** HarperCollins, 1990. 70 pp. ISBN 0-06-020729-9.

"Poppa has suffered a heart attack," is what the ten-year-old narrator's grandmother tells him, and his world is shaken. It was Poppa, his grandfather, who helped him learn to build things, who listened to every Yankees baseball game with him, and with whom he had the closest relationship. When Aunt Lucy, the local nurse, comes to help, she brings her nephew, Dooley. He convinces the boy that by switching his grandfather's soul with that of an animal, his grandfather will live. ★★★

2.10		Cannon, A. E. **Cal Cameron by Day, Spider-Man by Night.** Delacorte Press, 1988. 133 pp. ISBN 0-385-29635-5.

Cal Cameron plans to coast through his last two years at Scenic View High School as the big man on campus. Enter Marti Jeffs, a new student who is not the least bit interested in making a career of being popular. Cal and Marti become friends, but Cal is careful to keep his popular image and Marti separate. Through his double life, Cal discovers a different side of himself and comes to understand some of the complex relationships between his father, his grandfather, his brother, and himself.

2.11		Carkeet, David. **The Silent Treatment.** Harper and Row, 1988. 280 pp. ISBN 0-06-020979-8.

Ricky and his off-the-wall friend Nate eagerly anticipate summer vacation and the excitement of solving their county's Gold Rush treasure hunt for a $2,000 prize. Unfortunately, Ricky's "perfect" older brother and the beautiful but weird Cindy Cargill always seem one step ahead in solving the puzzle. Almost as puzzling as the clues for the treasure hunt are the secrets that Ricky's parents keep. Fortunately, Ricky makes progress with both puzzles.

2.12		Close, Jessie. **The Warping of Al.** Harper and Row, 1990. 281 pp. ISBN 0-06-021280-2.

Al doesn't know yet who he is, but he is pretty sure he can't become the person his father wants him to be. He can't seem to talk to his father—or to his mother, either. He loves his grandmother, Goopie, and is close to her. He can talk to his sister E (for Ethel), but he isn't close to his sisters Flavia and Dottie. He has a hard time finding meaning in his life and in the world around him.

2.13   Cole, Norma. **The Final Tide.** Margaret K. McElderry Books, 1990. 153 pp. ISBN 0-689-50510-8.

The Tennessee Valley Authority has told all of the families in low-lying farmland that they must move because a dam is being built and a reservoir will soon cover their homes. The Haws family, except for Grandma, accepts the inevitable and prepares for the move. Fourteen-year-old Geneva is given the task of convincing Grandma Haws that the move is for the best. Geneva also has the task of becoming a "young lady" because her mother thinks it is time for Geneva to drop her tomboy ways of dressing and playing.

2.14   Colman, Hila. **Forgotten Girl.** Crown, 1990. 153 pp. ISBN 0-517-57591-4.

As a fourteen year old, Kelly finds life difficult to face because her mother treats her as a forgotten girl. Ignoring her, Kelly's mother divides her time and energy between her mayoral campaign and her seventeen-year-old son, Eliot. When Kelly discovers that Eliot is living a secret life, she must decide what to do. Her friendship with Dan helps her deal with her troubles.

2.15   Cooney, Caroline B. **Family Reunion.** Bantam Books, 1989. 167 pp. ISBN 0-553-05836-3.

Shelley is nervous when her "blended" New York family plans a visit to her cousins in Iowa. She's always thought of them as "The Perfects," and doesn't know whether to be relieved or disappointed to find that her aunt's family isn't so perfect after all. ★

2.16   Cresswell, Helen. **The Bagthorpes Liberated: Being the Seventh Part of the Bagthorpe Saga.** Macmillan, 1989. 186 pp. ISBN 0-02-725441-0.

When the Bagthorpes return from a holiday in Wales to find forty-one pints of sour milk in the drive, a tramp sleeping in Jack's bed, and the refrigerator and freezer full of slimy, rotting food, it doesn't take a municipal judge to see the injustice of leaving all the cleaning up to Mrs. Bagthorpe, especially since it was Mr. Bagthorpe who turned off the electricity. Liberation is called for! But liberating the wildly eccentric brood of Bagthorpe offspring, grandparents, relatives, and guests turns out to produce more hilarity than equality.

2.17   Danziger, Paula. **Everyone Else's Parents Said Yes.** Delacorte Press, 1989. 115 pp. ISBN 0-385-29805-6.

Matthew Martin will be eleven years old in just five days, and he wants a sleepover birthday party for all the boys in his class. Matthew also wants a big, sugary birthday cake and treats galore, a major problem for his health-nut mother. His mother will grant this small request—if only Matthew agrees to stop bugging his older sister, who plans to have her first date on the same evening as the birthday party. He doesn't know if he can stop teasing his sister—or any of the girls in his class, for that matter. That is, until they all decide to gang up on him and declare him a natural disaster.

2.18   Deaver, Julie Reece. **First Wedding, Once Removed.** Harper and Row, 1990. 216 pp. ISBN 0-06-021427-9.

Pokie is thirteen, and her brother Gib is eighteen. They spend hours together watching airplanes and dreaming about flying them, but then Gib goes off to college and Pokie starts high school. When Gib comes home at Christmas, he brings a girlfriend, whom Pokie resents. This is Pokie's own story of how she comes to terms with change.

2.19   Deuker, Carl. **On the Devil's Court.** Little, Brown/Joy Street Books, 1988. 252 pp. ISBN 0-316-18147-1.

Seventeen-year-old Joe Faust's first summer in Seattle is wet and dreary until he stumbles across a basketball court and meets Ross, the local high school's star shooter. Joe and Ross become friends, and their days are filled with buckets, jump shots, and dunks until the game becomes an obsession for Joe. Joe and his father don't get along, and Joe vows to use basketball to prove he's better than his father—even if it means making a pact with the Devil. ★

2.20   Diggs, Lucy. **Moon in the Water.** Atheneum, 1988. 234 pp. ISBN 0-689-31337-3.

In 1955, fourteen-year-old JoBob works at Slim's horse stable in rural California. His father, who stages cock fights behind their house, beats him, and his mother is powerless. So JoBob spends most of his time at the stable. When his secret training of Blue Chip, a beginner's horse, is discovered, he is given the horse and allowed to enter riding competitions. He and Blue are friends who work as a team, but as JoBob makes himself a part of the world of horses and riding, he comes into conflict with his family.

2.21 Draper, C. G. **A Holiday Year.** Little, Brown, 1988. 149 pp. ISBN 0-316-19203-1.

Ned and his family live near Boston but celebrate the major holidays of the year in a cottage on Cape Cod near their grandparents' house. Ned's sisters, Sally and Pat, and his cousins, Henri and Frank, play parts in each holiday story. His parents and his grandparents are also important characters in these lighthearted celebrations.

2.22 Ethridge, Kenneth E. **Viola, Furgy, Bobbi, and Me.** Holiday House, 1989. 164 pp. ISBN 0-8234-0746-2.

Stephen White needs money, so he starts doing yard work for Viola Spencer, the old woman down the street. He is surprised to discover that she's an avid Detroit Tigers fan, as he is. She turns out to be so much fun that soon he, his girlfriend Bobbi, and his crazy pal Furgy are spending lots of time with her—doing yard work, watching baseball games, and eating popcorn. When Viola's daughters find out, they're furious and try to take Viola away. Stephen and his friends fight for Viola's independence and learn about themselves in the process.

2.23 Facklam, Margery. **The Trouble with Mothers.** Clarion Books, 1989. 135 pp. ISBN 0-89919-773-6.

Thirteen-year-old Luke Troy wants to be noticed for his swimming abilities. Instead, he is seen only as the son of the history teacher who wrote a "dirty" novel. Troy resents defending the book, but he fights to support his mother and the principles of freedom. ★★

2.24 Farish, Terry. **Why I'm Already Blue.** Greenwillow Books, 1989. 152 pp. ISBN 0-688-09096-6.

Lucy likes being in her bed in her own room with the covers pulled up over her head. Now that her older sister has left for nursing school, it's better than facing her bleak life alone. Her mother is cold and distant, and her father's drinking has shrunk his dental practice to almost nothing. They continually fight with each other. The only bright spot for Lucy is her friendship with Gus, the wheelchair-bound boy next door.

2.25   Ferris, Jean. **Across the Grain.** Farrar, Straus and Giroux, 1990. 216 pp. ISBN 0-374-30030-5.

Although Will is younger than his sister Paige, he promises his dying mother that he will watch over Paige. But Paige is his legal guardian, and what choice does Will have when Paige takes a job in the desert? He hates moving from their house on the beach but has little choice. He meets Sam and a girl his own age, Mike, and they give him a new perspective on life. With their help, he reaches his eighteenth birthday more able to leave his sister to make her own mistakes, while he heads off for college and a future on his own. ★

2.26   Fine, Anne. **Alias Madame Doubtfire.** Little, Brown/Joy Street Books, 1988. 199 pp. ISBN 0-316-28313-4.

Lydia, Christopher, and Natalie's parents aren't just divorced—they're at war, and the children are hostages shuttled grudgingly back and forth. Their mother is *so* demanding, and they hardly ever have enough time to spend with their offbeat actor father. When Madame Doubtfire answers Mother's ad for a housekeeper, new fun—and problems—begin. Part Mary Poppins, part Groucho Marx, Madame Doubtfire is very capable, and the kids love her. But what if Mother finds out who she really is? ★

2.27   Fine, Anne. **My War with Goggle-Eyes.** Little, Brown/Joy Street Books, 1989. 160 pp. ISBN 0-316-28314-2.

Kitty's teacher asks her to help an unhappy classmate who doesn't like the man her mother is going to marry. Kitty's a good person to take on this task. She's been through it with her own stepdad, a man she now likes but started out calling "Goggle-Eyes." ★

2.28   Gaeddert, Louann. **A Summer like Turnips.** Henry Holt, 1989. 71 pp. ISBN 0-8050-0839-X.

Twelve-year-old Bruce Hardy adores visiting Gramps for the summer when they swim, golf, and get to be "good buddies" again. This summer, however, Gramps is mourning the death of Grandma, and his grief hurts Bruce. Bruce, a spirited girl, and a mangy old dog join forces to comfort Gramps and show him the true beauty of life.

2.29   Gleeson, Libby. **Eleanor, Elizabeth.** Holiday House, 1990. 136 pp. ISBN 0-8234-0804-3.

Eleanor Wheeler isn't happy when her family moves to her mother's childhood home. But then one day while she's feeling bored, she comes across her grandmother's diary in a shed behind the house. In the diary, she learns of her grandmother's secrets and of a secret hiding place near the creek bed. From then on, Eleanor's attitude changes toward both her grandmother and her new home.

2.30 Greenberg, Jan. **Just the Two of Us.** Farrar, Straus and Giroux, 1988. 128 pp. ISBN 0-374-36198-3.

Twelve-year-old Holly doesn't realize how much she loves living in New York with her mother until she finds out that they are moving to Iowa. The news couldn't be worse, thinks Holly, who immediately hatches a plan to stay in New York with the Applebaum family. When summer arrives and Holly's mother drives off in the U-Haul, Holly doesn't feel as excited about living with the glamorous Applebaums as she had expected. And before long, in spite of the fun she and Max have catering "Parties with Pizzazz," she's wondering if she's truly cut out for living on her own in New York City.

2.31 Grove, Vicki. **Good-Bye, My Wishing Star.** G. P. Putnam's Sons, 1988. 128 pp. ISBN 0-399-21532-8.

Twelve-year-old Jens Tucker's family is forced to sell their dairy. Jens learns to look through fresh eyes at both the good and bad things about being part of a farm family as she comes to accept the change in her life.

2.32 Hall, Barbara. **Dixie Storms.** Harcourt Brace Jovanovich, 1990. 197 pp. ISBN 0-15-223825-5.

Fourteen-year-old Dutch, who lives on a Southern farm as part of an extended family, already has her share of teenage worries and problems. But then her seemingly sophisticated cousin Norma comes from the city and makes Dutch's summer even worse. Along with the summer storm that finally arrives, comes relief for Dutch as she comes to terms with her feelings about herself and the members of her family—including cousin Norma. ★★★★

2.33 Hamilton, Virginia. **Cousins.** Philomel Books, 1990. 125 pp. ISBN 0-399-22164-6.

Cammy lives with her grandmother and her cousin Patty Ann, which isn't always easy for her. Cammy is jealous of the almost-perfect Patty Ann. But when Patty Ann drowns while rescuing another cousin, Cammy feels guilt and sorrow. To add to her troubles, she has fears about her grandmother dying. ★★★

2.34   Henkes, Kelvin. **The Zebra Wall.** Greenwillow Books, 1988. 147 pp. ISBN 0-688-07568-1.

When the Vorlob girls' mother has a new baby, Aunt Irene comes to help. The girls go out of their way to make her feel unwelcome in hopes that she will pack up and go home. Things change when they discover that she's the one who needs help.

2.35   Holl, Kristi D. **No Strings Attached.** Atheneum, 1988. 128 pp. ISBN 0-689-31399-3.

When June and her mother move in with seventy-three-year-old Franklin, June is delighted to have a home where she thinks her school friends will be welcome. But Franklin wants his privacy and is critical of her friends. In this sequel to *Just Like a Real Family*, both old and young must learn that there are limits to friendship.

2.36   Jones, Rebecca C. **The Believers.** Arcade, 1989. 144 pp. ISBN 1-55970-035-1.

Tibby Taylor's mother is an ambitious television news reporter who leaves Tibby in her hometown under the care of Aunt Evelyn. On the outside, Tibby is confident and carefree, almost a smart aleck, but inside she desperately wants attention from her mother. When she becomes friends with the Milners, who are members of a fundamentalist religious group, she joins in their belief and convinces herself that if she prays hard enough, her mother will come home.

2.37   Joosse, Barbara M. **Pieces of the Picture.** J. B. Lippincott, 1989. 136 pp. ISBN 0-397-32343-3.

Twelve-year-old Emily sees her newly widowed mother as joyless and hard working. She operates an inn in Door County, Wisconsin, where the only excitement for Emily is spying on guests and exploring old boxes in the attic. A Canadian goose becomes Emily's special friend, as this warm-hearted and spunky girl tries to understand her mother and adapt to her father's death.

2.38   Killien, Christi. **Artie's Brief: The Whole Truth and Nothing But.** Illustrated by Pamela Johnson. Houghton Mifflin, 1989. 93 pp. ISBN 0-395-49697-7.

When Artie's brother Tom killed himself, Artie was troubled that their father didn't show more emotion. And now that Artie's classmate Gilbert Flowers keeps getting into fights at school, Artie decides that Gilbert, like Tom, is up against an unfair and hostile world. His desire to help people and his dream of becoming a lawyer lead Artie to take Gilbert's case and defend him as a lawyer would. This approach has its flaws and leaves Artie wondering just which battles are worth fighting.

2.39 Kropp, Paul. **Moonkid and Liberty.** Little, Brown, 1990. 167 pp. ISBN 0-316-50485-8.

Sixteen-year-old Liberty wants desperately to be accepted by the "in" group, while her thirteen-year-old brother Ian is convinced he is an alien lodged in a human body. The two must confront the realities of their lives: a mother who left them and an aging hippie father. They learn to love and respect one another all over again when a family crisis forces them to affirm their loyalties.

2.40 Laird, Elizabeth. **Loving Ben.** Delacorte Press, 1989. 183 pp. ISBN 0-385-29810-2.

Twelve-year-old Anna Peacock and her family are thrilled to have a new baby, but they are saddened that he is very sick. Although he can't do what other babies do, the family loves him and is devastated when he dies after only two years. ★★

2.41 Levin, Betty. **The Trouble with Gramary.** Greenwillow Books, 1988. 198 pp. ISBN 0-688-07372-7.

Merkka and Ben's family live in their grandmother's seaside house in a small Maine village. Gramary, as they call her, is not the kind of grandmother you usually find in children's picture books: she runs a welding shop in the front yard. Although Merkka loves the way Gramary accomplishes such tasks as helping to rescue a dog stranded on an old wrecked ship, Merkka has mixed feelings about her, especially when the townspeople start to complain about the messy front yard. When developers want to turn the waterfront into a tourist attraction, Merkka starts to see that some things are more important than real estate. ★

2.42 Levy, Marilyn. **No Way Home.** Fawcett Junior Books, 1990. 153 pp. ISBN 0-449-70326-6.

When his father goes to Europe for six weeks, Billy is sent to California to stay with his mother who abandoned the family three years earlier. But to Billy's disappointment, he doesn't get to spend his time at Disneyland or at the beach. His mother now goes by the name Indra, and Billy is confined to Omkara, the religious commune where she lives. He begins learning the strange ways of this group while still trying to re-establish contact with his family in Chicago and ends up learning as much about himself as about his mother and the Omkaras.

2.43   MacLachlan, Patricia. **The Facts and Fictions of Minna Pratt.** Harper and Row/Charlotte Zolotow Books, 1988. 136 pp. ISBN 0-06-024117-9.

Eleven-year-old Minna Pratt wishes that parents would listen to their children, that her mother liked to cook something other than oatmeal stirred into a mass of beige lumps, and that her family had even a tiny bit of order to it. But what budding cellist Minna wishes more than anything else is that she could perfect her vibrato—that little tremor in the strings that makes the tone so warm and beautiful. Then she meets Lucas Ellerby, a violist who has a lovely vibrato and is a newcomer to her weekly chamber group. She finds that he is charmed by her eccentric family, while she envies his oh-so-civilized parents and his orderly, quiet life. As their friendship grows, both begin to find things about their own families that they can love and respect. Now, will Minna ever get the hang of that vibrato? ★★

2.44   Martin, Ann M. **Ten Kids, No Pets.** Holiday House, 1988. 174 pp. ISBN 0-8234-0691-1.

The ten children in the Rosso family are named in alphabetical order, sit in the van in alphabetical order, and leave the house for school in alphabetical order. Life doesn't stay so orderly when the Rossos move from New York City to the country. However, the kids can all agree on one thing: they should have a pet. Can they get Mrs. Rosso to think so, too?

2.45   Mazer, Harry. **Someone's Mother Is Missing.** Delacorte Press, 1990. 166 pp. ISBN 0-385-30161-8.

Lisa and Sam have very different lifestyles in spite of being cousins. Lisa's is country clubs and tennis lessons, while Sam's is adequate but nothing fancy. Then Lisa's father dies, and her dream world comes crashing down. The money is gone, and Lisa's mother can't cope, so she leaves Lisa and her sister. Sam tries to piece all this together, to support his cousins, and to help in the search to bring their mother back.

2.46 McNair, Joseph. **Commander Coatrack Returns.** Houghton Mifflin, 1989. 188 pp. ISBN 0-395-48295-X.

When little Cody was born, Mom and Dad knew he had special needs, but they were too sad to be able to help him. Big sister Lisa stepped in, caring for him, comforting him, and making up stories for him—stories she could lose herself in, too. Now Mom and Dad finally begin to take care of Cody themselves, and Lisa feels lost. Then she meets Robert, a boy at school who pretends to be someone different all the time. She joins his game and almost gets swallowed up by it. ★

2.47 Mickle, Shelley Fraser. **The Queen of October.** Algonquin Books, 1989. 301 pp. ISBN 0-945575-21-1.

Sally feels as if her parents' love is a fraud when she is sent to live with her grandparents while the details of her parents' divorce are worked out. Not only does she have to deal with the divorce and with growing up, but she must also adjust to small-town life.

2.48 Miklowitz, Gloria D. **Suddenly Super Rich.** Bantam Books, 1989. 150 pp. ISBN 0-553-05845-2.

Danielle can't believe her eyes as she watches the numbers go by on the screen. They're her mother's numbers, the ones she plays in the lottery every week. And instantly, the Ormandy family is five million dollars richer! Imagine going shopping when *nothing* is too expensive! A new house, new cars, new friends, and also lots of changes that aren't so pleasant leave Danielle and her family confused and unbalanced. Maybe money isn't everything after all. ★

2.49 Miller, Judi. **The Middle of the Sandwich Is the Best Part.** Simon and Schuster/Minstrel Books, 1990. 149 pp. ISBN 0-671-66575-8.

Betsi, a preteen, keeps a diary throughout this book. She is the middle child in her family, with a studious older sister and a musical genius for a younger brother. She fears she is never going to be special. Her grandmother and members of a school club are her confidantes and helpers as she tries various schemes to become special.

2.50   Murrow, Liza Ketchum. **Dancing on the Table.** Illustrated by
             Ronald Himler. Holiday House, 1990. 120 pp. ISBN 0-8234-0808-
             6.

             Jenny has a special relationship with her fun-loving grandmother,
             Nana. But when Nana announces that she is marrying Charlie
             Streeter, whom Jenny thinks of as "the Gray Man," Jenny feels
             betrayed, thinking that Nana will abandon their friendship.

2.51   Murrow, Liza Ketchum. **Fire in the Heart.** Holiday House, 1989.
             264 pp. ISBN 0-8234-0750-0.

             A packet of photographs, century-old letters, a tragic accident—
             all are parts of the puzzle that lead fourteen-year-old Molly closer
             to knowing her mother, who died when Molly was five. Her quest
             to know more leads Molly from her home in Vermont to an old
             mining camp in Northern California. There, with help from
             young, handsome Ramon of the historical society and from her
             photographer stepmother, Molly hunts for treasure buried by a
             relative during the Gold Rush days. Through exploring the past,
             Molly gains renewed love for the family she lives with now.

2.52   Nixon, Joan Lowery. **Hollywood Daughters: A Family Trilogy.**
             Bantam Books, 1990. 160–196 pp. each.

             The three books in this trilogy are *Star Baby* (ISBN 0-553-28957-
             8), *Overnight Sensation* (ISBN 0-553-29019-3), and *Encore*
             (ISBN 0-553-07024-X). In *Overnight Sensation*, which is set in the
             1960s, Cassie, the daughter of an actress, is struggling to find her
             own identity. She has a chance to help her new boyfriend finance
             a film, and she struggles with the question of whether to hurt her
             mother in hopes of gaining approval and love from her boyfriend.
             Encore takes place a generation later when Cassie's daughter,
             sixteen-year-old Erin Jinkens, is already a has-been. Erin was a
             cast member in a long-running TV series which has been
             cancelled. Erin turns for understanding to her grandmother, who
             still feels the lure of the stage lights. Can Erin find a way to save
             her career and rekindle her grandmother's? Even the ending is
             Hollywood.

2.53   Okimoto, Jean Davies. **Take a Chance, Gramps!** Little, Brown,
             1990. 135 pp. ISBN 0-316-63812-9.

             Shy Jane is best friends with outgoing Alicia. They are looking
             forward to starting junior high when disaster strikes—Alicia has
             to move, and Jane is left alone with nothing but her fear. Then

Jane reaches out to help her widowed grandfather and in the process learns some things about taking chances and making friends no matter what age you are.

2.54   Park, Barbara. **My Mother Got Married (and Other Disasters).** Alfred A. Knopf, 1989. 138 pp. ISBN 0-394-92149-6.

"Be patient!"—that's what Mother tells Charles as his world is invaded by a new stepfamily. Charles has to share his room with a pesky five year old, his new stepsister hogs both the bathroom and the telephone, and there is a new man sitting at his father's place at the table. Will Charles ever adjust to all these changes?

2.55   Paterson, Katherine. **Park's Quest.** Lodestar Books, 1988. 160 pp. ISBN 0-525-67258-3.

Eleven-year-old Park sets out on a quest, but he finds that his quest has very little of the glory of the quests of medieval knights. Park travels to his grandfather's farm to meet his father's family. Because his mother will not or cannot share her memories with him, Park knows nothing about his father, except that he was a soldier killed in Vietnam. In this complex story, Park learns some things about his father, and he also learns that real-life quests are longer and more complicated than riding forth to slay a dragon. ★

2.56   Reading, J. P. **The Summer of Sassy Jo.** Houghton Mifflin, 1989. 164 pp. ISBN 0-395-48950-4.

How do you get even with a mother who abandoned you? This is the problem that thirteen-year-old Sara Jo faces when Aunt Mimi, who has raised her, sends her to live with her mother for the summer. Her mother is now a recovering alcoholic with a stable second family. Thanks to help from several people, including a first boyfriend, Sara Jo is able to overcome her bitterness and build a new relationship with her mother. ★

2.57   Robinson, Barbara. **My Brother Louis Measures Worms and Other Louis Stories.** Harper and Row/Trophy, 1990. 149 pp. ISBN 0-06-440362-9.

Louis's family is not by any means typical. His mother is detached and oblivious to many of life's routines. Her artsy mind lets her avoid thinking about ordinary details. To survive, Louis's sister has become a keen observer, and Louis has become the world's most unique eight year old. Their father fits in somewhere, but no one is sure where. In this loosely connected series of events about one family and its different lifestyle, you get a humorous look at the adults as the kids see them.

2.58   Rocklin, Joanne. **Dear Baby.** Harper and Row, 1988. 96 pp. ISBN 0-02-777320-5.

Before Farla has time to get used to her mother's new husband, she finds she also has to get used to the idea of a new baby. She almost decides to run away and live with her grandmother, but then her grandmother gets a boyfriend, and Farla has to make yet another adjustment. In an effort to help her cope, Farla's mother and teacher encourage her to write letters to the unborn baby. Through these letters, you get to see how a new and sometimes awkward family grows into something old and comfortable.

2.59   Rodowsky, Colby. **Sydney, Herself.** Farrar, Straus and Giroux, 1989. 182 pp. ISBN 0-374-30649-4.

Sydney's English teacher assigns the class a self-awareness journal, and *Sydney, Herself* is the result. As you read it, you'll not only get to know a likable girl, you'll also get to know her mother and watch the two of them come to terms with their relationship and their individual dreams. ★★

2.60   Ruckman, Ivy. **Who Invited the Undertaker?** Thomas Y. Crowell, 1989. 186 pp. ISBN 0-690-04834-3.

Since his father died over two years ago, Dale Purcell has tried to be the man of the house—and that's not easy for a seventh grader. He fixes dinner, babysits, and does odd jobs. His mom is getting forgetful and depressed. Bills are piling up. So he and his friend Jeff decide to find his mother a husband. First, they put an ad in the personals column. Then, they set her up to sing at the supermarket on "singles night." Meanwhile, Dale's mind is full of fantasies for his own life—dreams of Lizette, the prettiest girl in school. Did *she* pass him the mysterious pink note in English class?

2.61   Rylant, Cynthia. **A Kindness.** Orchard/Richard Jackson Books, 1988. 117 pp. ISBN 0-531-08367-5.

Fifteen-year-old Chip is accustomed to handling all the practical matters in his single-parent family, including budgeting, shopping, and following directions on how to put things together—even his own Christmas presents. He and his mother are especially close—until she shares the news that she's pregnant. He's hurt that she won't tell him any more than that, but in the year that follows, he begins to understand some things about privacy and responsibility. ★★

2.62 Schenker, Dona. **Throw a Hungry Loop.** Alfred A. Knopf, 1990. 114 pp. ISBN 0-679-90332-1.

Thirteen-year-old "Tres" Bomer's name means "three" in Spanish. He uses this unusual name because he's named after his father and his grandfather, and his father already goes by "Junior." The three men share the same name—but not a whole lot else. Tres, who lives with the other two men on a Texas ranch, wants to become a rodeo cowboy—a dream his grandfather has no patience with. And Tres's father is wrapped up in his own problems. But thanks to a heifer calf, a stubborn and unappreciated mule, and a girl named Robin, Tres's story ends a lot happier than it begins. ★

2.63 Slote, Alfred. **A Friend like That.** J. B. Lippincott, 1988. 152 pp. ISBN 0-397-32311-5.

Robby is so fearful that his widowed father will remarry that he takes a drastic step and runs away. It takes a new friend, the first girl he has ever liked, to help him deal with his own family.

2.64 Slote, Alfred. **The Trading Game.** J. B. Lippincott, 1990. 200 pp. ISBN 0-397-32398-0.

This is a baseball story—sort of. Andy Harris's grandpa is a retired professional ball player, and Andy aspires to follow in his footsteps, but for right now, his big interest is in collecting baseball cards. In the midst of his passion for getting a complete set, he learns some things about people, especially his father and his grandfather. ★

2.65 Smith, Marya. **Across the Creek.** Arcade, 1989. 126 pp. ISBN 1-55970-041-6.

After the death of his young mother, Ryerson "Rye" comes to stay on his grandmother's farm while his father looks for a new home. The farm is where his mother grew up. He misses her greatly, and since his grandmother does little to make him feel needed, he begins to explore his surroundings and finds vivid reminders of the childhood his mother told him about. When he sees a young girl who resembles her, he is convinced he has met the child form of his mother.

2.66   Smith, Robert Kimmel. **The Squeaky Wheel.** Delacorte Press, 1990. 182 pp. ISBN 0-385-30155-3.

After the split between his parents, Mark Baker finds himself in totally new surroundings, and he feels lonely, unhappy, and angry. He hates his new apartment, hates his new school, and hates the new town. His mother won't discuss the divorce, and his father is never around. Mark thinks he has lost everything that matters in life—his house, his friends, and his family. But slowly he begins to discover life after divorce, as he adapts to the changes and starts to communicate with his parents.

2.67   Snyder, Zilpha Keatley. **Libby on Wednesday.** Delacorte Press, 1990. 196 pp. ISBN 0-385-29979-6.

If you harbor suspicions that your family is a bit different and that you're ever so special, you'll probably enjoy Libby's story. Her family really is different, and they choose to educate their adorable Libby at home. Eventually, though, she enrolls in middle school, where she views her classmates as uneducated, and they view her as peculiar. As long as Libby can remember, she has written down her feelings and ideas, and now at public school, she finds solace and pleasure in a writers' club that meets every Wednesday. You'll get to know not only Libby and her feelings, but also the ideas and feelings of a very real group of her fellow students. ★★

2.68   Springer, Nancy. **Not on a White Horse.** Alfred A. Knopf, 1990. 182 pp. ISBN 0-394-82965-4.

Ree's father is unemployed, her mother is overworked and exhausted, and her sister Dierdre is lovesick. When Ree begins a tireless search for a runaway horse she privately calls Angel, it leads her to an unexpected friendship with the blacksmith Chickie Miller and his family—and to a more mature relationship with her own family. From Chickie, Ree also learns about caring for a sick, maltreated horse and about setting out to accomplish her goal of becoming a veterinarian.

2.69   Sweeney, Joyce. **The Dream Collector.** Delacorte Press, 1989. 196 pp. ISBN 0-385-29813-7.

The plot of this story is an old one put in a new setting. Sixteen-year-old Becky Seville gets a book for her family that's guaranteed to show them how to get whatever they wish for. The Sevilles make their dreams come true, but the results aren't quite what they had anticipated. ★

2.70   Terris, Susan. **Author! Author!** Farrar, Straus and Giroux, 1990. 172 pp. ISBN 0-374-34995-9.

As if it isn't hard enough for Valerie to be the only middle school student with a published children's book, her parents seem totally shaken by her success and her newfound relationship with their old friend, Tekla Reis. It was Tekla who helped Val get published, and it is Tekla who seems so much more like Val than her own conventional parents. Maybe Tekla is her *real* mother! Valerie tries to unravel the secrets of Tekla and her parents as she struggles with finding her own identity as a writer and a person.

2.71   Tolan, Stephanie S. **A Good Courage.** William Morrow, 1988. 240 pp. ISBN 0-680-07446-4.

Tie-Dye's mother is a hippie left over from the 1960s, and she drags fourteen-year-old Tie-Dye from one bad experience to another. They finally end up in a commune run by religious fanatic Brother Daniel. In order to survive, Tie-Dye has to bring forth a kind of courage he didn't know he had. ★

2.72   Wilson, Johnniece Marshall. **Oh, Brother.** Scholastic, 1988. 121 pp. ISBN 0-590-41363-5.

Alex is more responsible than his older brother Andrew, and this leads to conflict. One day, Andrew borrows Alex's bicycle and has a run-in with a gang who beats up Andrew and steals the bike. But then the brothers grow closer together, and Andrew becomes more responsible, while Alex learns to stand up for himself.

2.73   Zable, Rona S. **Landing on Marvin Gardens.** Bantam Books, 1989. 136 pp. ISBN 0-553-05839-8.

What fifteen-year-old Katie and her divorced mother get into isn't as much fun as playing Monopoly, the game this book's title comes from. Their apartment building is being turned into condominiums, and they have to move in with Aunt Rose, who is not the kindly aunt you might expect. ★

2.74   Zirpoli, Jane. **Roots in the Outfield.** Houghton Mifflin, 1988.

Josh Morris is having a miserable summer. First, he loses the game for his baseball team, earning the nickname "Roots" when he freezes and misses the ball. Then, he has to spend the summer with his father, his new stepmother, and his awful stepsister, Wendy. As if that isn't enough, Slug Smith, his favorite baseball player of all time, has disappeared, so that even major league baseball doesn't seem much fun. As the summer goes on, Josh finds that his life is changing, and he has a few surprising discoveries in store.

Series

2.75   **Sisters.** Harcourt Brace Jovanovich/Gulliver Books.

Marilyn Kaye is the author of these stories about a family of four sisters. In *A Friend Like Phoebe*, Phoebe, the youngest of the four sisters, is proud but also envious of her sisters' accomplishments. When she learns that her class will be the subject of a television documentary and one student will be interviewed, she decides this is her chance to shine. But when her best friends nominate someone else, she is forced to come to terms with her own feelings about friendship, her sympathy for a friend whose mother has died, and her desire to do something she really wants.

2.76   **The Sisters.** Fawcett Books.

These books by Jennifer Cole revolve around the lives of Mollie and Cindy and their older sister Nicole, who goes off to college partway through the series. The first book is titled *Three's a Crowd*; there are now nearly twenty books in the series, including *And Then There Were Two*, *College Bound*, *The Boy Next Door*, *Campus Fever*, and *Making Up*.

2.77   **Sugar and Spice.** Ballantine/Ivy Books.

This series by Janet Quin-Harkin follows the lives of two girls who are related by blood but are opposite in temperament. The nearly twenty titles currently include *Blind Date*, *It's My Turn*, and *Home Sweet Home*.

Recommended Books about Family Relationships Published before 1988

Alcock, Vivien. *The Cuckoo Sister*. Delacorte Press, 1986.
Bond, Nancy. *A Place to Come Back To*. Atheneum, 1984.

Brancato, Robin. *Sweet Bells Jangled Out of Tune*. Alfred A. Knopf, 1982.

Branscum, Robbie. *Johnny May*. Doubleday, 1975.

Bridgers, Sue Ellen. *Home before Dark*. Alfred A. Knopf, 1976.

Bridgers, Sue Ellen. *Notes for Another Life*. Alfred A. Knopf, 1981.

Brooks, Bruce. *Midnight Hour Encores*. Harper and Row, 1986.

Burch, Robert. *Ida Early Comes over the Mountain*. Penguin/Puffin, 1980.

Byars, Betsy. *The Animal, the Vegetable, and John D. Jones*. Delacorte Press, 1982.

Byars, Betsy. *The Night Swimmers*. Delacorte Press, 1980.

Cassedy, Sylvia. *M.E. and Morton*. Thomas Y. Crowell, 1987.

Childress, Alice. *A Hero Ain't Nothin' but a Sandwich*. Putnam/Coward-McCann, 1973.

Childress, Alice. *Rainbow Jordan*. Putnam/Coward-McCann, 1981.

Cleaver, Vera, and Bill Cleaver. *Where the Lilies Bloom*. Harper and Row, 1969.

Clements, Bruce. *I Tell a Lie Every So Often*. Farrar, Straus and Giroux, 1974.

Danziger, Paula. *Can You Sue Your Parents for Malpractice?* Delacorte Press, 1979.

Danziger, Paula. *The Divorce Express*. Delacorte Press, 1982.

Delton, Judy. *Angel's Mother's Wedding*. Houghton Mifflin, 1987.

Engebrecht, P. A. *Under the Haystack*. Thomas Nelson, 1973.

Fleischman, Paul. *Rear-View Mirrors*. Harper and Row, 1986.

Fox, Paula. *The Moonlight Man*. Bradbury Press, 1986.

Gaines, Ernest J. *A Long Day in November*. Dial Press, 1971.

Geller, Mark. *What I Heard*. Harper and Row, 1987.

Hinton, S. E. *Rumblefish*. Delacorte Press, 1979.

Hinton, S. E. *Tex*. Delacorte Press, 1979.

Kerr, M. E. *Dinky Hocker Shoots Smack!* Harper and Row, 1972.

Kerr, M. E. *The Son of Someone Famous*. Harper and Row, 1974.

Klein, Norma. *Mom, the Wolfman, and Me*. Pantheon Books, 1972.

Mazer, Norma Fox. *After the Rain*. William Morrow, 1987.

Morgan, Alison. *Paul's Kite*. Atheneum, 1982.

Nelson, Theresa. *The Twenty-Five Cent Miracle*. Bradbury Press, 1986.

Paterson, Katherine. *The Great Gilly Hopkins*. Thomas Y. Crowell, 1978.

Paterson, Katherine. *Jacob Have I Loved*. Thomas Y. Crowell, 1980.

Pearce, Phillipa. *The Way to Sattin Shore*. Greenwillow Books, 1984.

Peck, Richard. *Father Figure*. Viking, 1978.

Peck, Robert Newton. *A Day No Pigs Would Die*. Alfred A. Knopf, 1973.

Pfeffer, Susan Beth. *The Year without Michael*. Bantam Books, 1987.

Sachs, Marilyn. *The Truth about Mary Rose*. Doubleday, 1973.
Smith, Doris Buchanan. *Return to Bitter Creek*. Viking Penguin, 1986.
Voigt, Cynthia. *Dicey's Song*. Atheneum, 1982.
Voigt, Cynthia. *Sons from Afar*. Atheneum, 1987.
Willey, Margaret. *Finding David Dolores*. Harper and Row, 1986.

3 Connecting with Friends and Foes: School and Community Relationships

3.1   Alcock, Vivien. **The Trial of Anna Cotman.** Delacorte Press, 1990. 160 pp. ISBN 0-385-29981-8.

Fourteen-year-old Anna is a newcomer, so she is happy when Lindy invites her to join the secret "Society of Masks," a club organized by Lindy's older brother and his friends. But after Yellow Lord joins, the club takes on mean and sinister tones, and Alice finds herself in trouble when she challenges some of its actions. ★

3.2   Blair, Cynthia. **Crazy in Love.** Fawcett/Juniper Books, 1988. 171 pp. ISBN 0-449-70189-1.

Sallie and Rachel are closer than best friends—they're more like soul sisters. Their friendship is threatened by Sallie's songwriting partner Saul—first because Saul is attracted to Rachel rather than Sallie and then because Rachel's Jewish heritage forces her to reject Saul because of his Puerto Rican background.

3.3   Blue, Rose. **The Secret Papers of Camp Get Around.** Penguin/New American Library, 1988. 159 pp. ISBN 0-451-15301-4.

Under protest, fourteen-year-old Marcy is off to summer camp with her "pestiferous" little brother. To her delight, Marcy meets up with sixteen-year-old Steve. Steve and Marcy share an interest in journalism, and they decide to make their own newspaper to cover the gossip of Camp Get Around. But as they dig for dirt, they find more than they anticipated.

3.4   Brittain, Bill. **The Fantastic Freshman.** Harper and Row, 1988. 160 pp. ISBN 0-06-020719-1.

More than anything, Stanley Muffet wants to be special when he goes to high school. With a little help from a mysterious stranger and an even more mysterious keepsake, he gets his wish, but it isn't as satisfying as he thought it would be. ★

3.5   Bunting, Eve. **Our Sixth Grade Sugar Babies.** J. B. Lippincott, 1990. 146 pp. ISBN 0-397-32452-9.

All the sixth graders are to carry five-pound sacks of sugar everywhere they go for a week. The assignment is meant to teach them responsibility and awareness of the amount of time and energy needed to care for a small child. Vicki and Ellie dub their sacks "sugar babies," and Vicki hopes the assignment will convince her mother that she's responsible enough to travel to another city and care for her half-sister for a week. But what seems like an easy task gets complicated when Vicki decides to leave her "sugar baby" with a senile neighbor so she can go to the library with the terrific hunk who just moved into the neighborhood. ★

3.6   Busselle, Rebecca. **Bathing Ugly.** Orchard Books, 1988. 184 pp. ISBN 0-531-05801-8.

Betsy Sherman wants to be like all the other girls at Camp Sunny Days. She is, and more—about fifty pounds more. Named her cabin's entry in the "Bathing Ugly" contest, she comes to realize that beauty is only skin deep—and a good deal of work. By sheer will and determination, she cuts out candy and cuts back on food and snacks. In doing so, she learns a few good lessons about herself and the obstacle called growing up. ★

3.7   Carris, Joan. **The Greatest Idea Ever.** J. B. Lippincott, 1990. 167 pp. ISBN 0-397-32378-6.

Gus, a fifth grader, is famous for his great ideas, most of which involve his two best friends, Pep and Buzzer. The boys need a great idea now—they want to settle the score with Nanny Vincent, the class tattletale. Gus plans for the ultimate revenge during the May Day parade!

3.8   Cohen, Barbara. **Tell Us Your Secret.** Bantam Books, 1989. 171 pp. ISBN 0-553-05810-X.

Crunch Oliver, Eve Streitman, and ten other aspiring young writing students attend a two-week writers' conference at Marygrove mansion. In addition to acquiring some sophisticated writing skills, they form deep friendships as they begin to tell each other their personal secrets and fears. Can two weeks at summer camp change the rest of your life?

3.9   Colman, Hila. **The Double Life of Angela Jones.** William Morrow, 1988. 156 pp. ISBN 0-688-06781-6.

Angela's father wants something better for his daughter than their crowded and poor New York neighborhood school. He arranges a scholarship for her to go to an exclusive boarding school in New Hampshire, where she learns a lot about social prejudices—those directed at her and those she dishes out. The main lesson comes through two friendships, one with her wealthy roommate and one with a boy she meets at the gas station while she's driving her roommate's Porsche.

3.10   Coombs, Karen. **Samantha Gill, Belly Dancer.** Avon/Camelot Books, 1989. 128 pp. ISBN 0-380-75737-0.

At the end of fifth grade, Samantha dreads the boredom of summer. The problem is what to do on a miniature budget! Sam and her best friend Abby investigate all kinds of promising hobbies until they run across a belly-dancing record in the library. Sam hopes belly dancing will cure her clumsiness, and her father even offers to buy her a snake as an accessory. But by summer's end, Sam has to admit that belly dancing is not the hobby for her.

3.11   Danziger, Paula. **Make like a Tree and Leave.** Delacorte Press, 1990. 117 pp. ISBN 0-385-30151-0.

Matthew Martin and his three pals, Billy, Joshua, and Brian, are all boys who want to succeed. Sometimes they try too hard, as when they put Brian in a plaster cast to make their mummy project more realistic and then can't get the cast off! But when Mrs. Nickles, who lives next to the school and bakes the world's best chocolate chip cookies, falls and hurts herself, Brian, his friends, the school, and the whole town rally round in a real-life project to help someone in need.

3.12   Derby, Pat. **Goodbye Emily, Hello.** Farrar, Straus and Giroux, 1989. 153 pp. ISBN 0-374-32744-0.

Robin and Emily meet each other at the beginning of elementary school, and for the next eight years they have a close but uneven friendship. The outgoing Emily is confident enough to make all the decisions for herself and for the less-assertive Robin. But when they start high school, Emily drops her best friend to become part of a more popular group. Eventually, she finds that she still needs Robin's friendship, but what develops is not the same lopsided relationship.

3.13   Dines, Carol. **Best Friends Tell the Best Lies.** Delacorte Press, 1989. 213 pp. ISBN 0-385-50131-8.

Leah and Tamara are best friends, drawn together partly because both of them have divorced parents. Tamara copes with her frustrations by telling lies, which disappoints and angers Leah. But from this rocky point in their friendship, both girls grow and gain new understandings of themselves and those around them.

3.14   Ellis, Sarah. **Next-Door Neighbors.** Margaret K. McElderry Books, 1990. 154 pp. ISBN 0-689-50495-0.

Twelve-year-old Peggy is moving to another town in Canada where her father will serve as the minister at the local church. Peggy's fears mount as she thinks of all the new people in her school and community. When she lies to try to impress the kids at school, she is left without friends. She turns to George, the custodian's son, for friendship. As they work on a project, they enlist the help of Sing, a Chinese man who works for an eccentric and abusive neighbor. When Sing disappears, they do some sleuth work to find him. ★

3.15   Geller, Mark. **The Strange Case of the Reluctant Partners.** Harper and Row, 1990. 88 pp. ISBN 0-06-021973-4.

Thomas Trible has been assigned to Elaine Moore as her partner in an English class assignment in which each partner is to write a biography about the other. Why couldn't Thomas have been assigned to someone like Brigette Cortes, who is cute and exciting to be around? Elaine is quiet and studious and different. But as the assignment develops, so does their friendship and their understanding of what makes a good friend.

3.16   Gelman, Jan. **Marci's Secret Book of Flirting: Don't Go Out without It!** Alfred A. Knopf/Bullseye Books, 1990. 104 pp. ISBN 0-394-81931-4.

Marci and her best friend Pam are in seventh grade. Junior high is new, exciting, difficult, and scary, but fun. They're worried, though—they ought to be learning to talk to boys, but they haven't a clue as to how to go about it. Should they imitate Marci's sixteen-year-old sister, Darlene? Or take lessons from Cathy, Marci's sister in college? They decide to do both and to take notes on what they learn. Marci's how-to-flirt guidebook is the result.

3.17   Gerson, Corrine. **My Grandfather the Spy.** Walker, 1990. 121 pp. ISBN 0-8027-6955-1.

Danny travels from Chicago, Illinois, to Paradise, Vermont, to spend the summer on a farm. When he arrives, he falls in love with the farm and the family who lives there. Soon after his arrival, an old man whom he met on the bus trip appears at the farm. After meeting the man, the family asks him to give up his rented cottage and join them and Danny on the farm. The summer is filled with friendship, activity, mystery, and surprises.

3.18 Gibbons, Faye. **King Shoes and Clown Pockets.** William Morrow, 1989. 231 pp. ISBN 0-688-06592-9.

When Raymond's father gets a new job, the family moves to a trailer park in rural Alabama. But Raymond hates to leave his grandfather and their beautiful Tennessee farm. He's lonely in his new home. His sister ignores him, his brother treats him like a pesky fly, and his parents are always busy. Then Raymond meets Bruce, the freewheeling son of the neighborhood junk dealer and handyman. They roam the woods, adopt a dog, create a secret hideout, and together face Miss Autrey, the meanest fifth-grade teacher *ever*.

3.19 Grove, Vicki. **The Fastest Friend in the West.** G. P. Putnam's Sons, 1990. 174 pp. ISBN 0-399-22184-0.

Lori can't believe it. Her best friend has moved out of the locker they've shared since seventh grade and has gone to join the popular group. Lori feels so lonely that she decides to paint her room like the ocean and stay there by herself with her aquarium. When Vern, a new girl at school, tries to be friendly, Lori hardly knows what to do. Vern is *so* weird. She wears the same messy clothes every day and a rusty old key on a chain around her neck. Lori is mystified when Vern explains that she has time to make only one friend. When Vern's father abruptly withdraws her from school and takes her away, Lori is shocked to discover Vern's secret.

3.20 Hall, Lynn. **The Secret Life of Dagmar Schultz.** Charles Scribner's Sons, 1988. 89 pp. ISBN 0-684-18915-1.

Dagmar is convinced that all she needs is a boyfriend, her thirteenth birthday, and a secret life. She is so jealous of her best friend that she creates for herself an imaginary sixteen-year-old boyfriend named Doug. One lie leads to another and then another until Dagmar isn't sure where fantasy ends and reality begins.

3.21   Haven, Susan. **Is It Them or Is It Me?** G. P. Putnam's Sons, 1990.
174 pp. ISBN 0-399-21916-1.

Molly Snyder is excited about starting high school. She's a bit
unhappy that her best friend Kathy is going to a different school,
but she has a chance to work on the school paper, and she's
making new friends. However, two things are troubling her: she
has Henry Frack—"Frack the Hack"—for history, and something seems to be wrong with her mom's health.

3.22   Haven, Susan. **Maybe I'll Move to the Lost and Found.** G. P.
Putnam's Sons, 1988. 158 pp. ISBN 0-399-21509-3.

Gilly Miles lives in a New York City apartment house, which, in
a way, is its own community. Among the kids who live there, she
has a boyfriend—sort of—named Arnold. Then Victory Norton
moves in and sweeps Arnold off his feet. Now when he kisses
Gilly, it's only to practice for kissing Victory—but that's only one
of Gilly's problems. ★

3.23   Hermes, Patricia. **I Hate Being Gifted.** G. P. Putnam's Sons,
1990. 119 pp. ISBN 0-399-21687-1.

K.T. and her two best friends, Melinda and Chrissy, are all set to
begin sixth grade together until L.E.A.P.—the Learning Enrich-
ment Activity Program—enters the picture. K.T. has tested for
the program and will spend three afternoons a week away from
the class and her pals. At a time when friends and friendship are
especially important, K.T. feels left out and shunned when plans
for projects and partnerships go on without her. Teachers,
parents, and even her brothers begin to notice that K.T. is
miserable. Finally, K.T. gets advice and support from a most
unexpected source.

3.24   Hopkins, Lila. **Talking Turkey.** Franklin Watts, 1989. 152 pp.
ISBN 0-531-10797-3.

Seventh-grader Croaker learns that you can't always tell what
people are like just by looking at them. Because of his looks, he's
accused of taking money from his classroom, but he knows that
it's Angela who did it. He accuses her of being the thief, and in the
complications that follow, he falls and breaks his arm, Angela
confesses, and several other surprising facts about fellow students
come to light.

3.25 Hurwitz, Johanna. **Class President.** William Morrow, 1990. 85 pp. ISBN 0-688-09114-8.

Meet Julio, Lucas, and Cricket—the most vocal members of Mr. Flores's fifth-grade class. When Mr. Flores announces that the class is going to hold an election for a class president, Cricket and Lucas square off for the race. Julio becomes Lucas's manager; after all, nobody would vote for Julio, would they?

3.26 Jane, Pamela. **Just Plain Penny.** Houghton Mifflin, 1990. 146 pp. ISBN 0-395-52807-0.

Eleven-year-old Penny Poppen has a vivid imagination from wide reading and watching old movies on TV. To get through a boring summer, she writes a play. Then she and her neighborhood friends rush to a used-clothing store to buy costumes. Although the play includes a real-life mysterious stranger and a surprise transformation, it cannot drown out the voices of Penny's parents. She overhears their nightly conversations but cannot interpret what they are saying. Will the surprise they greet her with be too much to handle?

3.27 Jones, Rebecca C. **Germy Blew the Bugle.** Arcade, 1990. 136 pp. ISBN 1-55970-088-2.

Jeremy Bluett, "Germy" to his friends, is in sixth grade and wants to earn some money. He suggests a school newspaper to his friends, thinking that with subscriptions and advertising fees, he will have a money-maker. The principal soon hears of his plans and makes arrangements for the printing but won't let him collect the fees. And Germy soon discovers that producing a newspaper takes a lot of hard work.

3.28 Jukes, Mavis. **Getting Even.** Alfred A. Knopf, 1988. 163 pp. ISBN 0-394-82593-4.

How do you deal with someone like Corky Newton? He puts hair in people's sandwiches, snoops in desks, and blackmails other kids for candy. The worst part is he seems to get away with it because he's the Cleanup Captain and the principal's nephew. Maggie and her wild friend Iris decide to get even, but each idea gets them in deeper and deeper trouble, both at home and at school.

3.29 Kennedy, S. A. **Hey, Didi Darling.** Bantam/Skylark Books, 1989. 150 pp. ISBN 0-533-15708-6.

In this funny story, five good friends—all girls—start a band. They succeed in making fine music, but nobody wants an all-girl band, so they dress themselves as boys and become Tommy and the Tigers.

3.30   Killien, Christi. **Rusty Fertlanger, Lady's Man.** Houghton Mifflin, 1988. 133 pp. ISBN 0-395-46762-4.

What to do? Rusty is no jock, but school rules require everyone to participate on a team. Rusty just wants to maintain his low profile and keep drawing cartoons of Molar Maximillian, the character that he's developing. He chooses to join the wrestling team because he thinks it will be the least distracting. But as a lightweight, his first opponent is a girl, and it's not at all clear that he's going to be able to keep his low profile. ★

3.31   Kleinbaum, N. H. **Dead Poets Society.** Bantam Books, 1989. 166 pp. ISBN 0-553-28298-0.

At Welton Academy discipline, excellence, tradition, and honor reign until a group of students are inspired by the flamboyant teaching of Mr. Keating. Poetry is the passion of his life, and with Keating's interpretations of Byron, Shelley, and Keats, the boys begin to live for the moment. Can their passion live and flourish under the rigid atmosphere of Welton? Based on the motion picture (screenplay by Tom Schulman). Mature situations.

3.32   Maguire, Jesse. **Just Friends.** Ballantine/Ivy Books, 1990. 185 pp. ISBN 0-8041-0445-X.

When rich and elegant Darcy Jenner gets kicked out of her elite boarding school, she enrolls at Norwell High School. There she meets Josh, Caro, and T.J. They welcome her to their hideout at Split River Station but don't quite accept her into their working-class lives. The four friends are all escaping painful homes and families. They're trying to learn to trust each other and accept their differences as they seek their own identities.

3.33   Malmgren, Dallin. **The Ninth Issue.** Delacorte Press, 1989. 181 pp. ISBN 0-385-29691-6.

Blue Hocker is *not* happy about moving to Texas. When he doesn't make the football team, he punches the quarterback and gets three days' suspension and a schedule change into the journalism class that runs the school newspaper. *The Town Crier* is a boring paper that no one reads, but the new advisor, Mr.

Choate, inspires the newspaper staff. By the April issue, they can't print enough copies to meet the demand, but they find that success, too, has its demands.

3.34 Marek, Margot. **Matt's Crusade.** Aflred A. Knopf/Borzoi Sprinters, 1988. 147 pp. ISBN 0-394-82585-3.

To Matt Tyson, the most important thing in the world is making the football team at his junior high school. His friend, Allie Behringer, however, has other concerns. She and her father, Matt's social studies teacher, are worried about the possibility that nuclear weapons are going to be housed at the local army base. They are planning to protest the nuclear missile placement. Matt's father is on the opposite side. All of Matt's priorities and values—his friendships, his family loyalties, his allegiance to his team—are called into question as he makes his choices on the nuclear issue.

3.35 Matthews, Phoebe. **Switchstance.** Avon/Flare Books, 1989. 169 pp. ISBN 0-380-75729-X.

Deserted—that's how Elvy feels. Dad has moved to California and Mom to New York, dumping Elvy at her grandmother's. Lonely in her new school, Elvy makes some bad choices about friends and activities—until the right boy comes along.

3.36 Moore, Emily. **Whose Side Are You On?** Farrar, Straus and Giroux, 1988. 133 pp. ISBN 0-374-38409-6.

Sixth-grader Barbara fails math, and the teacher assigns her oldest rival, T.J. Brodie, to be her tutor. Fortunately, the situation turns out better than Barbara had anticipated, and she and T.J. actually become friends. Then T.J. disappears from school, and Barbara sets out to find out why—she's sure his grandfather has sent him to a home.

3.37 Morris, Judy K. **The Kid Who Ran for Principal.** J. B. Lippincott, 1989. 212 pp. ISBN 0-397-32360-3.

When the principal of Daniel Webster Elementary School dies unexpectedly, the sixth graders discover that the interim principal will be elected by the whole school community. They decide to have an exercise in democracy and sponsor their own candidate, Bonnie Mann. Tired of being the cooperative goody-goody, Bonnie accepts the challenge, determined to improve the school. But can she really do it? Can a kid run for principal and win?

Change the lunchroom? Fix the swings? Get a soccer coach? And, hardest of all, fire their incompetent sixth-grade teacher, Mr. Locke?

3.38   Orgel, Doris. **Crack in the Heart.** Fawcett/Juniper Books, 1989. 155 pp. ISBN 0-449-70204-9.

After Zanna's father dies in an auto accident, she and her mother begin a new life in New York. Zanna is unhappy to leave her friends, but her mother has taken a job as a nurse in a very exclusive school for girls. Zanna's tuition is part of the package. Zanna doesn't fit in there until she begins babysitting a teacher's infant and meets the teacher's older, renegade son, Jeff.

3.39   Park, Barbara. **Partners in Crime.** Alfred A. Knopf, 1990. 116 pp. ISBN 0-679-90212-0.

Earl hates to read aloud. Maxie is tired of his classmates making fun of his good grades. And Rosie loves to tattle. But how did these three relative strangers end up in the school dumpster together? And what fantastic story will they concoct to tell the principal on Monday morning?

3.40   Pinkwater, Jill. **Buffalo Brenda.** Macmillan, 1989. 203 pp. ISBN 0-02-774631-3.

India Ink Teidlebaum and Brenda Tuna are not your typical high school freshmen. They don't want to be like everyone else, and indeed they aren't. When they're expelled from the school newspaper staff, they start their own underground paper. But this zany pair's biggest accomplishment comes when they manage to adopt a bison from the federal government to serve as the school mascot. ★★

3.41   Posner, Richard. **Sparrow's Flight.** M. Evans, 1988. 256 pp. ISBN 0-87131-544-0.

Julie Hoffman is new at Westfield High School, alone and lonely until she is invited to join the Clan. The Clan inhabits a fantasy world in which members use elf names and share Clan secrets. Julie is happy to be included; she has only been on the fringes of groups before. Besides, her home life has been more and more unhappy since her father disappeared and her relationship with her mother started going downhill. But some of the Clan secrets begin to seem ominous, and Julie has to figure out where fantasy and game playing end and where reality begins.

3.42   Reilly, Pat. **Columbus Circle.** Dell/Yearling Books, 1988. 108 pp. ISBN 0-440-40036-8.

When his father declares bankruptcy, Gardner Waterford must move from his Park Avenue home. His family finds a tiny apartment on Columbus Circle, but Gardner dreads the neighborhood kids who race around on skateboards, dress in the latest fad outfits, and carry cassette radios on their shoulders. And the kids don't like Gardner or his snobbish mother either. So when she takes away their toys, Gardner knows trouble is going to erupt as they seek revenge.

3.43   Ryan, Mary C. **The Voice from the Mendelsohn's Maple.** Little, Brown, 1990. 132 pp. ISBN 0-316-76360-8.

Penny Egan is surprised when she hears the neighbor's tree calling for help. When she decides to solve the mystery, Penny discovers that it's not the tree that's talking; instead it's a little old lady, Miss Katherine Cooper, who has climbed up the tree. This incident begins a summer of mystery and new friendships for Penny as she gets involved with the elderly residents of Beacon Manor Home.

3.44   Shannon, Jacqueline. **Faking It.** Avon Books, 1989. 170 pp. ISBN 0-380-75601-3.

Denny, Mandy, and Fleur are all keeping secrets. Denny doesn't want the other girls to know that she is not yet physically mature or interested in boys; Mandy knows nothing about her father, not even his name; and Fleur is afraid that if the kids find out that she failed seventh grade, they will make fun of her. But together the three learn something about friendship.

3.45   Shura, Mary Francis. **Polly Panic.** G. P. Putnam's Sons, 1990. 127 pp. ISBN 0-399-22214-6.

Polly has been looking forward to being one of the big kids as a sixth grader in elementary school. But then the school board moves the sixth graders to the junior high, and she's one of the youngest. To make things worse, her best friend Staci seems to have dumped her in favor of the "in" crowd, and her dad may be losing his job—again. Worst of all, she's made an enemy of the class bully. Luckily, Polly has the support of her family and her friends to help her cope with her up-and-down life.

3.46   Singer, Marilyn. **Twenty Ways to Lose Your Best Friend.** Harper and Row, 1990. 121 pp. ISBN 0-06-025642-7.

"Most people have small minds," Emma's mother says. When it comes time for tryouts for the school play, Emma decides to prove she is not "most people." She votes for Marguerite, who isn't very likable but is a better performer than her friend Sandy. Emma puts her friendship with Sandy on the line and learns that defending what she believes to be right has a price.

3.47   Slepian, Jan. **The Broccoli Tapes.** Philomel Books, 1989. 134 pp. ISBN 0-399-21712-6.

While most people are thrilled to go to Hawaii for a vacation, twelve-year-old Sara and her thirteen-year-old brother Sam aren't so happy to be living there for five months. They are lonely and bored until they rescue a wildcat they name Broccoli. Sara sends cassette tapes home to her teacher and classmates telling them all about the adventure. You get to read firsthand what's on the tapes. ★★★

3.48   Spinelli, Jerry. **Dump Days.** Little, Brown, 1988. 159 pp. ISBN 0-316-80706-0.

J.D. and his best friend Duke face the beginning of summer vacation with enthusiasm and grand plans. They decide to have one *perfect* day during their vacation. All they need is a little money, and surely that will be easy to raise—or maybe not so easy.

3.49   Sweeney, Joyce. **Face the Dragon.** Delacorte Press, 1990. 231 pp. ISBN 0-385-30164-2.

Eric Henderson and Paul Price, both fourteen, enter an accelerated program at their high school. At first, Eric fears everything there—the school, the classes, the girls. But slowly Eric gains confidence, and as he begins to succeed in school, he pulls away from his best friend Paul. He now looks on Paul as a rival, but ultimately he must "face his dragon" and decide between friendship and fame.

3.50   Thesman, Jean. **Couldn't I Start Over?** Avon/Flare Books, 1989. 170 pp. ISBN 0-380-75717-6.

Shiloh, the best pianist at North Seattle High, is on the brink of having a great year. She has a best friend, a special boyfriend, and a teacher who cares. But then comes Lovey Sullivan. She's

gorgeous and clever and has the heart of a barracuda. If you've
ever been the victim of a master manipulator, you'll recognize
Lovey. For a while, it seems that Shiloh's only friends are her
rock-musician brother and a fellow piano student named Ben,
who longs for a more important place in Shiloh's life.

3.51   Towne, Mary. **Their House.** Atheneum, 1990. 198 pp. ISBN 0-
689-31562-7.

Molly Jackson isn't too happy about moving to a big house in the
country. She's afraid of the changes this elegant neighborhood
might bring. But when her parents take her to see the new place,
she becomes fascinated with the Warrens, the strange old couple
who've always lived there. The Jacksons begin renovating the old
house, and Molly gets to know Mrs. Warren, but she's puzzled at
why the Warrens are stalling about moving out of their part of the
house. Whose house is this anyway? In trying to unravel the
mystery of the Warrens, Molly helps prevent tragedy and saves
three lives.

3.52   Walker, Paul Robert. **The Method.** Harcourt Brace Jovanovich,
1990. 256 pp. ISBN 0-15-299528-5.

Fifteen-year-old Albie Jensen wants to be an actor more than
anything. He auditions for The Company, a small, privileged
summer theater group, as a way to gain experience and make a
few friends. This elite group, headed by the highly respected
teacher, Mr. Pierce, undergoes intense training for six weeks.
During these six weeks, Albie learns difficult lessons in love and
friendship, but the hardest lesson is to separate acting from being
his real self.

3.53   Wyss, Thelma Hatch. **Here at the Scenic-Vu Motel.** Harper
Keypoint Books, 1988. 154 pp. ISBN 0-06-447001-6.

Their parents were mostly refugees from the sixties who hoped to
escape to a simpler life in Bear Flats, Idaho. So the kids are
isolated from the "real life" of pick-up trucks and cruising in
town—until the school board refuses to pay for busing them to the
nearest high school. Then the teenagers have to stay at the Scenic-
Vu Motel during the school week. Senior Jake Callahan finds
himself in charge of the six others and learns that being a leader is
more work than he thought. ★★

Series

3.54   **The Baby-Sitters Club.** Scholastic.

Seven girls join as partners to form a baby-sitters' club. In some ways, they're typical teenagers, but their experiences are hardly average. In *California Girls*, they've won the lottery and go to California for an adventure, while in *Poor Mallory!* they pitch in to help Mallory when her father loses his job. By the end of 1990, there were forty-nine different titles in this series by Ann M. Martin.

3.55   **Center Stage.** Fawcett Books.

In *Star Struck*, Barri Gillette and her best friend, Melanie, compete to be in the local cast of *Romeo and Juliet*. Romeo is going to be played by Ward McKenna, a nationally famous star. The complication is that if Barri gets the part, she'll have to let down a lot of people by dropping out of the school play. In the second book in the series, *Barri, Take Two*, Melanie and Barri aspire to go to New York to meet the characters in their favorite TV soap opera. Written by Ellen Ashley.

3.56   **The Fabulous Five.** Bantam/Skylark Books.

This series by Betsy Haynes follows the story of five girls who form a club with the idea of keeping up with snobby Taffy Sinclair. But when they get to Wakeman Junior High, they find all kinds of challenges to their friendship. In *Playing the Part*, Beth gets a part in the school play, but then her boyfriend starts dating her friend Christie. In *The Fabulous Five in Trouble*, fantasy enters the picture when the girls have a slumber party and wake up in the wrong bodies.

3.57   **Pen Pals.** Dell/Yearling Books.

In this series by Sharon Dennis Wyeth, four freshman girls are roommates at a private boarding school in New Hampshire. They have acquired pen pals from a nearby boys' school. The girls struggle with the difficulties of getting along, growing up, and dreaming of romance and the future. A few titles include *No Creeps Need Apply*, *Sam the Sham*, *Amy's Song*, *Handle with Care*, and *Sealed with a Kiss*.

3.58   **The Pink Parrots.** Little, Brown/Sports Illustrated for Kids Books.

Five friends—Breezy, Jazz, Kim, Terry, and Crystal—are on an all-girl baseball team sponsored by the Pink Parrots Beauty Salon. Their coach, owner, and manager is Rose Ann DiMona, whom they call Ro. The first book is *The Girls Strike Back: The Making of the Pink Parrots*, and the second is *All That Jazz*, in which Jasmine falls head over heels in love with baseball instead of just with the boys who play it. The series was created by Lucy Ellis; the books are about 120 pages each.

3.59   **River Heights.** Archway Paperbacks.

Readers of the Nancy Drew books by Carolyn Keene are already familiar with the town of River Heights, from which this series gets its name. Nikki Masters and Brittany Tate take center stage in these books, with Nancy Drew making only cameo appearances. Like the Sweet Valley High stories, these stories focus on romance. Titles include *Love Times Three*, *Guilty Secrets*, and *Going Too Far*.

3.60   **Roommates.** Ballantine/Ivy Books.

The Roommates series by Allison Blair might not show college life exactly the way it really is, but older readers will particularly enjoy these stories of Stacy, Roni, Terry, and Sam. The four young women are about as different from each other as they could be: Stacy's a wealthy snob, Roni's a rebellious Southern belle, Terry's a serious student, and Sam's an all-American farm girl. Some of the most recent titles are *Major Attraction*, *Love by the Book*, *Social Studies*, *Back to School*, and *Study Break*.

3.61   **Satin Slippers.** Fawcett Books.

Leah Stephenson and her friends are fifteen-year-old students at the San Francisco Ballet Academy. They are dedicated to becoming fine ballerinas. In their struggles and triumphs you'll see that they are talented but still typical teenagers. Some recent titles are *Summer Dance*, *Starting Over*, *Rising Star*, *Chance to Love*, *Stepping Out*, *Temptations*, *Curtain Call*, *Second Best*, and *Changing Partners*. Written by Elizabeth Bernard.

3.62   **Silver Skates.** Fawcett Books.

Barbara J. Mumma's stories center on the boys and girls at Coach Gregory Mastroni's Lake Placid Skating School. Titles so far include *Breaking the Ice*, *Face the Music*, *Ice Follies*, *Two to Tango*, *Winner's Waltz*, and *World Class*.

3.63   Super Seniors. Dell.

Eileen Goudge's super seniors are a group of girls from Glenwood High whose adventures and romances take place in a number of settings. Look for *Old Enough*; *Hawaiian Christmas*; *Something Borrowed, Something Blue*; and *Deep-Sea Summer*.

3.64   Sweet Valley Twins. Bantam/Skylark Books.

Younger readers will enjoy Francine Pascal's Sweet Valley Twins, which features Sweet Valley High's Jessica and Elizabeth Wakefield when they were preteens. In *The Big Camp Secret*, the girls enjoy their first vacation away from home and by themselves; in *Elizabeth's New Hero*, a gymnastics team from East Germany visits Sweet Valley for a week, and the boy staying in the twins' home decides to defect; and in *Danny Means Trouble*, Elizabeth tries to help a boy in the sixth grade who's become a troublemaker to cover up the fact that he can't read.

3.65   The Treehouse Times. Avon/Camelot Books.

Page McBrier's stories follow a group of neighborhood friends who have the luxury of owning a treehouse. In the series' first book, *Under Twelve Not Allowed*, Amy and her friends start a neighborhood newspaper with their office in the treehouse. Their first really exciting story leads them to discover some very interesting facts about the people in their neighborhood. In *The Kickball Crisis*, the kickball field is for sale, and Erin Valez decides, along with the rest of the gang, to set out to save the field. What they find out may cause more problems than anyone could have imagined. Other titles include *Spaghetti Breath*, *First Course Trouble*, *Press Mess*, and *The Great Rip Off*.

3.66   West Mount High Trilogy. Archway Paperbacks.

These three books by Janice Harrell involve five best friends in high school who interact in the joys and struggles that come with growing up. The titles are *Wild Times at West Mount High*, *Easy Answers*, and *Senior Year at Last*. In the last book, Ann Lee feels changed by her summer in Belgium, but no one seems to notice; Michael is involved in a passionate relationship with the wild and dangerous C.G.; and Rainey is torn between the rich and mellow Tucker and the devotion and friendship of Blake. Tensions peak at the homecoming game.

**Recommended Books about School and Community Relationships
Published before 1988**

Bonham, Frank. *Durango Street*. E. P. Dutton, 1967.

Brancato, Robin. *Blinded by the Light*. Alfred A. Knopf, 1978.

Branscum, Robbie. *The Saving of P.S.* Doubleday, 1977.

Brooks, Bruce. *The Moves Make the Man*. Harper and Row, 1984.

Byars, Betsy. *The Pinballs*. Harper and Row, 1977.

Callen, Larry. *The Deadly Mandrake*. Little, Brown, 1978.

Cawley, Winifred. *Gran at Coalgate*. Holt, Rinehart and Winston, 1975.

Cole, Brock. *The Goats*. Farrar, Straus and Giroux, 1987.

Cormier, Robert. *The Chocolate War*. Pantheon Books, 1974.

Cross, Gillian. *The Dark behind the Curtain*. Oxford University Press, 1984.

Hahn, Mary Downing. *Daphne's Book*. Clarion Books, 1983.

Hamilton, Virginia. *The Planet of Junior Brown*. Macmillan, 1971.

Hinton, S. E. *The Outsiders*. Viking, 1967.

Hinton, S. E. *Rumblefish*. Delacorte Press, 1979.

Kerr, M. E. *Fell*. Harper and Row, 1987.

Kerr, M. E. *Is That You, Miss Blue?* Harper and Row, 1975.

Kerr, M. E. *What I Really Think of You*. Harper and Row, 1982.

Kidd, Ronald. *Sizzle and Splat*. Lodestar Books, 1983.

Lisle, Janet Taylor. *Sirens and Spies*. Bradbury Press, 1985.

Mazer, Norma Fox. *Downtown*. William Morrow, 1984.

Peck, Richard. *Dreamland Lake*. Holt, Rinehart and Winston, 1973.

Peck, Richard *Princess Ashley*. Delacorte Press, 1987.

Phipson, Joan. *The Watcher in the Garden*. Atheneum, 1982.

Robinson, Barbara. *The Best Christmas Pageant Ever*. Harper and Row, 1972.

Swarthout, Glendon. *Bless the Beasts and Children*. Doubleday, 1970.

Zindel, Paul. *My Darling, My Hamburger*. Harper and Row, 1969.

Zindel, Paul. *Pardon Me, You're Stepping on My Eyeball*. Harper and Row, 1976.

Zindel, Paul. *The Pigman*. Harper and Row, 1968.

4 Connecting with Boyfriends and Girlfriends: Love and Romance

4.1 Busselle, Rebecca. **A Frog's Eye View.** Orchard Books, 1990. 191 pp. ISBN 0-531-05907-3.

Summer has come and with it the freedom of doing nothing. But for Neela, it gets off to a bad start. Her boyfriend is busy with his job, with his band, and with the new girl singer. Neela's best friend is gone for a month, and out of boredom and jealousy, Neela begins to follow her boyfriend and take pictures of him without his knowledge. As might be predicted, this is the beginning of the end of Neela's romance, but she does learn a few things about human relationships.

4.2 Byars, Betsy. **Bingo Brown and the Language of Love.** Viking Penguin, 1989. 160 pp. ISBN 0-670-82791-6.

In this funny sequel to *The Burning Questions of Bingo Brown*, Melissa moves to Bixby, Oklahoma, and Bingo has to cook thirty-six dinners for his parents to pay for his long-distance phone calls to her. But since he's such an expert at talking to girls, he tries to teach Wentworth how to talk to them. And finally, in a surprising turn of events, he learns that he's going to have the opportunity to become a big brother. ★★

4.3 Byars, Betsy. **Bingo Brown, Gypsy Lover.** Viking Penguin, 1990. 160 pp. ISBN 0-670-83322-3.

If you're lucky, you've already met Harrison "Bingo" Brown, a likable and funny kid from two earlier books by Betsy Byars. In this book Bingo is preoccupied with keeping a romance going with his girlfriend, Melissa, who has moved off to Bixby, Oklahoma. He's also worried that his routine is going to change when a new baby arrives. But when the baby comes unexpectedly early, and no one is sure he's going to survive, Bingo learns about priorities. ★★

4.4 Clements, Bruce. **Tom Loves Anna Loves Tom.** Farrar, Straus and Giroux, 1990. 167 pp. ISBN 0-374-37673-5.

After glimpsing Anna in the hardware store and following her to eight o'clock Mass, sixteen-year-old Tom has to make every day with her count, for in two weeks she will leave her invalid aunt to return to her family in Chicago. He gains Anna's love and respect, and she tells him her fearful secret about Walter, her dead brother's friend. Fortunately, Tom is able to help. ★

4.5 Cooney, Caroline B. **Camp Girl-Meets-Boy.** Bantam Books, 1988. 160 pp. ISBN 0-553-27273-X.

What could be more convenient for summer fun and romance than having a boys' camp and a girls' camp next to each other? Vi and Marissa take jobs as counselors at the girls' camp, which makes meetings with counselors at the boys' camp quite easy— that is, until the stunning and talented Cathy shows up. Can ordinary girls like Vi and Marissa stand a chance against her?

4.6 Cooney, Caroline B. **The Girl Who Invented Romance.** Bantam/ Starfire Books, 1988. 176 pp. ISBN 0-533-05473-2.

Sixteen-year-old Kelly William decides that since love seems to be a game, she'll invent a new board game—Romance. But real life is not always played by rules, and Kelly finds, through watching her friends, her parents, and her older brother, Parker, and through her own disastrous first date that finding love is not determined by a roll of the dice. In a happy ending, she learns that "on a board game, there isn't room for even a fraction of what love is." ★

4.7 Davis, Jenny. **Sex Education.** Orchard/Richard Jackson Books, 1988. 150 pp. ISBN 0-531-08356-X.

Livvie and David are surprised when their high school biology teacher announces that the first term will be devoted to sex education. They're even more surprised when they get their first major assignment, which is to care about someone. They choose a new neighbor who is pregnant, and as the tragic story unfolds, Livvie learns that caring is both complicated and risky. ★★★

4.8 Gerber, Merrill Joan. **I'd Rather Think about Robby.** Harper and Row, 1989. 153 pp. ISBN 0-06-022283-2.

Eleven-year-old Marilyn Carlin finds herself thinking a lot about the birds and the bees, or the bees and the boys, or is it the bees and Robby? Her group, the Four Roses, is going to have a party with dates. Marilyn invites Robby to be her date, but he also wants to invite the pretty and sophisticated Holly. In spite of this shaky start, Marilyn and her friends learn to like Holly for herself.

4.9   Hall, Lynn. **Fair Maiden.** Charles Scribner's Sons, 1990. 120 pp. ISBN 0-684-19213-6.

An unstable brother is just one of the many problems Jennifer Dean escapes by getting involved in a medieval fair. But there she confronts a world with its own set of problems. She falls in love with an older man, who is also seeking escape from reality. In the end, both must face the real world, realize their individual roles, and question the true basis for their relationship. It's not a perfect world, but it holds hope for a stronger Jennifer.

4.10   Hermes, Patricia. **Be Still My Heart.** G. P. Putnam's Sons, 1989. 144 pp. ISBN 0-399-21917-X.

Unlike her best friend Leslie, who has all the looks, Allison thinks she is unattractive to boys. She has to make do with working on the school newspaper, just to be near David, the editor and Leslie's current boyfriend. When Ms. Adams, the paper's sponsor and a very popular teacher, almost loses her job because her husband has AIDS, Allison shows what she is made of by organizing student support for her advisor and teacher. In the end, Allison sees that David is more interested in her abilities than in Leslie's "California golden girl" looks. ★

4.11   Herrick, Ann. **The Perfect Guy.** Bantam Books, 1989. 160 pp. ISBN 0-553-279270-0.

When her mother marries the English teacher, Rebecca gets a new stepbrother, "the perfect guy." She's disappointed that "the perfect guy" is only interested in being a brother, but all's well that ends well in this wish-fulfilling romance.

4.12   Kaplow, Robert. **Alessandra in Love.** J. B. Lippincott, 1989. 153 pp. ISBN 0-397-32282-8.

Alessandra is a witty, vivacious fifteen year old with an overwhelming interest in Wyn, a talented but self-centered new boy at her school. It is a rocky romance since they seem to have little in common and bicker most of the time—that is, when Wyn is not talking about himself or seeing his former girlfriend. ★

4.13   Killien, Christi. **Fickle Fever.** Houghton Mifflin, 1988. 123 pp. ISBN 0-395-48159-7.

Skeeter (whom readers might already have met in *Putting On an Act*) is in search of love, the big "L" word. Skeeter sets her sights on Terry, her former pen pal; then on Rodney Kline, the bowling champ; then on Chet Dimmit, her brother's car-fancying friend; then on the religiously conservative Alan Reedy; and finally on her best friend's cousin. But then something happens which forces Skeeter to realize that there are different kinds of love. ★

4.14   Lantz, Francess. **The Truth about Making Out.** Bantam/Skylark Books, 1990. 152 pp. ISBN 0-553-15813-9.

Having big sisters has some advantages—at least that's what Amanda and Leigh decide when no one will answer their questions about what it's like to have a boyfriend and to kiss. This story gets to be like a television comedy when Amanda and Leigh decide the only way to find out about making out is to follow their sisters and spy.

4.15   Lowry, Lois. **Your Move, J.P.!** Houghton Mifflin, 1990. 122 pp. ISBN 0-395-53639-1.

J.P. Tate falls in love with the beautiful Angela Galsworthy, who has recently arrived from London to join his seventh-grade class. As J.P.'s sister Caroline and his old friend Hope keep careful watch, his attempts to win Angela's affection grow increasingly complex.

4.16   Makris, Kathryn. **A Different Way.** Avon/Flare Books, 1989. 182 pp. ISBN 0-380-75728-1.

Steve finds the adjustment from Pennsylvania to Texas a difficult one. He longs for acceptance by the "in" crowd, but learns that *he* has the power to accept and reject as well.

4.17   Matthews, Phoebe. **The Boy on the Cover.** Avon/Flare Books, 1988. 154 pp. ISBN 0-380-75407-X.

When Cyndi Carlisle falls head over heels for the boy on the cover of one of her romance books, she becomes obsessed with finding him. And when he shows up in her own high school, she can't believe her luck. Fortunately, he gets to know her first and doesn't realize she's been obsessed with him for months; after all, one misunderstanding can lead to another in the game of love.

4.18   Mazer, Harry. **City Light.** Scholastic, 1988. 192 pp. ISBN 0-590-40511-X.

George is not a gracious loser when Julie tells him their romance is finished. But eventually, he gathers his dignity and his resources and is ready to forge ahead with Rosemary, a girl he meets through a computer bulletin board. ★

4.19   Mazer, Norma Fox, and Harry Mazer. **Heartbeat.** Bantam Books, 1989. 165 pp. ISBN 0-553-05808-8.

Tod Ellerbee and Amos Vaccaro have been friends for years—ever since Amos saved Tod from drowning. Now, Amos wants Tod to set him up with Hilary, a mature girl who attends the same school as Tod. Tod plays matchmaker, but he, too, is smitten with love. How can a love triangle have a happy ending? ★

4.20   Paulsen, Gary. **The Boy Who Owned the School.** Orchard/ Richard Jackson Books, 1990. 85 pp. ISBN 0-531-08465-5.

Jacob Freisten thinks he's the "ugliest boy in history except for one." At school he works hard to be invisible because when people pay attention to him, it always seems to end in disaster. He's failing English and, desperate for extra credit, he agrees to help with the school's production of *The Wizard of Oz*. In the process he learns that he's not so much of a tin woodsman or cowardly lion as he thought. Happily, he also learns that Maria, the most perfect girl in school, has a heart.

4.21   Sonnenmark, Laura. **Something's Rotten in the State of Maryland.** Scholastic, 1990. 192 pp. ISBN 0-590-42876-4.

Marie describes herself as a Snow White look-alike who could be even better looking if she tried. She rewrites Shakespeare's *Hamlet*, and when the school's drama club decides to produce it, she gets more involved than she thought she would. She works hard on the play and gives an amusing account of her relationship with her boyfriend Simon. ★

4.22   Stine, R. L. **How I Broke Up with Ernie.** Archway Paperbacks, 1990. 136 pp. ISBN 0-671-69496-0.

Amy is popular but not entirely successful—she can't seem to break up with Ernie. She keeps trying, but he won't go away. ★

4.23   Swallow, Pamela Curtis. **No Promises.** G. P. Putnam's Sons, 1989. 173 pp. ISBN 0-399-21561-1.

When Jared, a transfer student from France, takes an interest in sophomore Dana McGarren, Dana begins to have trouble with her best friend Lynn, who also likes Jared, *and* her boyfriend Paul. She thinks over her emotions and tries to decide what is right for her. Fortunately, everyone involved acts with sensitivity, honesty, and maturity, even when fate intervenes. ★

4.24 Trivelpiece, Laurel. **Just a Little Bit Lost.** Scholastic/Apple Paperbacks, 1988. 186 pp. ISBN 0-590-41465-8.

The freshman class hike turns into a test of courage for Bennet Kinnell. As a spoiled only child, she's never had challenging responsibilities. But now, she's accidentally left behind by the other hikers. Fortunately, Phillip Hargrove finds her, but they have a difficult four days as they work and wait to be rescued. ★

4.25 Wersba, Barbara. **Beautiful Losers.** Harper and Row, 1988. 149 pp. ISBN 0-06-026363-6.

Rita is in an unusual situation. She is eighteen, fat, and in love with Arnold Bromberg, who is twice her age! Arnold is a writer and a reader of great poetry, a cook and a painter, but he never seems to have a job for very long. Rita struggles to understand her parents' disappointment as she pursues this unusual relationship.

Series

4.26 **First Kiss.** Ballantine/Ivy Books.

Head Over Heels, Love Song, Falling for You, The Perfect Couple, and *Right Boy, Wrong Girl* are some of the books in this romance series where problems come up quickly and are solved just as suddenly. Suzanne Weyn and Janice Boies are among the different authors who have written books in the series.

4.27 **Heartbreak Café.** Fawcett Books.

Debbie's parents divorce, and she takes a job at a beach café so she can afford to keep her car. She works hard to earn her boss's respect and eventually becomes friends with the regular customers. This series by Janet Quin-Harkin follows her adventures and romances at the café. Titles include *No Experience Required, The Main Attraction, At Your Service, Catch of the Day, Love to Go,* and *Just Desserts.*

4.28 **Linda Stories.** Archway Paperbacks.

Linda Berman is a conscientious and considerate high school student whose romantic adventures are the basis of this series by

Linda Lewis. Titles include *We Hate Everything but Boys*, *Is There Life after Boys?*, *We Love Only Older Boys*, *My Heart Belongs to That Boy*, and *All for the Love of That Boy*.

4.29   Meg and Stanley Stories. Archway Paperbacks.

Emily Hallin's first three books in this series are *Partners*, *Changes*, and *Risks*. In them, Megan Royce and Stanley Stoneman attempt to keep seeing each other in spite of Stanley's mom, who would rather that Stanley date debutante Daphne Wainwright.

4.30   Sebastian Sisters. Bantam Books.

This series features the four Sebastian sisters with a book about each of them at age sixteen. In the first one, *Evvie at Sixteen*, Evvie is asked to take care of her rich great-aunt Grace for the summer. Aunt Grace has the money and social prestige the Sebastian family lacks, and while visiting, Evvie discovers a secret about her handsome, loving father. A later book, *Meg at Sixteen*, is framed by the question "How many people get to see the moment when their parents met? The moment they fell in love?" In this story, the sisters try to adjust to their mother's impending remarriage by retelling the story of their parents' meeting and falling in love and recording it on tape.

4.31   Sweet Dreams. Bantam Books.

The Sweet Dreams series was one of the first to be written just for teenagers. It now includes almost 200 titles written by many different authors. All the books are romances, and many bring in other subjects. In Susan Wallach's *Acting on Impulse*, the class takes a trip to England; in Judy Baer's *Working at Love*, teens run their own business; and in Stephanie St. Pierre's *A Brush with Love*, characters struggle with a love triangle.

4.32   Sweet Valley High. Bantam Books.

Francine Pascal wrote the first few books in this series about twins Jessica and Elizabeth Wakefield. By now, dozens of writers have contributed to the more than 100 titles. The twins' experiences cover a wide range. In *Lost at Sea*, a science field trip ends in a shipwreck, and in *Two-Boy Weekend*, Jessica's steady boyfriend is away for the weekend, and when she flirts with the mysterious and good-looking Christopher, the results are more than she anticipated.

Recommended Books about Love and Romance Published before 1988

Daly, Maureen. *Seventeenth Summer*. Dodd, Mead, 1942.

Fox, Paula. *A Place Apart*. Farrar, Straus and Giroux, 1980.

Hamilton, Virginia. *A Little Love*. G. P. Putnam's Sons, 1984.

Hunt, Irene. *Up a Road Slowly*. Follett Press, 1966.

Hunter, Mollie. *Hold on to Love*. Harper and Row, 1984.

Hunter, Mollie. *A Sound of Chariots*. Harper and Row, 1982.

Jordan, June. *His Own Where*. Thomas Y. Crowell, 1971.

Kerr, M. E. *Gentlehands*. Harper and Row, 1978.

Kerr, M. E. *If I Love You, Am I Trapped Forever?* Harper and Row, 1973.

Kerr, M. E. *I'll Love You When You're More Like Me*. Harper and Row, 1977.

Kerr, M. E. *Little Little*. Harper and Row, 1971.

Kidd, Ronald. *Sizzle and Splat*. Lodestar Books, 1983.

LeGuin, Ursula. *Very Far Away from Anywhere Else*. Atheneum, 1976.

Levoy, Myron. *Alan and Naomi*. Harper and Row, 1977.

Levoy, Myron. *Three Friends*. Harper and Row, 1984.

Mahy, Margaret. *The Catalogue of the Universe*. Macmillan, 1986.

Mazer, Harry. *I Love You, Stupid!* Harper and Row, 1981.

Mazer, Norma Fox. *Someone to Love*. Delacorte Press, 1983.

Myers, Walter Dean. *Motown and Didi: A Love Story*. Viking Kestrel, 1984.

Peck, Richard. *Close Enough to Touch*. Delacorte Press, 1981.

Robinson, Barbara. *Temporary Times, Temporary Places*. Harper and Row, 1982.

Singer, Marilyn. *The Course of True Love Never Did Run Smooth*. Harper and Row, 1983.

Wersba, Barbara. *Fat: A Love Story*. Harper and Row, 1987.

Wersba, Barbara. *Love Is the Crooked Thing*. Harper and Row, 1987.

Wilkinson, Brenda. *Ludell and Willie*. Harper and Row, 1977.

II Understandings

What does it mean to understand someone? Children often feel that their parents or their teachers don't understand them, and sometimes husbands and wives feel the same way about each other. Understanding goes deeper than just knowing the facts; feelings are involved. When you understand people, you sympathize with them, and you use your imagination to think how you would feel if you were in their position. You can never understand someone completely, probably not even yourself, but the more you know about the world and about people's experiences, the closer you can come to gaining understanding. In your own lifetime, you could not possibly live through as many experiences as you can read about, so books are a good way to help develop understanding.

The books in this section are about people's experiences in many different situations. Some of the stories come straight out of their authors' imaginations, while others are true accounts, as in the chapter on biographies; still others are based on real people or real events but with fictional touches, such as made-up conversations and descriptive details. We have divided these books into chapters according to what seemed to us to be the most important topic in each one, but you should be aware that the books will often deal with other topics, since fully developed stories have many aspects. For instance, we have not put all the books about characters from various ethnic backgrounds into one chapter, but instead have put only the books that focus on ethnic relationships there. Books in other chapters may also feature characters with strong ethnic identities. Whatever a book's topic, we hope that reading it will help you understand human nature.

5 Understanding the Troubled: Problems

5.1   Adler, C. S. **Ghost Brother.** Clarion Books, 1990. 150 pp. ISBN 0-395-52592-6.

Wally can't believe his older brother Jon is really dead. Jon was always the brave one, the exciting one, the successful athlete, Mom's favorite. Without him, Wally doesn't know how he can stand his bossy Aunt Flo or help his grieving mother. Jon's ghost begins appearing to Wally and giving him advice. He even helps Wally learn to skateboard. But Wally isn't like Jon, and every time he follows Jon's advice, he gets into trouble. How can he hold on to his brother's memory and still have the confidence to be himself?

5.2   Allen, Richard E. **Ozzy on the Outside.** Delacorte Press, 1989. 196 pp. ISBN 0-385-29741-6.

Ozzy Mills is very close to his mother, who encourages him to be special and individualistic. This suits both his outsider image at school and his desire to be a famous novelist. His mother's sudden death and the family's reactions drive Ozzy to run away, but an impulsive young woman on the bus helps him through his guilt and grief.

5.3   Bennett, James. **I Can Hear the Mourning Dove.** Houghton Mifflin, 1990. 224 pp. ISBN 0-395-53623-5.

Grace Braun spends most of her sixteenth year in a mental institution recovering from a suicide attempt. The sudden death of her father hit her hard, but her confidence is slowly rebuilding through relationships with a psychologist, a teacher, and a classmate. Then another tragic episode lands Grace back in the hospital, where she strikes up a friendship with Luke, a rebellious delinquent who's been shuffled from one foster home to another. Although she has difficulty reaching out to him, Grace not only helps Luke deal with his problems, but begins to come to terms with her own. ★

5.4   Bunting, Eve. **Such Nice Kids.** Clarion Books, 1990. 120 pp. ISBN
0-395-54998-1.

Jason, Meeker, and Pidge are all good buddies who all have dates
on the same evening. Jason is going with Destiny, whom he wants
to impress. Since Meeker's car only holds two people, Pidge is left
stranded. Meeker convinces Jason to lend his mother's car to
Pidge—without her permission. One bad decision leads to a lie,
which leads to an endless stream of events that brings about an
accident and the end of innocence and friendships.

5.5   Bunting, Eve. **A Sudden Silence.** Harcourt Brace Jovanovich,
1988. 112 pp. ISBN 0-15-282058-2.

Jesse's younger brother, Bryan, who is deaf, is killed by a drunk
hit-and-run driver. Jesse and Chloe, Bryan's girlfriend, set out to
find the driver. They learn that justice, guilt, alcoholism, and grief
are more complicated than placing blame. ★

5.6   Byars, Betsy. **The Burning Questions of Bingo Brown.** Viking
Penguin, 1988. 160 pp. ISBN 0-670-81932-8.

Sixth-grader Bingo Brown uses his school journal to write down
his burning questions. Not all of these questions are somber, but
one is—it's about Mr. Markham, his favorite teacher. Mr.
Markham's latest writing assignment was to write a letter
convincing someone not to commit suicide. When Mr. Markham
goes riding on his motorcycle—minus his helmet—and has an
accident, Bingo worries that the assignment was a cry for help. ★★

5.7   Carter, Alden R. **RoboDad.** G. P. Putnam's Sons, 1990. 144 pp.
ISBN 0-399-22191-3.

Fourteen-year-old Shar has a strange autumn after her father
develops a mental condition. Although the doctor does not
promise a full recovery, Shar does not give up hope. But she has
other problems, too. Her best friend forsakes Shar and gives all
her time and attention to a new boyfriend; her twin brothers don't
help around the house; and her mother seems more interested in
her male co-worker than in her family. Meanwhile, Shar gains a
lot of weight. After making a list of reasons for dieting—
boyfriend, other people's criticism, and clothing size—she settles
on only one, and that is herself.

5.8   Carter, Alden R. **Up Country.** G. P. Putnam's Sons, 1989. 224 pp.
ISBN 0-389-21583-2.

Sixteen-year-old Carl's mother is alcoholic. Until she got in a hit-and-run accident, Carl had been able to manage their lives fairly well. But now his mother must go away for treatment, and he's sent off to live with relatives he barely knows. He finds that making a new life for himself is a challenge. ★★

5.9   Cassedy, Sylvia. **Lucie Babbidge's House.** Thomas Y. Crowell, 1989. 243 pp. ISBN 0-690-04798-3.

Miss Pimm tells Lucie Babbidge she is plain and stubborn. The other girls at Norwood Hall make fun of her clothes and the way she acts, calling her a stupid slob. They nickname her "Goosey-Loosey" and say she's crazy. But they don't know about the other Lucie and her special house where Mumma and Dadda love her and play games, and where she and her brother Emmett take piano lessons from the strange yet elegant Mr. Broome. These are parts of Lucie's secret life, apart from the painful past and the dismal present.

5.10   Cohen, Barbara. **The Long Way Home.** Greenwillow Books, 1990. 160 pp. ISBN 0-688-09674-3.

Every summer, the Berg kids go to the shore to be with the rest of their family. But this year, they are being packed off to camp; nothing is like it usually is. Even the twins, Emily and Sally, are not confiding in each other. When the tension at home gets to be too much, they have a conference. Everyone is scared—scared of the same thing: Mom may die. The chemotherapy may not help. But then a family camp counselor steps in and the family begins to pull together.

5.11   Conrad, Pam. **Taking the Ferry Home.** Harper and Row, 1988. 180 pp. ISBN 0-06-021317-5.

Ali Mintz's father, a well-known writer and recovering alcoholic, rents a cottage on Dune Island one summer. It belongs to beautiful Simone Silver's family. The two sixteen year olds have a rocky start because Ali is jealous of Simone's wealth and beauty, but they become friends, and Simone shares the distress she feels over her mother's addiction to drugs and alcohol. But then a boy enters the picture.

5.12   Crutcher, Chris. **Chinese Handcuffs.** Greenwillow Books, 1989. 192 pp. ISBN 0-688-08345-5.

Rebellious Dillon witnessed the suicide of his older brother, and before he is over the trauma, he gets wrapped up in the problems of his two favorite girls—Stacy, his brother's girlfriend, and Jan, the basketball star. The emotional intensity and action in this novel come through in mature situations and language. ★

5.13   Deaver, Julie Reece. **Say Goodnight, Gracie.** Harper and Row, 1988. 214 pp. ISBN 0-06-021419-8.

Morgan is a seventeen-year-old aspiring actress who learns that you really don't realize how much someone means until they're gone—her life-long best friend Jimmy has been killed by a drunk driver. Jimmy was an excellent dancer and a practical joker. He was good at bringing Morgan out of her shyness. Now that he is gone, Morgan must cope alone with something much more difficult than the kinds of problems that the two of them used to share. ★★★

5.14   DeClements, Barthe. **Monkey See, Monkey Do.** Delacorte Press, 1990. 146 pp. ISBN 0-385-30158-8.

Jerry Johnson, Jr., is the son of Jerry Johnson, Sr., former inmate. Everything the younger Jerry had hoped for with his father's parole is ruined when he finds his father with two former "colleagues." As all his dad's promises to reform are broken, Jerry becomes more and more withdrawn from school and his class-mates. Only the next-door neighbor Grace, a PK (preacher's kid), stays friends with him, even when Jerry's dad is publicly arrested for shoplifting. It takes strength for Jerry to accept that his dad is the way he is and won't likely change.

5.15   Doren, Marion. **Nell of Blue Harbor.** Harcourt Brace Jovano-vich, 1990. 153 pp. ISBN 0-15-256889-1.

Nell has lived all her life on The Farm, a commune in Vermont where her family has lived since her father and some other Vietnam veterans bought it. When her family is forced to leave the commune, Nell isn't sure she is ready to go. It soon becomes clear that her parents are even less ready than Nell. Her mother retreats into poetry writing, leaving eleven-year-old Nell to take most of the responsibility for the house and her baby sister. Her father does little to help and seems unable to cope. Finally, Nell is forced to make hard choices in order to come to grips with her problems.

5.16   Ellis, Sarah. **A Family Project.** Macmillan, 1988. 128 pp. ISBN 0-689-50444-6.

Eleven-year-old Jessica and her parents are happy when the new baby is born. But then, after waiting so long for the birth, they are dropped into sadness when the baby dies of crib death. You'll feel sorry along with them, but you'll be glad you got to know this family in both its sad and its happy moments. ★★

5.17   Farish, Terry. **Shelter for a Seabird.** Greenwillow Books, 1990. 176 pp. ISBN 0-688-09627-1.

Andrea comes back to her island home after having a baby that she gave up for adoption. Her family never mentions her three-month absence. But things are not the same—Andrea is not the same. School is a failure, and developers are buying the island piece by piece for tourism. But then Swede shows up. He is lost, too. Forced into the army by his father, he is AWOL. It's Easter weekend, and Andrea and Swede share two lifetimes in six short days.

5.18   Ferris, Jean. **Looking for Home.** Farrar, Straus and Giroux, 1989. 167 pp. ISBN 0-374-34649-6.

Daphne's home life is a long way from what it should be, and even a longer way from what she dreams of. When she becomes pregnant, she doesn't want to tell the boy who was involved, nor does she dare tell her father. Her solution is to leave school and move to a city where she gets a job as a waitress and finds herself a new sort of family. It still isn't the family she dreams of, but it's what she needs at the time. ★

5.19   Forman, James D. **Cry Havoc.** Charles Scribner's Sons, 1988. 199 pp. ISBN 0-684-18838-4.

Fifteen-year-old Cathy Cooper has been expelled from her exclusive private school. Her mother, high-strung and artistic, is between stays at mental hospitals where she has lived for much of Cathy's life. Cathy's father seems discouraged and unhappy. As if these personal problems weren't enough, the town where she lives is under attack by someone—or something. All of Cathy's world is threatened—either by her parents' dreadful unhappiness or by the mayhem that is building in the world outside.

5.20   Fosburgh, Lisa. **The Wrong Way Home.** Bantam Books, 1990. 180 pp. ISBN 0-553-05883-5.

Fifteen-year-old Bent has to accept the fact that her divorced mother's illness has ruined her ability to be the caregiver for the family. This forces Bent into a difficult situation. When her mother is taken to a nursing home, Bent's father and stepmother welcome her into their home, but she is not ready to accept the facts of her parents' divorce and her father's remarriage, much less a new home and family. She finally runs away—to find what was there all along.

5.21   Fox, Paula. **The Village by the Sea.** Orchard Books, 1988. 147 pp. ISBN 0-531-08388-8.

It's bad enough that Emma's father has to have an operation, but being sent off to live with Aunt Bea is almost more than Emma can bear. At first, things are as bad as Emma feared, but then she learns that Aunt Bea's gruff outside doesn't necessarily show what she's like deep inside. ★★★

5.22   Grant, Cynthia D. **Phoenix Rising: or How to Survive Your Life.** Atheneum, 1989. 152 pp. ISBN 0-689-31458-2.

Jessie is just a year younger than her eighteen-year-old sister, who has died from cancer. Jessie's whole family reels under the loss, but for Jessie, it's especially bad. She is angry and also suffers depression, panic, and nightmares. Then she finds her sister's diary. Reading it and sharing her dying sister's experience help her to accept her sister's death. ★★★

5.23   Hall, Lynn. **Halsey's Pride.** Charles Scribner's Sons, 1990. 119 pp. ISBN 0-684-19155-5.

March Halsey is thirteen and epileptic. Her mother has decided that she is too much to handle and dumps her off at her father's— permanently. Here, March has two goals: to keep her epilepsy a secret at her new school and to make her father's dog kennel a success. March loves Pride, her father's prized dog, and it's through Pride that March gets to know her father and establish a new relationship with him while learning to accept herself as she is. ★

5.24   Hinton, S. E. **Taming the Star Runner.** Delacorte Press, 1988. 144 pp. ISBN 0-449-50058-3.

After getting in trouble and serving time in a detention center, fifteen-year-old Travis lands at his uncle's horse ranch where everyone hopes he will be rehabilitated. But Travis isn't the typical delinquent—he's written a book that he's trying to get published. ★★

5.25   Holland, Isabelle. **The Unfrightened Dark.** Little, Brown, 1990. 121 pp. ISBN 0-316-37173-4.

When Jocelyn Hunter was twelve, she lost her sight in an accident—the same accident that killed her parents. Jocelyn now lives with her Aunt Marion. She depends on her guide dog, Brace, and friends like Pip Mowbray for help and support. But neither of them can help her when she encounters people who claim that her dog is "imprisoned" and should be set free.

5.26   Holman, Felice. **Secret City, U.S.A.** Charles Scribner's Sons, 1990. 197 pp. ISBN 0-684-19168-7.

Thirteen-year-old Benno hates the crowded tenement where he lives. The only thing that had made it tolerable was the loving attention of his grandfather, whose death has left Benno frightened and lonely. Wandering the city, Benno and his friend Moon find a wasteland of wrecked and abandoned buildings. One house is still standing, and the two boys decide to make it a livable place for homeless people. They call it Secret City. With help from several street children and a few friends, Benno and Moon face wild dogs, the angry Poison gang, and the strange Mr. McWhat as they try to build an oasis of hope amid the decay of their city.

5.27   Hopper, Nancy J. **Wake Me When the Band Starts Playing.** Lodestar Books, 1988. 128 pp. ISBN 0-525-67244-3.

When it comes to eating, sixteen-year-old Mike Thatcher's a junkaholic; when it comes to exercise, he's a couch potato. But all this changes when he gets on the school swim team and becomes a successful diver. ★

5.28   Hughes, Dean. **Family Pose.** Atheneum, 1989. 184 pp. ISBN 0-689-31396-9.

Living on the streets of Seattle is much harder than eleven-year-old David expects. It's cold and often rainy, and the loneliness is even worse than it was when he lived with the Poulters. He sneaks into the Hotel Jefferson, finds a warm room where a Coke machine is, and sits down to rest. And that's where Paul, the night bellboy, finds him sound asleep. ★

5.29   Irwin, Hadley. **Can't Hear You Listening.** Margaret K. McElderry Books, 1990. 202 pp. ISBN 0-689-50513-2.

Sixteen-year-old Tracy Spencer constantly argues with her mother and also has to deal with her parents' trial separation. On top of all of these problems, Tracy sees changes in her childhood friend Stanley. Stanley was always a smart, responsible person, but suddenly he has become a party animal. Tracy knows that he has been using drugs, including alcohol. Now she has a difficult question to answer: How can you remain loyal to a friend and help him at the same time?

5.30 Irwin, Hadley. **So Long at the Fair.** Margaret K. McElderry Books, 1988. 208 pp. ISBN 0-689-50454-3.

Joel spends a week living at the state fair, but it isn't a week of fun and games. Instead, he spends the time trying to figure out why his friend Ashley committed suicide. The answers don't come easily, but Joel learns a lot about himself in this unusual week.

5.31 Klein, Norma. **Learning How to Fall.** Bantam Books, 1989. 181 pp. ISBN 0-553-05809-6.

Dusty Penrose suddenly finds himself in a psychiatric hospital when he can't cope with breaking up with his girlfriend Star. Dusty's father, a recovering alcoholic, had committed Dusty, and Dusty is angry with him for doing so. Amelia Eagan befriends Dusty, and they form a close relationship—until Star reenters the picture. Dusty feels confused and tormented as he tries to adjust to change, lost dreams, and missed opportunities. He doesn't know if he can survive without any emotional scars. Mature situations.

5.32 Klein, Norma. **No More Saturday Nights.** Alfred A. Knopf, 1988. 278 pp. ISBN 0-394-81944-6.

Tim Weber has had a hard time communicating with his father since his mother's death six years earlier. Bound for college, Tim makes the gap even wider when he decides that he will raise his child alone. He finds that parenting is demanding but not without joy—and he makes small inroads in the relationship with his own father.

5.33 Levitin, Sonia. **Incident at Loring Groves.** Dial Books for Young Readers, 1988. 192 pp. ISBN 0-8037-0455-0.

A teenage girl disappears. Later, a group of her classmates break into an unoccupied cottage and find her body. They decide not to tell anyone, but two of the group aren't sure that's the right decision. Based on a true story. ★

5.34 Levy, Marilyn. **Touching.** Fawcett/Juniper Books, 1988. 165 pp. ISBN 0-449-70267-7.

Wonderful things are beginning to happen for sixteen-year-old Eve Morrison. She has a part in the school play, and she has met the man of her dreams—his name is Torbin Black, and he looks just like Tom Cruise. But then life comes crashing down. Eve's father is an alcoholic, and Eve must learn to live with him as well as with the situation. ★

5.35 Lyon, George Ella. **Red Rover, Red Rover.** Orchard/Richard Jackson Books, 1989. 131 pp. ISBN 0-531-08432-9.

Eleven-year-old Sumi Mitchell misses her older brother Drake, who has left to attend prep school. She grieves her grandfather's sudden death from a heart attack. Sumi also loses her best friend, Keezie, who moves out of town. During this turbulent year, Sumi learns to cope with loss and find her own identity in her rapidly changing world.

5.36 Maggio, Rosalie. **The Music Box Christmas.** Morrow Junior Books, 1990. 128 pp. ISBN 0-688-08851-1.

Nick Latimar's grandmother has just died, and his father is in prison for cheating when he sold used cars. With only five days until Christmas, things don't look too good for the three Latimar kids. Mom isn't able to function without grandmother Gabby, who took care of them all after dad went to prison. The situation gets more complicated when Dad shows up unannounced—and unreleased. But Gabby's music box brings Nick around and guides the family through the holiday with the true Christmas spirit.

5.37 Mahy, Margaret. **Memory.** Margaret K. McElderry Books, 1988. 240 pp. ISBN 0-689-50445-2.

Nineteen-year-old Jonny Dart feels partially responsible for his sister's death. He struggles with painfully clear memories while Sophie, an elderly Alzheimer's victim, has painfully jumbled memories. Because of their friendship, the memories become less painful for Jonny as well as for Sophie. ★★★★

5.38 Marino, Jan. **Eighty-Eight Steps to September.** Little, Brown, 1989. 162 pp. ISBN 0-316-54620-8.

This summer for Amy promises to be the best. She has the excitement of a new dog, a brother to help build a doghouse, and a best friend. Even the steps up the hill in town are a pleasant nuisance—all eighty-eight of them. That is, until she beats her brother racing up them. She's never done that before. He is tired all the time—so tired that he must go to the hospital in Boston. The summer passes, but nothing goes right. The kids say Robbi won't ever come home. Are they correct or just being mean?

5.39   Mazer, Norma Fox. **Silver.** William Morrow, 1988. 261 pp. ISBN 0-688-06865-0.

Moving to a new school presents new problems and dilemmas for Sarabeth Silver. As she meets new friends, she finds that friendship requires more than simple telephone conversations and trips to the shopping mall. Asa, Grant, Patty, and Jennifer all become important parts of Sarabeth's life. When Patty shares the painful secret that her uncle is molesting her, Sarabeth must make decisions that are not easy. ★

5.40   McDaniel, Lurlene. **Too Young to Die.** Bantam/Starfire Books, 1989. 166 pp. ISBN 0-553-28008-2.

Melissa and her best friend Jory are evidence that opposites attract. Melissa is serious, studious, and goal oriented. Jory is a little rich girl who likes to party. She shows she is loyal when Melissa gets leukemia.

5.41   McDonnell, Christine. **Friends First.** Viking Penguin, 1990. 176 pp. ISBN 0-670-81923-9.

Fourteen-year-old Miranda is going through a lot of changes. She has been best friends with Gus and his family since infancy, but now that they're both growing up, Miranda feels confused and awkward. She's especially troubled about sexuality, particularly after someone tries to attack her in the hallway of her apartment house. Gradually, she comes to a new but different relationship with her old friend Gus.

5.42   McQuaid, Sandra. **Blindfold.** Holiday House, 1990. 167 pp. ISBN 0-8234-0811-6.

The whole town seems to blame Sally for the double suicide of her best friends, Benji and his blind brother Joel. Sally doesn't understand the tragedy any more than anyone else, and she seeks help from a psychiatrist to deal with her sense of loss, grief, and guilt.

5.43   Myers, Walter Dean. **Scorpions.** Harper and Row, 1988. 216 pp. ISBN 0-06-024365-1.

Jamal's brother Randy, leader of the Scorpions, is in jail—accused of murder. Randy says he's innocent, and his lawyer says they need money for an appeal, but there is barely enough money for food, and Jamal can hardly stand the desperation in Mama's eyes. About the only good thing in Jamal's life is his best friend, Tito. Then an old gang member brings word to Jamal that he is to take over as leader of the Scorpions until Randy gets out of jail. He also brings Jamal a gun—a way to show the older, tougher gang members that a twelve year old can be their leader. Tito tries to get Jamal to destroy the gun, but Jamal has already seen its power. His mistake is thinking he can handle it. ★★

5.44   Naughton, Jim. **My Brother Stealing Second.** Harper and Row, 1989. 213 pp. ISBN 0-06-024375-9.

Sixteen-year-old Bobby Connely is having trouble dealing with the death of his older brother. His parents aren't handling it much better and have moved from Ryder to Reese Point, the next town over. Bobby doesn't want to try out for baseball because it reminds him of Billy, who was a star shortstop. But through the wisdom of an older friend and a new girlfriend, Bobby begins to break out of his shell and heal—but then he discovers the awful truth about the accident that killed his brother. ★

5.45   Naylor, Phyllis R. **Send No Blessings.** Atheneum, 1990. 231 pp. ISBN 0-689-31582-1.

Fifteen-year-old Beth is the oldest of eight children, or "blessings," as her parents call them. She isn't excited about all of these "blessings" because most of the work involved falls on her. She prays that no more "blessings" will come to her family, which is already cramped, living in a trailer. Two teachers help Beth cope with her present situation as she plans the kind of life she wants for herself. ★

5.46   Pevsner, Stella. **How Could You Do It, Diane?** Clarion Books, 1989. 183 pp. ISBN 0-395-51041-4.

Her family is shattered when fifteen-year-old Diane commits suicide. Her stepsister Bethany thinks that finding the reason will help them understand her death. Even though they never find *the* reason, the family gradually begins healing as they go about their daily tasks. ★★★

5.47   Roberts, Nadine. **With Love, from Sam and Me.** Fawcett/
             Juniper Books, 1990. 135 pp. ISBN 0-449-70368-1.

             Although Marylou can tolerate the cold and sometimes harsh
             treatment she gets from her foster parents, their abuse of her new
             foster brother, a mere toddler whom she loves, is more than she
             can bear. She makes off with him one night, a decision which leads
             her through some frightening situations.

5.48   Samuels, Barbara. **Yours, Brett.** Lodestar Books, 1988. 192 pp.
             ISBN 0-525-67255-9.

             For ten long years, Brett was transferred from one foster home to
             another. Finally, she lands in Second-Chance House and begins
             to accept and appreciate her own strengths. For Brett, there's a
             happy ending, but some of her friends aren't so fortunate.

5.49   Schnur, Steven. **Hannah and Cyclops.** Bantam/Skylark Books,
             1990. 80 pp. ISBN 0-553-15796-5.

             Rafi comes to school with so many cuts and bruises that the kids
             think he's a real klutz; the teacher calls him accident prone. When
             he shows up with a black eye, his classmates nickname him
             "Cyclops," but Hannah begins to wonder whether Rafi's injuries
             really are accidental. But no one—not her parents, her teacher, or
             her friend, Judge Gilbert—believes her when she tries to tell them
             that Rafi is in serious trouble.

5.50   Schusterman, Neal. **The Shadow Club.** Little, Brown, 1988.
             183 pp. ISBN 0-316-77540-1.

             The kids in this book are competitors, and they join together to
             play practical jokes on their competition. The jokes get out of
             hand, so that pretty soon they aren't funny, even to their creators.

5.51   Slepian, Jan. **Risk n' Roses.** Philomel Books, 1990. 175 pp. ISBN
             0-399-22219-7.

             Having just moved to the Bronx, Skip is anxious to join the "in"
             group on her street, led by the wild, daring Jean Persico; but she
             sees innocent, guileless Angela, her mentally retarded sister, as a
             drawback to being accepted. While carrying out the "dares"
             concocted by Jean for initiation into her club, Skip realizes her
             own strengths and loyalties. ★

5.52   Smith, Marya. **Winter-Broken.** Arcade, 1990. 120 pp. ISBN 1-
             55970-064-5.

Twelve-year-old Dawn's father is an alcoholic who emotionally and physically abuses his wife and children. Dawn's one pleasure in life is helping a neighbor care for a horse that she names Wildfire. Her love for the horse, even after it is sold, helps Dawn cope with the grim situation at home.

5.53 Tolan, Stephanie S. **Plague Year.** Morrow Junior Books, 1990. 198 pp. ISBN 0-688-08801-5.

David Watson tells the story of Bran Slocum from his first day in Ridgewood to his last. The jocks and their followers at school immediately dislike Bran because he looks weird, wears strange clothes, and acts mysteriously. Molly, David's best friend, leads the defense of Bran from the school bullies and the bigoted townspeople, who discover the secret of the newcomer's strange behavior as a wave of fear and hatred plague the once ordinary Ridgewood.

5.54 Van Raven, Pieter. **The Great Man's Secret.** Charles Scribner's Sons, 1989. 176 pp. ISBN 0-684-19041-9.

Jerry Huffaker's journalism teacher sends him to interview a famous author who just turned down the Nobel Prize for Literature. The "great man" lost his legs in an accident several years earlier and since then has been a recluse. Perhaps he's tired of being alone, or perhaps he enjoys the irony of having an interview in a high school newspaper instead of all the glory of the Nobel Prize, or maybe he just thinks Jerry's a good kid. Whatever the reason, the great man warms up to Jerry, and they become friends. ★

5.55 Wallace, Bill. **The Christmas Spurs.** Holiday House, 1990. 119 pp. ISBN 0-8-234-0831-0.

Eleven-year-old Nick and his younger brother Jimmy have an unusual relationship. Despite the difference in their ages, the two of them are extremely close as they grow up surrounded by cowboys, horses, and big rigs in Oklahoma. But when Jimmy is diagnosed with leukemia, Nick begins to see his brother in a different light. He is torn between the values his parents taught him, ideas about miracles and God's love he has learned in church, and his own feelings of loss and loneliness. A small, personal Christmas miracle helps Nick come to terms with his brother's illness and his own feelings.

5.56   Willey, Margaret. **If Not for You.** Harper Keypoint Books, 1990. 154 pp. ISBN 0-06-447015-6.

When Linda and her boyfriend, both high school seniors, elope, Bonnie thinks it's too glamorous to be true. But when they come back married and with a baby, Bonnie's view of them and of her own life changes.

5.57   Wolff, Virginia Euwer. **Probably Still Nick Swansen.** Henry Holt, 1988. 144 pp. ISBN 0-8050-0701-6.

Nick Swansen, a high school student with learning disabilities, is self-conscious about being placed in a special resource room. But in this class, he meets Shana, who accepts his invitation to go to the prom. What happens there, however, is nothing like what Nick was expecting. ★★★★

5.58   Zindel, Paul. **A Begonia for Miss Applebaum.** Harper and Row, 1989. 180 pp. ISBN 0-06-026877-8.

Miss Applebaum earned her nickname "The Shocker" through the wonderful revelations she regularly surprises her high school science classes with. When Henry and Zelda, best friends who share a devotion to Miss Applebaum, discover that their mentor is terminally ill, they join her in countless, colorful, enlightening romps through New York City that make her last weeks full and exciting. ★

Recommended Books about Problems Published before 1988

Anonymous. *Go Ask Alice.* Prentice-Hall, 1971.
Arrick, Fran. *Chernowitz.* Bradbury Press, 1981.
Arrick, Fran. *Tunnel Vision.* Bradbury Press, 1980.
Bach, Alice. *Waiting for Johnny Miracle.* Harper and Row, 1980.
Beckman, Gunnel. *Admission to the Feast.* Dell, 1973.
Brancato, Robin. *Winning.* Alfred A. Knopf, 1977.
Byars, Betsy. *Cracker Jackson.* Viking, 1985.
Byars, Betsy. *The Two-Thousand Pound Goldfish.* Harper and Row, 1982.
Cleary, Beverly. *Dear Mr. Henshaw.* William Morrow, 1983.
Cleaver, Vera, and Bill Cleaver. *Grover.* J. B. Lippincott, 1976.
Cleaver, Vera, and Bill Cleaver. *Trial Valley.* J. B. Lippincott, 1977.
Cleaver, Vera, and Bill Cleaver. *Where the Lilies Bloom.* J. B. Lippincott, 1969.

Cormier, Robert. *I Am the Cheese.* Pantheon Books, 1977.

Craven, Margaret. *I Heard the Owl Call My Name.* Doubleday, 1973.

Crutcher, Chris. *The Crazy Horse Electric Game.* Greenwillow Books, 1987.

Cunningham, Julia. *Come to the Edge.* Pantheon Books, 1977.

Cunningham, Julia. *Dorp Dead.* Pantheon Books, 1965.

Danziger, Paula. *The Cat Ate My Gymsuit.* Delacorte Press, 1974.

Fox, Paula. *One-Eyed Cat.* Bradbury Press, 1984.

Greene, Constance C. *Beat the Turtle Drum.* Viking Penguin, 1976.

Hautzig, Deborah. *Second Star to the Right.* Greenwillow Books, 1981.

Holland, Isabelle. *The Man without a Face.* J. B. Lippincott, 1971.

Holman, Felice. *Slake's Limbo.* Charles Scribner's Sons, 1974.

Hughes, Monica. *Hunter in the Dark.* Atheneum, 1983.

Hunt, Irene. *The Lottery Rose.* Charles Scribner's Sons, 1976.

Kerr, M. E. *Little Little.* Harper and Row, 1981.

Kerr, M. E. *Night Kites.* Harper and Row, 1986.

Levenkron, Steven. *The Best Little Girl in the World.* Contemporary Books, 1978.

Levitin, Sonia. *The Return.* Atheneum, 1987.

Lowry, Lois. *A Summer To Die.* Houghton Mifflin, 1977.

Major, Kevin. *Far from Shore.* Delacorte Press, 1981.

Mathis, Sharon Bell. *Teacup Full of Roses.* Penguin/Puffin, 1972.

Olsen, Violet. *Never Brought to Mind.* Atheneum, 1985.

Oneal, Zibby. *A Formal Feeling.* Viking Penguin, 1982.

Paterson, Katherine. *Bridge to Terabithia.* Thomas Y. Crowell, 1977.

Peck, Richard. *Are You in the House Alone?* Viking Penguin, 1976.

Peck, Richard. *Remembering the Good Times.* Delacorte Press, 1985.

Peck, Richard. *Something for Joey.* Bantam Books, 1978.

Rodowsky, Colby. *The Gathering Room.* Farrar, Straus and Giroux, 1981.

Slepian, Jan. *The Alfred Summer.* Macmillan, 1980.

Smith, Doris B. *A Taste of Blackberries.* Thomas Y. Crowell, 1973.

Voigt, Cynthia. *Izzy, Willy-Nilly.* Atheneum, 1986.

Winthrop, Elizabeth. *A Little Demonstration of Affection.* Harper and Row, 1975.

6 Understanding Ourselves: Ethnic Relationships (Historical and Contemporary)

6.1 Barrie, Barbara. **Lone Star.** Delacorte Press, 1990. 182 pp. ISBN 0-385-30156-1.

It is 1944, and young Jane Miller and her family have moved from Chicago to Corpus Christi, Texas, in an attempt to make a new start. The Millers have left behind friends, relatives, and strong ties to their Jewish faith. Now Jane must grapple with a new city, a new school, new friends, and new and different customs. While Jane is trying to sort out her new life, her parents and grandfather are fighting to keep their Jewish traditions alive. At the same time, everyone is haunted by the fierce battles that Hitler is waging in Europe.

6.2 Cannon, A. E. **The Shadow Brothers.** Delacorte Press, 1990. 180 pp. ISBN 0-385-29982-6.

When he was seven years old, Henry Yazzie left his Navajo family to move in with the Jenkinses. He grew up as a foster brother to Marcus Jenkins, and now that they are in high school, they are enjoying the typical fun and challenges of dating, working, and participating in athletics. Then a boy from the Hopi tribe comes to their high school, and he teases Henry for his white ways. He calls him an apple—red on the outside but white on the inside. The effect on Henry is deep and causes him to rethink his whole life. ★

6.3 Crew, Linda. **Children of the River.** Delacorte Press, 1989. 213 pp. ISBN 0-385-29690-8.

Four years before this story begins, thirteen-year-old Sundara had been swinging on a breezy porch in a Cambodian fishing village, dreaming of her coming marriage to Chamroeun. Then the Khmer Rouge brought war to her country and separated her from her family. After six weeks on a crowded boat, she and her aunt's family arrived in the Philippines and finally in Oregon. Now seventeen and an honors student, Sundara tries to adapt to American customs—and to handle her growing love for Jonathan, the handsome football star.

6.4   Guy, Rosa. **The Ups and Downs of Carl Davis III.** Delacorte Press, 1989. 113 pp. ISBN 0-385-29724-6.

Twelve-year-old Carl Davis III feels confused and betrayed when he is suddenly sent from his New York City home to live with his grandmother in a small southern town. His teacher and fellow students don't like his pompous displays of brilliance or his insistence on an awareness of black heritage. Eventually, he learns the mystery of his banishment and some valuable lessons in life.

6.5   Hernández, Irene Beltran. **Across the Great River.** Arte Público Press, 1989. 136 pp. ISBN 0-934770-96-4.

Growing up fast is not what little Kata had planned, but the journey across the Rio Grande certainly speeds up that process. As her family travels from Mexico to America, the land of opportunity, her father is drowned, and her mother is wounded. The image of the giant man with a tattoo on his wrist, who helped her family cross the river, haunts her day and night. Adjusting to this promised land becomes a test of endurance, and Kata must survive many hardships.

6.6   Hobbs, Will. **Bearstone.** Atheneum, 1989. 144 pp. ISBN 0-689-31496-5.

Fourteen-year-old Cloyd is a Ute Indian who would rather be living in the southern Utah canyons than going to school, where he feels that the system, as well as individual classmates and teachers, are against him. Cloyd's mother is dead, and his father is kept alive only by machines. He resents being sent to spend the summer as a helper to an elderly farmer whose wife recently died.
★

6.7   Okimoto, Jean Davies. **Molly by Any Other Name.** Scholastic, 1990. 276 pp. ISBN 0-590-42993-0.

Molly is a seventeen-year-old Asian girl who was adopted and now grows curious about her heritage. She knows the agency that can put her in touch with her birth mother, but how can she tell her adoptive parents? When she breaks the news, her mother is supportive, but her father fears he will lose Molly. Eventually, he tries to understand, especially after meeting others like Molly. When the court opens her records, Molly has a big decision to make. Does she really want to meet her birth mother? And will the person who gave Molly away seventeen years ago want to see her?

6.8   Paulsen, Gary. **Canyons.** Delacorte Press, 1990. 184 pp. ISBN 0-385-30153-7.

A century ago, a Native American boy, Canyon Runs, hoped to gain his manhood by going on a raid with the men of his tribe. His dream ended with a bullet in his head, and his spirit cannot rest because his body was not buried properly. A contemporary teenager, Brennan Cole, wants to earn a feeling of independence by camping out for a spell and living on his own. Brennan finds a skull, and it's as if a compulsion guides him to do the right thing.

6.9   Pitts, Paul. **Racing the Sun.** Avon/Camelot Books, 1988. 150 pp. ISBN 0-380-75496-7.

The smell of cedarwood smoke and other bits of Navajo culture invade twelve-year-old Brandon Rogers's home when his grandfather comes from the reservation to stay with Brandon's family. Keith Rogers, Brandon's dad, has long since adopted the culture of the white American suburbs, even changing his Indian name. But Brandon's grandfather teaches Brandon something about Navajo ways as he learns to "race the sun."

6.10   Robinson, Margaret A. **A Woman of Her Tribe.** Charles Scribner's Sons, 1990. 131 pp. ISBN 0-684-19223-3.

Annette is fifteen and in-between: half Anglo and half Nootka Indian. She must choose between the country, where she was raised by her family and her Granmaw, and the city, which she finds frightening yet thrilling and full of exciting new people. Must she choose between the demands of her Native American heritage and her own dreams of the future?

6.11   Rosofsky, Iris. **Miriam.** Harper and Row, 1988. 192 pp. ISBN 0-06-024854-8.

Sometimes life is full of joy, and sometimes it's full of sorrow. Miriam tells about growing up in a traditional Jewish family with all its celebrations and rituals. She also tells about her brother's life from the time he is born until he dies at age thirteen. The tragedy leads Miriam to question her faith and also to reflect on her own life's purpose. You'll feel you know Miriam and can understand her struggle to find her own way while not leaving behind all that her family and faith have given her.

6.12   Singer, Marilyn. **Several Kinds of Silence.** Harper and Row, 1988. 275 pp. ISBN 0-06-025627-3.

Sixteen-year-old Franny resents sharing her room with her diabetic grandmother; her younger sister, Lainie, is a brat; and her father hates anything Japanese. When Franny's job as a flower shop assistant furthers her relationship with the Japanese American Dragon Boy of her fantasies, she moves farther away from family and friends and becomes more and more anguished. She has always used her silence to keep peace in the family, but the price is becoming too high.

6.13   Smith, K. **Skeeter.** Houghton Mifflin, 1989. 208 pp. ISBN 0-395-49603-9.

Even though their personalities are almost opposite, Joey and Steve are best friends, drawn together by their love of hunting in the woods of rural Tennessee. The boys are white, and when they meet elderly Skeeter Hawkins, who is black and known for his skill as a hunter, they're shy. But over the next few months, this unlikely trio learns more than just hunting skills.

6.14   Spinelli, Jerry. **Maniac Magee.** Little, Brown, 1990. 184 pp. ISBN 0-316-80722-2.

When white Jeffrey Magee is orphaned at age three, he is sent to live with an aunt and uncle who feud constantly. After eight years of that tense atmosphere, the boy runs away. Now the incredible adventures begin, and he truly earns the nickname "Maniac." Eventually, Jeffrey is taken in by a black family, and they all learn some things about racism. ★★★

6.15   Taylor, Mildred D. **The Road to Memphis.** Dial Press, 1990. 288 pp. ISBN 0-8037-0340-6.

If you've read *Roll of Thunder, Hear My Cry* or *Let the Circle Be Unbroken*, then you already know the spunky heroine of *The Road to Memphis*. She is Cassie Logan, who by now is seventeen years old and is being forced to learn about the realities of racism in Mississippi during the 1940s. The unfairness that Cassie sees all around her makes her decide to become a lawyer, even though she realizes full well that it's going to take more than the law to solve the problems she observes. ★

6.16   Todd, Leonard. **Squaring Off.** Viking Penguin, 1990. 150 pp. ISBN 0-670-83377-0.

Thirteen-year-old Willy Stamp is attempting to come to terms with his life in Savannah, Georgia, during the mid-1950s.

Segregation is an issue, but more important to motherless Willy is his relationship to his father and his father's relationship to LuJane Jessup, a striptease dancer. The title comes from Willy's attempts to "square off" with his problems, which by the end of the story, he manages to do. ★

6.17   Van Raven, Pieter. **Pickle and Price.** Charles Scribner's Sons, 1990. 202 pp. ISBN 0-784-19162-8.

It's the early 1950s, and two unlikely young men join forces. They meet on a prison farm while Price, who is black, is doing time for a crime he didn't commit. Pickle is the white, fourteen-year-old son of the farm's manager. When Price is released, Pickle decides this would be a good time to steal the farm truck and run away from his abusive father. They get to Price's old home in Detroit, where all is not well, and so they head out for California and a summer filled with adventure. ★

6.18   Yarbrough, Camille. **The Shimmershine Queens.** G. P. Putnam's Sons, 1989. 144 pp. ISBN 0-399-21465-8.

Angie's elderly cousin tells her about "shimmershine." This is her cousin's word for good feelings of pride and satisfaction in her African heritage. Angie desperately needs some shimmershine to make her feel better about herself and about the troubles her parents are having. By the end of the book, thanks to a good friend and a good teacher, Angie begins to glow with some of her own shimmershine. ★

Recommended Books about Ethnic Relationships Published before 1988

Armstrong, William H. *Sounder.* Harper and Row, 1969.
Brooks, Bruce. *The Moves Make the Man.* Harper and Row, 1984.
Childress, Alice. *A Hero Ain't Nothin' but a Sandwich.* Putnam/Coward-McCann, 1973.
Childress, Alice. *Rainbow Jordan.* Putnam/Coward-McCann, 1981.
Forman, James. *The Life and Death of Yellow Bird.* Farrar, Straus and Giroux, 1973.
Fox, Paula. *The Slave Dancer.* Bradbury Press, 1973.
George, Jean. *Julie of the Wolves.* Harper and Row, 1972.
Guy, Rosa. *The Friends.* Henry Holt, 1973.
Hamilton, Virginia. *Arilla Sun Down.* Greenwillow Books, 1976.
Hamilton, Virginia. *M. C. Higgins the Great.* Macmillan, 1974.

Highwater, Jamake. *Legend Days*. Harper and Row, 1984.

Levoy, Myron. *Alan and Naomi*. Harper and Row, 1977.

Mazer, Harry. *The War on Villa Street*. Delacorte Press, 1978.

Mohr, Nicholasa. *El Bronx Remembered*. Harper and Row, 1975.

Mohr, Nicholasa. *Going Home*. Dial Books for Young Readers, 1986.

Mohr, Nicholasa. *In Nueva York*. Dial Press, 1977.

Myers, Walter Dean. *Fast Sam, Cool Clyde, and Stuff*. Viking Penguin, 1975.

O'Dell, Scott. *Island of the Blue Dolphins*. Houghton Mifflin, 1960.

O'Dell, Scott. *The King's Fifth*. Houghton Mifflin, 1966.

Paulsen, Gary. *Dogsong*. Bradbury Press, 1985.

Sebestyen, Ouida. *Words by Heart*. Atlantic Monthly Press, 1979.

Speare, Elizabeth George. *The Sign of the Beaver*. Houghton Mifflin, 1983.

Voigt, Cynthia. *Come a Stranger*. Atheneum, 1986.

Wilkinson, Brenda. *Ludell*. Harper and Row, 1975.

Wilkinson, Brenda. *Ludell and Willie*. Harper and Row, 1977.

Williams-Garcia, Rita. *Blue Tights*. Lodestar Books, 1987.

Yep, Laurence. *Child of the Owl*. Harper and Row, 1977.

Yep, Laurence. *Dragonwings*. Harper and Row, 1975.

Yep, Laurence. *Sea Glass*. Harper and Row, 1979.

7 Understanding the Past: Realistic Books Set in the United States before 1960

7.1 Cameron, Eleanor. **The Private Worlds of Julia Redfern.** E. P. Dutton, 1988. 224 pp. ISBN 0-525-44394-0.

Julia first appeared in *A Room Made of Windows*, and now, five books later, she's a mature young woman who faces her father's death and her first love. The book is set in Berkeley, California, just after World War I, but you'll see many similarities between your own successes and problems and Julia's. ★

7.2 Collier, James Lincoln. **The Winchesters.** Macmillan, 1988. 169 pp. ISBN 0-02-722831-2.

The mill workers are about to strike because they resent their treatment by the powerful Winchester family, owners of the company and most of the town. Even though fourteen-year-old Chris is only a poor relation, he is about to lose his best friend and his girlfriend just because he bears the family name. But despite suffering and injustice, he refuses to perpetuate further injustices, and this means standing up to the Winchester barons.

7.3 Conrad, Pam. **My Daniel.** Harper and Row, 1989. 137 pp. ISBN 0-06-021313-2.

Twelve-year-old Ellie and her younger brother spend an enchanting day in New York's Natural History Museum with their eighty-year-old grandmother, Julia. Julia recollects her girlhood on a Nebraska farm; she was Ellie's age during the memorable year that she and her brother discovered a full dinosaur skeleton, which Julia is now seeing for the first time in the museum as she shares the experience with her grandchildren. ★★

7.4 Defelice, Cynthia. **Weasel.** Macmillan, 1990. 119 pp. ISBN 0-02-726457-2.

Fear clutches the hearts of two pioneer children, Nathan and Molly. A mysterious, mute stranger comes to their cabin door late one dark evening. In hopes of finding their pa, who has been missing for six days, they follow the man into the dark depths of the forest. The tension mounts when eleven-year-old Nathan comes face to face with the dreaded man the Indians call Weasel. His family and friends have been tortured and terrorized by this demon for many years. Nathan faces a struggle between his urge for revenge and his sense of what's right. ★★

7.5   Downing, Warwick. **Kid Curry's Last Ride.** Orchard Books, 1989. 166 pp. ISBN 0-531-05802-6.

Alexander Penrose III is shipped off to Sheridan, Wyoming to spend the summer of 1935 with his grandmother while his parents sail away to France. Compared to his hometown of Denver, Sheridan is just a hole in the wall, close to the real Hole in the Wall of Butch Cassidy and the Sundance Kid. Alex makes friends with an old geezer, who claims to be Kid Curry, a leftover from Butch Cassidy's gang. In the end, Alex gets more excitement and adventure than he would ever have found if he'd stayed home in Denver.

7.6   Edwards, Pat. **Little John and Plutie.** Houghton Mifflin, 1988. 180 pp. ISBN 0-395-48223-2.

John Greer is excited that his dad is returning from Memphis. The mules he's bringing back are to be part of a new beginning for the family after a series of misfortunes. The changes that occur, though, aren't quite what John had anticipated, especially the move to town to live with his grandmother. But there he discovers a special friend in the bold and upbeat Pluto. John is white and Pluto is black, and the limits placed on the friendship surprise John and awaken him to some harsh realities of the turn-of-the-century South.

7.7   Fleischman, Paul. **Saturnalia.** Harper and Row, 1990. 113 pp. ISBN 0-06-021912-2.

In ancient Rome, masters and slaves exchanged places during Saturnalia. As plans are being made for a Saturnalia celebration in colonial Boston, the lives of a tithingman, a printer, a printer's apprentice, a captured Narraganset Indian, a wigmaker, and the wigmaker's dishonest servant become interwoven. ★★★

7.8   Hamilton, Virginia. **Anthony Burns: The Defeat and Triumph of a Fugitive Slave.** Alfred A. Knopf, 1988. 193 pp. ISBN 0-394-98185-5.

Prize-winning writer Virginia Hamilton brings to life the true story of Anthony Burns, a twenty-year-old slave. Burns escaped to Boston in 1854, and when his owner came to take him back to the South, thousands of abolitionists rose to defend him. The legal and physical struggles that ensued foreshadowed the Civil War. Because no one kept information on Anthony Burns until he became famous, Hamilton had to "backfill" much of the information about his early life based on her research of the period and the events. ★★★★

7.9   Hamm, Diane Johnston. **Bunkhouse Journal.** Charles Scribner's Sons, 1990. 112 pp. ISBN 0-684-19206-3.

It is 1910, and sixteen-year-old Sandy Mannix has run away from Denver and his alcoholic father. He's living on a ranch in Wyoming, where he works for his cousin and her husband, and for the first time, he feels that he has a real family and friends. Yet he worries about his father and his brother and whether or not he should return to help them.

7.10 Hansen, Joyce. **Out from This Place.** Walker, 1988. 135 pp. ISBN 0-8027-6817-2.

This book continues the pre-Civil War story told in *Which Way Freedom*. Easter joins a group of runaway slaves who work on an island plantation for pay. She learns to read and then faces the painful choice of whether to try to go to school or wait for Obi, who has promised to join her. ★

7.11 Hotze, Sollace. **A Circle Unbroken.** Clarion Books, 1988. 224 pp. ISBN 0-89919-733-7.

Based on true events, this is the story of ten-year-old Rachel Porter, a frontier child captured and abused in an Indian raid in which her mother and siblings are killed. After the raid, she is adopted by a chief of the Dakota Sioux and raised as Kata Wi ("Burning Sun," after her red hair). When at age seventeen she is returned to her embittered father and white society, Rachel spends a difficult year trying to figure out who she is and where she belongs.

7.12 Houston, Gloria. **Littlejim.** Philomel Books, 1990. 172 pp. ISBN 0-399-22220-0.

Twelve-year-old Littlejim, growing up in the Appalachians early in this century, wants to become a writer. He has a chance to win a contest and have his essay published in the *Kansas City Star*. But his father insists on Littlejim's doing "man's work" on the farm and at the lumber mill instead of indulging in the "tomfoolery" that he learns at school. Luckily, Littlejim has wise allies in his mother, his sister, his teacher, and other people in his community.

7.13   Howard, Ellen. **Her Own Song.** Atheneum, 1988. 193 pp. ISBN 0-689-31444-2.

Ten-year-old Mellie knows she's adopted, but she doesn't know that she has had two adoptive families and that the first one was Chinese. She lives in Seattle in 1905, and widespread prejudice against Chinese immigrants there presents her with intriguing challenges as she adjusts to her family situation.

7.14   Hudson, Jan. **Sweetgrass.** Philomel Books, 1989. 157 pp. ISBN 0-399-21721-5.

Sweetgrass is a fifteen-year-old Blackfoot girl, living with her tribe in western Canada. She is anxious to be married to Eagle-Sun, but her parents feel she is not yet mature enough. She tolerates her brother, ponders a woman's unrecognized place, toils, dreams, and helps her tribe survive a bitter winter and a devastating outbreak of smallpox. ★★★★★

7.15   Kadohata, Cynthia. **The Floating World.** Viking Penguin, 1989. 196 pp. ISBN 0-670-82680-4.

At twelve, Olivia was pinched unmercifully by her Japanese grandmother; by the time she's in her twenties, she lives with her boyfriend Andy who wrecks cars for a living. Her memories of growing up include her first boyfriend Tan, her job at a chicken hatchery, and the many towns she and her family lived in because of the difficulty Japanese Americans had finding work in the years just after World War II.

7.16   Karr, Kathleen. **It Ain't Always Easy.** Farrar, Straus and Giroux, 1990. 229 pp. ISBN 0-374-33645-8.

Eleven-year-old Jack McConnell has been taking care of himself since his family died in an epidemic. Eight-year-old Mandy Kerrigan seeks his help to learn survival on the streets, and they become a team. When they are found sleeping in a hallway, they are taken by the Children's Aid Society of New York to be sent West for adoption. Jack and Mandy then begin a quest to find a safe place to be together with good adults and relative security. In spite of many setbacks and disappointments, Jack never gives up until his search takes him back to New York where he began.

7.17 Lasky, Kathryn. **The Bone Wars.** William Morrow, 1988. 378 pp. ISBN 0-688-07433-2.

In 1885, teenagers Julian DeMott and Thaddeus Longsworth team up to uncover dinosaur remains in the Badlands of Montana. They face such obstacles as Indian wars, competition between opposing teams of paleontologists, and interference from army generals and government officials. ★

7.18 Levitin, Sonia. **Silver Days.** Atheneum, 1989. 190 pp. ISBN 0-689-31563-5.

A German family reunites in New York in 1940. Their "silver days" occur between 1940 and 1943, when they move to California, and Lisa can again study dancing, as she did before they left Germany. This book continues the story begun in *Journey to America.* ★

7.19 Luhrmann, Winifred Bruce. **Only Brave Tomorrows.** Houghton Mifflin, 1989. 190 pp. ISBN 0-395-47983-5.

Faith Ralston has been raised in seventeenth-century England by her Aunt Abbie, and she expects life to go on in the same genteel, ladylike fashion. Suddenly, her father arrives to reclaim her and take her back to the Massachusetts colony where he now lives. Faith is strong and resourceful, and although life on the American Frontier presents a challenge, she manages. But then she is caught up in King Philip's War and is forced to face the deaths of fellow colonists as well as her isolation in the New World.

7.20 Lyon, George Ella. **Borrowed Children.** Orchard Books, 1988. 160 pp. ISBN 0-531-08351-9.

It's the Depression in Kentucky, and when Mandy's mother has to stay in bed for six weeks after the birth of a new brother, Mandy must stay home from school to take care of the family. After the crisis is over, Mandy gets to visit her grandparents in Memphis where she is surprised to learn that even though her grandparents have money, her mother's childhood hadn't been so different from Mandy's. ★★

7.21 Martin, Katherine. **Night Riding.** Alfred A. Knopf/Borzoi Sprinters, 1989. 197 pp. ISBN 0-679-90064-0.

Prin's summer starts off badly and doesn't improve with time. Two days after school is out, her father has to go to the hospital for tuberculosis treatments, leaving Prin, eleven, her sister, Jo Lynn, fifteen, and their mother to deal with their farm and their business. Prin's mother is expecting a baby, and their family situation becomes worse when their Aunt May comes to live with them. But even worse, the Hammonds next door are causing problems. Mary Faith, the fifteen-year-old daughter, is pregnant, and B.Z., the father, is menacing. When Prin takes to riding her father's horses at night, new problems surface.

7.22   Moore, Robin. **The Bread Sister of Sinking Creek.** J. B. Lippincott, 1990. 154 pp. ISBN 0-397-32418-9.

Maggie is a young orphaned girl who lives in Pennsylvania in the 1800s. She finds her way deep into the hills there where she finds strength within herself and an opportunity to carve her niche in the wilderness. Her gift is that of bread making, handed down to her by her Irish aunt. Maggie shares her gift with others, bringing a bit of happiness to the difficult lives of the pioneers.

7.23   Moore, Robin. **Maggie among the Seneca.** J. B. Lippincott, 1990. 144 pp. ISBN 0-397-32456-1.

The year is 1778, and in this sequel to *The Bread Sister of Sinking Creek*, sixteen-year-old Maggie Callahan is captured by Seneca Indians in central Pennsylvania. She lives with the Seneca for several years, marrying a Seneca man and giving birth to his child. After her husband is killed by a wolf and her baby is taken from her, she manages to make her way back to the Allegheny River and the tavern which her aunt manages.

7.24   Peck, Robert Newton. **Arly.** Walker, 1989. 160 pp. ISBN 0-8027-6856-3.

"The roaring twenties" are usually thought of as a time of prosperity—at least until the stock market crash and the Great Depression came in 1929. But for Arly's family, field-workers in Jailtown, Florida, the stock market crash doesn't make much difference. They are already as poor as they can be. But when the first schoolteacher comes to the community, Arly's father makes Arly go to school, because he knows the world isn't always going to be like it is in Jailtown.

7.25   Peck, Robert Newton. **The Horse Hunters.** Random House, 1988. 215 pp. ISBN 0-394-56980-6.

Fifteen-year-old Ladd Bodeen sets out through the Florida wilds in 1932. He's after a herd of mares and a white stallion that has evaded capture for over thirty years. Hoping to win his unyielding older brother's respect and to bring in some much needed cash to the ranch, Ladd becomes a horse hunter. His adventures with the young girl Cora and his father's former partner, Dodge Yardell, give him insight into what it takes to be a man.

7.26   Perez, N. A. **Breaker.** Houghton Mifflin, 1988. 207 pp. ISBN 0-395-45537-5.

A mine cave-in kills Patrick McFarlane's father in turn-of-the-century northeastern Pennsylvania. Fourteen-year-old Patrick is then forced to leave school and go to work as a breaker in the mines, sorting coal and breathing the heavy coal dust. But times are changing for the miners; frustrated and angry over the inhumane conditions, they are threatening to strike. If that happens, Patrick and his family will be caught in the middle of the violence. This book is based on the true story of the mine workers' strike of 1902.

7.27   Pople, Maureen. **A Nugget of Gold.** Henry Holt, 1988. 183 pp. ISBN 0-8050-0984-1.

The lives of sixteen-year-old Sally Matthews, a modern teenager, and Ann Bird Shipton, a young woman who lived a hundred years before, become entangled when Sally finds a golden brooch. The brooch compels Sally to investigate a mystery from the past.

7.28   Poynter, Margaret. **A Time Too Swift.** Atheneum, 1990. 216 pp. ISBN 0-689-31146-X.

Living in San Diego in 1941, Marjorie learns that war brings more horror than glamor as her friends, family, and first boyfriend suffer its effects.

7.29   Reeder, Carolyn. **Shades of Gray.** Macmillan, 1989. 176 pp. ISBN 0-02-775810-9.

The Civil War is over, and Will Page finds himself an orphan. He is sent to live with some relatives that he can't respect because they had not joined the Confederate cause. But eventually, as he sees how hard they must work to keep their farm going, he begins to think about them in a different way. ★

7.30   Rinaldi, Ann. **The Last Silk Dress.** Holiday House, 1988. 350 pp. ISBN 0-8234-0690-3.

Fourteen-year-old Susan Chilmark decides to please her mother and aid the Confederate Army during the Civil War by collecting the last silk dresses of the southern ladies to make a spy balloon. As she matures, she begins to question the Southern way of life as well as her actions to aid the Confederacy. She must make decisions that could isolate her from her family as well as her country. ★

7.31   Ross, Rhea Beth. **The Bet's On, Lizzie Bingman!** Illustrated by Pamela Johnson. Houghton Mifflin, 1988. 186 pp. ISBN 0-395-44472-1.

In the summer of 1914, fourteen-year-old Lizzie Bingman declares her independence from men. Lizzie wants to vote, to walk the streets of Granby unescorted by her brothers, and to pick and choose her own friends without the interference of her family. And so she makes a bet with her older brother that she can take care of herself. Little does Lizzie realize that not only adventure but real danger await her as she investigates her world alone.

7.32   Thesman, Jean. **Rachel Chance.** Houghton Mifflin, 1990. 175 pp. ISBN 0-395-50934-3.

It is 1940, and Rachel Chance's family faces many problems. The most serious is the kidnapping of Rider, her two-year-old half brother. His being born out of wedlock does not keep fifteen-year-old Rachel from loving him. Since a preacher's friends set fire to her grandfather's field, Rachel believes they stole Rider. She sets out to get him back, taking an unusual assortment of helpers: her grandfather, a teenage farm hand, and a fortune-teller. They trace the route of the preacher and his gang until they come upon a big surprise! ★

7.33   Van Raven, Pieter. **A Time of Troubles.** Charles Scribner's Sons, 1990. 192 pp. ISBN 0-684-19212-8.

Roy Purdy faithfully visits his father Harlow each month for the four years Harlow is imprisoned for arson. Upon Harlow's release, the two set out across the United States with the promise of a new life, new ways, and a guaranteed job in Depression era California. But old habits die hard, and Roy must accept the fact that prison has added even more troublesome traits to his father's character. The choices are not easy, but Roy survived while his father was away and will do so again. He must.

7.34 Voigt, Cynthia. **Tree by Leaf.** Atheneum, 1988. 208 pp. ISBN 0-689-31403-5.

For twelve-year-old Clothilde the summer of 1920 is a time of hard work and inner reflection. The return of her disfigured father from World War I and the possible loss of her beloved Maine peninsula, Speer Point, bring frustration and despair. The need for understanding and inner strength involves Clothilde in a strange mystical experience.

7.35 White, Alana. **Come Next Spring.** Clarion Books, 1990. 170 pp. ISBN 0-395-52593-4.

Twelve-year-old Salina Harris lives in the Tennessee Smoky Mountains. World War II has been over for five years now, and the country is settling back into normal life. Salina isn't concerned with the rest of the country, though; she's struggling with the changes in her family relationships: her older sister Mary is engaged, and her older brother Paul spends all his time with his sickly pony. Salina's friends are enticed by fantasies of the "Big City," and Scooter, the new girl, has a different point of view on everything—even on the highway coming through Salina's beloved Smokey Mountains. Salina doesn't understand why everything can't just stay the same! Through the course of the year, Salina's adventures show her how to respect and accept the changes slowly creeping into her life.

7.36 White, Ruth. **Sweet Creek Holler.** Farrar, Straus and Giroux, 1988. 215 pp. ISBN 0-374-37360-4.

When Ginny Short's coal-mining father is killed, she and her mother and sister have to leave their company-owned house and move into a little shack set on Sweet Creek Holler in southwest Virginia. Ginny gets to know the people in Sweet Creek Holler intimately as she grows up among them. ★

7.37 Whitmore, Arvella. **The Bread Winner.** Houghton Mifflin, 1990. 138 pp. ISBN 0-395-537-053.

Afternoons at the movies, ice cream sodas, and fancy houses—these are the images that fill twelve-year-old Sarah Puckett's mind when her family leaves their farm to move to Waheegan. But it is 1932, in the midst of the Great Depression, and Sarah's dreams are quickly shattered when her family moves into Shantytown. When she truly realizes her family's dire financial straits, Sarah's lively, persistent, and curious nature helps to put the family back on its feet. She begins a bread-baking business that not only brings her family together, but helps to rally the town as well.

Series

7.38   Maggie Books. Ellen C. Temple.

In Judy Alter's *Maggie and a Horse Named Devildust*, fourteen-year-old Maggie Pickett cools her heels in Ponder, Texas. She envies Buffalo Bill and Annie Oakley, who are performing in Wild West shows. Maggie's family has moved to the city from their ranch and are even talking of sending Maggie to boarding school so she can learn to be a lady. Instead, she wants to ride Devildust, and so she and friend Davey take an adventurous journey to the Mulhall ranch in Oklahoma where Maggie proves she has the mettle to be a performer. A year later in *Maggie and the Search for Devildust*, the wonderful horse is stolen and the family embarks on a search. In the third book, *Maggie and Devildust Ridin' High*, Maggie is eighteen and gets an invitation from Buffalo Bill to join his Wild West show. By now, Davey Benson, once just her good friend, is decidedly more important to her.

7.39   The Orphan Train Quartet. Bantam Books.

Joan Lowry Nixon's stories are based on true history in the 1850s when abandoned or orphaned children from the streets of New York were sent by train to the Western frontier to be adopted, sometimes by families who had lost their own children or who needed young workers. Readers of *A Family Apart, Caught in the Act, In the Face of Danger*, and *A Place to Belong* will probably find that they have more in common than they thought with these young pioneers.

Recommended Historical Fiction Set in the United States Published before 1988

Armstrong, William H. *Sounder*. Harper and Row, 1969.
Burch, Robert. *Queenie Peavy*. Penguin/Puffin, 1987.
Clapp, Patricia. *The Tamarack Tree*. Lothrop, Lee and Shepard Books, 1986.
Conford, Ellen. *Lenny Kandell, Smart Aleck*. Little, Brown, 1983.
Coolidge, Olivia. *Come by Here*. Houghton Mifflin, 1970.
Ferry, Charles. *Raspberry One*. Houghton Mifflin, 1983.

Fitzgerald, John D. *The Great Brain*. Dial Books for Young Readers, 1967.

Fox, Paula. *The Slave Dancer*. Bradbury Press, 1973.

Howard, Ellen. *Edith Herself*. Atheneum, 1987.

Hurmence, Belinda. *Tancy*. Clarion Books, 1984.

MacLachlan, Patricia. *Sarah, Plain and Tall*. Harper and Row, 1985.

O'Dell, Scott. *Island of the Blue Dolphins*. Houghton Mifflin, 1960.

O'Dell, Scott. *The King's Fifth*. Houghton Mifflin, 1966.

O'Dell, Scott. *Streams to the River, River to the Sea*. Houghton Mifflin, 1986.

Rabe, Bernice. *Naomi*. Thomas Nelson, 1975.

Schlee, Ann. *Ask Me No Questions*. Holt, Rinehart and Winston, 1982.

Sebestyen, Ouida. *Words by Heart*. Atlantic Monthly Press, 1979.

Skurzynski, Gloria. *The Tempering*. Clarion Books, 1983.

Speare, Elizabeth George. *The Sign of the Beaver*. Houghton Mifflin, 1983.

Thrasher, Crystal. *End of a Dark Road*. Atheneum, 1982.

Yep, Laurence. *Dragonwings*. Harper and Row, 1975.

8 Understanding Others: People outside the United States (Historical and Contemporary)

8.1   Aamundsen, Nina Ring. **Two Short and One Long.** Translated from Norwegian by the author. Houghton Mifflin, 1990. 103 pp. ISBN 0-395-52434-2.

Set in Oslo, Norway, this book is about two sixth-grade boys, Einar and Jonas. The book gets its name from the way they show their friendship—through belching. But their friendship isn't all games—as strong as Jonas's friendship with Einar is, it's threatened when a new boy from Afghanistan comes to school and Einar refuses to accept this "foreigner." Finally, Einar learns that accepting oneself makes it easier to accept others. ★★

8.2   Bergman, Tamar. **The Boy from Over There.** Translated from Hebrew by Hillel Halkin. Houghton Mifflin, 1988. 181 pp. ISBN 0-395-43077-1.

World War II has ended, and although Rina's father has not found his way to the kibbutz where she now lives in the Jordan Valley, she is sure he will appear someday. Avramik is the new boy in the kibbutz—the boy from "over there," meaning Europe—and he refuses to acknowledge that his mother may be dead. Together, Avramik and Rina face the difficulties of holding onto hope against incredible odds and of growing up in a new country and a new way of life.

8.3   Clarke, J. **The Heroic Life of Al Capsella.** Henry Holt, 1990. 152 pp. ISBN 0-8050-1310-5.

All Al Capsella wants is to be normal, that is, to have normal parents living an ordinary Canadian life in a typical Canadian house. But nothing about Al's parents is normal. Mrs. Capsella wears a leather jacket, rides an old bicycle, writes romance novels, and visits his school at every opportunity. Mr. Capsella is a college professor who wears the same sweater every day and stays up late every night drinking coffee and grading papers. Their house is a mess, and since laundry isn't a high priority, Al can never find a pair of clean, matching socks—hence, his school nickname of "Rainbow Feet." Can a kid reform his parents? ★★

8.4   Conlon-McKenna, Marita. **Under the Hawthorn Tree.** Illustrated by Donald Tesky. Holiday House, 1990. 153 pp. ISBN 0-8234-0838-8.

During the Irish potato famine, three children are left alone while their mother searches for their father, who has gone to look for work. There is little to eat, and their landlord has threatened to send them to the workhouse. The three decide to run away to their aunts, whom they have heard a lot about but never visited. Many problems hinder their progress, including malnutrition, accidents, and fear. Originally published in Ireland.

8.5   Cross, Gillian. **A Map of Nowhere.** Holiday House, 1989. 150 pp. ISBN 0-8234-0741-1.

The line between fantasy and reality, between good and evil, is not always clear. Nick walks this thin line when he is drawn into a role-playing game with Joseph Fisher and his sister Ruth and a dangerous bet with his brother's motorcycle gang, The Company. Set in England.

8.6   Degens, T. **On the Third Ward.** Harper and Row, 1990. 256 pp. ISBN 0-06-021429-5.

World War II has been over for six years, but the people of Germany are still suffering. This is the story of Wanda, P.B., and Carla, who are tuberculosis patients in a children's hospital. Life in the hospital, along with the winter fog outside the windows, is so dreary that the girls escape through fantasies, taking readers along with them.

8.7   Doherty, Berlie. **White Peak Farm.** Orchard Books, 1990. 112 pp. ISBN 0-531-08467-1.

Jeannie is the narrator of this story, which she presents through short sketches about each member of her Derbyshire, England, farm family. She confides that "we were a house of secrets," and the sketches show how each member adapts to or fights the changes that come to every family as it grows. Jeannie's family members do not understand each other's dreams, nor do they know how to talk about their expectations. Although their problems aren't solved as neatly as they might be in a television show, you'll come away feeling like you've shared in an honest portrayal of a family working its way forward. ★★★★

8.8 Duder, Tessa. **In Lane Three, Alex Archer.** Houghton Mifflin, 1989. 180 pp. ISBN 0-395-50927-0.

Alexandra Archer is self-motivated and excels in almost everything: school, music, dance, and above all, swimming. She is one of the two girls most likely to represent New Zealand in the 1960 Rome Olympics. The pressure is great, and she is almost convinced by spiteful gossip to pull out of the race. Only with the understanding help and love of her boyfriend Andy is Alex able to win the most important prize of all: control of herself in spite of having all the odds against her. ★★★

8.9 Dunlop, Beverley. **The Poetry Girl.** Houghton Mifflin, 1989. 209 pp. ISBN 0-395-49679-9.

Twelve-year-old Natalia lives on a farm in New Zealand. She is discouraged by being held back a year in school, but this is only the beginning of her troubles. Her family moves from the farm she loves, her father has a nervous breakdown, and she has an unsympathetic teacher at school. The book's title comes from the way Natalia escapes from life by reciting poetry she has memorized. Fortunately, by the end of the book, her troubles seem to be taking a turn for the better.

8.10 Garfield, Leon. **Young Nick and Jubilee.** Delacorte Press, 1989. 134 pp. ISBN 0-385-29777-7.

At eleven, young Nick finds himself and his little sister Jubilee orphaned and alone on the sordid streets of the London of yesteryear. Nick worries about marrying off Jubilee and thinks if he can only get her a good education someone will want her. He discovers the Blewcoat charity school, but to qualify, they must have a father to sponsor them. Nick convinces Mr. Christmas Owen, a kindly scoundrel and thief, to take on fatherhood. And so begins an adventure in family life which ends in love.

8.11 George, Jean Craighead. **Shark beneath the Reef.** Illustrated by Robert Sabin. Harper and Row, 1989. 182 pp. ISBN 0-06-021993-9.

Tomás Torres, a fourteen-year-old Mexican boy, must make a far-reaching decision about whether to continue his education or to become a fisher with his grandfather and his uncle. He loves his island home, the Sea of Cortez, and the many fish which are threatened by large, commercial fishing ships. He calls upon the gods of his ancestors to help him spear the great whale shark as proof of his manhood, but as he learns, there's no such simple solution for himself or his village.

8.12   Gleeson, Libby. **I Am Susannah.** Holiday House, 1989. 124 pp. ISBN 0-8234-0742-X.

Susie is a young Australian teenager whose always-best-forever friend moves away and appears to forget her. Susie's father, whom she's never known, may be on his way to Australia from Italy, and her mother's mind isn't on Susie. A big school project is almost due, and there is going to be a party with boys and kissing. Amidst all this confusion, Susie finds an unexpected and, in many ways, an unlikely new friend.

8.13   Gordon, Sheila. **The Middle of Somewhere: A Story of South Africa.** Orchard Books, 1990. 154 pp. ISBN 0-531-08508-2.

Even though Rebecca is a child who is more interested in playing with dolls than in worrying about the political strife and the hardships around her, it's impossible for her and her family to stay out of the conflict when their village is to be moved. Rebecca's family has quite a reaction when Nelson Mandela is released from prison.

8.14   Hartling, Peter. **Crutches.** Translated from German by Elizabeth Crawford. Lothrop, Lee and Shepard Books, 1988. 160 pp. ISBN 0-688-07991-1.

World War II has just ended, and Thomas and his mother are travelling to Vienna in search of his Aunt Wanda. Thomas becomes separated from his mother. He is befriended by a former German soldier who's lost a leg and is nicknamed "Crutches." It's almost two years before they manage to find Thomas's mother. ★★

8.15   Hartling, Peter. **Old John.** Translated by Elizabeth Crawford. Illustrated by Ted Lewin. Lothrop, Lee and Shepard Books, 1990. 128 pp. ISBN 0-688-08734-3.

Old John, the seventy-five-year-old grandfather of Jacob and Laura Schirmer, moves in with the family. Over the next year-and-a-half, a series of arguments, adventures, projects, quarrels, and unexpected incidents of love arise. Old John becomes something of a celebrity when he takes in Sabine Laemmle, a young girl who has problems with an abusive father. Her father is a strong figure in the town, and it's surprising that only Old John dares to stand up against him. Originally published in Germany in 1981. ★

8.16   Ho, Minfong. **Rice without Rain.** Lothrop, Lee and Shepard Books, 1990. 208 pp. ISBN 0-688-06355-1.

Seventeen-year-old Jinda lives in a poor village in Thailand. Because of droughts, the rice fields are barren, and prospects for a crop that will feed her family and pay the rent are bleak. When strangers come from the city universities to help, their ideas for change threaten the village elders and their centuries-old relationship with greedy landlords. Sri, a young doctor, comes with modern medicines that challenge the village healer. Ned brings revolutionary politics that both excite and scare Jinda. And the situation becomes more complicated when Jinda's father is imprisoned. Jinda falls in love with Ned, and the spreading revolutionary fervor erupts in a bloody demonstration in Bangkok. ★★

8.17   Horvath, Polly. **No More Cornflakes.** Farrar, Straus and Giroux, 1990. 134 pp. ISBN 0-374-35530-4.

Growing up in a Canadian household with a teenage sister, an eccentric aunt, and a father and mother who hop around the house like rabbits is no easy matter. Hortense Himple gets herself in some humorous situations trying to cope with her family and her friends. Desperation drives Hortense to try one wacky scheme after another to help the family's state of affairs and keep her friends at the same time.

8.18   Jonsson, Reidar. **My Life as a Dog.** Farrar, Straus and Giroux, 1990. 220 pp. ISBN 0-374-35108-2.

Set in Sweden in the late 1950s, this is the story of thirteen-year-old Ingemar's view of life, his problems, and why trouble seems to haunt him. Ingemar lives with relatives and friends at a children's home because his mother has tuberculosis and his father is away at sea. He bravely faces his many scrapes with humor. An internationally known film of the same name was based on this story.

8.19   Korman, Gordon. **Losing Joe's Place.** Scholastic, 1990. 192 pp. ISBN 0-590-42768-7.

Jason and his friends, Don and Ferguson, are thrilled when they get a chance to sublet Jason's brother's apartment in Toronto the summer before their senior year. But the complications of a seemingly simple arrangement are endless. The apartment is above a deli, and the boys end up helping the landlord save his business, getting Jason's brother's Camaro mistakenly confiscated by the police as a stolen vehicle, and entertaining one of Jason's brother's peculiar friends, who is used to wandering in and out. ★★

8.20   Levin, Betty. **Brother Moose.** Greenwillow Books, 1990. 213 pp. ISBN 0-688-09266-7.

In the late 1800s, poor and orphaned children from England were shipped to Canada where they were adopted or placed in foster homes where they could help the families with household and farm work. This is the story of two such girls, Nell and Louisa. Nell is small and intelligent, while Louisa is large, clumsy, and not very bright. When Louisa's foster family is mean to her, Nell rescues her and with the help of new friends, including an elderly Glooskeb Indian, sets out for Maine, where Nell is supposed to find her foster mother. ★

8.21   Marsden, John. **So Much to Tell You.** Little Brown/Joy Street Books, 1989. 112 pp. ISBN 0-316-54877-4.

Fourteen-year-old Australian Marina's face has been terribly disfigured, and as a result she has lost her desire to speak. This book is Marina's journal, which her English teacher has all his students keep. At first she is afraid of the journal, but as she begins to write and put her feelings down, she remembers the details of her accident, and finally she is able to face her attacker and to slowly begin to relate to her dorm mates. ★

8.22   Naidoo, Beverley. **Chain of Fire.** J. B. Lippincott, 1990. 245 pp. ISBN 0-397-32427-8.

You'll meet the same characters here that were featured in *Journey to Jo'Burg: A South African Story.* Teenagers Naledi and Taolo are among the residents of the village of Bophelong who are being forced to leave their homes and go back to the barren land that is said to be their homeland. They help to lead a resistance, a movement of poor people who "join together to become like a chain, so that together [they] can be strong." ★

8.23 Newth, Mette. **The Abduction.** Translated from Norwegian by Tiina Nunnally and Steve Murray. Farrar, Straus and Giroux, 1989. 247 pp. ISBN 0-374-30008-9.

Norwegian sailors raid Greenland and abduct two Eskimos, Osuqo and the young man she plans to marry. On the ship back to Norway, Christine, a servant girl, is assigned to guard them, and the clash between European and Eskimo values becomes clear as power and fear shape Osuqo's and Christine's stories. ★★

8.24 Pershall, Mary K. **You Take the High Road.** Dial Books for Young Readers, 1990. 256 pp. ISBN 0-8037-0700-2.

Samantha lives near Melbourne, Australia, but the focus of this story is on her family, not its setting. Sam's family is unstable and becomes more so when her two-year-old brother accidentally drowns. With the help of Greg Baker, her English teacher, and through her growing interest in Tony Russell, a classmate, Sam gains a new understanding of life and her role in it. The book ends with Samantha flying to the United States to spend time with her grandmother. ★

8.25 Prochazkova, Iva. **The Season of Secret Wishes.** Translated by Elizabeth D. Crawford. Lothrop, Lee and Shepard Books, 1989. 208 pp. ISBN 0-688-08735-3.

What has it been like to live with limited freedom in Czechoslovakia? Eleven-year-old Kapka moves to Prague and discovers a roof she can walk on, a boy who collects people, a girl who is a real actress, and a terrifying old woman. She begins to see her parents in a different way when her father is taken away for interrogation because someone in the government doesn't like his sculptures. Originally published in Germany in 1988.

8.26 Pullman, Philip. **Shadow in the North.** Alfred A. Knopf, 1988. 331 pp. ISBN 0-394-89453-7.

In this sequel to *The Ruby in the Smoke*, twenty-two-year-old Sally Lockhart is a detective in Victorian London. Her investigation into the failure of a shipping company leads her and her friends into the world of politics and high finance. With her discovery of the mysterious North Star Corporation, Sally places them all in danger. After a series of adventures and several deaths, she confronts Axel Bellmann, who is the powerful force behind the North Star Corporation. ★★

8.27   Raymond, Patrick. **Daniel and Esther.** Macmillan, 1990. 165 pp. ISBN 0-689-50404-3.

This coming-of-age story is set in England before the outbreak of World War II. In the midst of the chaos that is soon to swallow them up, Daniel and Esther experience their first intense, often bittersweet love as they both grow and take on new responsibilities. ★

8.28   Roe, Elaine Corbeil. **Circle of Light.** Harper and Row, 1989. 248 pp. ISBN 0-06-025079-8.

Lucy Delacorte's teasing brother at home and the difficult hours she must spend in the nuns' study become almost too much for her. How could she let Sister Andrew talk her into competing for a scholarship? Even in an isolated room, she has trouble concentrating. Two deaths in the family and her hopeless love for Gabriel cause her to retreat further than is good for her. The award she finally receives takes second place to her success in getting Claire and Alice together. Sister Andrew's plan wasn't such a bad idea after all for this smart French Canadian teenager.

8.29   Sacks, Margaret. **Beyond Safe Boundaries.** Lodestar Books, 1989. 155 pp. ISBN 0-525-67281-8.

It's the 1950s in South Africa, and Elizabeth is pleased that her father is remarrying. Her older sister Evie is not so pleased, and the family is almost relieved when she leaves for college. But when Evie becomes involved in anti-apartheid demonstrations, the family has to look beyond itself and begin to weigh the values and customs that it has always taken for granted. ★★

8.30   Savage, Deborah. **Flight of the Albatross.** Houghton Mifflin, 1989. 236 pp. ISBN 0-395-45711-4.

Sarah's mother is an ornithologist, a person who studies birds, working in New Zealand. Sarah goes to New Zealand to spend the summer with her mother, but her mother is working so hard that she has little time for Sarah. So Sarah has time for her own adventures, which are much more interesting than what she could have found at home.

8.31   Schami, Rafik. **A Hand Full of Stars.** Translated from Arabic by Rika Lesser. E. P. Dutton, 1990. 224 pp. ISBN 0-525-44535-8.

The young narrator of this story lives in Damascus, Syria, and you may be surprised to learn how much you have in common with him. But you may also be surprised at the challenges he faces in his desire to be a journalist. Censorship problems in the United States seem small compared to what he faces in Syria. ★★★

8.32 Shaw, Margret. **A Wider Tomorrow.** Holiday House, 1990. 130 pp. ISBN 0-8234-0837-X.

Living in England, seventeen-year-old Roberta gets an offer to visit America. Meanwhile, the university accepts her. Now she can't decide which invitation to take. While trying to decide, she talks with her grandmother, an unusual woman with a varied background. Roberta pointedly asks this former member of Parliament, WWI ambulance driver, and fighter for women's rights why she never married. When the elderly woman tells how she and her sisters, as children, were controlled by men, Roberta begins to understand her heritage as a woman. What she learns convinces her that she must be responsible for her own future.

8.33 Southall, Ivan. **Blackbird.** Farrar, Straus and Giroux, 1988. 112 pp. ISBN 0-374-30783-0.

The world is at war, and Will's family has fled to the very southern part of Australia to escape the invading Japanese. His father, a colonel, is away, and it is left to Will to protect his mother and their new home. At least that's the way he sees it in his partly serious and partly playful imaginings. He climbs to the top of the roof to watch for invaders, but instead, he encounters personal tests for himself.

8.34 Staples, Suzanne Fisher. **Shabanu, Daughter of the Wind.** Alfred A. Knopf/Borzoi Sprinters, 1989. 246 pp. ISBN 0-394-94815-7.

Shabanu and her sister Phulan are daughters of nomads living in the Cholistan Desert in Pakistan. Thirteen-year-old Phulan will marry soon; Shabanu, twelve, is to be wed in a year or so. When plans for the girls to marry the brothers to whom they have been promised are destroyed, Shabanu is the daughter whose future is most changed. Suddenly her life turns in a direction she had never expected, and she is angry and hurt. ★★★★★

8.35 Stolz, Mary. **Bartholomew Fair.** Greenwillow Books, 1990. 152 pp. ISBN 0-688-09522-4.

The year is 1597 and six people, ranging from Queen Elizabeth to a scullery maid, are eagerly awaiting Bartholomew Fair in London. The story recounts the events of the day for each of these characters, beginning with their anticipation, how they travel, what they do at the fair, how they interact with each other, and their reflections after it's all over.

8.36   Stolz, Mary. **Pangur Ban.** Illustrated by Pamela Johnson. Harper and Row Junior Books, 1988. 182 pp. ISBN 0-06-025862-4.

Cormac, the fifteen-year-old son of a farmer in ninth-century Ireland, departs from tradition with his dislike of farming and his love of drawing. With his white cat, Pangur Ban, he is allowed to enter a monastery where he learns to illuminate manuscripts. As Cormac completes his own manuscript containing the story of St. Patrick, the Viking raiders come once again to Ireland. The place he chooses to hide his manuscript affects the life of another young monk many years later.

8.37   Swindells, Robert. **A Serpent's Tooth.** Holiday House, 1989. 136 pp. ISBN 0-8234-0743-8.

Thirteen-year-old Lucy's dreams are visions that mesh the past and the future. When her father takes a new job and the family moves to another part of England, she must face many of the same problems as her American counterparts: making new friends and adjusting to her new life. The family nearly breaks apart when her mother becomes an activist against a powerful corporation about to build a nuclear waste dump. Lucy must decide where she stands.

8.38   Vande Velde, Vivian. **A Well-Timed Enchantment.** Crown, 1990. 184 pp. ISBN 0-517-57319-9.

When Deanna goes to France for the summer, she is depressed because of her parents' divorce and her inability to speak French. But when she loses her Mickey Mouse watch down an old, unused well, she falls into more adventure than she ever could have at home.

8.39   Wignell, Edel. **Escape by Deluge.** Holiday House, 1990. 152 pp. ISBN 0-8234-0802-7.

Shelley Green, an Australian teenager, is awakened every night at midnight. She ignores her father's opinion that the loud "Boom-Boom-Boom! Yal-loooooo!" is just the evening traffic. She knows there has to be another explanation. She cannot concentrate in school or on her swimming because of the loud noises underneath her apartment building. When she decides to do a school project on the waterway underneath the city, she finds more than she is prepared for.

8.40 Zheleznikov, Vladimir. **Scarecrow.** Translated from Russian by Antonina W. Bouis. J. B. Lippincott, 1990. 148 pp. ISBN 0-397-32317-4.

In this story from pre-Perestroika Russia, Lena is a thin, fragile young girl who has come to live with her grandfather. She has a difficult time adjusting to her new home. Her grandfather is considered eccentric by the other villagers, and she is not easily accepted. Still, her friendship with Dimka, a boy in her class, offers some comfort. Then she is falsely accused of being a traitor to her group and becomes a victim, persecuted by her fellow students.

Recommended Books about People outside the United States Published before 1988

Avery, Gillian. *The Elephant War.* (England) Dell, 1988.*

Chukovsky, Kornei. *The Silver Crest: My Russian Boyhood.* (Russia) Holt, Rinehart and Winston, 1976.

Douglas, Lloyd. *The Robe.* (Ancient Rome) Houghton Mifflin, 1942.

Gordan, Sheila. *Waiting for the Rain.* (South Africa) Orchard Books, 1987.

Haugaard, Erik Christian. *The Untold Tale.* (Denmark) Houghton Mifflin, 1971.

James, Aldridge. *A Sporting Proposition.* (Australia) Little, Brown, 1973.

Koehn, Ilse. *Tilla.* (Germany) Greenwillow Books, 1981.

Konigsburg, E. L. *A Proud Taste for Scarlet and Miniver.* (England) Atheneum, 1973.

Kullman, Harry. *The Battle Horse.* (Sweden) Bradbury Press, 1981.

Linevski, A. *An Old Tale Carved out of Stone.* (Russia) Crown, 1973.

Major, Kevin. *Hold Fast.* (Newfoundland) Delacorte Press, 1980.

Matsubara, Hisako. *Cranes at Dusk.* (Japan) Doubleday, 1985.

Nostlinger, Christine. *Luke and Angela.* (Germany) Harcourt Brace Jovanovich, 1981.

---

*This is the date that this book was reprinted. It was originally published before 1988.

Nostlinger, Christine. *Marrying Off Mother*. (Germany) Harcourt Brace
    Jovanovich, 1982.
Paterson, Katherine. *The Master Puppeteer*. (Japan) Thomas Y. Crowell,
    1976.
Paterson, Katherine. *Rebels of the Heavenly Kingdom*. (China) Lodestar
    Books, 1973.
Patterson, Sarah. *The Distant Summer*. (England) Archway Paperbacks,
    1977.
Speare, Elizabeth. *The Bronze Bow*. (Biblical Galilee) Houghton Mifflin,
    1961.

9 Understanding Competition: Sports

Fiction

9.1 Baczewski, Paul. **Just for Kicks.** J. B. Lippincott, 1990. 192 pp. ISBN 0-397-32465-0.

You can see from the title that this book isn't to be taken too seriously. It's almost a spoof of sports books. It's about Brandon Lewis and his superjock family. Brandon is a basketball player and manager of the football team where his brother is the star quarterback and his sister is the punter and field-goal kicker. The ending is too good to be true, and getting there is a lot of fun. ★

9.2 Christopher, Matt. **Tackle without a Team.** Illustrated by Margaret Sanfilippo. Little, Brown, 1989. 145 pp. ISBN 0-316-14067-8.

"Down! Set! Hep, Hep, Hep!" Scott Kramer experiences all the excitement of football until his coach finds marijuana in his sports bag. "I don't smoke, coach!" isn't enough of a defense, and Scott soon finds himself trying to win back the trust of his parents, coach, and best friend after he is kicked off the team. He has to do some quick and clever detective work to find out who planted the drugs on him.

9.3 Dygard, Thomas. **Forward Pass.** William Morrow, 1989. 186 pp. ISBN 0-688-07961-X.

Frank Gardner, football coach at Aldridge High, discovers a cure for his mediocre team: Jill Winston. An outstanding girls' basketball player and natural athlete, she's the only one in the school talented enough to catch the bullet passes of quarterback Scott Butler. When Jill and her parents agree, private practices begin, and in the game against the Randville Tigers, Coach Gardner unleashes his secret weapon: number 89—a *girl*! and a great wide receiver. But in the midst of the successful football season, girls' basketball starts, and Jill is torn between her two sports.

9.4   Smith, Robert Kimmel. **Bobby Baseball.** Illustrated by Alan
Tiegreen. Delacorte Press, 1989. 165 pp. ISBN 0-385-29807-2.

Ten-year-old Robert E. Ellis, who calls himself "Bobby Baseball,"
believes he is destined to become a major league baseball player.
However, his constant daydreaming about the sport gets him into
trouble. He is a good pitcher, but it is difficult for him to accept
being treated like all the other players by his coach. Bobby's desire
for special treatment causes him to embarrass himself and others.
Luckily, a close friend helps him control his strong temper. An
added bonus at the end of each chapter is baseball trivia facts that
prove the author loves baseball as much as he hopes his readers
will.

9.5   Tunis, John R. **Highpockets.** William Morrow, 1990. 192 pp.
ISBN 0-688-09288-8.

In this new edition of an all-time favorite, a baseball player learns
not to give up.

9.6   Tunis, John R. **Keystone Kids.** Harcourt Brace Jovanovich, 1990.
239 pp. ISBN 0-15-242389-3.

Keystone Kids reveals what happens when after struggling to put
together a baseball team, the players must overcome their
prejudice against a rookie catcher, Jocko Klein. Being winners
means scoring a victory against anti-Semitism, regaining their
confidence in each other, and pulling together as a team.

9.7   Tunis, John R. **The Kid Comes Back.** Edited by David Rather.
William Morrow, 1990. 248 pp. ISBN 0-688-09290-X.

Roy Tucker, "The Kid," returns from World War II and decides
to go back to playing baseball. A plane crash has left him with one
leg shorter than the other, and even after surgery, his doctor,
manager, and teammates aren't sure he'll ever recover the athletic
skill that had made him the "speediest man in the National
League." The Kid has come back from hard times before, but will
he be able to overcome the fear that is holding him back now?

9.8   Tunis, John R. **Rookie of the Year.** Harcourt Brace Jovanovich,
1990. 220 pp. ISBN 0-15-268881-1.

Spike Russell, the Dodger manager, tries to rally his team in their
drive for the championship. But their season is threatened by a
scheming team secretary and the seeming irresponsibility of their
team's newest star, a rookie pitcher.

Nonfiction

9.9   Abt, Samuel. **LeMond: The Incredible Comeback of an American Hero.** Random House, 1990. 206 pp. ISBN 0-394-58476-7.

Only recently have Americans begun to take bicycling as a serious
sport, and part of the reason for its new popularity is the success
of Greg LeMond, who in 1986 won the Tour de France, a 2,000-
mile bicycle race that goes for twenty-three days. As the first
American to win this prestigious race, he was an instant hero, but
within the next year he almost died when he was shot in a hunting
accident. Then just as he was getting his strength back in 1988, he
had to have his appendix taken out. Everyone was sure his career
was over, but in 1989 he surprised the world and became *Sports
Illustrated*'s "sportsman of the year" by winning the 1989 Tour de
France. He crossed the line eight seconds ahead of the expected
winner, Laurent Fignon.

9.10   Anderson, Dave. **The Story of Basketball.** William Morrow,
1988. 182 pp. ISBN 0-688-06748-4.

The year 1991 marks the centennial of basketball, and Dave
Anderson's book helps celebrate a century of this favorite sport.
A section on basic techniques of good ball playing includes action
photographs of well-known players and coaches. There's also a
good chapter on women's basketball and the direction it is taking.

9.11   Appel, Mary. **The First Book of Baseball.** Crown, 1988. 95 pp.
ISBN 0-517-56726-1.

The lively tone makes this introduction to baseball and its history
and rules fun to read. A section of most-asked questions, a
glossary, and several charts and lists also make it good for
reference.

9.12   Boyd, Brendan, and Robert Garrett. **Hoops: Behind the Scenes
with the Boston Celtics.** Photographs by Henry Horenstein.
Little, Brown, 1989. 128 pp. ISBN 0-316-37319-2.

The authors call this snapshot scrapbook of the Boston Celtics a
"family album" because of the way this professional basketball
team prides itself on a sense of family. Pictures and explanations
cover all aspects of the Celtic organization, from drafting players
to celebrating the playoffs.

9.13   Brenner, Richard J. **The Complete Super Bowl Story: Games I-XXIII.** Lerner, 1990. 112 pp. ISBN 0-8225-1503-2.

After an explanation of the growth of the upstart American Football League and how it resulted in a championship Super Bowl game between the new American Football League and the old National Football League, the author recalls the highlights of each game between 1967 and 1989. For real football fans.

9.14   Brenner, Richard J. **The World Series—The Great Contests.** Lerner, 1989. 81 pp. ISBN 0-8225-1502-4.

After giving a brief history of the World Series, the author describes and illustrates the greatest baseball games ever played: 1955's Brooklyn Dodgers versus New York Yankees, 1975's Cincinnati Reds versus Boston Red Sox, and 1988's Los Angeles Dodgers versus Oakland Athletics. Famous players and outstanding strategies are "replayed" in vivid detail.

9.15   Campbell, Nelson. **Grass Roots and Schoolyards: A High School Basketball Anthology.** Stephen Greene Press, 1988. 209 pp. ISBN 0-8289-0640-8.

The true basketball stories in this collection are divided into sections about little towns, big cities, and towns whose size lies in-between. Besides the stories gleaned from hometown newspapers and slick magazines like *Sports Illustrated*, each section includes short clips under the heading of "Weird and Wondrous." The book captures the spirit of high school basketball by featuring players ranging from Elvin Hayes to the Prairie City, Iowa, high school girls' team.

9.16   Goodman, Michael E. **Photo Finishes: Great Last-Second, Bottom-of-the-Ninth, Sudden-Death Victories.** Little, Brown/Sports Illustrated for Kids Books, 1990. 122 pp. ISBN 0-316-32023-4.

If you get discouraged easily and tend to give up too soon, this is just the book you need. It presents thirty exciting, real-life stories, complete with news photos showing that the game isn't over until it's over. These come-from-behind stories of winning in basketball, tennis, baseball, football, hockey, skiing, cycling, gymnastics, and track are fun to read whether you're a spectator or an athlete.

9.17   Gutman, Bill. **Pro Sports Champions.** Archway Paperbacks, 1990. 135 pp. ISBN 0-671-69334-4.

Popular sportswriter Bill Gutman has chosen his favorite teams and favorite individuals to feature in this book that contains biographies of Sugar Ray Robinson, Wayne Gretzky, Nolan Ryan, Kareem Abdul-Jabbar, and Michael Jordan. The teams he writes about include the 1969-1970 New York Knicks and the 1988 Dodgers. He also describes the 1958 game between the Giants and the Colts, calling it "the greatest game ever played."

9.18   Hammond, Tim. **Sports.** Illustrated by Mike Clowes. Alfred A. Knopf, 1988. 64 pp. ISBN 0-394-99616-X.

Have you ever wondered how a popular sport got started? Or what you should call the various pieces of equipment? If so, *Sports* has the answers for you. Soccer, football, tennis, bowling, and basketball are just a few of the sports discussed, along with more obscure games such as cricket, squash, archery, and martial arts. Top-quality pictures and a straightforward text make this book an excellent reference source as well as a pleasure to skim. Part of the Eyewitness series.

9.19   Hilgers, Laura. **Steffi Graf.** Little, Brown/Sports Illustrated for Kids Books, 1990. 118 pp. ISBN 0-316-36239-5.

The author is a writer and editor for *Sports Illustrated for Kids*, and so she had access to lots of good photographs and background information for this biography of the world's best woman tennis player. Steffi Graf earned that title in 1988 when she was only nineteen years old and won a Gold Medal in the Olympics and captured the Grand Slam (which means she came in first in the four biggest tournaments in the world). An interesting feature of this paperback is a thirty-two-page, full-color insert that includes photos and "fast facts" not only about Graf, but about some of the competitions she's been in and some of the people she's competed against, as well as about her fellow West German, Boris Becker.

9.20   Hollander, Phyllis, and Zander Hollander. **More Amazing but True Sports Stories.** Scholastic, 1990. 129 pp. ISBN 0-590-43876-X.

If you worry that your parents seem overly interested in your success as an athlete, you can take heart from reading the story in this book about the boxer whose mother jumped into the ring and belted her son's opponent—at least your mother probably hasn't done that! Other stories in this sequel to *Amazing but True Sports Stories* include one about an outfielder who was arrested when he threw a ball that killed a seagull, one about a baseball commissioner who developed his interest in baseball while recovering from an injury that would keep him from ever playing sports, and one about an injured high school football player who in 1927 was called from the audience to kick a field goal—he was dressed in street clothes and shoes but made a successful kick, and when the other team protested, rules were changed all across the country so that now all players must be dressed in official uniforms to play.

9.21 Jennings, Jay. **Long Shots: They Beat the Odds.** Silver Burdett Press, 1990. 57 pp. ISBN 0-382-24105-3.

The athletes featured in this book all overcame the odds against them. Although the author calls them "long shots," he's sure they wouldn't include themselves in that category. The five chapters feature "Basketball's Little Big Man," Spud Webb; "Track's Golden Gazelle," Wilma Rudolph; "Queen of the Drag Strip," Shirley Muldowney; "Baseball's Wonder Boy," Jim Abbott; and "Destiny's Team," the 1969 New York Mets. Part of the Sports Triumphs Books series.

9.22 Jones, Ron. **B-Ball: The Team That Never Lost a Game.** Bantam Books, 1990. 153 pp. ISBN 0-553-05867-3.

Coach Ron Jones chronicles his experiences working with the San Francisco Special Olympics basketball team. He shows his personal warmth, humor, and compassion in teaching his team to play basketball and to face the world with greater confidence and joy.

9.23 Miller, J. David. **The Super Book of Football.** Little, Brown/ Sports Illustrated for Kids Books, 1990. 136 pp. ISBN 0-316-57370-1.

Lots of photos, many of them in color, and boldface headings make this an easy book to skim. It's written for kids, but older readers will enjoy it, too. It's divided into four sections: "The Origins of Football," "In the Huddle," "Weekend Warriors," and "Inside the NFL." The final pages include a glossary of terms and a summary of Super Bowl results and record holders for touchdown passes, catches, rushing yardage, and more.

9.24   Nash, Bruce, and Allan Zullo. **Freebies for Sports Fans!** Illustrated by Roy Doty. Simon and Schuster, 1990. 96 pp. ISBN 0-671-70339-0.

Over 150 free or nearly free sports items are described in this paperback, designed for sports collectors and/or people who just like to get mail. None of the items costs more than $1.00, although you may have to pay for postage and handling. And you should realize that as time goes on, more and more of the items will become unavailable because those offering them will have moved or gone out of business.

9.25   Riffenburgh, Beau, and David Boss. **Great Ones: NFL Quarterbacks from Baugh to Montana.** Viking Penguin, 1989. 192 pp. ISBN 0-670-82979-X.

This oversize book has almost life-size close-ups of the faces of ten outstanding football players. The rest of the book is filled with anecdotes, statistics, essays, and more pictures, most in full color. It brings professional and college football even closer than the television screen can.

9.26   Ritter, Lawrence S. **The Story of Baseball,** revised and expanded edition. William Morrow, 1990. 224 pp. ISBN 0-688-09056-7.

Although people have always played with sticks and balls, the first game that looked like modern baseball was played in Hoboken, New Jersey, in 1846. Professional baseball started in 1869. In the foreword to this book, Ted Williams says, "Tradition means a lot in baseball"—to really enjoy the game, you have to know not only how it's played but also the stars of today and the great stars who came before them. When Williams was playing, he never felt he was playing just against nine people on the opposing team—he always had the greats, like Babe Ruth, Ty Cobb, Rogers Hornsby, and Bill Terry, in the back of his mind as he measured his own playing against theirs.

9.27   Sherman, Eric. **365 Amazing Days in Sports: A Day-by-Day Look at Sports History.** Little, Brown/Sports Illustrated for Kids Books, 1990. 378 pp. ISBN 0-316-78537-7.

This book follows a calendar year from January 1 to December 31 and tells you the great sports events that took place on each date, covering events as far back as the Civil War. For example, on October 15, 1986, the New York Mets and the Houston Astros played the longest playoff game in baseball history, while on

December 28, 1958, the New York Giants and the Baltimore Colts played the first overtime football game.

9.28 St. John, Jetty. **Monaco Grand Prix.** Lerner, 1989. 64 pp. ISBN 0-8225-0530-4.

Every May, thousands of racing fans gather at the tiny Mediterranean country of Monaco for one of the most important Formula One races of the year, the Monaco Grand Prix. This book describes the race's history and looks in detail at the 1986 race. It follows one of the racers, Nelson Piquet, through practices, qualifying, and the race itself. Full-color and historic black-and-white photographs, maps, and a glossary of racing terms add to the interest of the book's text.

9.29 Sullivan, George. **All about Baseball.** G. P. Putnam's Sons, 1989. 126 pp. ISBN 0-399-61226-2.

Whether you've never played baseball and need to learn about it from the beginning or you just need to check on a rule, this is a good book for reference or browsing. Clear photos help illustrate the points.

9.30 Sullivan, George. **Big League Spring Training.** Henry Holt, 1989. 118 pp. ISBN 0-8050-0838-1.

Some people mark the beginning of spring by the first robin, others by the blooming of jonquils or dogwood trees, but for baseball lovers, spring comes when baseball gear, uniforms, and pitching machines are hauled out of winter storage and taken to baseball fields in such sunny states as Florida, Arizona, Texas, and California. The book shows what's involved as major league players get ready for the long summer ahead.

9.31 Teitelbaum, Michael. **Playbook! Baseball: You Are the Manager, You Call the Shots.** Little, Brown/Sports Illustrated for Kids Books, 1990. 96 pp. ISBN 0-316-83624-9.

This book assumes you already know a lot about baseball and that you are ready to take charge. It's modeled after the popular Choose Your Own Adventure series. After a few introductory pages, various game situations are described, and you as the manager make a decision on the best play. Depending on which decision you make, you turn to the page indicated to see what happens.

9.32 Teitelbaum, Michael. **Playbook! Football: You Are the Quarter-back, You Call the Shots.** Little, Brown/Sports Illustrated for Kids Books, 1990. 96 pp. ISBN 0-316-83623-0.

This book about football is written in the same format as a Choose Your Own Adventure book. You are the quarterback who decides on the plays, then you turn to the specified pages to see the results of your choices.

Series

9.33 **The Gymnasts.** Scholastic/Apple Paperbacks.

Among the titles in this series are *The Beginners, First Meet, Bad Break, Crush on the Coach,* and *Mystery at the Meet.* In this series by Elizabeth Levy, Cindi, Ti An, Darlene, and Lauren are all on the Pinecones gymnastics team. In *World-Class Gymnast,* the Pinecones find that they can help the famous Heidi Ferguson recover from anorexia. Fiction.

9.34 **The High Fives.** Simon and Schuster/Minstrel Books.

The first book in this series is *Soccer Is a Kick* by S. S. Gorman. Five athletic and fun-loving boys hang out together and use their nicknames to show that they're really one, like a hand. Jack, the shortest, is called "Thumbs-up"; Gadget is called "Index"; Stretch, who is the tallest, goes by "Center"; Chris is called "Ringo," partly because he's the ringleader; and Jack's little brother is called "P.K." for Pinky. They're all on the Tornadoes soccer team, and they team up for more than just beating the Hurricanes. Other titles include *Slam Dunk* and *Homerun Stretch.* Fiction.

9.35 **Make the Team.** Little, Brown/Sports Illustrated for Kids Books.

Soccer: A Heads-up Guide to Super Soccer! and *Basketball: A Slammin' Jammin' Guide to Super Hoops* are two of the books in this series by Richard J. Brenner. Both books have chapters on developing skills, and in addition, there are chapters on mental conditioning and on handling problems with coaches, parents, and other players. Photos and drawings illustrate the various points. Nonfiction.

9.36 **Official Pro Football Hall of Fame Books.** Simon and Schuster.

These books come in both paperback and hardback and are intended for football fans of all ages. They include posters, stickers, activities, facts, and interesting trivia. Titles include *Answer Book* by Joe Horrigan, *Fun and Fact Sticker Book* by Bob Carroll (with paintings by Mark Rucker), *Book of Superstars* by Don R. Smith, and *Pro Football Hall of Fame Playbook* by Rick Korch. Nonfiction.

9.37   Perfect Ten. Fawcett Books.

As high school freshmen, Monica, Casey, and Jo are best friends. But more importantly, they are gymnastics competitors who are determined to be champions. One girl is featured in each of these books by Holly Simpson. Among the titles in the series are *Dream Time*, *To Be the Best*, *Breaking the Rules*, and *Casey and the Coach*. Fiction.

9.38   Rookies. Ballantine Books.

Although written for young baseball fans, the Rookies series by Mark Freeman features adult characters in major league baseball. The plots are nonstop sports action and chatter. Titles include *Play Ball*, *Squeeze Play*, *Spring Training*, *Big League Break*, and *Playoff Pressure*. Fiction.

9.39   Young Fans' Edition. Archway Paperbacks.

The authors have collected unusual happenings, tricks, bloopers, and mistakes to publish in the books in this series. Titles include *The Football Hall of Shame*, *The Baseball Hall of Shame*, and *The Sports Hall of Shame for Young Fans*. They are sort of like the *Guinness Book of World Records*, except that all the incidents are sports related, and for the most part, people didn't try to get their names in these books! Nonfiction.

Recommended Books about Sports Published before 1988

Brancato, Robin. *Winning.* Alfred A. Knopf, 1977.
Brooks, Bruce. *The Moves Make the Man.* Harper and Row, 1984.
Crutcher, Chris. *The Crazy Horse Electric Game.* Greenwillow Books, 1987.
Crutcher, Chris. *Stotan!* Greenwillow Books, 1986.
Dygard, Thomas J. *Halfback Tough.* William Morrow, 1986.
Knudson, R. R. *Fox Running.* Harper and Row, 1975.

Knudson, R. R. *Rinehart Shouts*. Farrar, Straus and Giroux, 1987.

Knudson, R. R. *Zan Hagen's Marathon*. Farrar, Straus and Giroux, 1984.

Knudson, R. R. *Zanballer*. Delacorte Press, 1972.

Knudson, R. R. *Zanbanger*. Harper and Row, 1977.

Knudson, R. R. *Zanboomer*. Harper and Row, 1978.

Lipsyte, Robert. *The Contender*. Harper and Row, 1967.

Morris, Jeannie. *Brian Piccolo: A Short Season*. Dell, 1972.

Myers, Walter Dean. *The Outside Shot*. Dell/Laurel-Leaf Books, 1987.

Peck, Richard E. *Something for Joey*. Bantam Books, 1978.

Salassi, Otto R. *On the Ropes*. Greenwillow Books, 1981.

Sayers, Gayle. *I Am Third*. Viking, 1970.

Smith, Doris Buchanan. *Karate Dancer*. G. P. Putnam's Sons, 1987.

Voigt, Cynthia. *The Runner*. Atheneum, 1985.

10 Understanding Wars: National and International Conflicts

10.1   Baklanov, Grigory. **Forever Nineteen.** Translated from Russian by Antonina W. Bouis. J. B. Lippincott, 1989. 166 pp. ISBN 0-397-32297-6.

In World War II, nineteen-year-old Volodya Tretyakov optimistically leaves his mother, his sister, and his small Russian village to become a soldier. His dreams of great battles and heroic deeds are quickly replaced by harsh realities—cold and lonely nights, hours and days of waiting, sniper shots, dying companions, and the possibility of death.

10.2   Bawden, Nina. **Henry.** Illustrated by Joyce Powzyk. Lothrop, Lee and Shepard Books, 1988. 99 pp. ISBN 0-688-07894-X.

The unlikely hero of this World War II story is a baby red squirrel, adopted for a few months by an English family evacuated from London and assigned to live with a Welsh farm family. The squirrel was dumped out of its nest, much like the family was dumped out of its life in London; it comes to symbolize the family's unstable position. But being a symbol means nothing to the fun-loving squirrel, nor when it goes back to the woods does it realize what it did to bring two families together in a time of need. ★★

10.3   Beatty, Patricia, and Phillip Robbins. **Eben Tyne, Powdermonkey.** Morrow Junior Books, 1990. 227 pp. ISBN 0-688-08884-8.

Eben Tyne is thirteen years old, the youngest in a long line of seagoing men. When the Union blockade of Confederate shipping threatens to strangle the South, desperate times come and inspire Southerners to build the ironclad ship, the *Merrimack*. Eben, who has already proven his bravery, is made a powder monkey, with the job of bringing gunpowder from below deck. In the *Merrimack*'s battle with the *Monitor*, Eben loses his illusions about the glory of ships, battles, and war and ends up in a Yankee prison camp under some unusual conditions.

10.4   Chang, Margaret, and Raymond Chang. **In the Eye of War.** Margaret K. McElderry Books, 1990. 197 pp. ISBN 0-689-50503-5.

Growing up in Shanghai in 1944, Shao-Shao is surrounded by warfare, yet largely untouched by its violence. Although the city is occupied by the cruel Japanese forces, Shao-Shao's life revolves around his family, his school, flying kites, and playing with his friends. His own father sometimes seems harsher than the Japanese. No matter what Shao-Shao does, it is never good enough to please his father.

10.5   Fluek, Toby Knobel. **Memories of My Life in a Polish Village 1930–1949.** Alfred A. Knopf, 1990. 110 pp. ISBN 0-394-58617-4.

The author, who now lives in New York City, was a small Jewish girl living in the village of Czernica, Poland when World War II broke out. Her family was forced to move to a Jewish ghetto and later to scurry from one hiding place to another. She and her mother were the only ones from her family to survive the war. She is now an artist, and she tells her story through both pictures and words. Each page has only a few lines of type, illustrated by a painting.

10.6   Foreman, Michael. **War Boy: A Country Childhood.** Little, Brown, 1989. 92 pp. ISBN 1-55970-049-1.

British artist Michael Foreman tells the story of World War II from his own memories that start with a fire bomb coming through the ceiling of his house in the village of Pakefield. ★

10.7   Friedman, Ina R. **The Other Victims: First-Person Stories of Non-Jews Persecuted by the Nazis.** Houghton Mifflin, 1990. 214 pp. ISBN 0-395-50212-8.

Besides the six million Jews killed in the Holocaust, there were five million others who were either killed directly or forced into labor camps where they died of disease, malnutrition, and overwork. Their stories are organized into the following categories: "Those 'Unworthy of Life,' " "The War against the Church," "Racial Purification: Breeding the Master Race," "Mind Control," and "Slaves for the Nazi Empire." ★

10.8   Fritz, Jean. **China's Long March: 6,000 Miles of Danger.** Illustrated by Yang Zhr Cheng. G. P. Putnam's Sons, 1988. 124 pp. ISBN 0-399-21512-3.

Jean Fritz is an author who specializes in personalizing history, and this book is no exception. She shows what it was like for the men and women in the Chinese Communist Red Army who in 1934–1935 had to march 6,000 miles as they escaped from Chiang Kai-shek and marched across China to the Northwest frontier. ★★

10.9   Jensen, Kathryn. **Pocket Change.** Bradbury Press, 1989. 172 pp. ISBN 0-02-747731-2.

Sixteen-year-old Josie Monroe thinks life is just fine, but then her father begins to change dramatically, and Josie is the only one who figures out that he is having flashbacks to Vietnam. The book's title comes from Josie's observation that old memories finally work their way to the surface, just as pocket change eventually wears through cloth. ★

10.10   Jones, Adrienne. **Long Time Passing.** Harper and Row, 1990. 244 pp. ISBN 0-06-023055-X.

It is the Vietnam era, an era of protests and student unrest, and Jonas Duncan is being pulled in two directions. His father is a career Marine officer, and Jonas has been raised in the military life. Yet, with his mother dead, he's been sent to live with a cousin in northern California where he has discovered new friends and is drawn to a different lifestyle. He is attracted to the lovely Auleen and her commune friends, but his father wants him to join the military. Everyone seems to pull him in a new direction, and Jonas is having trouble coming to terms with what he wants to do.

10.11   Laird, Christa. **Shadow of the Wall.** Greenwillow Books, 1990. 144 pp. ISBN 0-688-09336-1.

The stark terror and uncertainties of daily life in the Warsaw Ghetto from 1939 to 1942 are vividly detailed in the story of thirteen-year-old Mischa and his sisters. As inmates of Dr. Janusz Korzcak's orphanage, the children have a measure of protection—or do they? The ever-tightening noose of Nazi repression brings the reader into the story as it comes to its inevitable conclusion. Mischa is a fictional character, but the novel is based on historical documents and records. A map and a five-page postscript help readers understand the sweep of events.

10.12   Lingard, Joan. **Tug of War.** Lodestar Books, 1990. 194 pp. ISBN 0-525-67306-7.

Hugo and Astra are fourteen-year-old twins in a Latvian family fleeing before the Russian invasion of their country in 1944. In the confusion, Hugo is separated from the family and ends up in Hamburg where he is cared for by a German family. The others wait out the war in a refugee camp. Fortunately, the family is reunited at the end, but by then, Hugo is in love with a German woman and now has a difficult choice to make.

10.13   Lowry, Lois. **Number the Stars.** Houghton Mifflin, 1989. 137 pp. ISBN 0-395-51060-0.

Ten-year-old Annemarie Johansen lives in German-occupied Copenhagen in 1943. She despises the Nazi soldiers who stand on each street corner. She misses the frosted cakes and ham dinners, unavailable since the Germans took control of Denmark and started monitoring the food supply. Most of all, Annemarie fears for the life of Ellen Rosen, her Jewish best friend. Can she help Ellen escape the clutches of the Nazis and save her from certain death? ★★★★

10.14   Matas, Carol. **Code Name *KRIS*** Charles Scribner's Sons, 1990. 152 pp. ISBN 0-684-19208-X.

During the second world war, Jesper takes the code name "KRIS" for his underground espionage against the German soldiers who occupy his beloved Denmark. He has been helping Jews escape, but now as the threat of a Nazi takeover escalates, he must renew his resistance fighting by helping to produce Danish newspapers, plant sabotage bombs, and remain silent after capture—even through torture. Will he survive the experience without becoming a murderer himself, or will he seek revenge?

10.15   Meltzer, Milton. **Columbus and the World around Him.** Franklin Watts, 1990. 192 pp. ISBN 0-531-10899-6.

As we celebrate the 500th anniversary of Columbus's first voyage to America, Milton Meltzer's biography of Columbus will be especially valuable because of the way Meltzer builds upon the few facts that are known about the brave and stubborn Italian who changed the world's history. Meltzer presents both good and bad sides of Columbus's character and actions. If you start up your own research project, you'll be especially interested in Meltzer's explanations of where he got his information and how he sorted, weighed, and analyzed it. ★★★★

10.16   Moeri, Louise. **The Forty-Third War.** Houghton Mifflin, 1989. 200 pp. ISBN 0-395-50215-2.

Uno, Lolo, and Macio are "recruited" at gunpoint to join the Revolutionaries in the forty-third war of their Central American country against the Loyalists. The war has already touched their families by taking away their fathers and other older men. Uno's sister hasn't been the same since the Loyalist troops came through their village and raped her. But who will work the banana-loading sheds to earn money to keep their families alive if they go? They are given no choice. They train for three days, patrol on day four, and enter full-scale battle by day eight. Boys become men quickly and gain a mature understanding of their future.

10.17   Myers, Walter Dean. **Fallen Angels.** Scholastic, 1988. 336 pp. ISBN 0-590-40942-5.

Appropriate for older readers, this Vietnam War book is the gripping story of seventeen-year-old Richie Perry, who joins the army mostly to get away from everyday life in Harlem. He finds Vietnam so far from everyday life that he has a hard time realizing that he isn't in a movie or on TV. What happens to Richie and his buddies is crushingly real, and it doesn't change when the lights go on or the set is turned off. ★★★★★★

10.18   Nelson, Theresa. **And One for All.** Orchard Books, 1989. 192 pp. ISBN 0-531-08404-3.

It wasn't just in Vietnam that wars were fought in the late 1960s. Seventh-grader Geraldine Brennan fights her own war against grief and anger when her brother Wing is killed. At first, Geraldine wants to blame her brother's best friend, Sam Daily, because he was home marching in demonstrations against the war while Wing was marching through jungles and getting shot at. But gradually, Geraldine and her family are able to make room in their hearts for Sam and the grief that he, too, must endure. ★★★★★

10.19   Pople, Maureen. **The Other Side of the Family.** Henry Holt, 1988. 167 pp. ISBN 0-8050-0758-X.

During World War II, Katherine Tucker is sent from London to live with her mother's parents in Australia. But when Japanese submarines enter the Sydney harbor, Katherine is sent inland to stay with her father's mother. Katherine expects to find a wealthy woman, one who disowned her son because she was so disappointed in his choice of a bride. Instead, she finds an elderly woman so poor that she has to steal coal from the railroad tracks. ★

10.20   Rostkowski, Margaret I. **The Best of Friends.** Harper and Row, 1989. 183 pp. ISBN 0-06-025105-0.

In the 1960s during the Vietnam War protests, high school students Dan and Will and Dan's sister, Sarah, face the radically shifting sands of time. They must make decisions about personal goals, group responsibility, relationships, friendships, and growing up that will affect their whole lives.

10.21   Roth-Hano, Renée. **Touch Wood: A Girlhood in Occupied France.** Four Winds Press, 1988. 304 pp. ISBN 0-02-777340-X.

Renée Roth-Hano was a Jewish child in France during World War II. She writes her story in the form of a diary. Her family is divided by the war, and she and her younger sisters are cared for by Catholic nuns. There's a happy ending: Renée's family is reunited after the Allied invasion. But the details of the experience are presented so realistically that it's easy to understand the frustration and anger that Renée feels. ★

10.22   Sevela, Ephraim. **We Were Not Like Other People.** Harper and Row, 1989. 216 pp. ISBN 0-06-025508-0.

A young Russian boy is separated from his family during Stalin's purge in the 1930s. He survives on his own in wartime Russia, traveling from place to place and meeting all kinds of people. The boy is Jewish in heritage but was raised without religion as a true son of the Revolution. His views are shattered as necessity leads him from one situation to the next. He meets several strong, kind, courageous people—and he loses them, one after another. At the end of six years, the war is over, and the boy makes his way across Russia in search of his family. ★

10.23   Westall, Robert. **Blitzcat.** Scholastic, 1989. 230 pp. ISBN 0-590-42770-9.

This unusual account of England during World War II comes from Lord Gort, a cat separated from her owner when he joins the British Royal Air Force. She follows him across Britain, beginning with the dropping of the first bombs. The violence of war and the tremendous pressures that people must face are reflected in mature language and situations. ★

Recommended Books about War Published before 1988

Bawden, Nina. *Carrie's War*. J. B. Lippincott, 1973.

Bedoukian, Kerap. *Some of Us Survived*. Farrar, Straus and Giroux, 1979.

Benchley, Nathaniel. *Bright Candles*. Harper and Row, 1974.

Bykov, Vasil. *Pack of Wolves*. Thomas Y. Crowell, 1981.

Clapp, Patricia. *I'm Deborah Sampson*. Lothrop, Lee and Shepard, 1977.

Coerr, Eleanor B. *Sadako and the Thousand Paper Cranes*. G. P. Putnam's Sons, 1977.

Collier, James L., and Christopher Collier. *My Brother Sam Is Dead*. Four Winds Press, 1974.

Cummings, Betty S. *Hew against the Grain*. Atheneum, 1977.

Davies, Andrew. *Conrad's War*. Crown, 1980.

Degens, T. *Transport 7-41-R*. Viking, 1974.

Forman, James. *My Enemy, My Brother*. Hawthorn Books, 1969.

Frank, Anne. *The Diary of a Young Girl*. W. W. Norton, 1957.

Greene, Bette. *Summer of My German Soldier*. Dial Books for Young Readers, 1973.

Hannam, Charles. *A Boy in That Situation: An Autobiography*. Harper and Row, 1978.

Haugaard, Erik Christian. *Cromwell's Boy*. Houghton Mifflin, 1978.

Haugaard, Erik Christian. *The Little Fishes*. Houghton Mifflin, 1967.

Houston, Jeanne Wakatsuki, and James D. Houston. *Farewell to Manzanar*. Houghton Mifflin, 1973.

Hunt, Irene. *Across Five Aprils*. Grosset and Dunlap, 1965.

Hunter, Mollie. *The Stronghold*. Harper and Row, 1974.

Kerr, Judith. *When Hitler Stole Pink Rabbit*. Putnam/Coward-McCann, 1972.

Kerr, M. E. *Gentlehands*. Harper and Row, 1978.

Kherdian, David. *The Road from Home: The Story of an Armenian Girl*. Greenwillow Books, 1979.

Koehn, Ilse. *Mischling, Second Degree: My Childhood in Nazi Germany*. Greenwillow Books, 1979.

Mazer, Harry. *The Last Mission*. Delacorte Press, 1979.

McCutcheon, Elsie. *Summer of the Zeppelin*. Farrar, Straus and Giroux, 1985.

Patterson, Sarah. *The Distant Summer*. Simon and Schuster, 1976.

Reiss, Johanna. *The Upstairs Room*. Thomas Y. Crowell, 1972.

Siegal, Aranka. *Upon the Head of the Goat: A Childhood in Hungary*. Farrar, Straus and Giroux, 1981.

Southall, Ivan. *The Long Night Watch*. Farrar, Straus and Giroux, 1984.
Sutcliff, Rosemary. *The Lantern Bearers*. Henry Z. Walck, 1959.
Westall, Robert. *The Machine Gunners*. Greenwillow Books, 1976.
Wiesel, Elie. *Night*. Farrar, Straus and Giroux, 1960.

11 Understanding Real People: Biographies and Biographical Fiction

11.1 Aaseng, Nathan. **Midstream Changes.** Lerner, 1990. 78 pp. ISBN 0-8225-0681-5.

Colonel Sanders, Milton Bradley, and Mary Kay Ash all started out with nothing and turned ideas into million-dollar businesses. Here you can read their stories and stories of others who have turned dreams into thriving businesses. Photos bring these people to life for you.

11.2 Aaseng, Nathan. **The Rejects: People and Products That Outsmarted the Experts.** Lerner, 1989. 80 pp. ISBN 0-8225-0677-7.

Chester Carlson invented the Xerox machine; William Lear built a small and inexpensive jet plane which revolutionized aviation; and Charles Darrow refined the game of Monopoly, bringing enjoyment to millions. Their stories are included with six other accounts of people who pursued their dreams in spite of discouraging rejections.

11.3 Bentley, Judith. **Archbishop Tutu of South Africa.** Enslow, 1988. 96 pp. ISBN 0-89490-180.

Desmond Tutu grew up under apartheid in South Africa where as a black child he questioned the fairness of the system. He's still asking the same questions but of a much broader audience.

11.4 Blassingame, Wyatt. **The Look-It-Up Book of Presidents: From George Washington through Ronald Reagan.** Random House, 1988. 154 pp. ISBN 0-394-86839-5.

George Washington was elected president in Philadelphia in the summer of 1787. This book gives a short biography of our first president—and of the thirty-nine others through Ronald Reagan. Each biography tells you that president's major achievements, and maps and charts show the presidents' birthplaces, the number of electoral votes they got in each state, and how the United States has grown since its beginnings. Photos—including one of George Washington's false teeth—add interest.

11.5 Bober, Natalie S. **Thomas Jefferson: Man on a Mountain.** Atheneum, 1988. 288 pp. ISBN 0-689-31154-0.

The author uses Thomas Jefferson's own writings and what his contemporaries wrote about him to bring her story to life. Readers get to share in the troubles and doubts as well as in the successes of this unusual American hero.

11.6 Briggs, Carole S. **Women in Space: Reaching the Last Frontier.** Lerner, 1988. 80 pp. ISBN 0-8225-1581-4.

Although the focus is on women astronauts, beginning with Russia's Valentina Tereshkova who made a 1963 flight into space, this book gives an overview of both men's and women's accomplishments. There are photos, several in full color, along with the personal stories of the astronauts.

11.7 Brooks, Polly Schoyer. **Beyond the Myth: The Story of Joan of Arc.** J. B. Lippincott, 1990. 176 pp. ISBN 0-397-32423-5.

This story is taken from what is known about the Middle Ages as well as from the extraordinary trial record which was kept by the men who condemned Joan of Arc to death by fire. The record was translated into modern French in the late 1800s and then into many other languages, making Joan of Arc one of the most famous women in history. But even though we know a lot about her, there is great disagreement over who she was, what she did, and what she believed. ★

11.8 Carpenter, Angelica Shirley, and Jean Shirley. **Frances Hodgson Burnett: Beyond the Secret Garden.** Lerner, 1990. 128 pp. ISBN 0-8225-4905-0.

If you've read *The Secret Garden*, *Little Lord Fauntleroy*, or *A Little Princess*, then you are likely to be interested in this biography of their author, who began publishing stories when she was only eighteen. She was born in Manchester, England, during the Industrial Revolution. Her father died when she was only three, and her once comfortable family found itself hard up for money. They moved to a poorer neighborhood where Frances had many of the experiences that she would later put into her rags-to-riches stories. When she was a teenager, Frances's family emigrated to America, and she began her writing career in Knoxville, Tennessee, an area still suffering from the effects of the American Civil War.

11.9   Cleary, Beverly. **A Girl from Yamhill: A Memoir.** William Morrow, 1988. 256 pp. ISBN 0-688-07800-1.

Anyone who grew up reading Beverly Cleary's books will probably also enjoy Cleary's own story of her life as a child and a teenager, first on a farm and later in Portland. She tells you about neighborhood games and friends, the thrill of discovering books, and the demands of trying to please her difficult mother. ★★★

11.10   Cosner, Sharon. **War Nurses.** Walker, 1988. 106 pp. ISBN 0-8027-6828-8.

Nearly everyone has heard of Clara Barton, the American Civil War nurse who helped found the American Red Cross, and of Florence Nightingale, who in the 1850s revolutionized the way the British Army managed its battlefront hospitals. But these two women are not the only ones who deserve credit for outstanding contributions to the field of health care under war conditions, and this book tells the stories of nurses you may never have heard of.

11.11   Davidson, Margaret. **The Story of Alexander Graham Bell: Inventor of the Telephone.** Dell/Yearling Books, 1989. 92 pp. ISBN 0-440-40228-X.

There is much more to the career of Scottish-born Alexander Graham Bell than the invention of the telephone. Not only was he a family man and a teacher of the deaf, but he invented all kinds of things, including one of the first air conditioners—in the bottom of his swimming pool.

11.12   Freedman, Russell. **Franklin Delano Roosevelt.** Clarion Books, 1990. 200 pp. ISBN 0-89919-379-X.

Franklin Delano Roosevelt was the last president to serve before Congress limited presidents to two terms (eight years) in office. Roosevelt was elected four times but died in office soon after his fourth term began. Nearly everyone as old as your grandparents will have a strong opinion—either positive or negative—about President Roosevelt. He came into office in the midst of the Great Depression and saw the United States through most of World War II. The author has gone to original sources to get much of his information about this unusual man and how his life was shaped by world events and conditions, and how he in turn shaped those events and conditions. Photographs add interest. ★★★★

11.13   Fritz, Jean. **The Great Little Madison.** G. P. Putnam's Sons, 1989. 159 pp. ISBN 0-399-21768-1.

His tombstone reads simply "Madison." Although weak in voice and small in stature, James Madison was a major figure in American history, serving his country from his twenties until well into his eighties. He was an intelligent, logical voice in the writing of the United States Constitution, arguing stringently for the concept of balance of powers. And his presidency saw the unpopular War of 1812 with Great Britain, a war that cemented American independence. ★★★★★

11.14   Gallo, Donald R., editor. **Speaking for Ourselves: Autobiographical Sketches by Notable Authors of Books for Young Adults.** National Council of Teachers of English, 1990. 231 pp. ISBN 0-8141-4625-2.

If you've read a lot of books written specifically for teenagers or if you aspire to be a writer, you will probably want to skim through this book and find information on your favorite authors. Over eighty writers each contribute a two-page biography. Most of them also contribute a photograph, while the editor provides a list of their books. You'll get more out of your reading when you know something about the authors and can picture the faces behind the words. ★

11.15   Gherman, Beverly. **Agnes de Mille: Dancing Off the Earth.** Atheneum, 1990. 122 pp. ISBN 0-689-31441-8.

Agnes de Mille should never have been a dancer. She was not built correctly, her father disapproved, and she began lessons too late in life. But in spite of all those handicaps, de Mille persevered and became a wonderful dancer and choreographer, working until she was over eighty years old. One of her accomplishments was to bring classical dance techniques into popular art forms, including the Broadway musicals "Carousel" and "Oklahoma!"

11.16   Gilman, Michael. **Mathew Henson: Explorer.** Chelsea House, 1988. 110 pp. ISBN 1-55546-590-0.

Mathew Henson was a black explorer. For twenty-three years he was one of the most informed and valuable members of Robert Peary's team of explorers. He learned to speak with the North Greenland Eskimos and developed many Eskimo skills, such as dogsledding and building shelters and boats. He was the only member of the team whom Peary chose to accompany him and the four Eskimos who reached the North Pole on April 6, 1909.

11.17   Goodall, Jane. **My Life with the Chimpanzees.** Simon and Schuster/Minstrel Books, 1988. 123 pp. ISBN 0-671-66095-0.

Goodall's autobiography is especially interesting because she shares so many of her observations. She tells you about the chimpanzees and also about her son, Grub, and her husband, Hugo, and the life they lived at the Gombe Stream Research Center in Tanzania where Goodall worked as a naturalist.

11.18   Haskins, James. **Sports Great Magic Johnson.** Enslow, 1989. 64 pp. ISBN 0-89490-160-5.

The success that Magic Johnson has had on the basketball court may remind you of the saying, "Give him the name, he'll play the game." But actually, his success came first. Ever since high school, whatever team he played on met "magical" success, and that's how this well-known basketball genius and likable teammate got the name "Magic." ★

11.19   Hodges, Margaret. **Making a Difference: The Story of an American Family.** Charles Scribner's Sons, 1989. 208 pp. ISBN 0-684-18979-8.

This is the biography of a whole family—one raised by single parent Mary Sherwood at the turn of the century. Sherwood's friend Eleanor Roosevelt admired her because of the way she raised her children to care about and contribute to society. Sherwood's daughters have been active in working for environmental issues, health care, and education, while her son contributed through a career in international relations.

11.20   Hughes, Libby. **Benazir Bhutto: From Prison to Prime Minister.** Dillon Press, 1990. 123 pp. ISBN 0-87518-438-3.

Even though Benazir Bhutto lost her position as prime minister of Pakistan in August of 1990, she made a mark as the first woman ever to become leader of a Muslim state. This story outlines her political upbringing as the daughter of another prime minister of Pakistan, the founder of the Pakistan People's Party (PPP). After graduation from Radcliffe College and Oxford University, Benazir returned home to political unrest. Following a 1977 overthrow, her father was arrested and later executed, and Benazir began leading the PPP and fighting for democracy in Pakistan. In

1988, after ten years spent in and out of prisons and political exile, her continued popularity resulted in her election as the first woman prime minister of Pakistan at the age of thirty-five.

11.21   Lawlor, Laurie. **Daniel Boone.** Illustrated by Bert Dodson. Albert Whitman, 1988. 160 pp. ISBN 0-8075-1462-4.

Daniel Boone the man has become Daniel Boone "the model American frontier hero." This biography traces Boone's life from his birth in Pennsylvania in 1734 to his death in Missouri in 1820. In the years between, he saw the United States' birth, unification, and expansion. He was a leader in the first, shaky steps toward that expansion, pushing the frontier beyond the Appalachian Mountains. You will understand the dangers and rewards of a frontier life as you follow Boone's experience of Indian attacks, captivity, and the establishment of Boonesborough, Kentucky. Illustrations, photos, and maps help you understand the America of Daniel Boone. ★

11.22   Levert, Suzanne. **The Doubleday Book of Famous Americans.** Doubleday, 1989. 305 pp. ISBN 0-385-23699-9.

Ever wonder . . . If Joe Namath finished college? Who invented the atomic bomb? Who brought Ernest Hemingway to the attention of the world? Who was the "Most Valuable Player" of the National League in 1949? This collection of 101 short, lively biographical sketches will answer these and many other questions and make you a guaranteed winner in Trivial Pursuit and Jeopardy. The collection, which includes stories of twenty-two women, will also help you understand the wide range of modern and historical figures whose diverse accomplishments have made America great.

11.23   Little, Jean. **Little by Little: A Writer's Education.** Viking Penguin, 1988. 233 pp. ISBN 0-670-81649-3.

You will especially enjoy this autobiography if you've read some of Jean Little's novels. As a child, she was legally blind, but that didn't stop her from discovering the joys of reading and of imagination that led her to become a writer. Her story tells of the difficulties and triumphs of growing up in Taiwan and Canada, going to school, overcoming her handicap, and eventually becoming a published writer. ★★

11.24   Lyons, Mary E. **Sorrow's Kitchen: The Life and Folklore of Zora Neale Hurston.** Charles Scribner's Sons, 1990. 125 pp. ISBN 0-684-19198-9.

Zora Neale Hurston is one of this century's most notable black writers, and this is her story. She was born in Florida and travelled North, seeking freedom and meaning through her writing. She brought African American folklore to national attention in her accounts of her native Southern heritage. ★

11.25   Marrin, Albert. **Stalin: Russia's Man of Steel.** Viking Penguin, 1988. 256 pp. ISBN 0-670-82101-0.

The power that one man can wield is vividly demonstrated in this biography of Stalin, Russia's first Communist dictator. You'll learn enough of the history of the U.S.S.R. to be able to comprehend just how important the changes now occurring are. ★

11.26   Meltzer, Milton. **Benjamin Franklin: The New American.** Franklin Watts, 1988. 287 pp. ISBN 0-531-10582-2.

Milton Meltzer uses original sources and illustrations to bring Benjamin Franklin's story closer to you. You'll learn about Franklin's many careers—as a printer, author, scientist, inventor, humanitarian, politician, and diplomat. This book shows Franklin to have been a warm and ambitious, although not perfect, person. ★

11.27   Meltzer, Milton. **Rescue: The Story of How Gentiles Saved Jews in the Holocaust.** Harper and Row, 1988. 192 pp. ISBN 0-06-024210-8.

This book offers a different look at the Holocaust because the focus is away from the atrocities and on examples of bravery and courage of people who hid and fed Jews during the Nazi occupation. It includes stories from Germany, Poland, Austria, Italy, and other Western European countries and pays tribute through them to those who helped, as well as to those who survived because of that help. ★★★★

11.28   Meltzer, Milton. **Starting from Home: A Writer's Beginnings.** Viking Penguin, 1988. 145 pp. ISBN 0-670-81604-3.

Milton Meltzer has brought different periods of history alive for thousands of young readers, and now he does the same thing for the early 1900s as he tells about his family and his childhood.

11.29   Meltzer, Milton. **Underground Man.** Harcourt Brace Jovanovich, 1990. 261 pp. ISBN 0-15-200617-6.

Young Joshua Bowen doesn't know what his calling in life is until he discovers abolitionism and becomes involved in smuggling runaway slaves into Ohio. The work is doubly dangerous: it could mean death for the slaves and prison for Joshua. Nevertheless, he takes on the job. When he is caught and imprisoned, he thinks he will die of misery and loneliness. He lives, though, and by helping other prisoners through an epidemic of cholera, he earns his freedom. Then the chance to continue his work on the Underground Railroad is offered once more. Should he take the risk? Does he dare?

11.30 Miller, Douglas T. **Frederick Douglass and the Fight for Freedom.** Facts on File, 1988. 152 pp. ISBN 0-8160-1617-8.

As an acknowledged spokesperson for blacks prior to the Civil War, Douglass holds a unique position in American history. You'll read not only about Douglass's life, but also about the period in which he lived and his relationship to the social structure and the political beliefs of the day. Part of the Makers of America series.

11.31 Miller, Jim Wayne. **Newfound.** Orchard/Richard Jackson Books, 1989. 256 pp. ISBN 0-531-08445-0.

Jim Wayne Miller tells about his life from when he is in sixth grade and his parents separate until he goes away to college. After the separation, he and his brother, sister, and mother go to live in Newfound, Tennessee, where all four grandparents live. You'll get to know and appreciate the people and the life of the community of Newfound. ★

11.32 Mills, Judie. **John F. Kennedy.** Franklin Watts, 1988. 370 pp. ISBN 0-531-10520-2.

You can learn a lot about the man who became president from this biography of John F. Kennedy. You'll learn how political events shaped his personal life and philosophy and how he grew under the responsibility of the presidency. ★

11.33 Moskin, Marietta D. **Margaret Thatcher of Great Britain.** Julian Messner, 1990. 128 pp. ISBN 0-671-69632-7.

Even though Margaret Thatcher is no longer Britain's prime minister, she's still a fascinating woman, and for a long time people will be debating her place in history. The concluding chapter of this book is a seven-page "Postscript" which acknowledges the controversial nature of Mrs. Thatcher's recent decisions and discusses the possibility of her losing her position. It also comments on her personal life, her husband, and her children. A glossary of terms will help you to understand news accounts from Britain and to see some of the differences between British and American government. Part of the In Focus Biography series.

11.34 Neimark, Anne E. **Ché! Latin America's Legendary Guerilla Leader.** J. B. Lippincott, 1989. 107 pp. ISBN 0-397-32309-3.

Ernesto Guevara earned the title "Ché" for his famous military exploits in Latin America. Inspired by all the poor people he saw, Ché fought to bring social justice to Latin America through revolutionary change. With a small band of devoted guerilla fighters, he battled against the inequality and injustice of greedy governments—and won! This is the story of the rebel and the hero.

11.35 Patent, Gregory. **Shanghai Passage.** Illustrated by Ted Lewin. Clarion Books, 1990. 115 pp. ISBN 0-89919-743-4.

Gregory Patent was born to Russian and Iraqi parents in Hong Kong in 1929. He spent his childhood in Shanghai. The story begins near the end of World War II when the Americans are bombing the Japanese-occupied colony. Patent describes his experiences after the war as a British school boy and describes his family's struggle to emigrate to America. The book ends in 1950 when the family arrives in San Francisco.

11.36 Paulsen, Gary. **Woodsong.** Illustrated by Ruth Wright Paulsen. Bradbury Press, 1990. 132 pp. ISBN 0-02-770221-9.

Gary Paulsen's story isn't an autobiography in the traditional sense. Instead, it's an account of some of the experiences he's had with animals and nature. They climax with his thoughts and feelings when he and his dogs run for two and a half weeks in the Iditarod sled race in Alaska. If you have enjoyed Paulsen's fiction, you will be especially interested in these glimpses into the experiences that prepared him to write such books as *Dogsong* and *Hatchet*. ★★★★★

11.37 Peet, Bill. **Bill Peet, an Autobiography.** Houghton Mifflin, 1989. 190 pp. ISBN 0-395-50932-7.

As a young painter, Bill Peet was hired by a greeting card company, but the prospect of a whole season of sympathy cards was too much for him, and he made his way west to try his luck with the Walt Disney studio in Los Angeles. He had two careers, one as an animator for Disney films and one as a writer and illustrator of children's books. He has illustrated his autobiography with many cartoon-style drawings. ★★★★

11.38 Rowland, Della. **The Story of Sacajawea, Guide to Lewis and Clark.** Dell/Yearling Books, 1989. 92 pp. ISBN 0-440-40215-8.

In 1803 Lewis and Clark were commissioned by President Jefferson to locate a land-water route west to the Pacific. They hired a French Canadian fur trader, Charbonneau, and his Native American wife Sacajawea to help them. Sacajawea was Shoshoni by birth; she had been enslaved by the Minnataree nation and sold to Charbonneau. A new mother, Sacajawea strapped her son to her back and accompanied her husband. Foul weather, illness, and stolen supplies hindered the group of fewer than fifty. Sacajawea's bravery and knowledge of the land enabled the expedition to end successfully.

11.39 Salerno-Sonnenberg, Nadja. **Nadja on My Way.** Crown, 1989. 84 pp. ISBN 0-517-57391-1.

In this book, Nadja Salerno-Sonnenberg, a famous musician, recalls her childhood, her musician family, her friends, and her life in famous music schools where she did not always get along with her teachers. While Nadja was competing for the coveted Naumburg Prize, she was nearly evicted from her New York apartment. When she won it, she decided to dedicate her life to playing the violin. She shows that dedication and luck are key ingredients to a successful career in music.

11.40 Sibley, Brian. **The Land of Narnia.** Illustrated by Pauline Baynes. Harper and Row, 1990. 96 pp. ISBN 0-06-025625-7.

This is a book for readers who have fond memories of *The Lion, the Witch, and the Wardrobe* and the other Chronicles of Narnia books. The first part of the book shows how C. S. Lewis's experiences helped him write the Narnia stories, while the second half talks about each of the books. Photographs, reproductions, and original drawings make this book a pleasure to look at as well as to read.

11.41 Stanley, Diane, and Peter Vennema. **Good Queen Bess: The Story of Elizabeth I of England.** Four Winds Press, 1990. 40 pp. ISBN 0-02-786810-9.

This looks like just a picture book, but children who read picture books usually don't know enough about the world to be interested in the life of the Queen of England in the last part of the sixteenth century. So instead of being for young children, *Good Queen Bess* is a good introduction to world history for young teens. You'll learn how Elizabeth I guided England in its growth from a weak, strife-torn country into a great world power. ★★

11.42   Sullivan, George. **George Bush.** Julian Messner, 1989. 169 pp. ISBN 0-671-64599-4.

In 1988 when George Bush became the forty-first president of the United States, he brought to the office twenty-five years of experience in public office. In earlier years, he was a successful Texas businessperson and an outstanding scholar and athlete at Yale University. And while he was growing up, his father, a United States senator, instilled in him the importance of public service.

11.43   Ventura, Piero. **Great Composers.** G. P. Putnam's Sons, 1989. 124 pp. ISBN 0-399-21746-0.

Nearly 100 composers each have their stories told on one or two beautifully illustrated, large pages. In addition to biographical information, you'll read about different eras and types of music. The first composer in the book is Pope Gregory, who between 590 and 604 A.D. contributed greatly to the importance of music in the Catholic Church. The book ends with pages on such people as Benny Goodman, Duke Ellington, and the Beatles. Notes at the end provide further details on each of the featured musicians.

11.44   Weidhorn, Manfred. **Robert E. Lee.** Atheneum, 1988. 150 pp. ISBN 0-689-31340-3.

This biography offers anecdotes and discussions about Robert E. Lee's weaknesses as well as his strengths. It also includes photographs and background information about various aspects of the Civil War.

11.45   White, Ellen Emerson. **Bo Jackson: Playing the Games.** Scholastic, 1990. 86 pp. ISBN 0-590-44075-6.

Bo Jackson is one of the few athletes to succeed in two major league sports—baseball and football. But when he was a student at Auburn University, he also ran track. This paperback biography traces Jackson's life from being the eighth of ten children supported and raised mainly by his mother, who worked as a maid at the Holiday Inn in Alabama, to his present worldwide fame. It is made more interesting by a full-color photo-album insert.

11.46 Worth, Richard. **Robert Mugabe of Zimbabwe.** Julian Messner, 1990. 111 pp. ISBN 0-671-68987-8.

Robert Mugabe is the president of Zimbabwe, and this book tells as much about the country as about the person. A time line, a glossary, and a bibliography for further study make this a good resource book for social studies classes or for providing background information to understanding current events in Africa. Part of the In Focus Biography series.

Series

11.47 **The Achievers.** Lerner.

These biographies, written by several different authors and illustrated with photographs, show that it takes more than the usual to accomplish the unusual. For example, *Florence Griffith Joyner: Dazzling Olympian* tells how Joyner started her running career by chasing jackrabbits in the Mohave Desert, where her father lived. And *Joe Montana: Comeback Quarterback* tells how Montana almost gave up on football when he didn't get to play at Notre Dame until his third year.

11.48 **Alvin Josephy's Biography Series of American Indians.** Silver Burdett Press.

Geronimo and the Struggle for Apache Freedom, Hiawatha and the Iroquois League, King Philip and the War with the Colonists, Sequoyah and the Cherokee Alphabet, Sitting Bull and the Battle of the Little Bighorn, and *Tecumseh and the Dream of an American Indian Nation* are included in this series of biographies written by different authors about famous Native Americans. The book about Sequoyah illustrates how the conflict between the new ways of the white people and the old ways of the Cherokees was a source of great turmoil for Sequoyah and his people. Yet out of the wars, the broken treaties, and the pain rose this brilliant artist, storyteller, trader, and craftsperson, who invented a writing system for the Cherokee language.

11.49 **The American Dream: Business Leaders of the Twentieth Century.** Silver Burdett Press.

Lots of photos accompany these stories of people who succeeded in business. The books include information about both the bad and good parts of these people's lives. Those featured include Elizabeth Arden, Andrew Carnegie, Samuel Goldwyn, William Randolph Hearst, and John D. Rockefeller.

11.50   Genius! The Artist and the Process. Silver Burdett Press.

These 128-page biographies focus on creative people and how their triumphs and disappointments are reflected in their work. The first three books are written about playwright Arthur Miller, painter Pablo Picasso, and architect Frank Lloyd Wright. The next three are about poet Maya Angelou, dancer Mikhail Baryshnikov, and musician Duke Ellington. A chronology, glossary, index, and bibliography at the end of each book make them good sources for research as well as for leisure reading.

11.51   Great Lives. Fawcett/Columbine.

This series now includes eighteen biographies, including those of Mikhail Gorbachev, Christopher Columbus, John F. Kennedy, Abraham Lincoln, and Harriet Tubman. One example is *Sally Ride: Shooting for the Stars*, which tells the story of Sally Ride, who was a successful astronaut and also served as a member of the Rogers Commission to investigate the Challenger disaster.

11.52   Lerner Biography. Lerner.

This series' eight titles, written by six different authors, tell the stories of men and women in politics, the military, and the arts. *Dwight D. Eisenhower: A Man Called Ike* reveals Ike the person, Ike the soldier, and Ike the politician. *Douglas MacArthur* recounts MacArthur's life from his childhood in the Wild West of the 1880s, to his student days at West Point, and then his nearly fifty years as a soldier, with his most challenging command being the leadership of the American armed forces in the Philippines during World War II.

11.53   Pioneers in Change. Silver Burdett Press.

Thomas Alva Edison, Margaret Mead, and *Alexander Graham Bell* are titles included in this series written by various authors. The books in this series will help you understand the situations and the social structures from which a number of unique individuals made their contributions. Vincent Buranelli's *Thomas Alva Edison* traces Edison's life from his childhood in poverty to his great success and fame. *Margaret Mead* by Julie Castiglia presents Mead as a woman ahead of her time; she got a college degree when few women did so, and she went on to become one of the most famous anthropologists in America. And Kathy Pelta's *Alexander Graham Bell* shows how the son of a Scottish speech teacher ended up inventing the telephone.

11.54   What Made Them Great. Silver Burdett Press.

These biographies of famous people like Christopher Columbus, Marie Curie, Anne Frank, Abraham Lincoln, Ferdinand Magellan, Florence Nightingale, Albert Schweitzer, and Leonardo da Vinci are about 100 pages each. They each feature a "Historical Chronology" at the back, which sets a context for the events covered.

**Recommended Biographies and Biographical Fiction
Published before 1988**

Atkinson, Linda. *In Kindling Flame: The Story of Hannah Senesh 1921–1944*. Lothrop, Lee and Shepard Books, 1985.
Blume, Judy. *Starring Sally J. Freedman as Herself*. Bradbury Press, 1977.
Brenner, Barbara. *On the Frontier with Mr. Audubon*. Putnam/Coward-McCann, 1977.
Brooks, Polly Schoyer. *Queen Eleanor, Independent Spirit of the Medieval World: A Biography of Eleanor of Aquitaine*. J. B. Lippincott, 1983.
Carter, Forest. *The Education of Little Tree*. Delacorte Press, 1979.
DePauw, Linda Grant. *Seafaring Women*. Houghton Mifflin, 1982.
Drimmer, Frederick. *The Elephant Man*. G. P. Putnam's Sons, 1985.
Freedman, Russell. *Lincoln: A Photobiography*. Clarion Books, 1987.
Fritz, Jean. *China Homecoming*. G. P. Putnam's Sons, 1985.
Fritz, Jean. *The Double Life of Pocahontas*. G. P. Putnam's Sons, 1983.
Fritz, Jean. *Homesick*. G. P. Putnam's Sons, 1982.
Fritz, Jean. *Traitor: The Case of Benedict Arnold*. G. P. Putnam's Sons, 1981.
Gherman, Beverly. *Georgia O'Keeffe: The "Wideness and Wonder" of Her World*. Atheneum, 1986.
Graham, Robin Lee, and Derek L. T. Gill. *Dove*. Harper and Row, 1972.
Hamilton, Virginia. *Paul Robeson: The Life and Times of a Free Black Man*. Harper and Row, 1974.

Haskins, James. *The Life and Death of Martin Luther King, Jr.* Lothrop, Lee and Shepard Books, 1977.

Kerr, M. E. *ME ME ME ME ME.* Harper and Row, 1983.

Kherdian, David. *The Road from Home: The Story of an Armenian Girl.* Greenwillow Books, 1979.

Meltzer, Milton. *Dorothea Lange: Life through the Camera.* Viking Penguin, 1985.

Meltzer, Milton. *Mary McLeod Bethune: Voice of Black Hope.* Viking Kestrel, 1987.

Watkins, Yoko Kawashima. *So Far from the Bamboo Grove.* Lothrop, Lee and Shepard Books, 1986.

III Imaginings

Writing and storytelling always tap into imagination, but you'll find that the stories in this section are especially imaginative. The first chapter groups together stories about animals—it takes a lot of imagination to write about what it's like to belong to another species! The next group of books sticks with human situations, but exciting and adventurous ones that most of us never experience. Then come science fiction and fantasy books. We put them together partly because it isn't always easy to tell the difference between them. Technically, science fiction stories are supposed to be possible under the physical laws of the universe, while fantasy stories are made possible through purely imagined breaks with reality. It's fun to think that they might occur, but the fantasy writer doesn't have to explain things through technology, as does the science fiction writer. There's a similar difference between the next two types of stories we grouped together—mystery stories and stories of the supernatural. The mystery writer must stick to real-world rules, while the author who chooses to bring in supernatural elements has much more freedom. Either way, the books listed under "Mysteries and the Supernatural" are designed to bring goose bumps—if not nightmares. We conclude this section with collections of myths and legends because after you've read a few modern examples of imaginative stories, you'll want to compare them with stories created and cherished by our ancestors and see that certain aspects of the human imagination have remained the same across many generations.

12 Imagining Our Fellow Creatures: Animals

12.1   Corcoran, Barbara. **Annie's Monster.** Atheneum, 1990. 188 pp. ISBN 0-689-31632-1.

Thirteen-year-old Annie MacDougal is thrilled when her father allows her to have an Irish wolfhound puppy. She names him Flanagan and begins enjoying his lively personality. However, the neighbors aren't so thrilled with Flanagan. They fear that he is unsafe because he is so big and energetic. But when Annie finds a homeless woman hiding in a shack in the woods, Flanagan proves his worth.

12.2   George, Jean Craighead. **On the Far Side of the Mountain.** E. P. Dutton, 1990. 170 pp. ISBN 0-525-44563-3.

You may have already read Jean Craighead George's *My Side of the Mountain* about Sam Gribley and his survival through a winter he spent living in the woods alone except for his falcon Frightful. In this sequel, Sam relates to more people, partly because his beloved falcon is confiscated, and he gets involved in ecological issues. ★

12.3   Hall, Lynn. **The Tormentors.** Harcourt Brace Jovanovich, 1990. 102 pp. ISBN 0-15-289470-5.

Sox Newmann is devoted to his black German shepherd, Heidi. When she disappears from the back of his brother's pickup truck, he has reason to believe she has been stolen. As he investigates her disappearance, he discovers that not only Heidi has been taken, but other dogs are also missing. The evidence points to the fact that the dogs are being stolen systematically for an ugly and inhumane purpose.

12.4   Hudson, Jan. **Dawn Rider.** Philomel Books, 1990. 170 pp. ISBN 0-399-22178-6.

Kit Fox is not worth much in the daily scheme of her people, the "Bloods." She does not see things or feel things or dream of things as do the other young girls in her tribe. She is not a warrior woman, even though she's good with a bow. She is not destined to be a healing woman, even though she's skilled and gentle. Nor does she dream of sharing a tepee and husband as a co-wife with her sister Many Deer. What she does want is to understand the new beast stolen from the "Snakes," which could carry her tribe over the plains and into the hunt. In an act of bravery, she becomes accepted for who she is. ★

12.5   Malterre, Elona. **The Last Wolf of Ireland.** Clarion Books, 1990. 127 pp. ISBN 0-395-54281-9.

This story takes place three hundred years ago. While Devin is exploring in the mist-covered woods near his Irish home, he encounters a wolf. He is surprised when the wolf does not hurt him because the Irish believe that wolves are evil and dangerous, as well as signs of bad luck. Wolves are killed for money, and as Devin watches, a hunter kills the wolf. Devin discovers that the wolf has left behind three pups. He decides to hide these wolf pups from the hunters, even though he knows that such an act is likely to bring him ridicule or punishment.

12.6   Murphy, Barbara Beasley. **Annie and the Animals.** Bantam/ Skylark Books, 1989. 104 pp. ISBN 0-553-15749-3.

Annie lives a comfortable life with her parents who love her, but she can't have a pet because of her dad's allergies. She loves animals, especially a dog named Fritz, who is owned by a woman who seems to have little interest in him. Annie makes plans to save Fritz from bad treatment. Her success eventually leads to a new understanding between Annie and Fritz's owner.

12.7   Namioka, Lensey. **Island of Ogres.** Harper and Row, 1989. 197 pp. ISBN 0-06-024373-2.

Set in sixteenth-century Japan on an island populated by fishers and nuns, this romantic samurai tale mixes humor, adventure, historically accurate details of Japanese life, and a complex mystery plot. Kajiro, an unemployed and out-of-shape young samurai with a slight drinking problem, is mistaken for an expert sword fighter and becomes involved in a mysterious plot to overthrow a local commander, whose island seems to be overrun with animal-eating ogres. Kajiro falls in love with the exasperating young Lady Yuri and is led into and out of danger by her troublesome pet cat.

12.8   O'Dell, Scott. **Black Star, Bright Dawn.** Houghton Mifflin, 1988. 134 pp. ISBN 0-395-47778-6.

Bright Dawn's father Bartok has been asked to run his dogs in the Iditarod, the thousand-mile sled race between Anchorage and Nome, Alaska. Bright Dawn helps him train, and when he is injured, the sponsors ask her to take his place—to run the race herself. During the race, Bright Dawn faces the dangers of the terrible cold, a blinding whiteout, and the treacherous ice. She comes to depend more and more on her lead dog Black Star, who proves to be her greatest asset on the punishing trip.

12.9   Peyton, K. M. **Darkling.** Delacorte Press, 1990. 256 pp. ISBN 0-385-30086-7.

Darkling is the thoroughbred foal that Jenny's grandfather gives her. As Jenny trains the horse to become a successful racehorse, she, too, grows and develops. Mixed in with the dual story of Jenny and her horse are some interesting characters, including the handsome boy next door and Jenny's unconventional family.

12.10   Scholes, Katherine. **The Landing: A Night of Birds.** Doubleday, 1989. 65 pp. ISBN 0-385-26191-8.

Muttonbirds are caught in a violent storm as they make their way toward the Aleutian Islands. Only the strongest survive to find rest in an old boathouse on a remote Australian coast. There, Annie, a young girl, learns to communicate with them. After the storm ends and the birds are ready to travel on, their leader Tyne entrusts Annie with the care of Solar. She hopes the huge, white bird will make his home with her. Originally published in Australia in 1987.

12.11   Taylor, Theodore. **Sniper.** Harcourt Brace Jovanovich, 1989. 227 pp. ISBN 0-15-276420-8.

Fifteen-year-old Ben Jepson's parents own a wild animal preserve, and while they are traveling in Africa, they leave him in charge. Usually, this would be no problem, but this time, the man who cares for the animals is seriously injured, and then a sniper begins shooting at the big cats. It's up to Ben to call for help and to make the right decisions in capturing the sniper and saving the animals. ★

12.12   Thiele, Colin. **Jodie's Journey.** Harper and Row, 1988. 169 pp. ISBN 0-06-026132-3.

It's difficult to say which is harder for Jodie Carpenter to bear: the incredible pain of the crippling arthritis that she has developed or the knowledge that because of it, she will never again ride her beloved horse Monarch. Before the disease took over her body, Jodie was a trophy-winning rider, and now, only a few months later, she is confined to a wheelchair. But being handicapped does not mean being helpless, as Jodie proves when circumstances force her to save herself and Monarch.

12.13 Wallace, Bill. **Beauty.** Holiday House, 1988. 192 pp. ISBN 0-8234-0715-2.

Eleven-year-old Luke is self-centered and angry when he has to move to his grandfather's Oklahoma farm. The one redeeming feature of his new life is his friendship with Beauty, an elderly mare that he takes care of and confides in. He learns enough from both Beauty and his grandfather that when tragedy strikes, he's able to cope with it.

Series

12.14 **The Blue Ribbon.** Fawcett Books.

Kate Wiley, Jessie Robeson, and Dana Cooper, three girls with very different backgrounds, share a common love of horses. They find challenges and friendship in the arena of thoroughbred horse competition. You can follow their adventures through all the *Blue Ribbon* books, including *Riding High*, *A Horse of Her Own*, *Kate's Challenge*, *Golden Girl*, *Time-Out for Jessie*, and *The Main Event*. By Chris St. John.

Recommended Animal Stories Published before 1988

Adams, Richard. *Watership Down*. Macmillan, 1975.
Annixter, Paul. *Swiftwater*. A. A. Wyn, 1950.
Bodker, Cecil. *Silas and the Black Mare*. Translated from Danish by Sheila La Farge. Delacorte Press, 1978.
Brenner, Barbara. *A Killing Season*. Four Winds Press, 1981.
Burnford, Sheila. *Bel Ria*. Little, Brown, 1978.
Burnford, Sheila. *The Incredible Journey*. Little, Brown, 1961.
Donovan, John. *Wild in the World*. Harper and Row, 1971.
Eckert, Allen. *Incident at Hawk's Hill*. Little, Brown, 1971.
Farley, Walter. *The Great Dane Thor*. Random House, 1980.

Fox, Paula. *One-Eyed Cat*. Bradbury Press, 1984.

George, Jean Craighead. *Julie of the Wolves*. Harper and Row, 1972.

George, Jean Craighead. *My Side of the Mountain*. E. P. Dutton, 1990.*

Gipson, Fred. *Curly and the Wild Boar*. Harper and Row, 1979.

Gipson, Fred. *Old Yeller*. Harper and Row, 1976.

Hall, Lynn. *The Horse Trader*. Charles Scribner's Sons, 1981.

Hall, Lynn. *Ride a Dark Horse*. William Morrow, 1987.

Hemingway, Ernest. *The Old Man and the Sea*. Charles Scribner's Sons, 1961.

Herriot, James. *All Creatures Great and Small*. St. Martin's Press, 1972.

Paulsen, Gary. *The Night the White Deer Died*. Delacorte Press, 1990.

Rawls, Wilson. *Where the Red Fern Grows*. Doubleday, 1961.

Savage, Deborah. *A Rumour of Otters*. Houghton Mifflin, 1986.

Swarthout, Glendon. *Bless the Beasts and Children*. Doubleday, 1970.

---

*This is the date that this book was reprinted. It was originally published before 1988.

13 Imagining Excitement: Adventure Stories

13.1 Aiken, Joan. **The Teeth of the Gale.** Harper and Row/Charlotte Zolotow Books, 1988. 307 pp. ISBN 0-06-020045-6.

Set in Spain in the 1820s, *The Teeth of the Gale* is a continuation of *Go Saddle the Sea* and *Bridle the Wind*, but you needn't have read the earlier books to appreciate this one. Eighteen-year-old Felix, who is studying law at the University of Salamanca, is suddenly called home. He is sole heir to the holdings of a Spanish count and an English duke, and in revolutionary Spain plots are thick. He's also in love with Juana Esparza, who almost takes her final vows as a nun.

13.2 Alexander, Lloyd. **The Drackenberg Adventure.** E. P. Dutton, 1988. 152 pp. ISBN 0-525-44389-4.

The year is 1873 in this sequel to *The Illyrian Adventure* and *The El Dorado Adventure*, and seventeen-year-old heiress Vesper Holly travels to Drackenberg, where her guardians Brinnie and Mary are duke and duchess. Helvitius, an old enemy, plans to take the fortunes of Drackenberg as his own. Vesper teams up with local gypsies to restore justice.

13.3 Alexander, Lloyd. **The Philadelphia Adventure.** E. P. Dutton, 1990. 160 pp. ISBN 0-525-44564-1.

This fifth book in the Vesper Holly adventure series takes place in Philadelphia during the 1876 Centennial Exhibition. The Emperor of Brazil's grandchildren are kidnapped, and President Grant appeals for help. Vesper has the job of delivering the ransom, but that's only the beginning in this rollicking adventure.

13.4 Avi. **The True Confessions of Charlotte Doyle.** Orchard/Richard Jackson Books, 1990. 215 pp. ISBN 0-531-08493-0.

Set in England in 1832, this is the story of a young girl, Charlotte Doyle, who is scheduled to meet her parents in America. She is registered on the ship *Seahawk*, but discovers too late that she is the only passenger. Almost immediately, strange things happen, and Charlotte becomes entangled in a plot to overthrow the ship's captain. Adventure takes many forms on this voyage, and Charlotte performs tasks which seem impossible for a girl of her upbringing. You'll find the appendix of nautical terms helpful if you're new to stories of the sea. ★★★★★

13.5 Bauer, Marion Dane. **A Dream of Queens and Castles.** Clarion Books, 1990. 118 pp. ISBN 0-395-51330-8.

Diana hates the idea of spending a year in England away from her friends in Minneapolis, except for one thing: she dreams of meeting Diana, Princess of Wales, who shares her name and who will one day be queen of England. So when she meets an old man who tells her that he is Group Captain Somers and that he has business at Buckingham Palace, she willingly accompanies him on an adventure.

13.6 Brennan, J. H. **Shiva: An Adventure of the Ice Age.** J. B. Lippincott, 1989. 184 pp. ISBN 0-397-32454-5.

Some anthropologists think that during the ice age, several types of humans coexisted. This story tells of the meeting of Shiva, a more advanced Cro-Magnon girl, and Doban, a small, hairy Neanderthal boy. Doban saves Shiva from a wolf and follows her back to the village of the "weakling strangers," as his clan calls them. Frightened that Shiva has brought back an "ogre" the elders lock him up in a cage and plan to kill him. Fearful that more "ogres" may be nearby, they plan an attack. Meanwhile, Doban's family hunts for him. A bloody confrontation seems unavoidable.

13.7 French, Michael. **Split Image.** Bantam Books, 1990. 181 pp. ISBN 0-553-07021-5.

When seventeen-year-old Garrett Murchinson's mother is killed in an automobile accident, he finds himself on the way to Los Angeles to live with a father he hasn't seen since he was seven. You'll learn in the first couple of pages that there's something suspicious about Garrett's dad, but it takes Garrett longer to figure out such things as why his dad teaches him to use his high-tech cameras and why his dad makes frequent trips to North Korea. It's a hard experience for Garrett, but he emerges with a new appreciation of family.

13.8 Hendry, Frances Mary. **Quest for a Maid.** Farrar, Straus and Giroux, 1990. 270 pp. ISBN 0-374-36162-2.

When Alexander III, a thirteenth-century king of Scotland, died in an accident, his young granddaughter, the Maid of Norway, was sent to marry Prince Edward of England and thus become the rightful queen of Scotland. Most historical accounts state the girl was drowned at sea, but some stories report that a woman from Norway presented herself ten years later as the Maid of Norway, who was thought dead. This tale is told through the eyes of the thirteen-year-old daughter of a boat builder. The Maid became the girl's companion and her salvation. ★★

13.9   Maguire, Jesse. **Nowhere High.** Ballantine/Ivy Books, 1990. 185 pp. ISBN 0-8041-0444-1.

Moving from California to Pennsylvania is a harder experience for T.J. than he imagined it would be. The seventeen-year-old senior gets a surprise welcome to Ernest Norwell "Nowhere" High, and it takes a lot of talking with his new friends to discover why he is treated differently. Most of his problems can be traced to his father's relationship with the town's major industry, but that doesn't keep him from getting scared out of his wits.

13.10   Mooser, Stephen. **The Hitchhiking Vampire.** Delacorte Press, 1989. 119 pp. ISBN 0-385-29725-4.

This is a funny story about thirteen-year-old Jamie and her older brother Luke, who leave their flim-flam father in a California jail, drive to Utah to join their mother, pick up an old hitchhiker on the way, gamble with his life's savings, and finally convince him to go with them to Utah, where he can go into business with their grandfather. ★

13.11   Myers, Walter Dean. **The Mouse Rap.** Harper and Row, 1990. 186 pp. ISBN 0-06-024344-9.

Fourteen-year-old Frederick is called "Mouse" because he's so short, but that doesn't mean that he's short on imagination or on talk—especially not on talk. When he hears a TV newscast about the possibility that a gangster from Prohibition days, Tiger Moran, may have hidden $50,000 in the neighborhood, Mouse convinces his friends and a couple of old-timers to join in a cat (or in this case, tiger) and mouse game that stretches over time. They actually find the treasure, but equally interesting is Mouse's banter and the way readers get to know him and his feelings about his girlfriend, his father, and life in general. ★

13.12   Pullman, Philip. **The Tiger in the Well.** Alfred A. Knopf, 1990. 416 pp. ISBN 0-679-90214-7.

In this Victorian thriller, Sally Lockhart from *The Ruby in the Smoke* and *Shadow in the North* is now a young woman with a daughter named Harriet. Harriet's father has died, and Sally is struggling to manage life for herself and her young daughter when to her shock, she gets the news that a man she has never met is trying to obtain legal custody of Harriet. There's plenty of villainy and also plenty of action to keep you fascinated by this story of another time and place. ★

13.13   Regan, Dian Curtis. **A Game of Survival.** Avon/Flare Books, 1989. 132 pp. ISBN 0-380-75585-8.

Nicky is disappointed when he is paired with the new girl, rather than with his dream girl, for a wilderness scavenger hunt in the Colorado Rockies. He mocks her for being over prepared—until they are lost and caught in a blizzard. ★

13.14   Ruckman, Ivy. **No Way Out.** Thomas Y. Crowell, 1988. 212 pp. ISBN 0-690-04671-5.

Amy and Rick, along with Amy's younger brother Ben, are hiking the Zion Narrows where sandstone cliffs rise sharply above the riverbed. The hikers fear for their lives as a flash flood crashes around them. As they struggle to survive, they discover that they can be worn down by emotional pain as well as by their physical hardships.

13.15   Smith, Sherwood. **Wren to the Rescue.** Harcourt Brace Jovanovich/Jane Yolen Books, 1990. 216 pp. ISBN 0-15-200975-2.

When the orphan Wren learns that her good friend Tess is not an orphan but a princess being hidden in the orphanage, she is shocked. When she learns that she is to live with Tess as her companion, she is delighted, but the joy is short-lived. Tess is kidnapped by the evil King Andreus, and Wren, the magician's apprentice Tyron, and young Prince Connor Shaltar set out to try to rescue her. Their trip is long, difficult, and may even be deadly.

13.16   Sutcliff, Rosemary. **The Shining Company.** Farrar, Straus and Giroux, 1990. 240 pp. ISBN 0-374-36807-4.

Set in northern Britain in 600 A.D., this adventure story is based on "The Gododdin," an ancient poem telling about the struggles of tribes in Britain as they united to fight against the Saxons.

Betrayal, death, sacrifice, and bravery are all part of this account, which will be most appreciated by readers already familiar with Rosemary Sutcliff's other books set in England just after the Romans left, including *Blood Feud*, *The Shield Ring*, and *Dawn Wind*. ★★★

13.17   Thiele, Colin. **Shadow Shark.** Harper and Row, 1988. 224 pp. ISBN 0-06-026179-X.

Twelve-year-old Australian cousins Joe and Meg are excited when they get to go along as cooks on a shark hunt. Meg's dad owns the boat but has hired it out to a professional shark hunter. When the boat catches fire, the excitement of the hunt is forgotten, and Meg and Joe must combine all their abilities and resources to survive and to save Meg's father, who is injured and badly burned. ★

13.18   Thomas, Ruth. **The Runaways.** J. B. Lippincott, 1989. 296 pp. ISBN 0-397-32345-X.

Nathan and Julia are both in a sorry state. Nathan's fierce temper and Julia's constant bungling make them miserable, both at school and at home. Nathan's only real comfort is his hiding place, an old abandoned house, and when Julia accidentally blunders in, he thinks it's the last straw—that is, until they find the money.

13.19   Voigt, Cynthia. **On Fortune's Wheel.** Atheneum, 1990. 276 pp. ISBN 0-689-31636-4.

Birle, a medieval innkeeper's daughter, and Orien, a lord and future earl, are swept by "fortune's wheel" into high adventure when they are rescued from a sea accident, only to be sold as slaves in a far-off land. Their quest for freedom and home takes them through trials and dangers—and into romance. ★

13.20   Williams, Barbara. **The Crazy Gang Next Door.** Thomas Y. Crowell, 1990. 153 pp. ISBN 0-690-04868-8.

In this funny, slapstick story, Mrs. Overfield goes to New York, and Kim is supposed to look after her place. But before she can start attending to her duties, the place is invaded by four redheaded, bad-tempered kids. Or are they midgets? They claim to be Mrs. Overfield's niece and nephews, but Kim can't reach her neighbor to find out. The police won't investigate, and the young social worker who comes to check the place quits her job after one encounter with the gang. Meanwhile, they are wrecking Mrs. Overfield's house, and she's coming home soon—to what?

Series

13.21 Cadets. Ballantine Books.

In Ned Bannister's Cadets stories, the Pentagon has selected a team of five teenage recruits from the military academies for their special skills. They take part in an advanced cadet training program known as the Talon Group. Their covert operations are exciting and fast moving and are recommended for readers interested in espionage, technology, the military, or just plain old adventure. Each title begins with "Code Name," for example *Code Name: Snowball, Code Name: Sand Castle, Code Name: Retriever,* and *Code Name: Electron.*

13.22 Choose Your Own Adventure. Bantam Books.

These books make it easy for you to get involved. You direct the plot by making choices at critical points in the action and turning to the page indicated to continue the adventure. About a hundred different titles have been published in the last ten years. Some of the recent titles include *Mutiny in Space* by Edward Packard and R. A. Montgomery, *Return of the Ninja* by Jay Leibold, and *Stock Car Champion* by R. A. Montgomery. They include a variety of settings and subjects including car racing, mountain climbing, ocean exploring, and travelling in outer space and to exotic places on earth, like the Egyptian pyramids and the mountains of Japan.

Recommended Adventure Stories Published before 1988

Avi. *Wolf Rider: A Tale of Terror.* Bradbury Press, 1986.
Bellairs, John. *The Mummy, the Will, and the Crypt.* Dial Books for Young Readers, 1983.
Coldsmith, Don. *Return to the River.* Doubleday, 1987.
Dickinson, Peter. *Healer.* Delacorte Press, 1985.
Fleischman, Sid. *The Whipping Boy.* Greenwillow Books, 1986.
Garfield, Leon. *The December Rose.* Penguin/Puffin, 1987.
Garfield, Leon. *Smith.* Pantheon, 1967.
Garfield, Leon. *Sound of Coaches.* Viking, 1974.
Garfield, Leon. *The Strange Affair of Adelaide Harris.* Pantheon, 1971.

Hamilton, Virginia. *The House of Dies Drear*. Macmillan, 1968.

Lasky, Kathryn. *Beyond the Divide*. Macmillan, 1983.

Mazer, Harry. *Snowbound*. Delacorte Press, 1973.

Mazer, Norma Fox. *Downtown*. William Morrow, 1984.

Mazer, Norma Fox, and Harry Mazer. *The Solid Gold Kid*. Delacorte Press, 1977.

Pullman, Philip. *The Ruby in the Smoke*. Alfred A. Knopf, 1987.

Thompson, Julian F. *The Grounding of Group Six*. Avon Books, 1983.

White, Robb. *Deathwatch*. Doubleday, 1972.

14 Imagining What If: Science Fiction and Fantasy

14.1   Asch, Frank. **Journey to Terezor.** Holiday House, 1989. 160 pp. ISBN 0-8234-0751-9.

Matt Hilton and his family are rescued from a flood by an unusual helicopter, and when Matt awakens from a drug-induced sleep, he thinks he's on a set for a science fiction movie. But Ryan Morrison, a young scientist who has also been whisked away from earth, assures Matt it is not a movie set but the real thing. The two youths ally with Sara Hollings, another misplaced earthling, to begin a quest for freedom and a return to earth. Part one of a trilogy.

14.2   Asimov, Janet, and Isaac Asimov. **Norby and the Oldest Dragon.** Walker, 1990. 110 pp. ISBN 0-8027-6909-8.

Space Academy cadet Jeff Wells and his bossy robot friend Norby head off to the planet Jamyn to attend the Grand Dragon's birthday bash. Jeff is sure that this trip is going to be extremely boring until a cloud with a personality of its own breaks up the celebration. Can Jeff and Norby convince the lonely creature to leave Jamyn, or will all life on the planet cease to exist?

14.3   Baird, Thomas. **Smart Rats.** Harper and Row, 1990. 224 pp. ISBN 0-06-020365-S.

Adults in this futuristic horror story are hopelessly mired down, either because of discouragement or chemical poisoning, and so it's up to seventeen-year-old Laddie Grayson to save himself when the government decides to remove a child from each family that has more than one child. The book's title comes from the government's story that anyone escaping will be attacked by packs of "smart rats" that control areas outside of the settlements. ★

14.4   Baird, Thomas. **Where Time Ends.** Harper and Row, 1988. 230 pp. ISBN 0-06-020360-9.

Doug and Loop are best friends who go on a long-awaited camping trip in the Adirondacks. While they are there, Russia and the United States exchange biological bombs, and a casual week's hike turns into a struggle for survival. This is a grim look at a grim future.

14.5 Banks, Lynne Reid. **The Secret of the Indian.** Illustrated by Ted Lewin. Doubleday, 1989. 147 pp. ISBN 0-385-26292-2.

Omri and his cousin Patrick discover that the same magical cupboard which allowed them to bring cowboys and Indians from America's past into present-day England can be their own way back to the Old West. Unfortunately, time travel has side effects, and the travelers are only a few inches high when they arrive at their destinations. So when Patrick visits Texas, he's able to take a wild ride on a horse's hoof. You'll find adventure, suspense, and even romance in this sequel to *The Indian in the Cupboard* and *The Return of the Indian*.

14.6 Barron, Thomas A. **Heartlight.** Philomel Books, 1990. 272 pp. ISBN 0-300-22180-8.

From a laboratory in an old house in New England, Kate and her scientist grandfather set out to save the sun from destruction. Using an invention of the grandfather's, they start on a quest that takes them into space and to the star Trethoniel.

14.7 Bell, Clare. **Ratha and Thistle-Chaser.** Margaret K. McElderry Books, 1990. 232 pp. ISBN 0-689-50462-4.

Ratha is a young leader of the Named, a clan of intelligent cats who are battling starvation and possible extinction. With the aid of her trusted friend Thakur, she leads her clan to the seacoast where an abundant food supply awaits them, but only if the clan can learn to herd the beasts there. Their plans are thwarted by a stray cat who suffers from a disfigured leg and mysterious seizures. Thakur becomes friends with her, but does not win her trust. The clan's survival will depend on its ability to break with tradition. ★

14.8 Bellairs, John. **The Trolley to Yesterday.** Bantam Books, 1989. 183 pp. ISBN 0-553-15795-7.

Johnny and his friend Fergie are worried about the Professor. He is behaving in mysterious ways, and he seems to be talking to himself in his apartment. When he tells the boys about his time travel in the old trolley—well, they're sure he's gone off the deep end. That is, until they accompany him on a trip to Constantinople in 1453.

14.9 Brittain, Bill. **Professor Popkin's Prodigious Polish.** Illustrated by Andrew Glass. Harper and Row, 1990. 152 pp. ISBN 0-06-020727-2.

This story is set in the New England village of Coven Tree. It features young Luther Gilpin, who is tired of working on his family farm and so falls victim to Professor Popkin's promises of quick and easy money. All Luther has to do is sell the Professor's household polish. It proves to be devilishly effective in living up to its promise of bringing "new life to household objects." Other Coven Tree stories include *The Wish Giver, Devil's Donkey,* and *Dr. Dredd's Wagon of Wonders.*

14.10 Brooks, Bruce. **No Kidding.** Harper and Row, 1989. 207 pp. ISBN 0-06-020722-1.

In the twenty-first century, many of our problems have been solved. War and disease are rare. What's left is alcoholism and sterility caused by computer viewing. The few children there are usually take charge of things. At fourteen, Sam must make the important decisions for his family, including whether to put his alcoholic mother in an institution. He learns that he can't control everything—and that maybe he doesn't even want to. ★★★

14.11 Caraker, Mary. **The Snows of Jaspre.** Houghton Mifflin, 1989. 234 pp. ISBN 0-395-48292-5.

Morgan Farraday has come to Jaspre, a planet colonized by Earth, to serve as school superintendent. She is fascinated by the planet with its artificial sun and colored snows, but she is also worried by the unsettled political situation. She and her family are caught between the powers of the Space Exploratory Forces, who want to add another sun, and the snowgrubbers, a strange group led by Anders Ahlwen, who prefer to live in the frozen and mystical regions of the planet.

14.12 Charnas, Suzy McKee. **The Golden Thread.** Illustrated by Yvonne Gilbert. Bantam Books, 1989. 209 pp. ISBN 0-553-05821-5.

In this third book in the Sorcery Hall trilogy, fourteen-year-old Valentine Marsh discovers that she has inherited a magic power from her grandmother. Together with six friends, Valentine must fight the evil Bosanka Lonat, an alien witch from a dying planet. Valentine fears and despises Bosanka and her wicked spells until she learns compassion for all living things.

14.13   Charnas, Suzy McKee. **The Silver Glove.** Bantam Books, 1989. 162 pp. ISBN 0-553-27853-3.

Val's grandmother sends her a magical silver glove, and not long after, she finds out that the school psychologist is an evil magician who is stealing the souls of hundreds of people. Her mother has been dating him, and Val must join forces with her sorceress grandmother and act quickly and bravely before black magic takes over her mother's latent powers.

14.14   Chetwin, Grace. **Collidescope.** Bradbury Press, 1990. 240 pp. ISBN 0-02-718316-5.

An extraterrestrial cyborg (part human, part machine) named Hahn, a young Indian from precolonial times named Sky-Fire Trail, and a contemporary teenager named Frankie collide in space and time. They must use their space crystal to zoom through different dimensions in time and space to save Hahn, Sky-Fire Trail's tribe, and Earth itself from destruction. ★

14.15   Christopher, John. **When the Tripods Came.** E. P. Dutton, 1988. 151 pp. ISBN 0-525-44397-5.

Alien tripods sixty feet high with metal domes land on earth and embark on a path of destruction until they are destroyed by bombs. But after their destruction, some people form a cult in preparation for the next Tripod invasion. This story, told through the eyes of Laurie and Andy, two British young people, is a prequel to the Tripods trilogy which John Christopher wrote more than twenty years ago. If you enjoy this introduction, you'll probably also want to read *The White Mountains*, *The City of Gold and Lead*, and *The Pool of Fire*.

14.16   Conford, Ellen. **The Genie with the Light Blue Hair.** Bantam Books, 1989. 160 pp. ISBN 0-553-05806-1.

This humorous story begins when shy and withdrawn Jeannie Warren gets a strange lamp for her fifteenth birthday. Her ten-year-old brother teases her that it looks like Aladdin's magic lamp, and he's not too far wrong—except that the genie that comes from this lamp is a lot like Groucho Marx and is not about to grant three unconditional wishes. ★

14.17 Cooper, Clare. **Ashar of Oarius.** Harcourt Brace Jovanovich, 1990. 163 pp. ISBN 0-15-200409-2.

Kate is a bright teenager who leaves her space dome on the planet Plioctis with her young friend William to search for her missing cat Timmy. They find the cat, but when they return to the dome, they find that everyone has disappeared—except for a baby. Kate and William are forced to search for answers on their own after having lived under intergalactic law all their lives. Their only helper is the dome's computer system, "Grandpa," which gives them hope when all else has failed.

14.18 Corbalis, Judy. **The Ice Cream Heroes.** Illustrated by David Parkins. Little, Brown, 1989. 152 pp. ISBN 0-316-15648-5.

Henrietta is an orphan. Oskar might as well be, with his famous mountaineer mother Cornelia always off on a climb and his grandmother Elspeth always off on long-distance swims. When Elspeth sends Oskar alone to deliver a special ice pick to Cornelia in the Himalayas, Henrietta goes along and delivers it in her gorilla suit as a "gorillagram." Henrietta and Oskar escape from a pack of yetis, only to be taken captive by the evil Controller in his ice cream palace. Can they save themselves and other prisoners? And even more important, can they save the world's ice cream supply?

14.19 Cross, Gillian. **Twin and Super-Twin.** Holiday House, 1990. 169 pp. ISBN 0-8234-0840-X.

Twins David and Ben and their friend Mitch are the Nelson Square gang, rivals of the Wellington Street gang. The two London, England, gangs find their differences coming to a frightening climax at the Guy Fawkes Day bonfire. The bonfire is big enough for both gangs, but the "Nellies" decide to set it ablaze early when David's arm suddenly turns into a roman candle. David has become the unwilling tool of his twin Ben, who can transform David's arm into various forms. Attempts to disguise the new forms provide humorous episodes and even more complications. Eventually, the twins find a way to resolve their problems, but not until they've dealt with another surprise.

14.20 Curry, Ann. **The Book of Brendan.** Holiday House, 1990. 169 pp. ISBN 0-8234-0803-5.

Set in the time of King Arthur, this is the story of young Elric and his adventurous quest to free Holybury Abbey from the evil powers of Myrddin, the evil side of Merlin. Elric, Bridget, and their friend Father Brendan are the only ones to escape when Myrddin casts an evil spell. Father Brendan has written and illustrated a book about Saint Brendan, for whom he's named, and when help is needed most, the animals from Father Brendan's book come to life and lead the adventurers to help.

14.21   Dalton, Annie. **Out of the Ordinary.** Harper and Row, 1990. 243 pp. ISBN 0-06-021425-2.

Molly views herself as a most ordinary, even plain, young woman, but the adventure she gets into is far from ordinary and plain. When she sets out to get a summer job, she never dreams that she will become the protector of Floris, a young boy from another world and another time.

14.22   Danziger, Paula. **This Place Has No Atmosphere.** Dell/Yearling Books, 1989. 156 pp. ISBN 0-440-40205-0.

Fourteen-year-old Aurora Borreales Williams has an eleven-year-old sister named Starr. Their mother is a doctor, their father a dentist. In order to provide a better life for their family and to give it more space to grow, Aurora's parents agree to lend their medical talents for a pioneering venture on the moon. Even in the year 2057, Aurora experiences the usual upsets and frustrations of any teen leaving a familiar school and friends for the unknown. Traveling to the moon can be a drag, too! Never quite able to make the best of a bad situation, Aurora learns through a school project to adjust and make new friends.

14.23   De Lint, Charles. **The Dreaming Place.** Illustrated by Brian Froud. Atheneum, 1990. 138 pp. ISBN 0-689-31571-6.

Nina's cousin Ashley has been living with Nina and sharing her bedroom since Ashley's mother died three years ago. Nina doesn't like Ashley, and when she starts having horrible nightmares in which she feels that her soul is trapped in the bodies of animals, she's sure that Ashley is to blame. But the truth is worse than this, and only Ashley can help.

14.24   Dickinson, Peter. **Eva.** Delacorte Press, 1989. 219 pp. ISBN 0-385-29702-5.

In the world of the future, great strides have been made in medical technology. Following an automobile accident, thirteen-year-old

Eva is in an irreversible coma. Then doctors decide to try an experiment. They put her memory and brain patterns into a new body—that of a chimpanzee named Kelly. The new Eva/Kelly must learn to live in two worlds at once—the animal world and the human world. ★★★★★★

14.25 Dillon, Barbara. **A Mom by Magic.** Illustrated by Jeffrey Lindberg. J. B. Lippincott, 1990. 144 pp. ISBN 0-397-32449-9.

Jessica Slocum hasn't had a mother since she was two years old. She's now ten, and it's Christmastime. When she pulls a card from the wishing well at Milliman's department store, it promises her one wish, and she surprises even herself by wishing she could have a mother for the holiday season. What kind of a mother could a department store provide? A mannequin, of course. But in this story, the mannequin has come to life.

14.26 Follett, Ken. **The Power Twins.** William Morrow, 1990. 90 pp. ISBN 0-688-08723-X.

Uncle Grigoiran invites the twins, Fritz and Helen Price, along with their cousin Tubs to visit his sheep farm in Wales. But that's only the beginning of an adventure that includes a trip to Palassan, the capital of the Galactic Empire, where they act as arbitrators in a dispute involving forces on the Worm Planet. They receive special powers and learn to operate the space vehicle, Hypertrans. Formerly titled *The Power Twins and the Worm Puzzle*.

14.27 Forrester, John. **The Forbidden Beast.** Harper and Row, 1988. 132 pp. ISBN 0-06-447012-1.

You don't have to have read the first two books of Forrester's Bestiary trilogy to enjoy this third book, whose cast of characters is an interesting mixture of humans and nonhumans competing for power over both Luna and Old Earth. Among them are Tava and Ryland Langstrom, a talented geneticist couple devoted to restoring the plants and animals of Old Earth; Tamara and Drewyn, the Langstroms' sixteen-year-old twins; the Round Beast, a great and secretive power who has helped Tava's work on Old Earth; and the Forbidden Beast, who rules Luna and wants to wipe out all human beings.

14.28 Furlong, Monica. **Wise Child.** Alfred A. Knopf/Borzoi Sprinters, 1989. 228 pp. ISBN 0-394-82598-5.

The evil witch Maeve abandons her daughter Wise Child, who is then taken in by Juniper. Juniper is a kind sorceress, who mixes medicinal herbs and cares for the needy. She initiates Wise Child into the world of magical powers and unearthly places. But with Maeve's reentrance comes evil and temptation. Will Wise Child succumb or follow the path of the *doran*?

14.29 Gilden, Mel. **Harry Newberry and the Raiders of the Red Drink.** Henry Holt, 1989. 151 pp. ISBN 0-8050-0698-2.

This story is a cross between a high-adventure story and a spoof. Maps are disguised as pizzas, a robot as a vacuum cleaner, and weapons as cheese blight and chili. The main conflict is whether Harry and his mother, who he thinks is comic book heroine Tuatara, can prevent Bonnie Android from destroying Harry's hometown and stealing the magical red drink that Harry's grandfather invented.

14.30 Heinlein, Robert. **Time for the Stars.** Charles Scribner's Sons, 1990. 244 pp. ISBN 0-684-19211-X.

Science fiction fans love practically anything that Robert Heinlein wrote, but *Time for the Stars* may be especially interesting to you because the main characters are twin boys, born after their family has already used up its untaxed quota of three children. Pat and Tom communicate telepathically—both an advantage and a disadvantage—and as Tom tells the story, you are included in plenty of high-tech as well as human excitement.

14.31 Hilgartner, Beth. **Colors in the Dreamweaver's Loom.** Houghton Mifflin, 1989. 241 pp. ISBN 0-395-50214-4.

With the death of her father, sixteen-year-old Alexandra Scarsdale is left alone—again. Only this time it is permanent. Tired, lost, and scared, she falls asleep after running into the woods. She is discovered by some new friends, who lead her on a quest to help the Orathi, a gentle forest folk who do not bear arms. The Orathi must approach the gods to settle the dispute with the People of the City, who want their lands for expansion. They will abide by the gods' decision no matter how long it takes or what trials they must endure.

14.32 Jacobs, Paul Samuel. **Born into Light.** Scholastic, 1988. 144 pp. ISBN 0-590-40710-4.

Roger Westwood is the elderly narrator who looks back and tells what happened in his New England village at the turn of the century when an alien boy, first thought to be an abandoned child raised by animals, was taken into his family. The boy grew up and married Roger's sister. Now as an adult and father of his own family, the alien sets out to find other aliens on earth and to solve the mystery of why they are here. ★

14.33 Jacques, Brian. **Mattimeo.** Philomel Books, 1990. 446 pp. ISBN 0-399-21741-X.

Slagar the Cruel, his scarred face hidden behind a silk mask, plots revenge against the mouse warrior Matthias and the other creatures living in Redwall Abbey. He lulls the residents to sleep and steals several of the children to be slaves. One of the children is Matthias's son, Mattimeo, so Matthias and the rescue group from Redwall join Orlando the Axe, Jabez the hedgehog, and the Log-a-Log as they follow the dangerous and murderous path of Slagar.

14.34 Jones, Diana Wynne. **Eight Days of Luke.** Greenwillow Books, 1988. 150 pp. ISBN 0-688-08006-5.

David is spending his summer vacation with his aunts and uncles, and he is so upset about the constant need to feel grateful that he tries to put a curse on his relatives. But something goes wrong, and he finds himself fighting giant snakes—with the help of a strange boy named Luke. The mysterious Luke appears whenever a fire is lit. He's helpful, but he's also in some type of trouble. Will David be able to help?

14.35 Jones, Diana Wynne. **The Lives of Christopher Chant.** Greenwillow Books, 1988. 230 pp. ISBN 0-688-07806-0.

Christopher Chant, who just happens to have nine lives, is a boy of remarkable talent. Not only can he travel between dimensions, he can actually bring physical objects back from his dreams. His affectionate but shifty Uncle Ralph manipulates Christopher into performing experiments. Christopher innocently lands himself and his absentminded parents in a heap of trouble. But with the aid of a few other characters, Christopher begins to find his way out of trouble. ★★

14.36 Jordan, Sherryl. **A Time of Darkness.** Scholastic, 1990. 246 pp. ISBN 0-590-43763-6.

Until he is reunited with his family, Rocco doesn't know whether his life in the Valley of Anshur results from a trip into the future or into the past. But he does realize that the time he spends with his adopted brother Narvik, the wisewoman and healer Ayoshe, and his betrothed Ilsabeth teaches him much about friendship and responsibility. He also learns about himself from living in this primitive society that took him in and eventually made him their trusted leader.

14.37 Koontz, Dean R. **Oddkins: A Fable for All Ages.** Illustrated by Phil Parks. Warner Books, 1988. 183 pp. ISBN 0-446-51490-X.

The Oddkins are stuffed toy animals with magical powers to live as secret friends of children in need. With the death of their creator, Isaac Bodkins, the Oddkins begin a journey to the toyshop of Mrs. Shannon, another good toymaker. Along the way, they face many obstacles, from mongrel dogs to Rex, the malevolent marionette, and his gang of evil toys. The story is also a fable about Victor, Isaac's nephew, who is at first humorless, pinched, and unpleasant, but then learns that life has its magic, even for adults.

14.38 Lawrence, Louise. **The Warriors of Taan.** Harpercrest, 1988. 249 pp. ISBN 0-06-023736-8.

The Earthlings—Outworlders, as they are called—have built their cities on Taan. They call the world "New Earth," but the natives of Taan don't want them there for fear that the Outworlders will make the same mess of Taan that they made of their own world. Elana, a novice-healer in the sisterhood, is called on to risk her life and love to bring together the Outworlders, the warriors, and a mysterious group of creatures called Stonewraiths in an effort to heal the planet.

14.39 Le Guin, Ursula K. **Tehanu: The Last Book of Earthsea.** Atheneum, 1990. 226 pp. ISBN 0-689-31595-3.

From far away in the darklands, Sparrowhawk, the archmage of Earthsea, returns on the back of a dragon, barely alive and stripped of his magic. The Kargish widow Tenar restores his health and gives him refuge with her and a cruelly disfigured child, whose eyes hold dark mysteries and whose body burns with fire. Who exactly is the girl, and what will happen to Sparrowhawk now that he is powerless? ★

14.40 L'Engle, Madeleine. **An Acceptable Time.** Farrar, Straus and Giroux, 1989. 343 pp. ISBN 0-374-30027-5.

Eighteen-year-old Polly comes to Connecticut to live with her grandparents. She enjoys the knowledge and capabilities of her mother's parents but drifts away from them when a friend she met in Greece the summer before and Dr. Columbra, a retired priest, take her into another circle of time to meet with people who lived 3,000 years ago. She feels drawn to these people, and her study of Ogam helps her to communicate with them. But how will she get back to her own ring of time?

14.41 Levoy, Myron. **The Magic Hat of Mortimer Wintergreen.** Illustrated by Andrew Glass. Harpercrest, 1988. 211 pp. ISBN 0-06-023842-9.

It's the 1890s, and Amy and Joshua's parents are killed in a Sioux uprising. The children are taken in by mad old Aunt Vootch, who considers spending a night in a pigpen to be appropriate punishment even for breaking minor rules. In desperation, Amy and Joshua head east to find their grandparents. They throw in their lot with snake oil salesman Mortimer Wintergreen, who happens to have a magic hat that produces all sorts of amazing and useful items—but always in its own contrary way.

14.42 Lisle, Janet Taylor. **Afternoon of the Elves.** Orchard Books, 1989. 122 pp. ISBN 0-531-05837-9.

Nine-year-old Hillary and eleven-year-old Sara-Kate are next-door neighbors, but never friends until Hillary discovers an elfin village through the hedges in Sara-Kate's unkempt backyard. Hillary's parents and friends are worried when Sara-Kate reels Hillary in with her magical stories of the elves and their day-to-day comings and goings at the expense of her personal life. No one really knows what exists behind the tightly closed doors and heavily shaded windows of the Connelly house.

14.43 Logan, Carolyn F. **The Power of the Rellard.** Alfred A. Knopf, 1989. 278 pp. ISBN 0-394-82586-1.

Lucy is seriously ill, but that doesn't stop her brother and sister from crowning her Rellard, Keeper of the Power. Unfortunately, when she obtains mystical power, she must face more than her illness. Along with Georgie and Shelley, she must protect this power from an evil force that tries to destroy her family. This is difficult, since the evil takes many different forms, strangely working through members of her family. Lucy uses all her courage to fight it, but how long can she hold out against such a force?

14.44   Mace, Elisabeth. **Under Siege.** Orchard/Richard Jackson Books, 1990. 214 pp. ISBN 0-531-08471-X.

Morris gets a chance to play God with his uncle's computer-operated war game of peasants storming a medieval castle. But the game takes on eerie dimensions when the models come to life.

14.45   Maguire, Gregory. **I Feel Like the Morning Star.** Harper and Row, 1989. 277 pp. ISBN 0-06-024022-9.

Fifteen-year-old Sorb is roused night after night by the same dream—escape. For five years, this post–nuclear war colony of four hundred has settled into the normal routine of the twenty-first century, which includes living underground. Most people believe that the tunnels to the colony have collapsed and that there is no way back to the surface. But Sorb cannot ignore seeds of doubt and the hope of escape which tantalizes him. Will seeing the sun again be worth the risk?

14.46   Mooney, Bel. **The Stove Haunting.** Houghton Mifflin, 1988. 132 pp. ISBN 0-395-46764-0.

Daniel and his family have moved from London to an old home in a small town. Daniel doesn't know how he's going to like the change, and he scarcely has time to find out. An old stove is uncovered during the remodeling of the family's home, and Daniel finds himself mysteriously pulled into the 1800s when restless farm workers are beginning to unionize—a treasonable activity according to the laws of the day. Daniel needs to get back to the twentieth century, but he also needs to help these new friends from the past.

14.47   Morpurgo, Michael. **King of the Cloud Forests.** Viking Penguin, 1988. 145 pp. ISBN 0-670-82069-5.

This fantasy reads like historical fiction, set in the 1930s when the Japanese invade China. Fourteen-year-old Ashley Anderson escapes with his old family friend, Uncle Sung, and they set out to cross the Himalayas into India. Ashley is injured and then rescued by the Yeti, mystical people of the mountains who think he's come as a god to be their leader. ★

14.48   Moulton, Deborah. **The First Battle of Morn.** Dial Books for Young Readers, 1988. 171 pp. ISBN 0-8037-0550-6.

Torin's father is in charge of the winged horses ridden by the Teachers, who are the cruel rulers of the planet Morn. Torin helps in the stables until the birth of a special foal forces him out into a dangerous world, where he discovers that he must play a key role in the saving of his planet.

14.49 Murphy, Shirley Rousseau. **The Dragonbards.** Harper and Row, 1988. 288 pp. ISBN 0-06-024367-8.

This is the conclusion to the Dragonbard trilogy, which started with *Nightpool* and *The Ivory Lyre*. In it Meridien, the lost Queen of Auric, and her children are brought together; Kiri finds herself a dragon; and Teb and Camery become more than friends. The evil Quazelzeg marshals his forces to take control of the world. Can the dragonbards and their singing dragons keep him from victory?

14.50 Murphy, Shirley Rousseau, with Welch Suggs. **Medallion of the Black Hound.** Harper and Row, 1989. 182 pp. ISBN 0-06-024369-4.

David is distracted from high school soccer by a crazy dream; his attention is also carried away by the gold disc he wears around his neck. A gift from his father, the medallion is supposed to be a good luck charm. In spite of this, David seems headed for a showdown with his dreaded enemy. His father warned him of the charm's powers by telling him about its history. After he has many adventures in a strange medieval world, his parents gladly welcome him back home.

14.51 Peck, Sylvia. **Seal Child.** William Morrow, 1989. 200 pp. ISBN 0-688-08682-9.

From the moment of her sudden appearance on Ambrose Island where Molly's family is spending its winter break, Meara changes Molly's outlook on life. With Meara, everything is special, beautiful, and delightful. Meara lives with Ruby, Molly's adopted grandmother, and she seems somehow to be part of Ruby's stories of the ocean, the seals, and her past romance. When Molly's family returns for the whole summer, her little brother Douglas helps unravel some of the mystery surrounding Meara. But nothing prepares Molly for Meara's startling final action. Black-and-white pen-and-ink illustrations capture some of the text and characters.

14.52 Pendergraft, Patricia. **The Legend of Daisy Flowerdew.** Philomel Books, 1990. 190 pp. ISBN 0-399-22176-X.

Misunderstood and unwanted, thirteen-year-old Daisy Flower-dew has never known any peace or kindness, except when she's been alone in the woods with the flowers and birds or with Granny Henry. But when Granny Henry dies, Daisy is returned to the small country town of Vineland Flats, where she faces a mother and stepfather who treat her like an intruder. She also faces the terrible prospect of marrying the coarse and stupid Elmer Goots, who bought her for $10.00. Her only solace is in her paper dolls, Grace and Terence. They're the only ones she'll talk to, and Terence promises her that no matter what happens, wishes *can* come true.

14.53   Pierce, Meredith Ann. **The Pearl of the Soul of the World.** Little, Brown/Joy Street Books, 1990. 243 pp. ISBN 0-316-70743-0.

In this final book of the Darkangel trilogy, Aeriel continues her quest to release her husband Irrylath from the clutches of the White Witch. The sorceress Revenna bestows on Aeriel a white pearl which holds all the vast knowledge of the creators of World, and she speaks the last of the mysterious rhyme which holds the key to Aeriel's destiny. As the White Witch's drought plagues the land, Aeriel wonders if she has the strength to face the Witch and save not only her husband, but the world. ★

14.54   Pike, Christopher. **See You Later.** Archway Paperbacks, 1990. 226 pp. ISBN 0-671-67657-1.

Time travel, intrigue, and death are parts of this story, whose plot resembles a computer game. Mark has a crush on Becky, a clerk in a record store that carries the games he has created. But because Becky already has a boyfriend, she won't date Mark. Later in the same shop, Mark meets Vincent, a quiet young man also interested in computer games. Vincent and his roommate Kara change the course of Mark's and Becky's lives in this adventure.

14.55   Pinkwater, Daniel. **Borgel.** Macmillan, 1990. 170 pp. ISBN 0-02-774671-2.

Mysterious Uncle Borgel, who claims to be 111 years old, invites Melvin and his dog Fafner to accompany him on a late-night trip in his 1937 Dorbzeldge sedan. As "time-tourists," they visit Hapless Toad's Place and the Blue Moon Rest, and they row a Roman trireme across the River Styx.

14.56   Rubinstein, Gillian. **Space Demons.** Dial Books for Young Readers, 1988. 240 pp. ISBN 0-8037-0534-4.

Seventh-grader Andrew receives a new computer game. He shares it with his best friend and two others from school, hoping they can help him master its challenging format. The four are drawn into the game and find that mastering it is more than a matter of technology.

14.57 Sargent, Pamela. **Alien Child.** Harper and Row, 1988. 246 pp. ISBN 0-06-025202-2.

Nita has been raised by her guardian, the alien Llipel, in the belief that she is the only one of her kind remaining on earth—the last of the human race. Nita is, herself, a kind of accident. She was a frozen embryo brought to life by the aliens and raised in a laboratory. When she is fifteen, she discovers that the aliens have also raised a boy in the laboratory, and the two of them venture forth to see if they can find out what happened to the human race.

14.58 Service, Pamela F. **The Reluctant God.** Atheneum, 1988. 211 pp. ISBN 0-689-31404-3.

Have you ever read a story with a mummy for the good guy? Prince Ameni, son of Pharaoh Senusert II, lived in suspended animation for forty centuries until Lorna, an English schoolgirl accompanying her archaeologist father on a dig, found him. She teaches him to eat peanut butter and wear blue jeans, but the two of them don't spend all their time adjusting; they soon find themselves involved in an exciting cops-and-robbers adventure.

14.59 Service, Pamela F. **Under Alien Stars.** Atheneum, 1990. 214 pp. ISBN 0-689-31621-6.

Planet Earth is being used as a military base by Tsorian aliens and is under attack by Hykzoin forces. Human resisters capture the Tsorian military leader RogovJy while he is dining at the home of Jason Sikes's mother Marilyn. The attack by the Hykzoins makes Jason, Marilyn, RogovJy, and his daughter Aryl work together to survive the attack and save Earth.

14.60 Shachtman, Tom. **Beachmaster.** Henry Holt, 1988. 166 pp. ISBN 0-8050-0498-X.

Daniel au Fond is different from the other sea lions living in the cove. He takes risks and asks questions the others have forgotten or are afraid of. The bipeds who feed them are nice, but "nice" isn't enough. Escaping from the cove, Daniel is lured to a laboratory ship but escapes again—only to witness the slaughter of innocent seal pups. Forming his own colony, he returns once again to the cove, where he is named Beachmaster.

14.61   Silverberg, Robert. **Letters from Atlantis.** Atheneum, 1990. 136 pp. ISBN 0-689-31570-8.

Atlantis is a mythical island said to have vanished into the sea. Roy travels through time into the mind of the prince of Atlantis, while his partner Lora goes to the same time in Ice Age Europe. Their findings are very different. While Roy explores a city of modern technology, Lora finds a barren, desolate land with Neanderthal people using stone tools. How can Atlantis be so advanced while the rest of the world is shadowed in ignorance? ★

14.62   Singer, Marilyn. **The Charmed.** Macmillan, 1990. 219 pp. ISBN 0-789-31619-4.

Twelve-year-old Miranda has a friend named Bastable that no one else can see or hear. To Miranda, Bastable looks like a six-foot cat that walks upright. Then Miranda is given an old snake charmer's basket which turns out to be magical, and Miranda and Bastable are pulled into the basket, where they meet the snake goddess, Naja the Ever-Changing. They become involved in a struggle against an evil being that wants to conquer their worlds through mind control.

14.63   Sleator, William. **The Duplicate.** E. P. Dutton, 1988. 154 pp. ISBN 0-525-44390-8.

Have you ever wished you could be in two places at the same time? This is the story of David, who can do just that. David makes a copy of himself with a machine that duplicates organic matter. It seems like the perfect solution to all his problems, but when the duplicate also duplicates himself, David winds up with more problems than he started with. ★★★

14.64   Sleator, William. **Strange Attractors.** E. P. Dutton, 1989. 134 pp. ISBN 0-525-44530-7.

A scientist and his beautiful daughter from another universe make a careless mistake that has brought chaos to their planned time travel and landed them on earth. Could they be the "strange attractors" that upset the entire universe? It's up to a high school science student to keep this from happening. ★★

14.65   Smith, L. J. **Heart of Valor.** Macmillan, 1990. 227 pp. ISBN 0-02-785861-8.

The four children in the Hodges-Bradley family aren't exactly typical, nor are their adventures. In this sequel to *The Night of the Solstice*, they discover that what was a relatively minor earthquake in their town of Villa Park, California, has reopened passages to the Wildworld, and it's up to them to help the sorceress Morgana Shee save the earth.

14.66 Stannard, Russell. **The Time and Space of Uncle Albert.** Henry Holt, 1990. 120 pp. ISBN 0-8050-1309-1.

For her science project, Gedanken agrees to a journey into space in eccentric Uncle Albert's "thought bubble." Uncle Albert experiments with the law of relativity, and Gedanken is amazed to discover that time in the spacecraft is not the same as time on earth, that the spacecraft was "squeezed up" while in space, and that she weighs more in space than in Uncle Albert's study. At the end of her science project, Gedanken adds in a space quiz for her teacher—with complete answers. See the postscript to learn how these discoveries relate to the work of Albert Einstein and his "gedanken," or thought experiments.

14.67 Thomas, Jane Resh. **The Princess in the Pigpen.** Clarion Books, 1989. 128 pp. ISBN 0-395-51587-4.

Nine-year-old Princess Elizabeth is transported from a castle in seventeenth-century London to a pigpen in twentieth-century Iowa. The last thing she remembers was lying in her bed sick with a fever, and here she is a strange little girl in an even stranger situation. She's amazed by automobiles and electric lights, but most of all by penicillin, which helps her to get well. Now all she wants is to return home—but where is home, and how will she get there?

14.68 Townsend, John Rowe. **The Fortunate Isles.** J. B. Lippincott, 1989. 248 pp. ISBN 0-397-32366-2.

As surprised as everyone else to learn that she, a mere peasant girl and nonbeliever, is the Messenger to the Living God, Eleni willingly accepts her task. With the help of Andreas, a former assistant to the local priest, Eleni sets out on her quest to meet with the Living God. Their travels from the island of Molybdos to Malama on the Gold Island subject them to imprisonment and slavery. The faith of Andreas and the courage of Eleni are tested many times, yet their journey must be made in order to save their small island and fulfill the written prophesy.

14.69   Vardeman, Robert E. **Road to the Stars.** Harper and Row, 1988.
213 pp. ISBN 0-06-026288-5.

In 2088 ten billion people share the polluted earth and watch
excitedly as the first starships are launched to look for new homes
in space. Young Cliff Macklin has a goal closer to home: he wants
to go to a good university and launch a career in archaeology. But
when his father's company goes out of business, all of Cliff's plans
are changed. Cliff's parents and an uncle are accepted as crew
members on the starship Magellan, and Cliff faces a difficult
decision—to stay on Earth and become an archaeologist or "to
boldly go where no one has gone before."

14.70   Weiss, Ellen, and Mel Friedman. **The Tiny Parents.** Alfred A.
Knopf/Bullseye Books, 1989. 82 pp. ISBN 0-394-82418-0.

In this variation on the film *Honey, I Shrunk the Kids*, Marie and
Eddie Bicker are accustomed to their parents' odd behavior. Their
parents are inventors, after all, and not exactly ordinary. But
when they manage to shrink themselves down to two and a half
inches high, Marie and Eddie have to find a way to get them back
to normal—or at least as normal as they used to be--and they must
act quickly before their parents' speeded-up metabolisms burn
them out.

14.71   Westall, Robert. **Urn Burial.** Greenwillow Books, 1988. 160 pp.
ISBN   0-688-07595-9.

In this frightening adventure story, seventeen-year-old Ralph
finds the burial site of an alien and decides to open the coffin. In
it he finds equipment that he experiments with, bringing other
aliens to earth for some truly terrifying confrontations.

14.72   Woodruff, Elvira. **The Summer I Shrank My Grandmother.**
Holiday House, 1990. 153 pp. ISBN 0-8234-0832-9.

Hoping to keep her fun-loving grandmother from aging any
further, Nelly uses the mysterious chemistry set she finds in the
basement of their rented beach cottage to concoct a formula to
make her grandmother younger. And it works! Now Nelly's
dilemma is how to reverse the action, rescue her grandmother
from her own childhood, and explain the week's events to her
parents when they return.

14.73   Wrede, Patricia C. **Dealing with Dragons.** Harcourt Brace
Jovanovich/Jane Yolen Books, 1990. 212 pp. ISBN 0-15-222900-
0.

In this funny and fast-paced book, Cimorene is the youngest daughter of the King of Linderwall and should be happy, but alas, Cimorene hates the life of a princess. Her parents won't let her do any of the things that are fun, like learning magic or fencing or cooking. So, forced to choose between becoming the bride of handsome but dull Prince Therandil or running away to become a dragon's princess, she chooses the latter. She finds being a dragon's princess much more pleasant than being a proper princess—until she meets the wizard Zemenar and discovers what the wizards are plotting. ★★★

14.74 Yolen, Jane. **The Dragon's Boy.** Harper and Row, 1990. 120 pp. ISBN 0-06-026790-9.

If you were given the choice of being paid in gold, jewels, or wisdom, which would you choose? When young Artos is searching for Sir Ector's lost hound, he meets a magical dragon and is given just that choice. Although he is afraid of the dragon, he is drawn to him and with the beast's help begins his search for wisdom.

14.75 Zettner, Pat. **The Shadow Warrior.** Atheneum, 1990. 220 pp. ISBN 0-689-31486-8.

A world of giants, goblins, and Solgants (humans) is the setting for this unusual story of friendship and mutual respect. Llyndreth and her brother are pledged to fighting the goblins. Llyndreth, on her way to help her brother, enlists the help of one of the last of the giants. They come upon a wounded enemy goblin, who insists that they care for him until he recovers. You'll be happy about his recovery, which is more than physical.

Series

14.76 **The Firebrat.** Archway Paperbacks.

Shockwaves and *Thunder Mountain* are two titles in this science fiction series by Barbara and Scott Siegel. The setting is just after World War III, and America has been ruined by nuclear power. Matt and Dani set out across the country to reach Denver, where they hope that some semblance of civilization still exists.

14.77 **Planet Builders.** Ballantine/Ivy Books.

Robin Tallis's science fiction series tells the story of students who live on the newly colonized planet of Gaugin in the year 2520. The series begins with *Mountain of Stolen Dreams* and continues with *Night of Ghosts and Lightning.*

14.78   Trio: Rebels in the New World. Bantam Books.

The year is 2015, and it has been more than a decade since the United States government has collapsed, and the country has split into six factions. The older population has been wiped out by wars and political infighting, and it's up to the "trio" to restore order. See how Mimla Caceras and Matt Simpson, both in their early twenties, and teenager David Hasgard manage this difficult task. Titles in this series by Robert A. Montgomery include *Traitors from Within, Crossing Enemy Lines, Almost Lost, The Hidden Evil,* and *Escape from China.* (Author R. A. Montgomery also wrote books for the Choose Your Own Adventure series for younger readers.)

Recommended Science Fiction and Fantasy Published before 1988

Aiken, Joan. *The Wolves of Willoughby Chase.* Doubleday, 1963.
Alexander, Lloyd. *The Black Cauldron.* Henry Holt, 1965.
Alexander, Lloyd. *The Book of Three.* Henry Holt, 1964.
Alexander, Lloyd. *The Castle of Llyr.* Henry Holt, 1966.
Alexander, Lloyd. *The High King.* Henry Holt, 1968.
Alexander, Lloyd. *Taran Wanderer.* Henry Holt, 1967.
Alexander, Lloyd. *Westmark.* E. P. Dutton, 1981.
Babbit, Natalie. *Tuck Everlasting.* Farrar, Straus and Giroux, 1975.
Bell, Clare. *Ratha's Creature.* Atheneum, 1983.
Bethancourt, T. Ernesto. *The Dog Days of Arthur Cane.* Holiday House, 1976.
Cassedy, Sylvia. *Behind the Attic Wall.* Thomas Y. Crowell, 1983.
Cooper, Susan. *The Dark Is Rising.* Margaret K. McElderry, 1973.
Cooper, Susan. *Silver on the Tree.* Atheneum, 1977.
Corbett, W. J. *The Song of Pentecost.* E. P. Dutton, 1983.
Duane, Diane. *Deep Wizardry.* Delacorte Press, 1985.
Garner, Alan. *The Owl Service.* Philomel Books, 1979.
Greer, Gery, and Bob Ruddick. *Max and Me and the Time Machine.* Harcourt Brace Jovanovich, 1983.
Jacques, Brian. *Redwall.* Philomel Books, 1987.
Jones, Diana Wynne. *Archer's Goon.* Greenwillow Books, 1984.

Jones, Diana Wynne. *Charmed Life.* Alfred A. Knopf/Bullseye Books, 1989.*

Jones, Diana Wynne. *Howl's Moving Castle.* Greenwillow Books, 1986.

Langton, Jane. *The Fledgling.* Harper and Row, 1980.

Le Guin, Ursula K. *The Wizard of Earthsea.* Parnassus Press, 1968.

L'Engle, Madeleine. *A Wrinkle in Time.* Farrar, Straus and Giroux, 1962.

L'Engle, Madeleine. *The Young Unicorns.* Farrar, Straus and Giroux, 1968.

Lunn, Janet. *The Root Cellar.* Charles Scribner's Sons, 1983.

Macaulay, David. *Motel of the Mysteries.* Houghton Mifflin, 1979.

McKinley, Robin. *The Blue Sword.* Greenwillow Books, 1982.

McKinley, Robin. *The Hero and the Crown.* Greenwillow Books, 1984.

Merrill, Jean. *The Pushcart War.* W. R. Scott, 1964.

O'Brien, Robert. *Mrs. Frisby and the Rats of NIMH.* Atheneum, 1971.

O'Brien, Robert. *Z for Zachariah.* Atheneum, 1975.

Orwell, George. *Animal Farm.* Harcourt Brace Jovanovich, 1954.

Park, Ruth. *Playing Beatie Bow.* Atheneum, 1982.

Pierce, Meredith. *The Darkangel.* Little, Brown/Joy Street Books, 1982.

Pinkwater, Daniel M. *Alan Mendelsohn, the Boy from Mars.* E. P. Dutton, 1979.

Raskin, Ellen. *Figgs and Phantoms.* E. P. Dutton, 1974.

Rodgers, Mary. *Freaky Friday.* Harper and Row, 1973.

Rodgers, Mary. *Summer Switch.* Harper and Row, 1982.

Schlee, Ann. *The Vandal.* Crown, 1981.

Sleator, William. *The Boy Who Reversed Himself.* E. P. Dutton, 1986.

Sleator, William. *The Green Futures of Tycho.* E. P. Dutton, 1981.

Sleator, William. *Interstellar Pig.* E. P. Dutton, 1984.

Strieber, Whitley. *Wolf of Shadows.* Alfred A. Knopf, 1985.

Sutcliff, Rosemary. *The Light beyond the Forest.* E. P. Dutton, 1979.

Sutcliff, Rosemary. *The Road to Camlann.* E. P. Dutton, 1982.

Sutcliff, Rosemary. *The Sword and the Circle.* E. P. Dutton, 1981.

Tolkien, J. R. R. *The Hobbit, or There and Back Again.* Houghton Mifflin, 1938.

Voigt, Cynthia. *Building Blocks.* Atheneum, 1984.

Walsh, Jill Paton. *The Green Book.* Farrar, Straus and Giroux, 1982.

Wangerin, Walter, Jr. *The Book of the Dun Cow.* Harper and Row, 1978.

Yolen, Jane. *Dragon's Blood.* Delacorte Press, 1982.

---

*This is the date that this book was reprinted. It was originally published before 1988.

15 Imagining Chills and Thrills: Mysteries and the Supernatural

15.1 Angell, Judie. **Don't Rent My Room.** Bantam/Starfire Books, 1990. 138 pp. ISBN 0-553-07023-1.

Lucy's parents decide to leave New York City and Grandma to move to the coast of Massachusetts where they will run the Scottwood Inn. Lucy doesn't want to go and makes a deal with her parents. If she gives living at the inn a good try and still doesn't like it, she can move back to New York at the end of the summer and live with Grandma. Running an inn without much experience or help leaves Lucy's parents short on time and tempers, but Nathan, Lucy's youngest brother, is always good for a laugh. He even finds ghosts at Scottwood Inn. Now, what will Lucy decide?

15.2 Banks, Lynne Reid. **Melusine: A Mystery.** Harper and Row, 1988. 248 pp. ISBN 0-06-020395-1.

Roger goes on vacation with his family to an old French chateau, where he is drawn to Melusine, the strange daughter of the unpleasant chateau owner. There are hints that Melusine has another identity, but it turns out to be more awesome than Roger could have ever guessed. Part of her terrible secret becomes dangerous for Roger to know.

15.3 Bennett, Jay. **Sing Me a Death Song.** Franklin Watts, 1990. 160 pp. ISBN 0-531-10853-8.

Since Jason Feldon was ten years old, he has lived with the question of whether his mother is guilty of the murder she was put in a Florida prison for. It's now a week before his eighteenth birthday, and his mother is condemned to die. But then Jason gets a call from a detective on the case, and suddenly he has a chance to prove her innocence. ★

15.4 Bradbury, Ray. **The Halloween Tree.** Illustrated by Joseph Mugnaini. Alfred A. Knopf, 1988. 145 pp. ISBN 0-394-92409-6.

One Halloween, nine young boys put on costumes and innocently go around the neighborhood for tricks or treats. Seeking adventure, they dare to approach the haunted house of Mr. Moundshroud and the mysterious Halloween tree. Moundshroud takes the boys on a historical trip through Halloweens past where they meet mummies and gargoyles and witches galore.

15.5   Brandel, Marc. **An Ear for Danger.** Random House, 1989. 140 pp. ISBN 0-394-89943-1.

When Jupiter Jones, Pete Crenshaw, and Bob Andrews win a trip to a Mexican ranch, they have no idea of the danger that awaits them. After Jupiter senses that there is something unusual about this ranch and the man who runs it, the three investigators set out to uncover the mystery surrounding a burro named Blondie, a Mexican woman, and the rugged Sierra Madre.

15.6   Bunting, Eve. **The Ghost Children.** Clarion Books, 1989. 163 pp. ISBN 0-89919-843-0.

Thirteen-year-old Matt and his five-year-old sister Abby have lost their mother and must go to live with their only relative, Great Aunt Gerda. In her front yard, this eccentric woman keeps seven life-size dolls, which she calls her children. Her neighbors are embarrassed by the dolls, and some even think the dolls are bewitched. When two of the dolls are stolen, Matt, Abby, and their new friend Kristin make some exciting discoveries.

15.7   Bunting, Eve. **Is Anybody There?** J. B. Lippincott, 1988. 169 pp. ISBN 0-397-32303-4.

Marcus has a strong sense that someone has the key to the house where he and his mom live. Food, clocks, flashlights, and all kinds of things slowly disappear from the house. Marcus would like to blame Nick, the teacher who rents the small apartment on the property and who appears to be his mother's special friend. But Marcus's mom isn't so quick to agree with this easy solution.

15.8   Climo, Shirley. **T.J.'s Ghost.** Thomas Y. Crowell, 1989. 151 pp. ISBN 0-690-04689-8.

"Teeeejaaaay, Teeeejaaay," sounds a strange foghorn that seems to be calling T.J.'s name from the ocean mist that swirls around her Auntie Onion's house. But this isn't the only strange thing that happens to T.J. during her visit to her aunt and uncle on a beach in California. While looking for shells, she meets a young red-haired ghost from an Australian shipwreck of hundreds of years ago. Along with Winston, a pesky neighbor boy, she tries to help the Australian find a missing wedding ring and nearly drowns in the process.

15.9   Cohen, Daniel. **The Ghosts of War.** G. P. Putnam's Sons, 1990. 95 pp. ISBN 0-399-22200-6.

Some say ghosts are seen most often where people have died violently, so it's not surprising that so many ghost stories come out of wars. These spooky stories come from wars in England, Japan, the United States, and other countries.

15.10   Conrad, Pam. **Stonewords: A Ghost Story.** Harper and Row, 1990. 130 pp. ISBN 0-06-021315-9.

Zoe comes to live with her grandparents near a New England seacoast. She finds a special friend in the ghost who shares her name and her home, and in the nine years they spend together as friends, they experience the deepest meaning of love and forgiveness. Through the supernatural events she experiences, Zoe gets a glimpse of death and timelessness—and of the idea that both can somehow be changed by the present. ★

15.11   Cooney, Caroline B. **The Face on the Milk Carton.** Bantam Books, 1990. 184 pp. ISBN 0-553-05853-3.

Janie has the perfect life: a loving family, good friends, and a handsome boyfriend. Then by chance her life becomes a whirlwind of confusion, doubts, and fear when she recognizes her own face being advertised on a milk carton as a missing child. ★

15.12   Cross, Gilbert B. **A Witch across Time.** Atheneum, 1990. 216 pp. ISBN 0-689-31602-X.

Hannah Kincaid has just been released from a mental hospital and is sent to stay for the summer with a great aunt in Martha's Vineyard. Partly from staying in her aunt's eerie old house, Hannah begins having nightmares about a girl who had been wrongly hanged as a Salem witch. What at first looks like a reincarnation turns out to be a ghost trying to communicate her innocence. This intriguing tale shows what hatred and jealousy can do to individuals as well as to a community.

15.13   Cusick, Richie Tankersley. **The Lifeguard.** Scholastic, 1988. 192 pp. ISBN 0-590-41549-2.

Kelsey looks forward to a summer at Beverly Island, but instead of being the fun she anticipated, the vacation turns into a nightmare. When she begins looking into the disappearance of another teenage girl, she learns to her horror that not all lifeguards save lives—some take them. Mature situations.

15.14 Duffy, James. **The Man in the River.** Charles Scribner's Sons, 1990. 176 pp. ISBN 0-684-19161-X.

In this sequel to *Missing*, young Kate and her sister Sandy again need the help of the widowed, retired police officer Agatha Bates. She helps them solve the mystery of their long-absent father's sudden death.

15.15 Duffy, James. **Missing.** Charles Scribner's Sons, 1988. 137 pp. ISBN 0-684-18912-7.

Ten-year-old Kate Prescott has a reputation as a runaway in her rural New England community. She has run away twice so far, so is it any surprise that she is missing again? Even though the police are skeptical, her family is convinced that this time she has been kidnapped. With the help of retired police officer Agatha Bates, Kate's sister and mother uncover some important clues to her disappearance.

15.16 Duncan, Lois. **Don't Look behind You.** Delacorte Press, 1989. 179 pp. ISBN 0-440-501393-3.

April Corrigan is a star tennis player, her mother is a successful author of children's books, and she thinks her father is an airline executive. But then she finds out that her father has really been working undercover for the FBI, and when he testifies against a drug dealer, the family must go into the federal government's Witness Security Program. Changing the life of an individual isn't easy, and changing the lives of a whole family is even harder. ★★

15.17 Dunlap, Eileen. **The Valley of Deer.** Holiday House, 1989. 139 pp. ISBN 0-8234-0766-7.

Fourteen-year-old Anne Farrar thinks that living in an old, old house in a valley where her parents are doing archaeological work is boring. But then she discovers an old Bible with the name Alice Jardyne, born in 1701, mysteriously recorded along with some terrifying facts. Anne investigates and finds out that Alice was accused of witchcraft. Can Anne clear the name of a poor girl unjustly sentenced to death? Can history be changed?

15.18   Ehrlich, Amy. **Where It Stops, Nobody Knows.** Dial Books for Young Readers, 1988. 192 pp. ISBN 0-8037-0575-1.

What if you discovered that your mother wasn't your real mother but instead had kidnapped you as a baby? This is what happens to junior high student Nina Lewis, and that's why every time she gets settled in a new town and a new school, her "mother" decides it's time to move. What should Nina do? ★★

15.19   Feil, Hila. **Blue Moon.** Atheneum, 1990. 200 pp. ISBN 0-689-31607-0.

Julia's mother has decided being a nanny is just what Julia needs this summer. Julia is shipped off to Cape Cod to care for nine-year-old Molly. Upon arrival, Julia can see this will not be an easy job. Molly has lost her mother, her father is off in another country filming, and she has been left with a stepmother whom she doesn't like. Molly and Julia become entangled in a life-and-death situation, and after all has passed and the summer is over, neither girl's life will be the same.

15.20   Gabhart, Ann. **Wish Come True.** Avon/Flare Books, 1988. 137 pp. ISBN 0-380-75653-6.

Imagine owning a magic mirror, a mirror which grants all of your fondest wishes! Fifteen-year-old Alyssa's Aunt Reya gives her an old mirror for her birthday. Alyssa, who is upset about her family's recent move to Brookdale, wishes for friends in her new high school—and she's instantly popular. She continues wishing and wishing for more, until she realizes that there is something sinister about the mirror. Her aunt's warnings come too late: the mirror has already caused one death, and Alyssa knows that something terrible will happen again.

15.21   Garfield, Leon. **The Empty Sleeve.** Delacorte Press, 1988. 205 pp. ISBN 0-440-50049-4.

In this gripping adventure story, twins Peter and Paul Gannet are born at the chime of noon on a snowy January Saturday in the mid-1700s. At the time of their birth, Mr. Bagley, a smelly old ship's carpenter, prophesies trouble, especially for Peter, the first-born, who he says will see ghosts. Fourteen years later, Peter is being sent away to become an apprentice to a master locksmith. He would much rather go to sea, but standing between him and his dreams are all kinds of troubles—including a ghost who desperately wants something. ★★

15.22 Gates, Susan. **The Burnhope Wheel.** Holiday House, 1989. 96 pp. ISBN 0-8234-0767-5.

When a nearby town begins restoration of an old lead mine, history comes alive in a menacing and horrifying way for fifteen-year-old Ellen Peart. Violent spirits seem to be taking over Ellen's dreams and her life. Then she meets Dave, who is having the same awful dreams. Together they face evil, mystery, and death in the cave of the Burnhope Wheel.

15.23 Gifaldi, David. **Yours till Forever.** J. B. Lippincott, 1989. 90 pp. ISBN 0-397-32356-5.

Eighteen years ago on the day of his birth, Rick Haggstrom's parents were killed. Now, Rick learns that his two good friends, Pete and Sam (Pete's girlfriend), share his birthdate. That's interesting, but not earthshaking—until Pete gives Sam a necklace that looks exactly like the one Rick found in a box of his parents' belongings. It even has the same inscription. The coincidences keep adding up, and Rick begins to wonder what is really happening. Are Pete and Sam actually Rick's parents reincarnated? If so, Rick must prevent them from meeting the same tragic end his parents met. ★

15.24 Gilmore, Kate. **Enter Three Witches.** Houghton Mifflin, 1990. 210 pp. ISBN 0-395-50213-6.

Where do you take your girlfriend when your house is full of witches? This is a problem for sixteen-year-old Bren. His mother is a witch, his grandmother is a fortune-teller, and their boarder practices voodoo. Bren likes Erika, but he worries about her coming to his home. Then she gets the part of the First Witch in the school play, and one thing Bren doesn't have to worry about are the special effects for it. With all those witches in the audience, the results are more realistic than anyone could have imagined. ★★

15.25 Gripe, Maria. **Agnes Cecilia.** Translated from Swedish by Rika Lesser. Harper and Row, 1990. 288 pp. ISBN 0-06-022281-6.

Nora's parents have died in a car accident, so she has gone to live with her cousin, Dag, and his mother and father. She feels like an outsider, and when the family moves into an old house, she feels something else, too—a spirit trying to communicate with her. Through an antique doll named Agnes Cecilia, Nora slowly learns about her heritage and her family, and most importantly about herself. ★

15.26   Hahn, Mary Downing. **The Dead Man in Indian Creek.** Clarion Books, 1990. 130 pp. ISBN 0-395-52397-4.

Friends since kindergarten, twelve year olds Matt and Parker go on a late-summer overnight camping trip. However, Parker's dislike for Evans, his mother's employer and boyfriend, makes the trip turn out badly. When the boys discover a man's body in the nearby creek, Parker thinks he sees Evans on the bridge above the body and gets very suspicious. He gets Matt to join him in an attempt at solving the mystery. ★

15.27   Hahn, Mary Downing. **The Doll in the Garden: A Ghost Story.** Clarion Books, 1989. 128 pp. ISBN 0-89919-848-1.

A white cat that casts no shadow, an overgrown garden in the middle of a neatly kept lawn, and a child crying at night are just some of the things Ashley finds at the new apartment that she and her mom have taken above Miss Cooper's house. A newly found friend insists there are ghosts around. When Ashley investigates, she finds a doll buried in the garden, and this is only the beginning of her discoveries.

15.28   Hahn, Mary Downing. **Following the Mystery Man.** Avon/ Camelot Books, 1989. 192 pp. ISBN 0-380-70677-6.

Twelve-year-old Madigan imagines that someday her long-lost father will come back into her life and take her off to exotic places. Madigan thinks her dream has come true when a mysterious stranger comes to town and rents a room in her grandmother's house. The good-looking stranger offers her kindly advice, and so Madigan begins to sneak around trying to discover his true identity. This sneaking gets her involved in a robbery-and-kidnapping scheme which could cost her her life. Who is the mystery man?

15.29   Hall, Lynn. **Dagmar Schultz and the Angel Edna.** Charles Scribner's Sons, 1989. 86 pp. ISBN 0-684-19097-4.

At age thirteen, Dagmar Schultz at last has permission from her father to go out with boys. The problem is that no boys have asked her out. A further complication is that she has a guardian angel, the ghost of her great Aunt Edna, who has decided that she should be Dagmar's spiritual guide. Poor Dagmar. As if learning how to act like a teenager isn't already difficult enough!

15.30   Hall, Lynn. **A Killing Freeze.** William Morrow, 1988. 120 pp. ISBN 0-688-07867-2.

Clarie loved Mrs. Amling, and after her murder, it's not easy for Clarie to get excited about Winter Fest, a celebration that's crucial for the small town of Harmon Falls' snowmobile and other winter businesses. Clarie and her father try to keep everyone's spirits up for the sake of the festival, but when a second murder occurs, Clarie gets involved in the hunt for the killer and endangers her father and herself.

15.31   Hall, Lynn. **Murder in a Pig's Eye.** Harcourt Brace Jovanovich, 1990. 125 pp. ISBN 0-15-256268-0.

Sixteen-year-old Bodie enlists the help of his sister and his best friend to find the body of his employer's wife. He's sure that Henry, the elderly farmer who employed Bodie, has murdered his wife with a chain saw. It sounds grisly, but this isn't the kind of mystery that will make you break out with goose bumps; instead, it's more likely to make you break out laughing.

15.32   Howe, James. **Dew Drop Dead.** Atheneum, 1990. 156 pp. ISBN 0-689-31425-6.

Sebastian, Corrie, and David are best friends. While out riding bicycles late one afternoon, they happen upon an abandoned inn. Finding an open window, their curiosity overwhelms them, and the threesome enter the abandoned inn to investigate its contents. Their discovery involves them in a murder mystery.

15.33   James, J. Alison. **Sing for a Gentle Rain.** Atheneum, 1990. 211 pp. ISBN 0-689-32561-9.

High school junior James is fascinated with the ancient Anasazi Pueblo Indian culture. Haunted by dreams of the Anasazi, he leaves his grandfather and hikes into the desert seeking knowledge of it and of the source of his dreams. He comes face-to-face with Spring Rain, an Anasazi girl of the thirteenth century. Despite barriers of time and culture, love develops between them, and they fulfill a strange destiny. ★

15.34   Jarrow, Gail. **The Two-Ton Secret.** Avon/Camelot Books, 1989. 138 pp. ISBN 0-380-95904-7.

Thirteen-year-old Seth Findelson finds himself in deep trouble after he tells a tiny, little lie. Now bad luck follows him and his family. His father gets fired, his sister is badly injured in a hit-and-run accident, and, except for Phoebe, his friends desert him. When Seth becomes involved in the accident that injured his sister, he and Phoebe must take on the role of amateur detectives.

15.35   Johnston, Norma. **The Time of the Cranes.** Four Winds Press, 1990. 165 pp. ISBN 0-02-747713-4.

Stacy, a teenage actress, suddenly learns of the death of her beloved teacher Madame Karpova. Much to her surprise, Stacy inherits all of Madame's possessions. As she searches through Madame's belongings, she becomes curious about Madame Karpova's death. Her curiosity leads her to romance and intrigue as the truth about Madame Karpova's death unfolds.

15.36   Johnston, Norma. **Whisper of the Cat.** Bantam Books, 1988. 192 pp. ISBN 0-553-26947-X.

Suspense, intrigue, drugs, and superstition all play a part in this mystery that is set on an island off the coast of Georgia. A teenage girl goes to live with her father and stepmother in the old family mansion, and she finds life a far cry from the beauty and peace you'd expect from a beautiful Southern mansion.

15.37   Kerr, M. E. **Fell Back.** Harper and Row Junior Books, 1989. 181 pp. ISBN 0-06-023293-5.

Seventeen-year-old John Fell is convinced his prep school classmate Lasher's death was not suicide, but he is unprepared for the tangled path down which his curiosity leads him. A second apparent suicide casts further doubt and gloom on the Sevens, a secret organization whose members have enjoyed special privileges at the school for generations. In the middle of it all, Nina Deem, who is recovering from the trauma of her mother's death, finds a loyal friend and admirer in John.

15.38   Kidd, Ronald. **Second Fiddle: A Sizzle and Splat Mystery.** Lodestar Books, 1988. 167 pp. ISBN 0-525-67252-4.

Prudence Szyznowski (Sizzle) plays the trumpet. Arthur Hadley Reavis Pauling II (Splat) plays the tuba. These two unlikely detectives team up to discover who's behind a plot to stop the performance that will save the Pirelli Youth Orchestra. Following a trail of not always harmless practical jokes, Sizzle and Splat attempt to narrow their list of suspects and solve this baffling but funny mystery. *Second Fiddle* is a sequel to *Sizzle and Splat*, published in 1983.

15.39 Klause, Annette Curtis. **The Silver Kiss.** Delacorte Press, 1990. 198 pp. ISBN 0-385-30160-X.

A seventeen-year-old girl who is depressed because her mother is dying of cancer a young vampire in a park. As their friendship develops, they share their problems and help each other come to terms with what they must face. ★★★★

15.40 Levy, Elizabeth. **Cold as Ice.** Avon/Flare Books, 1989. 167 pp. ISBN 0-380-70315-7.

Kelly's dreams of meeting the handsome Olympic figure-skating stars during their tour of New York comes true—on her way to work at the Skating Dome, Kelly startles a mugger attacking Ken Swanson, one of the star skaters. Ken and Kelly become inseparable as attacks on the skaters increase, and the mystery over a motive deepens. Because of Ken's somewhat delinquent background, he fears that everyone suspects him. Kelly wants to believe his innocence, but can she be sure?

15.41 Major, Kevin. **Blood Red Ochre.** Delacorte Press, 1989. 147 pp. ISBN 0-385-29794-7.

David, a contemporary fifteen year old who lives in Newfoundland, is unhappy and restless until he meets Nancy, a strange but fascinating new girl at school. Dauoodaset, a Beothuk Indian of the 1800s who is struggling to keep his people alive, feels the same kind of restless dissatisfaction that David is experiencing. The two stories sweep back and forth between the past and the present until they collide when David and Nancy take a canoe trip as part of their research on the mysterious extinction of the Beothuk Indians. David finds that Nancy is both part of the mystery and part of its solution.

15.42 McBratney, Sam. **The Ghosts of Hungryhouse Lane.** Illustrated by Lisa Thiesing. Henry Holt, 1989. 118 pp. ISBN 0-8050-0985-X.

The Sweet family lives in a rented house—one that's haunted. Ghosts are supposed to intimidate people, but in this story, it's the children who intimidate the ghosts. There's a dispute over who owns the house, and the children help out by finding the will of the deceased owner.

15.43   Naylor, Phyllis R. **The Witch's Eye.** Delacorte Press, 1990. 179 pp. ISBN 0-385-30157-X.

Lynn Morley suspects something is wrong when her little brother starts to act strangely. He hits, screams, jabs, and howls for no reason. Then Lynn finds the evil witch's eye, and she knows Stevie has been entranced. To protect her family from evil untold, Lynn appoints herself as guardian of the eye, but as time passes, she, too, begins to look and act strangely. Only her good friend Mouse can save her from the deadly terror of witchcraft.

15.44   Nixon, Joan Lowery. **Whispers from the Dead.** Delacorte Press, 1989. 167 pp. ISBN 0-385-29809-9.

Ever since she nearly drowned a year ago, sixteen-year-old Sarah Darnell has been hearing voices. This makes her old friends uneasy, and they begin to avoid her. She looks forward to a fresh start when her family moves to Houston, but when they enter their new house, Sarah feels there's something wrong, and then she again begins hearing voices—only this time they're in Spanish. ★

15.45   Peck, Richard. **Voices after Midnight.** Delacorte Press, 1989. 181 pp. ISBN 0-385-29779-3.

When fourteen-year-old Chad is informed that his family will visit New York for two weeks, he dreams about snow, something he rarely sees in California, while his younger brother, Luke, is mainly curious about the past. Both interests come into play when the family rents a one-hundred-year-old townhouse. Seeking the truth about mysterious voices they hear, Chad, Luke, and their sister, Heidi, are drawn back to the great blizzard of 1888. ★

15.46   Pike, Christopher. **Fall into Darkness.** Archway Paperbacks, 1990. 213 pp. ISBN 0-671-67655-5.

Sharon is charged with the murder of her best friend, and although it is a frame-up, an intricate web of guilt ripples across her whole circle of friends before the mystery is unravelled.

15.47   Pike, Christopher. **Remember Me.** Archway Paperbacks, 1989. 230 pp. ISBN 0-671-67654-7.

Shari was killed in a fall from a fourth-floor balcony, and her death is initially thought to be a suicide. But Shari didn't intend to commit suicide, and so her spirit feels compelled to remain on earth, despite hazards and frustrations, to unravel the facts surrounding her "accident."

15.48   Pryor, Bonnie. **The Twenty-Four-Hour Lipstick Mystery.** Illustrated by Sheila Hamanaka. William Morrow, 1989. 135 pp. ISBN 0-688-08198-3.

Cassie Adams feels about as pretty as a frog and decides to earn enough money to enroll for a course at Mrs. Du Prey's School of Beauty and Charm. Miss Murdock, owner of a mysterious haunted house, hires Cassie, and the job leads her, her newfound friend, and her bratty younger brother on a mystery adventure.

15.49   Radford, Ken. **The Cellar.** Holiday House, 1989. 171 pp. ISBN 0-8234-0744-6.

In northern Wales near the border of England and Scotland lies Crud-yr-Awel, or Cradle of the Woods. It is occupied by a retired sea captain and his two sisters. An orphaned girl Sian comes to brighten up their days as a companion and helper. On her first night in the house, Sian hears someone calling for help. After finding a diary and toys in the attic, gossip in the community confirms her belief that the house was once the home of a child named Sarah Jane. With the aid of the diary and a neighbor boy, rumors and gossip of Sarah Jane's unhappy end are put to rest.

15.50   Radford, Ken. **Haunting at Mill Lane.** Holiday House, 1988. 153 pp. ISBN 0-8234-0676-8.

Sarah is twelve when her mother dies, and she has to move to Clyneway Cottage to live with her Aunt Liza and Uncle Jim. On her first night there, she finds an old rag doll which becomes her constant companion. She also meets a playmate named Sally-Anne, who insists that the rag doll belongs to her. Sarah is glad to have a friend in the lonely new place, but her aunt and uncle start to worry about her friendship because Sally-Anne is a ghost.

15.51   Reaver, Chap. **Mote.** Delacorte Press, 1990. 217 pp. ISBN 0-385-30163-4.

Chris Miller is shocked when he learns that one of his teachers has been murdered. He is even more surprised to learn that the police are looking for his good friend, Mote. Chris is sure that Mote is innocent, and so he and his buddy, Bill, along with two police officers, begin to hunt for clues and motives. They discover a world of powerful criminal figures and fanatics who will stop at nothing to achieve their deadly aims. Mature situations.

15.52   Roberts, Willo Davis. **Nightmare.** Atheneum, 1989. 224 pp. ISBN 0-690-31551-1.

The same day that seventeen-year-old Nick Correlli breaks up with his girlfriend, a man falls from an overpass and crashes into the windshield of Nick's car. The police rule it a suicide, but judging from the look on the man's face, Nick suspects it wasn't suicide. And judging from what happens afterwards, neither will you.

15.53   Roberts, Willo Davis. **To Grandmother's House We Go.** Atheneum, 1990. 187 pp. ISBN 0-689-31594-5.

Rosie, Kevin, and Nathan have already lost their father. When their mother has a stroke and it looks as if the three children will be sent to separate foster homes, they decide to run away. They run to the only relative they know of, a grandmother they have never seen. She is living with Uncle George in an old house that looks so spooky and run-down that the children think it must be abandoned. But are they really all alone there?

15.54   Schwandt, Stephen. **Guilt Trip.** Atheneum, 1990. 184 pp. ISBN 0-689-31557-0.

When Eddie Lymurek moves to Minneapolis to live with his Aunt Cyn, he has no idea of the mystery he's about to get involved in. He meets Angela Favor, the budding young star of the New Energy Theater Troupe, and becomes increasingly aware of the mysteries surrounding the recent murder of the Troupe's director, Corey Howe-Browne. As the investigation of the case builds, so does Eddie's interest in Angela until he realizes that sweet Angela has a side he hasn't seen—one that could prove dangerous. ★

15.55   Sebestyen, Ouida. **The Girl in the Box.** Little, Brown/Joy Street Books, 1988. 160 pp. ISBN 0-316-77935-0.

"If you have found this note in my pocket and need to identify me, I am Jackie McGee." This is one of the last notes that Jackie, the girl in the box, touch-types in the pitch-dark deep hole where her kidnapper has locked her. She has written many other notes, through which you'll learn about her life up to the moment she was kidnapped. She has very little food and very little water—yet she continues to write and to hope.

15.56   Silverstein, Herma. **Mad, Mad Monday.** Lodestar Books, 1988. 128 pp. ISBN 0-525-67239-7.

Fourteen-year-old Miranda Taylor has her reasons for choosing a cemetery as a setting for mixing a love potion. She's hoping to attract the boy she has a crush on, but instead, the potion brings a ghost in the form of "Teen Angel"—nicknamed Monday—a boy who died in the 1950s and has been mad ever since his old girlfriend betrayed his memory by marrying someone else. ★

15.57 Stine, R. L. **Curtains.** Archway Paperbacks, 1990. 139 pp. ISBN 0-671-69498-7.

This story starts with a murder, but fortunately it's only on stage. It's part of *Curtains*, a play that Rena is starring in at the Meritt Baxter Summer Theater Camp. But then something more serious than playacting occurs.

15.58 Swindells, Robert. **Follow a Shadow.** Holiday House, 1990. 148 pp. ISBN 0-8234-0839-6.

Fifteen-year-old Londoner Tim South isn't happy. He feels awkward and unattractive, and he's bored with his life. He upsets his family with his plan to drop out of school with his friends who experiment with drugs and alcohol. Then he discovers an old picture that bears a striking likeness to himself. He becomes obsessed with finding out who the picture is of. A talk with his grandmother and a field trip to the Bronte estate in Haworth provide clues about the portrait—and a change in Tim's life.

15.59 Thesman, Jean. **Appointment with a Stranger.** Houghton Mifflin, 1989. 166 pp. ISBN 0-395-49215-7.

Keller Parrish is having a difficult time at her new school. She has always been restricted from getting involved in school activities because of her asthma. But her life and her adjustment are made easier by a new friend, Tom Hurley. She first meets Tom when he pulls her from a pool near her grandmother's house. From then on, she meets him there frequently. Yet it is a puzzling friendship. No one else seems to know Tom. He doesn't go to her school or do anything with her friends. Who is he? Why is he so strangely isolated? Her friend Drew asks these same questions. Drew wants to be more to Keller than just a friend, and he believes that Tom Hurley stands in the way. ★

15.60 Trease, Geoffrey. **A Flight of Angels.** Lerner, 1989. 115 pp. ISBN 0-8225-0731-5.

Sheila wonders if her group can convince their teacher to let them do a project about the many caves that lie below the old parts of Nottingham. Her dad works for the old Peblow winery, so they can at least explore those cellars. What starts out as a school project becomes a major mystery that Sheila and her British classmates, Rodney, Debbie, and Kanshi, must solve.

15.61   Walker, Mary Alexander. **The Scathach and Maeve's Daughters.** Atheneum, 1990. 119 pp. ISBN 0-689-31638-0.

Scathach (rhymes with cat-hatch) is the greatest magical female in Celtic folklore, and in the eighth century, she grants sixteen-year-old Maeve a wish. Maeve words her wish in such a way that Scathach has to help Maeve's descendants for centuries to come. Scathach follows her charges from Ireland to England to Canada and to twenty-first century New York City, helping Maeve's descendants in their times of need and despair.

15.62   Wersba, Barbara. **The Best Place to Live Is the Ceiling.** Harper and Row, 1990. 184 pp. ISBN 0-06-026409-8.

Archie Smith is a loner, and his life is empty and depressing. He lives with twelve cats and his father, who is a professor of children's literature. As an emotional escape, Archie collects travel brochures and spends hours at Kennedy Airport where he fantasizes about travelling and watches the planes leave for faraway places. If he could just get on one of those planes, he could start his life over. He gets his chance when a stranger named Brian Chesterfield sits down at Archie's airport table and then collapses. The paramedics take him away, leaving Archie with his passport and a ticket to Switzerland. Archie boards the plane and begins a new life, one surprisingly full of criminals, street people, and a beautiful but strange girl named Polo. Strong language.

15.63   Westall, Robert. **Ghost Abbey.** Scholastic, 1989. 169 pp. ISBN 0-590-41692-8.

One of the characters in this story is an old house—actually an abbey—in Cheshire, England. After the death of Maggi's mother, she and her father and her younger twin brothers move to the abbey with the intention of repairing and restoring it. Maggi finds out that the mysterious old building has a mind of its own, especially when it's attacked by vandals.

15.64   Whelan, Gloria. **The Secret Keeper.** Alfred A. Knopf, 1990. 186 pp. ISBN 0-679-90572-3.

When Annie agrees to be ten-year-old Matt's "keeper" (he doesn't like the word "babysitter") for the summer, she has no idea of the secrets and mysteries that are about to unfold. As the secrets that Matt's grandparents have been keeping come out, it becomes obvious that the entire resort community he lives in is strangely involved in protecting Matt, and Annie realizes that her life could be in danger.

15.65   Wright, Betty Ren. **The Ghost of Ernie P.** Holiday House, 1990. 130 pp. ISBN 0-8234-0835-3.

Lightning knocks the minister down at Ernie P. Barber's funeral, and Jeff begins to suspect that Ernie's death was no accident. Ernie died in the middle of their secret project, "TSP." When mysterious things start happening, Jeff suspects that Ernie's ghost is haunting him, and things get even more mixed up when a witch enters the scene. Will Jeff be able to escape the wrath of Ernie and the witch?

15.66   Wright, Betty Ren. **The Pike River Phantom.** Holiday House, 1988. 153 pp. ISBN 0-8234-0721-7.

While selling candy bars for the middle school band, Charlie Hocking encounters a strange old woman in a run-down house outside of town. The next time he visits, he finds her grown strangely younger and discovers that the woman is a ghost set on revenge against this year's Sunbonnet Queen, his own cousin, Rachel. Charlie enters into a ghostly adventure and comes to know his long-absent father and to feel a part of the community.

Series

15.67   **Carly and Co. Mystery.** Fawcett.

In the first book in this series by Mel Cebalash, *Carly and Co.*, Carly wants to follow in her father's footsteps as a detective. So with the help of her Vietnamese friend, Sandy, she pursues bicycle thieves and drug dealers. In *Campground Caper: A Carly and Co. Mystery*, Carly's one-day trip into Phoenix turns into a compelling mystery when a neighbor, Ned Chute, is beaten up by two guys but doesn't want to call the police.

15.68   **Carter Colborn Mysteries.** Little, Brown/Joy Street Books.

Diana Shaw's Carter Colborn is something of a modern-day Nancy Drew. In *Gone Hollywood*, which follows *Lessons in Fear*, Carter goes to Los Angeles for the summer to live with her father, a television producer. When his teenage star becomes a missing person, Carter goes into action.

15.69   Fear Street. Archway Paperbacks.

The New Girl was the first of the Fear Street mysteries by R. L. Stine. Titles published since then include *The Surprise Party*, *The Overnight*, *Missing*, and *The Wrong Number*. In *The Sleepwalker*, Myra wakes up with a start. She's cold and damp; it's midnight, and she's standing on the sidewalk in her nightgown. This is especially unsettling because she's never before walked in her sleep, and this isn't the only strange event of the summer. There's also her job as caretaker for old Mrs. Cottler and her black cat, her new romance with Walker, a magician, and her friend Donna's near-fatal car accident. Maybe Mrs. Cottler really *is* a witch.

15.70   Hart and Soul. Bantam Books.

Kill the Story, *Play Dead*, *Speak No Evil*, *Get the Picture*, and *Too Hot to Handle* are among the titles in this series written by a husband and wife team under the pen name Jahnna N. Malcolm. They have also written five Sweet Dreams books, so as you might expect, these books include romance as well as mystery. Amanda Hart is editor of her school newspaper, while Mickey Soul is a tough kid from the other side of town. They get together to solve a mystery and then stay together—sort of—for what just might turn out to be a heart-and-soul romance.

15.71   Mike and Ally. Fawcett/Juniper Books.

Love Me Deadly was the first book in the Mike and Ally series by Blossom Elfman; then came *Tell Me No Lies* and *The Ghost Sitter*. In *The Ghost Sitter*, Ally befriends an old woman whose house is supposed to be haunted. When the woman disappears, no one will investigate—except Mike and Ally. Their discoveries include not only information about the victim and the neighborhood, but also about each other.

15.72   Nancy Drew and Hardy Boys Super Mystery. Archway Paperbacks.

In these revised and updated versions of Carolyn Keene's stories from a generation ago, Nancy Drew and the Hardy Boys join forces. Titles in this easy-to-read, fast-paced series include *A Crime for Christmas*, *The Last Resort*, and *Dangerous Games*.

15.73 **Private Eyes.** Bantam Books.

The Private Eyes series by Julia Winfield offers as much romance as mystery. In *Partners in Crime*, Christine and her boyfriend Andy play junior detectives as they investigate a star high school basketball player who appears to be intentionally causing their varsity team to lose games. In *Tug of Hearts*, they are called on to help one of Christine's friends from grade school find a missing will, but Andy worries that the friend is more interested in Christine than he is in the will.

15.74 **Sam and Dave Bean Mysteries.** Harper and Row.

Marilyn Singer is the author of these easy mysteries. In the *Case of the Fixed Election*, Sam and Dave are convinced that there is a plot to ruin the school elections. They're right! And in *The Hoax on You, Funtime* magazine offers a contest for the best hoax. While looking for a hoax to enter, Sam and Dave are out-hoaxed by a foreign-exchange student, a "Betsy Bee lady," and a guy collecting money for retired racehorses.

15.75 **Sweet Valley Twins Super Chiller.** Bantam/Skylark Books.

This new variation in the Sweet Valley Twins series for younger readers includes scary "super chiller" stories. The first two titles include *The Ghost in the Graveyard* and *The Christmas Ghost*, and they make readers wonder if Sweet Valley is haunted.

15.76 **The Three Investigators: Crimebusters.** Random House.

Robert Arthur came up with the idea for these adventure and mystery stories about Jupe, Pete, and Bob. The three are modern teenagers living in southern California, and they have an uncanny way of getting involved in solving dangerous mysteries. Titles include *Thriller Diller, Reel Trouble, Shoot the Works, Foul Play, Long Shot, Tough Stuff, Funny Business,* and *An Ear for Danger*.

Recommended Mysteries and Stories of the Supernatural Published before 1988

Bethancourt, T. Ernesto. *Doris Fein: Murder Is No Joke.* Holiday House, 1982.
Bethancourt, T. Ernesto. *Doris Fein: Quartz Boyer.* Holiday House, 1980.
Bonham, Frank. *Mystery of the Fat Cat.* E. P. Dutton, 1968.

Cross, Gillian. *On the Edge*. Holiday House, 1985.

Dickinson, Peter. *Annerton Pit*. Atlantic Monthly Press, 1977.

Duncan, Lois. *I Know What You Did Last Summer*. Little, Brown, 1973.

Duncan, Lois. *Killing Mr. Griffin*. Little, Brown, 1978.

Duncan, Lois. *Locked in Time*. Little, Brown, 1985.

Duncan, Lois. *Stranger with My Face*. Little, Brown, 1981.

Duncan, Lois. *Summer of Fear*. Little, Brown, 1976.

Duncan, Lois. *The Third Eye*. Little, Brown, 1984.

Hamilton, Virginia. *Sweet Whispers, Brother Rush*. Philomel Books, 1982.

Holman, Felice. *The Murderer*. Charles Scribner's Sons, 1978.

Jones, Diana Wynne. *Witch Week*. Greenwillow Books, 1982.

Kilgore, Kathleen. *The Wolfman of Beacon Hill*. Little, Brown, 1982.

Lively, Penelope. *The Ghost of Thomas Kempe*. E. P. Dutton, 1973.

Mahy, Margaret. *The Changeover: A Supernatural Romance*. Atheneum, 1984.

Mahy, Margaret. *The Haunting*. Atheneum, 1982.

Mahy, Margaret. *The Tricksters*. Margaret K. McElderry Books, 1987.

Peck, Richard. *The Ghost Belonged to Me*. Viking Penguin, 1975.

Peck, Richard. *Ghosts I Have Been*. Viking Penguin, 1977.

Peyton, K. M. *A Midsummer Night's Death*. William Collins, 1979.

Raskin, Ellen. *The Westing Game*. E. P. Dutton, 1978.

Sleator, William. *Fingers*. Atheneum, 1983.

Snyder, Zilpha Keatley. *The Egypt Game*. Atheneum, 1987.

Wells, Rosemary. *Leave Well Enough Alone*. Dial Press, 1977.

Wells, Rosemary. *When No One Was Looking*. Dial Press, 1980.

Westall, Robert. *Break of Dark*. Greenwillow Books, 1982.

Westall, Robert. *The Devil on the Road*. Greenwillow Books, 1979.

Westall, Robert. *Urn Burial*. Greenwillow Books, 1987.

Westall, Robert. *The Watch House*. Greenwillow Books, 1978.

Westall, Robert. *The Wind Eye*. Greenwillow Books, 1977.

Wiseman, David. *Jeremy Visick*. Houghton Mifflin, 1981.

Wrightson, Patricia. *The Nargun and the Stars*. Margaret K. McElderry Books, 1986.

16 Imaginings from Our Ancestors: Classics, Myths, Legends, and Folklore

16.1   Ash, Russell, and Bernard Higton, compilers. **Aesop's Fables: A Classic Illustrated Edition.** Chronicle Books, 1990. 95 pp. ISBN 0-87701-780-8.

You've probably heard many of these fifty-three stories, like "The Boy Who Cried Wolf," "The Fox and the Crow," and "The Hare and the Tortoise." But some of them will probably be new to you and so will most of the illustrations, all of which come from other editions of Aesop's fables. The book's compilers studied hundreds of old editions and chose their favorites for this book. It includes all kinds of illustrations, from ornate paintings to line drawings to cartoons and woodcuts.

16.2   Bach, Alice, and J. Cheryl Exum. **Moses' Ark: Stories from the Bible.** Illustrated by Leo and Diane Dillon. Delacorte Press, 1989. 185 pp. ISBN 0-385-29778-5.

The black-and-white drawings by prize-winning artists Leo and Diane Dillon add interest, but the really unusual aspect of this book of thirteen Bible stories is that the writers are biblical scholars who base their retellings on original Hebrew stories. Notes following each story explain uncertain meanings and Hebrew puns that are lost in English and place the stories in perspective. In the introduction, the authors explain how they got their details and how they looked for stories that include women.
★

16.3   Baum, L. Frank. **Dorothy and the Wizard in Oz.** Illustrated by John R. Neill. Morrow Junior Books, 1990. 272 pp. ISBN 0-688-09826-6.

Frank Baum's most famous book is *The Wonderful Wizard of Oz*, but he also went on to write thirteen more full-length books about Oz. This is the fourth book in the series, originally published in 1908, and it starts when Dorothy falls through a crack caused by a California earthquake. To her surprise, she is reunited with the Wizard of Oz, who by now has nine piglets to keep him company.

16.4   Berry, James. **Spiderman Anancy.** Illustrated by Joseph Olubo. Henry Holt, 1989. 144 pp. ISBN 0-85050-1207-9.

Anancy the spiderman is a trickster. Half man and half spider, he uses cunning and wit to win over his opponents. He is a hero and sometimes a fool, but he's always a lovable character in these Caribbean versions of stories most often associated with Africa.

16.5   Burkert, Nancy Ekholm. **Valentine and Orson.** Illustrated by the author. Farrar, Straus and Giroux/Floyd Yearout Books, 1989. 56 pp. ISBN 0-374-38078-3.

Nancy Burkert is a prize-winning artist, and this book circles around her twelve beautiful paintings that illustrate an old French story about a queen who is exiled to a deep forest. There, she gives birth to twin sons. One is stolen and raised as a prince, while the other one is raised in the forest by a bear. When they are eighteen, the prince is sent to kill the "wild man," but fortunately, fate prevents the killing. The story, told in rhyme, is meant to be read aloud as it would have been 500 years ago in a folk drama. ★

16.6   Carroll, Lewis. **Alice's Adventures in Wonderland.** Illustrated by Anthony Browne. Alfred A. Knopf, 1988. 117 pp. ISBN 0-394-90592-X.

The brand-new illustrations by Anthony Browne give a fresh look to this all-time favorite story of a girl who falls through a looking glass into a fantasy world. Browne includes unique little details that make his illustrations worth returning to for a second and even a third look. ★

16.7   Chaucer, Geoffrey. **Canterbury Tales.** Selected, translated from Middle English, and adapted by Barbara Cohen. Illustrated by Trina Schart Hyman. Lothrop, Lee and Shepard Books, 1988. 87 pp. ISBN 0-688-06201-6.

In Geoffrey Chaucer's long poem, a group of medieval people are taking a pilgrimage—a religious journey. They tell each other stories along the way to pass the time. This introductory version of Chaucer's famous poem retells several of the stories in modern English. Stories included in this book are "The Nun's Priest's Tale," "The Pardoner's Tale," "The Wife of Bath's Tale," and "The Franklin's Tale." Illustrated with watercolors. ★★

16.8   Collodi, Carlo. **The Adventures of Pinocchio.** Illustrated by Roberto Innocenti. Translated by E. Harden. Alfred A. Knopf, 1988. 142 pp. ISBN 0-394-82110-6.

Pinocchio comes alive in this illustrated version of the tale about a wooden puppet carved by the poor carpenter Geppetto. This version of the well-known tale is fast paced and filled with more adventures than the original. Besides Pinocchio's nose growing when he tells lies, he also finds himself in a seemingly endless series of adventures and mishaps, ranging from being turned into a donkey to growing a money tree in the Field of Miracles to being swallowed by a whale as big as a five-story house.

16.9 Dickinson, Peter. **Merlin Dreams.** Illustrated by Alan Lee. Delacorte Press, 1988. 160 pp. ISBN 0-440-50067-2.

The author goes back to ancient legend and myth to write about Merlin, King Arthur's advisor. According to some legends, Merlin chose at the end of his life to be bound underneath a rock where he would dream through the centuries. This is the basis for the stories in this collection, in which Merlin isn't treated as a magician, but instead as a tribal priest, a person with special knowledge and power. ★

16.10 Fonteyn, Margot, reteller. **Swan Lake.** Illustrated by Trina Schart Hyman. Harcourt Brace Jovanovich/Gulliver Books, 1989. 32 pp. ISBN 0-15-200600-1.

You can enjoy this illustrated version of an old legend that was made into a ballet whether or not you've ever seen the ballet, but dancers and dance fans will especially like it. Dancer Margot Fonteyn's two-page afterword gives the history of the ballet and talks about the atmosphere and spirit of the Swan Lake legend conveyed in the book.

16.11 Geras, Adele. **My Grandmother's Stories: A Collection of Jewish Folk Tales.** Illustrated by Jael Jordan. Alfred A. Knopf/Borzoi Sprinters, 1990. 96 pp. ISBN 0-679-90910-9.

These old tales include "Bavsi's Feast," "The Golden Shoes," "Saving the Pennies," "The Market of Miseries," "A Phantom at the Wedding," and five others. They are told through the eyes of a young girl visiting her grandmother and listening to the grandmother's stories as the two work in the kitchen. Illustrated.

16.12 Hamilton, Virginia. **The Dark Way: Stories of the Spirit World.** Illustrated by Lambert Davis. Harcourt Brace Jovanovich, 1990. 176 pp. ISBN 0-15-284215-2.

Virginia Hamilton is a well-known author of modern stories and science fiction who retells stories from around the world in this book. She makes comments after each story, and you can see that each one means something special to her, as she explains each of the stories' origins, makes comparisons to other stories, and highlights especially interesting details.

16.13   Hamilton, Virginia. **In the Beginning: Creation Stories from around the World.** Illustrated by Barry Moser. Harcourt Brace Jovanovich, 1988. 147 pp. ISBN 0-15-238740-4.

Most of us know two or three myths or stories about how the world was created, but in this book, you get twenty-five stories from around the world. Barry Moser's paintings illustrate the stories in their uniqueness. ★★★★★

16.14   Hastings, Selina. **A Selection from the Canterbury Tales.** Illustrated by Reg Cartwright. Henry Holt, 1988. 74 pp. ISBN 0-8050-0904-3.

This book introduces you to Geoffrey Chaucer's long poem about a group of travellers who decide to tell each other stories on their trip. The book tells you about the travellers' first meeting, when they decide to tell stories; Chaucer's descriptions of the story-tellers; and seven of the tales. The illustrations are beautiful, although this is not a picture book for children, but a modern English version of Chaucer's tales for advanced readers.

16.15   Hearn, Michael Patrick. **The Victorian Fairy Tale Book.** Pantheon Books, 1988. 385 pp. ISBN 0-679-73258-6.

"The Pied Piper of Hamelin" by Robert Browning, "The Magic Fish-Bone" by Charles Dickens, "The Golden Key" by George MacDonald, and "The Selfish Giant" by Oscar Wilde are some of the best-known stories among the seventeen included in this collection. Your parents or grandparents probably enjoyed these tales as they were growing up. You may even see some of the same pictures they did when they read the stories, since the book includes a lot of illustrations from older books of fairy tales.

16.16   Helprin, Mark, reteller. **Swan Lake.** Illustrated by Chris Van Allsburg. Houghton Mifflin, 1989. 81 pp. ISBN 0-395-49858-9.

This beautiful book has either decorative borders or a painting on each page. The Swan Lake legend, re-created in the famous ballet, is told here by an old man to the young daughter of its main characters, the Prince and Odette. You'll have fun comparing this version to Margot Fonteyn's (see 16.10).

16.17 Houston, James. **Akavak.** Harcourt Brace Jovanovich, 1990. 80 pp. ISBN 0-15-201731-3.

This is one of James Houston's three books on Inuit Eskimo legends, which he heard while he was living in the Canadian Arctic. In this legend, Akavak and his grandfather take a dangerous journey so that the grandfather can see his brother again before he dies. The wisdom of old age and the strength of youth are allied against the elemental forces of nature.

16.18 Houston, James. **Tikta'liktak.** Harcourt Brace Jovanovich, 1990. 64 pp. ISBN 0-15-287748-7.

James Houston lived in the Canadian Arctic for twelve years, and this is one of the Inuit Eskimo legends he heard there. A young Eskimo hunter is carried to sea one day on a drifting ice floe and must fight for survival for weeks as he tries to reach the mainland again.

16.19 Houston, James. **The White Archer.** Harcourt Brace Jovanovich, 1990. 96 pp. ISBN 0-15-696224-1.

In this Inuit Eskimo legend that James Houston heard while living in the Canadian Arctic, the young Eskimo Kungo seeks revenge against the raiders who killed his parents and kidnapped his sister. But when Kungo finally has the chance to kill, he gains a greater victory than revenge.

16.20 Hunter, Mollie. **The Mermaid Summer.** Harper and Row/ Charlotte Zolotow Books, 1988. 128 pp. ISBN 0-06-022628-5.

More than a hundred years ago, a mermaid ruled the cold, wild sea that washes around northern Scotland. This is the story of fisherman Eric Anderson, who refused to acknowledge her power. He and his men nearly drown, and he's driven into exile. Finally, it's up to his grandchildren Jon and Anna to stand up to the mermaid and bring their grandfather home. ★

16.21 Irving, Washington. **The Legend of Sleepy Hollow.** Illustrated by Arthur Rackham. Morrow Junior Books, 1990. 112 pp. ISBN 0-688-05276-2.

Ever since it came out in 1819, Washington Irving's story of the gangly schoolmaster Ichabod Crane and his pursuit of Katrina Van Tassel—along with her fortune—has amused listeners and readers. Nearly everyone has heard of the Headless Horseman, whether through cartoons, adapted stories, or jokes, but here is the original made all the better by Arthur Rackham's illustrations. A reproduction of the 1928 edition.

16.22 Kanawa, Kiri Te, compiler. **Land of the Long White Cloud: Maori Myths, Tales, and Legends.** Arcade, 1990. 118 pp. ISBN 1-55970-046-7.

Opera singer Kiri Te Kanawa, a native Maori, has selected nineteen tales from her childhood in New Zealand. Several deal with the trickster Maui: his birth, his catching the Great Fish (the South Island), and his taming of the sun. Also included are stories of Maori fairies: the tall, white-skinned *patupaiarehe*; and Taniwha, the black, man-eating monster who lives in deep water and under cliffs.

16.23 L'Engle, Madeleine. **The Glorious Impossible.** Simon and Schuster, 1990. 64 pp. ISBN 0-671-68690-9.

The title of this unusual retelling of the story of Jesus comes from Jesus's words, "For human beings it is impossible. For God nothing is impossible." The book is illustrated with paintings done by the Florentine artist Giotto in the 1300s for the Scrovegni Chapel in Padua, Italy. You'll find that they make the New Testament story believable in ordinary human terms.

16.24 Mayer, Marianna. **The Golden Swan.** Bantam/Skylark Books, 1990. 64 pp. ISBN 0-533-07054-1.

The Princess Damayanti has chosen King Nala for her husband, knowing that he is the only man she will ever love. But when she chooses this mortal over one of the gods, she offends Kali, the goddess of misfortune. Kali vows to seek revenge and brings disaster to King Nala. The story comes from the Sanskrit poem *The Mahabharata.* Part of the Timeless Tales series.

16.25 Mayer, Marianna. **Noble-Hearted Kate.** Bantam/Skylark Books, 1990. 64 pp. ISBN 0-533-07049-5.

Kate is devoted to her stepsister Meghan. When Kate's wicked mother puts a spell on Meghan, changing her head to a sheep's head, Kate is determined to find a way to break the spell. She has heard that the wisest being in the world is the Salmon of Wisdom, who lives in a river beneath the Tree of Knowledge. Kate and Meghan set out to find the Salmon, determined to seek his advice and follow his instructions, no matter how difficult the task may be. Part of the Timeless Tales series.

16.26 McKinley, Robin. **The Outlaws of Sherwood.** Greenwillow Books, 1988. 288 pp. ISBN 0-688-07178-3.

According to legend, Robin Hood was a twelfth-century English noble who became an outlaw. He and his band lived in Sherwood Forest, stealing from the rich and giving to the poor. Some of the characters in this author's retelling of the old story may surprise you with their ideas and attitudes, which seem more like they fit in the twentieth than the twelfth century. ★★★

16.27 Norman, Howard. **How Glooskap Outwits the Ice Giants and Other Tales of the Maritime Indians.** Wood engravings by Michael McCurdy. Little, Brown/Joy Street Books, 1989. 60 pp. ISBN 0-316-61181-6.

Native Americans living on the southeastern coast of Canada, near what is now Nova Scotia, had many stories about Glooskap, whose name means "Man from Nothing." He was thought of as the first human being, a great teacher, and a hero. These six easy-to-read stories include a creation myth and stories showing Glooskap's cleverness and strength against some unusual challenges.

16.28 Noyes, Alfred. **The Highwayman.** Illustrated by Neil Waldman. Harcourt Brace Jovanovich, 1990. 31 pp. ISBN 0-15-234340-7.

Generations have loved the rhythm and the tragic drama of Alfred Noyes's classic poem, *The Highwayman.* Bess, the innkeeper's daughter, plans to meet her lover at midnight, but King George's redcoats have planned a different meeting. Neil Waldman's watercolor illustrations, most of them two pages in size, add to the appeal of this romantic tale.

16.29 Price, Leontyne. **Aida.** Illustrated by Leo and Diane Dillon. Harcourt Brace Jovanovich/Gulliver Books, 1990. 32 pp. ISBN 0-15-200405-X.

One of the most famous of Giuseppe Verdi's operas is the story of Aida, an Ethiopian princess captured and taken into slavery by Egyptian soldiers. In Egypt she falls in love with Ramades, the soldier who is to lead the Egyptian army in its battle against her own father. Opera star Leontyne Price has played the tragic role of Aida many times, and here she tells the story from the princess's viewpoint. Her telling is made all the more vibrant by Leo and Diane Dillon's paintings and designs that decorate each page. ★★

16.30   Sandburg, Carl. **Rootabaga Stories.** Illustrated by Michael Hague. Harcourt Brace Jovanovich, 1989. 179 pp. ISBN 0-15-269061-1.

Have you met the Potato Face Blind Man? How about Slipfoot? Perhaps you have heard of Sky Blue or Feed Box. If you don't know these characters, you can meet them in this newly illustrated version of an old classic, originally published in 1923. Carl Sandburg's characters are not only people, but also animals, bugs, and other things that are fun to read about.

16.31   Sanfield, Steve. **The Adventures of High John the Conqueror.** Illustrated by John Ward. Orchard/Richard Jackson Books, 1989. 107 pp. ISBN 0-531-08407-8.

The legend of High John, a black slave and folk hero, originates from the storytelling traditions handed down from the time of slavery. John tricks and teases his white masters and evokes laughter and admiration from both his fellow slaves and his owners. Sixteen tales tell of his victory over bondage. ★

16.32   Sewell, Anna. **Black Beauty.** Illustrated by Charles Keeping. Farrar, Straus and Giroux, 1990. 216 pp. ISBN 0-374-30776-8.

Anna Sewell was devoted to protecting animals and wrote the story of Black Beauty, a London cab horse, as if told by the horse, as a plea for the better treatment of animals. You'll follow Black Beauty's story as he is traded from owner to owner, sometimes being treated well and sometimes cruelly. This new edition includes numerous drawings by Charles Keeping, one of England's foremost illustrators.

16.33   Spyri, Johanna. **Tomi Ungerer's** *Heidi.* Delacorte Press, 1990. 310 pp. ISBN 0-385-30244-4.

Heidi is the story of a young girl who lives in the Swiss Alps with her grandfather but then is taken to the city to be a companion to Klare, an invalid. Heidi's aunt Dete hopes Heidi will get an education and become more ladylike, but Heidi only grows despondent and ill. But in the end, both she and Klare return to Grandfather and the magic of the mountains. For this special edition, published to go along with Switzerland's 700th anniversary celebration, Tomi Ungerer has drawn and painted dozens of illustrations.

16.34 Weinrich, Beatrice Silverman, editor. **Yiddish Folktales.** Translated by Leonard Wolf. Pantheon, 1988. 416 pp. ISBN 0-394-54618-0.

This collection of Eastern European Jewish folktales is divided into parables, children's tales, magical tales, stories that teach lessons, humorous tales, legends, and tales of the supernatural. The *papirn-shnit* (paper cutting) decorations taken from Jewish folk art in Poland and Russia during the nineteenth and twentieth centuries add interest.

16.35 Yeats, W. B. **Fairy Tales of Ireland.** Selected and introduced by Neil Philip. Illustrated by P. J. Lynch. Delacorte Press, 1990. 160 pp. ISBN 0-385-30249-5.

The stories in this book are authentic Irish stories collected in the late 1800s by William Butler Yeats (who later became one of the world's most famous poets). They include "Daniel O'Rourke," "The Giant's Stairs," "A Legend of Knockmany," and "The Twelve Wild Geese." Since they are written in the rhythmic language of the original tellers, they're better when read aloud than to yourself.

16.36 Yep, Laurence. **The Rainbow People.** Harper and Row, 1989. 190 pp. ISBN 0-06-026761-5.

Twenty authentic folktales show the magic, mystery, and imagination of the Chinese culture. Dagger Claws, a monster, lures little children into his jaws until Shakey outsmarts him. Chung, a lazy but likeable idler, is dubbed the professor of smells and miraculously sniffs out lost items. A kind but poor peddler wins riches when he unselfishly seeks and finds a magic herb hidden in the woods. These delightful tales illustrate universal morals and the merits of honesty, the importance of courage, and the strength of love. ★★★

Series

16.37 **The Bank Street Collections.** Pocket Books.

These paperbacks are done in comic-book style, with each volume featuring a dozen or more stories adapted from the works of famous authors. The series includes *The Bank Street Book of*

Science Fiction, The Bank Street Book of Fantasy, The Bank Street Book of Creepy Tales, and *The Bank Street Book of Mystery.*

16.38   Junior Classics. Grosset and Dunlap.

Large type and illustrations make these abridgments of the classics easy for you to read. These paperbacks are only 90 to 125 pages each, and they have attractive covers. Titles include *Heidi, The Swiss Family Robinson, Black Beauty,* and *The Wind in the Willows.*

16.39   Step-Up Classic Chillers. Random House.

This series adapts and simplifies such classics as *Dracula, King Kong, Frankenstein, 20,000 Leagues under the Sea, Mysteries of Sherlock Holmes,* and *The Vampire* for easy reading. In *The Phantom of the Opera,* horrible deformities at birth make Eric lonely and angry. But they never stop his brilliant mind or his need to be loved. These are good introductions to the stories, and you'll want to return to the full versions in a few years to learn more of the characters' feelings and ideas.

16.40   Step-Up Classics. Random House.

Modern writers have taken favorite old stories and retold them in these easy-to-read, attractive paperbacks. Titles include H. G. Wells's *The Time Machine,* Charles Dickens's *Oliver Twist,* Robert Louis Stevenson's *Treasure Island,* and Anna Sewell's *Black Beauty.*

**Recommended Classics, Myths, Legends, and Folklore
Published before 1988**

Briggs, K. M. *Kate Crackernuts.* Greenwillow Books, 1980.
Brittain, Bill. *The Wish Giver: Three Tales of Coven Tree.* Harper and Row, 1983.
Curtis, Edward S., compiler. *The Girl Who Married a Ghost and Other Tales from the North American Indian.* Scholastic, 1978.
Fleischman, Sid. *Humbug Mountain.* Atlantic Monthly Press, 1978.
Garner, Alan. *Alan Garner's Book of British Fairy Tales.* Delacorte Press, 1985.
Hamilton, Virginia, reteller. *The People Could Fly: American Black Folk Tales.* Alfred A. Knopf, 1985.

Ish-Kishnor, Sulamith. *The Carpet of Solomon: A Hebrew Legend.* Pantheon, 1966.

McKinley, Robin. *Beauty: A Retelling of the Story of Beauty and the Beast.* Harper and Row, 1978.

Riordan, James. *The Woman in the Moon and Other Tales of Forgotten Heroines.* Dial Books for Young Readers, 1985.

Singer, Isaac Bashevis. *The Golem.* Farrar, Straus and Giroux, 1982.

Voigt, Cynthia. *Jackaroo.* Atheneum, 1985.

Yolen, Jane. *The Girl Who Cried Flowers and Other Tales.* Thomas Y. Crowell, 1974.

IV Contemporary Poetry and Short Stories

We've chosen the books in this section not because of their topics but because of their format. Poems and short stories are short enough to fit into today's hurry-up lifestyle. But don't try to speed-read poems or even short stories, because if you do, you will miss out on some of their value. They need to be savored, and you need time to think about one poem or one story before you go on to the next one.

If we weren't looking at the format of these stories and poems, then these books could be scattered throughout all the other lists because what the authors have written about is varied both in style and purpose. There are mysteries, adventures, history lessons, pleas for ecology, advice on how to get along with a friend, love stories, legends, opinions about war and politics, and probably any other topic you might wish to read about.

17 Books of Poetry

17.1 Agard, John, compiler. **Life Doesn't Frighten Me at All.** Henry Holt, 1990. 92 pp. ISBN 0-8050-1237-0.

John Agard planned this anthology "for those teenagers with an allergy to poetry." He has collected eighty-four unusual poems by poets from all over the world, from W. B. Yeats to reggae master Bob Marley to Attila the Stockbroker, and he proves what he set out to prove—that poems are about more than just dead leaves and frosted windows. Some of the poems include strong language. Black-and-white line drawings and photo collages add appeal to this book, which is small enough to tuck in a backpack or a large pocket. ★★

17.2 Aisenberg, Nadya, editor. **We Animals.** Sierra Club Books, 1989. 201 pp. ISBN 0-87156-685-0.

The goal of the Sierra Club, which produced this book, is to increase people's awareness of nature and the role we need to play to protect the environment. In keeping with that goal, this book offers poems from around the world about animals and their relationships with humans. ★

17.3 Aska, Warabe. **Seasons.** Poetry selected by Alberto Manguel. Doubleday, 1990. 48 pp. ISBN 0-385-41633-4.

Warabe Aska is a Japanese artist living in Canada. His paintings are fun to study because they include real people and real things but aren't anything you could photograph. The painting on the front cover, for example, blends together a piece of each painting in the book; and in one of the paintings inside the book, Warabe has hidden ten different animals. The paintings illustrate very simple poems, most of which set a mood or evoke feelings of wonder or nostalgia.

17.4 Elledge, Scott, editor. **Wider than the Sky: Poems to Grow Up With.** Harper and Row, 1990. 358 pp. ISBN 0-06-021787-1.

Scott Elledge presents here his favorite poems from contemporary poets, including Dr. Seuss and Shel Silverstein. He also
includes poets of the past, including William Shakespeare and
Emily Dickinson. At the back of the book, you'll find fifteen pages
of interesting notes about the origins of the poems, unusual words
or references in them, and their geographical settings.

17.5   Fleischman, Paul. **Joyful Noise: Poems for Two Voices.** Illustrated by Eric Beddows. Harper and Row/Charlotte Zolotow Books,
1988. 192 pp. ISBN 0-06-021852-5.

Paul Fleischman remembers that some of his most pleasant times
as a child were when his family read together. His father, Sid
Fleischman, was an author of some wonderfully funny children's
books, but even without a famous author in the family, Fleischman thinks that people can have fun sharing literature out loud.
So he wrote these funny poems about feeling and talking insects
for two people to read aloud to each other—they only make sense
with two voices. ★★★★

17.6   Glenn, Mel. **Back to Class.** Photographs by Michael J. Bernstein.
Clarion Books, 1988. 95 pp. ISBN 0-89919-656-X.

Each of these sixty-five poems is like reading a short story that has
been compacted. The poems, written in the same style as *Class
Dismissed* and *Class Dismissed II*, come from the voices of
students and teachers in a contemporary high school.

17.7   Janeczko, Paul B. **Brickyard Summer.** Illustrated by Ken Rush.
Orchard Books, 1989. 53 pp. ISBN 0-531-08446-9.

With the end of the school year comes the bonfire—spelling lists,
notebooks, all the reminders of school go up in smoke. The
narrator of these poems wanders through the summer thinking
about high school and getting to know the people in his
hometown. He discovers courage, vitality, and the importance of
friendship. ★★

17.8   Janeczko, Paul B., compiler. **The Music of What Happens:
Poems That Tell Stories.** Orchard Books, 1988. 208 pp. ISBN 0-
531-08357-8.

The stories told by these poems are more complex and take more
pondering, reading out loud, and discussion than did such grade
school favorites as "Casey at the Bat" and "The Cremation of Sam
McGhee." They're worth the extra effort, though; plus, there's the

advantage of getting acquainted with many of the best contemporary poets. ★★★

17.9 Janeczko, Paul B., editor. **The Place My Words Are Looking For.** Bradbury Press, 1990. 145 pp. ISBN 0-02-747671-5.

Paul Janeczko has selected thirty-nine American poets to talk to you about what they think poetry is and how to get started writing it. Their comments are simple and encouraging, yet profound. The poets describe many techniques--all true to life. A variety of children's poems by these authors and many more give the book flavor. The poets show you that poetry is fun! It is work, but it is working with yourself, a way of expressing your thoughts, feelings, and life experiences with your own kind of music. ★

17.10 Knudson, R. R., and May Swenson, compilers. **American Sports Poems.** Orchard Books, 1988. 226 pp. ISBN 0-531-08353-5.

If you thought all poetry was about flowers and springtime, here's a book to change your mind. Among the 158 poems, there's probably at least one on any sport you've ever participated in or watched. As an added bonus, the collectors, who are both well-known writers and poets, have included information on some of the poets and on the stories behind the poems. ★

17.11 Livingston, Myra Cohen, compiler. **If the Owl Calls Again: A Collection of Owl Poems.** Woodcuts by Antonio Fransconi. Margaret K. McElderry Books, 1990. 114 pp.ISBN 0-689-50501-9.

This collection of eighty poems about owls begins with Yuma and Papago Indian rhymes and then goes on to include humorous, thoughtful, reverential, and even frightening glimpses at this fascinating bird as seen by a wide range of poets. The collector of the poems asks if it's possible "that the owl is the mirror of our own hidden thoughts."

17.12 Mahy, Margaret. **Nonstop Nonsense.** Illustrated by Quentin Blake. Margaret K. McElderry Books, 1989. 120 pp. ISBN 0-689-50483-7.

Margaret Mahy usually writes imaginative novels, but here she's written funny poetry and rhythmic short stories. You'll meet the man from Fandango, who pays a visit once every five hundred years, and the word-wizard who casts her spell over the Delmonico family. Quentin Blake's drawings add to the fun.

17.13   McCullough, Frances, editor. **Earth, Air, Fire, and Water.**
Harper and Row/Charlotte Zolotow Books, 1989. 140 pp. ISBN
0-06-024208-6.

Poet Sylvia Plath once described her reaction to poetry: "I saw the
gooseflesh on my skin. I did not know what made it. I was not
cold. Had a ghost passed over? No, it was the poetry. . . . I wanted
to cry; I felt very odd. I had fallen into a new way of being happy."
Over 125 poems from the best modern poets are collected here
with the goal of getting the same reaction to poetry from you. A
prominent theme is reaching for wholeness— with nature, across
generations, and within yourself. ★

17.14   Morrison, Lillian, compiler. **Rhythm Road: Poems to Move To.**
Lothrop, Lee and Shepard Books, 1988. 147 pp. ISBN 0-688-
07098-1.

Here's a poetry book for movers and shakers—quite literally!
Each of the eighty-eight poems in this collection has to do with
movement. Obviously, there will be poems related to sports and
dance, but there are also poems about science, technology, and
thought. ★★

17.15   Morrison, Lillian, compiler. **Sprints and Distances: Sports in
Poetry and the Poetry in Sport.** Thomas Y. Crowell, 1989. 211 pp.
ISBN 0-690-04840-8.

Both poetry and sports are forms of play and ritual which take
people away from their everyday lives and lift them above
themselves. The collector of these poems succeeds in proving her
idea that poetry and sports "go together naturally wherever there
is a zest for life." The poems are as varied as "A Kite Is a Victim"
and "To Kate, Skating Better Than Her Date."

17.16   Morrison, Lillian, compiler. **Yours till Niagara Falls: A Book of
Autograph Verses.** Illustrated by Sylvie Wickstrom. Thomas Y.
Crowell, 1990. 183 pp. ISBN 0-690-04976-9.

"Remember me is all I ask, / But should remembrance be a task,
/ Forget me," and "When you get married and live upstairs, /
Don't come down and borrow my chairs" are two of the rhymes
in this collection of over 200 messages that kids have written over
the years in autograph books and yearbooks. The cartoon-style
drawings add to the fun.

17.17   Rylant, Cynthia. **Soda Jerk.** Illustrated by Peter Catalanotto. Or-
chard/Richard Jackson Books, 1990. 45 pp. ISBN 0-531-08464-7.

Although this book looks like a picture book for younger children, it's teenagers who will really understand it. It's set in Maxwell's Drugstore, where the narrator works the soda fountain. He observes that in his job, "Tips are okay. / But the secrets are better." In his poems, he shares some of those secrets as well as his observations about "perfect" rich kids, hippies, life with divorced parents, hunters who rejoice at the sight of a dead deer, and old ladies "who've been somebody's mom / for so long, / they have come begging / for a person to take an interest." ★

17.18   Steig, Jeanne. **Consider the Lemming.** Illustrated by William Steig. Farrar, Straus and Giroux / Michael di Capua Books, 1988. 48 pp. ISBN 0-374-31536-1.

Jeanne Steig's poems about animals and people's expectations about them are whimsical and surprising. The drawings bring extra enjoyment to this book, which is perfect for browsing.

17.19   Strauss, Gwen. **Trail of Stones.** Illustrated by Anthony Browne. David McKay, 1990. 35 pp. ISBN 0-679-80582-6.

These poems and paintings will take you beyond traditional fairy tales "into the woods" of imagination. This book shows you what the writer and the artist think might have happened after the original fairy tales ended. ★

17.20   Thayer, Ernest Lawrence. **Casey at the Bat.** Illustrated by Barry Moser. David R. Godine, 1988. 31 pp. ISBN 0-87923-772-8.

This version of an all-time favorite baseball poem is illustrated by some fresh and funny new drawings. You also get the bonus of a ten-page essay written by modern poet Donald Hall about baseball, poetry, and life in general.

17.21   Willard, Nancy. **The Ballad of Biddy Early.** Alfred A. Knopf, 1989. 36 pp. ISBN 0-394-88414-0.

Biddy Early, the wise woman of Clare, could read the future and cure sickness with her little crystal ball. All Ireland knows her stories of cats, ghosts, and humans. This book, illustrated by Barry Moser, retells the old stories in limericks, poems, and ballads.

17.22   Yolen, Jane. **Bird Watch.** Illustrated by Ted Lewin. Philomel Books, 1990. 48 pp. ISBN 0-399-21612-X.

Once you've read these poems about birds, they will come back to you the next time you see a bird perching on a tree or bringing food to one of its babies. You'll gain a new appreciation for these simple events. ★

Recommended Books of Poetry Published before 1988

Cassedy, Sylvia. *Roomrimes*. Thomas Y. Crowell, 1987.

Dunning, Stephen, and Others, compilers. *Reflections on a Gift of Watermelon Pickle . . . and other Modern Verse*. Lothrop, Lee and Shepard Books, 1967.

Dunning, Stephen, and Others, compilers. *Some Haystacks Don't Even Have Any Needle: And Other Complete Modern Poems*. Lothrop, Lee and Shepard Books, 1969.

Fleischman, Paul. *I Am Phoenix: Poems for Two Voices*. Harper and Row, 1985.

Glenn, Mel. *Class Dismissed: High School Poems*. Clarion Books, 1982.

Glenn, Mel. *Class Dismissed II: More High School Poems*. Clarion Books, 1986.

Gordon, Ruth, compiler. *Under All Silences: Shades of Love*. Harper and Row, 1987.

Hearne, Betsy. *Love Lines: Poetry in Person*. Margaret K. McElderry Books, 1987.

Hopkins, Lee Bennett, compiler. *Munching: Poems about Eating*. Little, Brown, 1985.

Hughes, Langston. *The Dream Keeper and Other Poems*. Alfred A. Knopf/Borzoi Sprinters, 1986.

Janeczko, Paul, compiler. *Don't Forget to Fly*. Bradbury Press, 1981.

Janeczko, Paul, compiler. *Going Over to Your Place: Poems for Each Other*. Bradbury Press, 1987.

Janeczko, Paul, compiler. *Pocket Poems: Selected for a Journey*. Bradbury Press, 1985.

Janeczko, Paul, compiler. *Poetspeak: In Their Work, about Their Work*. Bradbury Press, 1983.

Janeczko, Paul, compiler. *Postcard Poems: A Collection of Poetry for Sharing*. Bradbury Press, 1979.

Janeczko, Paul, compiler. *Strings: A Gathering of Family Poems*. Bradbury Press, 1984.

Janeczko, Paul, compiler. *This Delicious Day: Sixty-Five Poems*. Orchard Books, 1987.

Larrick, Nancy, compiler. *Tambourines! Tambourines to Glory! Prayers and Poems.* The Westminster Press/John Knox Press, 1982.

Livingston, Myra Cohen, editor. *What a Wonderful Bird the Frog Are: An Assortment of Humorous Poetry and Verse.* Harcourt Brace Jovanovich, 1973.

Lueders, Ed, and Primus St. John, editors. *Zero Makes Me Hungry: A Collection of Poems for Today.* Lothrop, Lee and Shepard Books, 1976.

McCullough, Frances, editor. *Love Is Like the Lion's Tooth: An Anthology of Love Poems.* Harper and Row, 1984.

Merriam, Eve. *Finding a Poem.* Atheneum, 1970.

Merriam, Eve. *If Only I Could Tell You: Poems for Young Lovers and Dreamers.* Alfred A. Knopf, 1983.

Merriam, Eve. *Out Loud.* Atheneum, 1973.

Merriam, Eve. *Rainbow Writing.* Atheneum, 1976.

Millay, Edna St. Vincent. *Poems: Selected for Young People.* Harper and Row, 1979.

Plotz, Helen, editor. *Eye's Delight: Poems of Art and Architecture.* Greenwillow Books, 1983.

Prelutsky, Jack. *Nightmares: Poems to Trouble Your Sleep.* Greenwillow Books, 1976.

Rylant, Cynthia. *Waiting to Waltz: A Childhood.* Bradbury Press, 1984.

Sandburg, Carl. *Rainbows Are Made: Poems by Carl Sandburg.* Selected by Lee Bennett Hopkins. Harcourt Brace Jovanovich, 1982.

Silverstein, Shel. *The Light in the Attic.* Harper and Row, 1983.

Silverstein, Shel. *Where the Sidewalk Ends: Poems and Drawings.* Harper and Row, 1974.

18 Collections of Short Stories

18.1 Aiken, Joan. **Give Yourself a Fright: Thirteen Stories of the Supernatural.** Delacorte Press, 1989. 180 pp. ISBN 0-440-50120-2.

In these thirteen stories, bizarre creatures disrupt the lives of ordinary characters. An ancient muse arrives on the doorstep of a sophisticated thief and nags him to write poetry. Twin brothers jealously want a mysterious locket which brings good luck and gives its owner the ability to detect ghosts. Possessed souls, specters, and living talismans prove that the world beyond presents strange phenomena to the unwary and unsuspecting.

18.2 Aiken, Joan. **The Last Slice of Rainbow.** Illustrated by Alix Berenzy. Harper and Row/Charlotte Zolotow Books, 1988. 144 pp. ISBN 0-06-020043-X.

Although these nine beautifully illustrated stories read like classical fairy tales, they may not be the stories you heard as a child because some of them are much too grim. Clem's dream is stolen by the Tooth Fairy, Cal is punished for being cruel when his legs run off without him, and Princess Christina hears horrible voices for years after she cuts off her cat's whiskers.

18.3 Aleksin, Anatoly, and Thomas Pettepiece, editors. **Face to Face: A Collection of Stories by Celebrated Soviet and American Writers.** Philomel Books, 1990. 256 pp. ISBN 0-399-21951-X.

With all the current interest in improving Soviet-American relations, *Face to Face* is a timely collection. The stories are written for young readers by eighteen noted authors, nine each from the United States and the Soviet Union. They compare experiences of growing up. The book is being released in the Soviet Union at the same time it is released in the United States. U.S. authors include Robert Cormier, Jean Fritz, Virginia Hamilton, Walter Dean Myers, Katherine Paterson, Cynthia Rylant, Cynthia Voigt, Jane Yolen, and Scott O'Dell, with an introduction by Hugh Downs.

18.4 Asimov, Isaac, and Martin H. Greenberg, editors. **Visions of Fantasy: Tales from the Masters.** Illustrated by Larry Elmore. Doubleday, 1989. 181 pp. ISBN 0-385-26359-7.

If you've read books by such writers as Jane Yolen, Marion Zimmer Bradley, and Isaac Asimov, then you know what kinds of stories to expect in this collection. Madeleine L'Engle writes about a mysterious girl and an unusual witch who live in a boarded-up plantation house after the Civil War, Ray Bradbury takes us to a Michigan lake where an almost-forgotten tragedy changes a young man's life, and Anne McCaffrey lets us share in the anxiety of the youngest dragonrider candidate. If you're not acquainted with these authors, then this rich collection of short stories is a good place to meet them.

18.5 Bird, E. J. **The Blizzard of 1896.** Carolrhoda Books, 1990. 72 pp. ISBN 0-87614-651-5.

"It all started with the wind that came sneaking across the mountains from the west and blew a few tumbleweeds into rows along the fences," goes the story of the great blizzard of 1896, which E. J. Bird uses as the center of this collection of stories he remembers hearing as a child some twenty years after the blizzard. Bird is also an artist whose drawings give life to the people and animals in these stories, like Miss Mary, Old Don Leeker, the bull that Sanya shot in the middle of the parlor, and the hungry grizzly that stole Joe Rupin's breakfast right out of the pan.

18.6 Brooke, William J. **A Telling of the Tales: Five Stories.** Harper and Row, 1990. 132 pp. ISBN 0-06-020688.

These new versions of old stories have some surprising endings. In "Sleeping Beauty," the princess does not like being kissed by the prince and doesn't believe that she's been asleep for 100 years. Cinderella doesn't cooperate with the prince, and when she tries on the shoe, it doesn't fit. Johnny Appleseed convinces Paul Bunyan to become an environmentalist. And John Henry trades his hammer for a steam machine, finishes his work, and goes home to Polly Ann.

18.7 Brooks, Martha. **Paradise Cafe and Other Stories.** Little, Brown/ Joy Street Books, 1990. 124 pp. ISBN 0-316-10978-9.

This prize-winning collection of fourteen stories includes one about Ardis, whose mother is going through early menopause while she's going through late puberty; another about Lulie, who has worn Graham Sanderson's father's signet ring until the tape on the back of it is "frayed and gray and caked as a miniature Egyptian mummy"; and one about Marie, whose parents fell in love when they playfully climbed into a big trash can on Highway 23. ★

18.8   Carlson, Lori M., and Cynthia L. Ventura, editors. **Where Angels Glide at Dawn: New Stories from Latin America.** J. B. Lippincott, 1990. 114 pp. ISBN 0-397-32425-1.

Ten stories from Latin America are included in this collection designed to bring some of the best Latin American short stories to you. The opening story begins, "I'm the bear in the pipes of the house," and goes on to explain how it's "my hair that keeps the conduits clean. . . . Once in a while I stick my paw out through a faucet and the girl on the third floor screams that she's scalded herself, or I growl at oven height on the second and Wilhelmina the cook complains that the chimney is drawing badly." Other equally unusual stories include "The Rebellion of the Magical Rabbits," "Paleton and the Musical Elephant," and "A Huge Black Umbrella." Introduction by Isabel Allende.

18.9   Carlstrom, Nancy White. **Light: Stories of a Small Kindness.** Illustrated by Lisa Desimini. Little, Brown, 1990. 42 pp. ISBN 0-316-12857-0.

The author tells why she wrote these stories about small kindnesses. She recalls being in a tiny village in Mexico where the people treated her kindly and presented her with "an egg, blazing white in the full, fierce sun" when she left. But while she was riding the bus away from the village, the egg broke, and she was ashamed of her carelessness and ever since has "been more careful with a small kindness." The seven stories in this beautifully illustrated book are set in Mexico, Guatemala, Haiti, and New York City.

18.10   Cohen, Daniel. **Phone Call from a Ghost: Strange Tales from Modern America.** Simon and Schuster/Minstrel Books, 1988. 112 pp. ISBN 0-671-68242-3.

You might expect most ghost stories to come from old castles in England and to be about Lord or Lady Something-or-Other who was beheaded in the fifteenth century. But not these stories—they are all set in America—except for one that's set in Canada. And they're all contemporary. The author doesn't claim they're true;

he just claims that he didn't make them up. He heard them from other people, and he's passing them on to you.

18.11 Coville, Bruce, compiler. **Herds of Thunder, Manes of Gold: A Collection of Horse Stories and Poems.** Illustrated by Ted Lewin. Doubleday, 1989. 176 pp. ISBN 0-385-24642-0.

These stories and poems come from all kinds of sources. Modern stories include Peter Roop's "Prairie Lightning" about a Black-foot boy's theft of an "elk-dog," which is what his people call horses, and Mary Stanton's "Sunrise," about a girl and her horse. There are also selected retellings of myths, King Henry V's description of his horse from the play by William Shakespeare, and "The Birth of a King," written by Marguerite Henry.

18.12 Dixon, Franklin W. **The Hardy Boys Ghost Stories.** Simon and Schuster/Minstrel Books, 1989. 137 pp. ISBN 0-671-69133-3.

These six stories have been taken from the famous Hardy Boys stories. In them, Frank and Joe are part detectives and part ghost hunters as they meet a fiendish scarecrow, get rescued by ghosts, and solve the "Mystery in Room 12."

18.13 Gelman, Mark. **Does God Have a Big Toe? Stories about Stories in the Bible.** Illustrated by Oscar de Mejo. Harper and Row, 1989. 88 pp. ISBN 0-06-022432-0.

You need to know the real Bible stories in order to appreciate the humor of the stories in this collection. The author is a rabbi who all his life has loved the characters in the Old Testament and has thought so much about what happened to them that it was easy for him to create new stories. The title story is about the Tower of Babel and how a little girl started the whole thing by arousing everyone's curiosity and desire to get a peek at God by asking if he had a big toe. ★

18.14 Jones, Diana Wynne. **Hidden Turnings: A Collection of Stories through Time and Space.** Greenwillow Books, 1990. 182 pp. ISBN 0-688-09163-6.

The settings and characters for these twelve fantasy and mystery tales range from ancient Greece to a twentieth-century disco, from Celtic fairies to a teenage banjo picker. One story is about a dream visit to a futuristic lab guarded by a trio of vicious wolves; another recalls someone's great aunt and her belief in the inhabitants in the sky. The selections are bound together by an element of the unexpected and supernatural which runs through them all: a hidden turning. Information about the authors is included, as is an introduction to the collection.

18.15   Jordan, Cathleen, and Cynthia Manson, compilers. **Tales from Alfred Hitchcock's Mystery Magazine.** William Morrow, 1988. 310 pp. ISBN 0-688-08176-2.

Humor, surprise, and hints of the horrifying are the threads that connect these twenty stories from *Alfred Hitchcock's Mystery Magazine.* Characters include yuppie vampires and the "real" Batman, and in one story rose-scented letters arrive from a mother who has been dead for over twenty years. Each story has just enough realism to make you wonder if it could possibly happen.

18.16   Macklin, John. **World's Strangest "True" Ghost Stories.** Sterling, 1990. 96 pp. ISBN 0-8069-5784-0.

If you enjoy the strange and bizarre headlines of tabloid newspapers, you will probably enjoy these stranger-than-fiction stories. Cases include a man who survived being swallowed by a whale and a horse who solved the mystery of a missing boy. Hauntings, fadings, and curses are the topics of other stories.

18.17   Martini, Teri. **The Secret Is Out: True Spy Stories.** Little, Brown, 1990. 133 pp. ISBN 0-316-54864-2.

These eleven true stories are arranged chronologically. A couple of them, such as the Benedict Arnold tale, are familiar, but others, such as the one about Lawrence of Arabia and the one about a soldier who was already dead when set adrift as a spy during World War II, probably won't be found in most history books. Illustrations add interest.

18.18   Pfeffer, Susan Beth. **Head of the Class.** Bantam/Starfire Books, 1989. 120 pp. ISBN 0-553-28190-9.

These stories are based on the popular TV series "Head of the Class." They begin with the introduction of Mr. Moore as substitute teacher for the Individualized Honors Program (IHP) at Fillmore High School and carry the class through five other episodes.

18.19   Pollack, Pamela, compiler. **The Random House Book of Humor for Children.** Illustrated by Paul O. Zelinsky. Random House, 1988. 311 pp. ISBN 0-394-98049-2.

If you're a person who reads through books looking for the funny parts, then this is the book for you. It gathers together the best chapters or sections of many funny books, including Judy Blume's *Tales of a Fourth Grade Nothing*, Richard Peck's *Ghosts I Have Been*, and Norton Juster's *The Phantom Tollbooth*. It also takes chapters from adult books, like James Thurber's *The Moth and the Star*, Frank Gilbreth and Ernestine Carey's *Cheaper by the Dozen*, and Garrison Keillor's *Lake Wobegon Days*.

18.20 Rochman, Hazel, compiler. **Somehow Tenderness Survives.** Harper Keypoint Books, 1988. 189 pp. ISBN 0-06-447063-6.

The language in these ten short stories is strong, factual, and realistic. This is a collection of autobiographical sketches of growing up, living, loving, and hating in South Africa under apartheid. The stories come from a cross section of racial and economic groups and will satisfy both adult and young readers.

18.21 Rylant, Cynthia. **A Couple of Kooks: And Other Stories about Love.** Orchard Books, 1990. 112 pp. ISBN 0-531-08500-7.

These eight stories each deal with a different kind of love. One story is about a retarded man who changes people by leaving flowers every Wednesday morning at 6:00 a.m. in front of the hardware store; another is about Boyd, the third son in a family, who has come in third all his life but finally comes in first the one time it really matters; and in another, the grandfather of a bride realizes at the wedding that "if one of those lovely women over there, near the violinists, crossed the lawn towards me, pulled this empty chair alongside mine, removed the mints and the champagne from my hands, leaned over in a mist of perfume and whispered in my ear, 'I love you,' I would follow her, with all my heart and soul." The final story, from which the collection gets its name, is about two sixteen year olds talking to their unborn baby to prepare it for the life it will have when they give it up for adoption. ★

18.22 Schulman, L. M., compiler. **The Random House Book of Sports Stories.** Illustrated by Thomas B. Allen. Random House, 1990. 247 pp. ISBN 0-394-92874-1.

These sixteen stories are all by well-known writers, ranging from old favorites like Ring Lardner, James Thurber, Jack London, and Ernest Hemingway to contemporary writers, including Toni Cade Bambara and Bruce Brooks. Besides the stories of sports you'd expect to read about, like basketball and football, there are also stories about skiing, boxing, hunting, tennis, running, horse racing, and Japanese martial arts.

18.23 Schwartz, Alvin. **Gold and Silver, Silver and Gold: Tales of Hidden Treasure.** Illustrated by David Christiana. Farrar, Straus and Giroux, 1988. 128 pp. ISBN 0-374-32690-8.

This author usually collects folktales, but this time the twenty-eight stories he has collected are based on supposedly true accounts of lost or hidden treasures that ambitious readers can go searching for—or at least dream about.

18.24 Sieruta, Peter. **Heartbeats.** Harper and Row, 1989. 216 pp. ISBN 0-06-025849-7.

These nine short stories highlight young people's relationships, including friendship, family relationships, romance, and school associations. Emery's brother goes out with Jodi, the girl of Emery's dreams; James O'Brien finds his life changed by a substitute teacher; Henry Tremain finds that with Joy Glass nothing is as it seems; and Jackie finds his first success in a grocery store. ★★★★★

18.25 Soto, Gary. **Baseball in April: And Other Stories.** Harcourt Brace Jovanovich, 1990. 109 pp. ISBN 0-15-205720-X.

Hispanic teenagers in central California are the characters in these eleven short stories that focus on the move from childhood into the teen years. Karate lessons, Little League baseball, family problems, and relating to the opposite sex are some of the experiences the stories tell about. A glossary of terms helps clarify some of the Spanish words used in the stories. ★★

18.26 Thomas, Joyce Carol, editor. **A Gathering of Flowers: Stories about Being Young in America.** Harper and Row, 1990. 236 pp. ISBN 0-06-026173-0.

The collector of these eleven stories started with the idea that all of us in America are somehow related, and so she set out to find short stories that would help Anglos, Hispanics, Asians, and Native and African Americans understand each other. The stories cover many different moods and experiences; for instance, Gary Soto's "First Love" is full of kisses and wishes, while Gerald Haslam's "Upstream" offers humor, and Al Young's "Going for the Moon" is mystical. Some of the authors whose writings you might already be familiar with include Lois Lowry, Jeanne Wakatsuki Houston, and Maxine Hong Kingston.

18.27   Yee, Paul. **Tales from Gold Mountain: Stories of the Chinese in the New World.** Illustrated by Simon Ng. Macmillan, 1990. 64 pp. ISBN 0-02-793621-X.

The eight stories in this collection show how Chinese immigrants to North America mixed their folklore traditions and beliefs with their new working and living conditions. They were able to keep their dreams and values, although in changed forms, when they entered a new life. A dreamlike painting accompanies each story.
★

18.28   Yolen, Jane, and Martin H. Greenberg, editors. **Werewolves: A Collection of Original Stories.** Harper and Row, 1988. 288 pp. ISBN 0-06-026798-4.

If you like books which send a chill down your back, you'll like this collection of stories about werewolves. Several famous authors of fantasy have contributed to this collection of werewolf stories, which range from an account of a frightening meeting between a werewolf and some Nazis to an amusing look at a werewolf who goes to college. There is even a story of a girl who plays in a band when she isn't being her wolflike other self.

Series

18.29   **Jack B. Quick: The World's Smartest Sports Detective!** Little, Brown/Sports Illustrated for Kids Books.

Jack and his friends are students at Central High, and as Jack proves, being sports champions takes lots of different kinds of "smarts." Titles include *The Case of the "Missing" Playbook: And Other Mysteries* and *The Case of the Basketball Joker: And Other Mysteries.*

Recommended Collections of Short Stories Published before 1988

Aiken, Joan. *A Whisper in the Night: Tales of Terror and Suspense.* Delacorte Press, 1984.
Asimov, Isaac. *Young Extraterrestrials.* Harper and Row, 1984.
Asimov, Isaac. *Young Ghosts.* Harper and Row, 1985.
Asimov, Isaac. *Young Mutants.* Harper and Row, 1984.

Asimov, Isaac. *Young Star Travelers*. Harper and Row, 1986.

Barrett, Peter A., editor. *To Break the Silence: Thirteen Short Stories for Young Readers*. Dell/Laurel-Leaf, 1986.

Caras, Roger. *Roger Caras' Treasury of Great Cat Stories*. E. P. Dutton, 1987.

Caras, Roger. *Roger Caras' Treasury of Great Dog Stories*. E. P. Dutton, 1987.

Conford, Ellen. *If This is Love, I'll Take Spaghetti*. Scholastic, 1983.

Edmonds, Walter D. *The Night Raider and Other Stories*. Little, Brown, 1980.

Fleischman, Paul. *Coming-and-Going Men: Four Tales*. Harper and Row, 1984.

Fleischman, Paul. *Graven Images: Three Stories*. Harper and Row, 1982.

Gallo, Donald R., editor. *Sixteen: Short Stories by Outstanding Young Adult Writers*. Delacorte Press, 1984.

Gallo, Donald R., editor. *Visions: Nineteen Short Stories by Outstanding Writers for Young Adults*. Delacorte Press, 1987.

Howker, Janni. *Badger on the Barge and Other Stories*. Greenwillow Books, 1985.

Mark, Jan. *Nothing to Be Afraid Of*. Harper and Row, 1982.

Mazer, Norma Fox. *Dear Bill, Remember Me? and Other Stories*. Delacorte Press, 1976.

Mazer, Norma Fox. *Summer Girls, Love Boys*. Delacorte Press, 1982.

Paulsen, Gary. *Sentries*. Bradbury Press, 1986.

Rylant, Cynthia. *Children of Christmas: Stories for the Season*. Orchard Books, 1987.

Rylant, Cynthia. *Every Living Thing*. Bradbury Press, 1985.

Schwartz, Alvin. *More Scary Stories to Tell in the Dark*. Harper and Row, 1984.

Schwartz, Alvin. *Scary Stories to Tell in the Dark*. Harper and Row, 1981.

Segel, Elizabeth, compiler. *Short Takes: A Short Story Collection for Young Readers*. Lothrop, Lee and Shepard Books, 1986.

Westall, Robert. *The Haunting of Chas. McGill and Other Stories*. Greenwillow Books, 1983.

Westall, Robert. *Rachel and the Angel and Other Stories*. Greenwillow Books, 1987.

Yolen, Jane, Martin H. Greenberg, and Charles G. Waugh, editors. *Spaceships and Spells*. Harper and Row, 1987.

V Books to Help with Schoolwork

Between the two covers of a textbook is a whole lot you might want to know about a topic—about math, science, grammar, history, politics, or any of the other subjects you study in school. But too often, textbooks leave little room for fascinating photographs and illustrations or for poetic language and metaphors. And textbook writers usually can't wander off the topic to explore those interesting stories that happen alongside the big ones or to fully discuss the various sides of controversial issues. Textbooks have to present the big picture to keep students moving toward a common goal. That's fine, but it's often more fun to stop along the way and explore the little pictures, and that's what the books in this section allow you to do. They present fuller and better-illustrated segments of information, opinion, and speculation than are often put into textbooks. And best of all, there are so many good information books on such a wide range of topics that no matter what your interests, you can probably find one or more books that will fit your needs exactly.

19 Physical Sciences, Math, and Technology

19.1 Berger, Melvin. **Solids, Liquids and Gases: From Superconductors to the Ozone Layer.** G. P. Putnam's Sons, 1989. 78 pp. ISBN 0-399-21731-2.

Besides giving directions for some simple home experiments, Berger's book also explains terms currently in the news, such as "acid rain," "heavy water," "semiconductors," and "troposphere."

19.2 Berliner, Don. **Research Airplanes: Testing the Boundaries of Flight.** Lerner, 1988. 64 pp. ISBN 0-8225-1582-2.

Stretching from the Wright brothers' first experimental gliders to today's space shuttles, the emphasis in this book is on how engineers test and modify planes to make them move in different and faster ways. The clear-cut organization makes this book a good source for information, while the photographs make it appropriate for pleasure-time browsing.

19.3 Booth, Nicholas. **Space: The Next 100 Years.** Crown/Orion Books, 1990. 127 pp. ISBN 0-517-57764-X.

Admiral Richard H. Truly, a NASA administrator, writes a foreword to this book that shows his excitement about all NASA has accomplished and the many things still to be explored in outer space. The book has four major sections: "Robot Explorers," "The High Frontier," "Extending the Frontier," and "The Far Future." Many drawings and full-color photographs make the fairly complex text easier to understand.

19.4 Branley, Franklyn M. **Uranus: The Seventh Planet.** Illustrated by Yvonne Buchanan. Thomas Y. Crowell, 1988. 53 pp. ISBN 0-690-04687-1.

When *Voyager 2* flew by Uranus in 1986, it sent back photos and information about this distant planet that made scientists revise many of their previously held theories. You'll learn not only about Uranus but also about methods of astronomical research.

19.5   Briggs, Carole S. **Research Balloons: Exploring Hidden Worlds.** Lerner, 1988. 64 pp. ISBN 0-8225-1585-7.

The author tells many stories of scientists using balloons for exploring space, predicting weather conditions, and studying the earth from afar. She starts with the story of the first balloon flight in 1783. Did you know its passengers were a sheep, a duck, and a rooster?

19.6   Cobb, Vicki. **Science Experiments You Can Eat.** Harper and Row/Trophy, 1989. 127 pp. ISBN 0-46-4460029.

How much moisture is in your popcorn? What food does yeast bacteria need to grow? What are the values of random sampling in a science experiment? Is honey more or less "hygroscopic" than sugar? And what is it about an egg yolk that is so important when making mayonnaise? These are just some of the questions answered in this upbeat science book. The experiments are explained well, and most of the ingredients are common items you can find in the kitchen or at a grocery store. Originally published in hardback in 1972.

19.7   Cobb, Vicki, and Kathy Darling. **Bet You Can: Science Possibilities to Fool You.** Illustrated by Stella Ormai. Greenwillow Books, 1990. 112 pp. ISBN 0-688-09865-7.

This book makes science fun—it's full of tricks that you can use to entertain and amaze your friends. Tricks include holding a friend on the ground with a thread, hanging a spoon from the end of your nose, and lifting water in an upside-down glass. But unlike a magician's tricks, there is a scientific explanation of how each of these tricks works. This book won the New York Academy of Science's Children's Book Award.

19.8   Donnelly, Judy, and Sydelle Kramer. **Space Junk: Pollution beyond the Earth.** Morrow Junior Books, 1990. 96 pp. ISBN 0-688-08679-9.

The notion of someone owning the moon used to be just an amusing idea, but today people are very serious about it. But even more important than the question of who owns space is the question of who's in charge of keeping it clean. Objects in space travel faster than they do in an atmosphere, so if something collides with a spaceship, there is a lot more damage than you would expect. For instance, in 1983 a chip of paint so tiny it would hardly be visible to the naked eye crashed into the window of the

Challenger and made a pea-sized pit. The window would surely have broken had it been hit by the glove that Ed White dropped on the first American space walk or the camera Michael Collins lost as he floated near *Gemini 10* or the bags of garbage, used-up space-walk equipment, and old weather and TV satellites that have been accumulating in space over the last twenty-five years.

19.9   Embry, Barbara, with Tom D. Crouch. **The Dream Is Alive: A Flight of Discovery aboard the Space Shuttle.** Harper Collins/ Trade Division, 1990. 64 pp. ISBN 0-06-021814-2.

The Smithsonian Institute and the Lockheed Company cooperated to make *The Dream Is Alive*, a film about flying in a space shuttle. This book is based on that film and the oversize, full-color pictures bring it home to you. Just as fascinating as the contemporary photographs of real astronauts doing real work are the old drawings showing how hundreds of years ago, people dreamed about space ships and flying to the moon. ★

19.10   Gatland, Kenneth. **The Illustrated Encyclopedia of Space Technology,** second edition. Crown/Orion Books, 1989. 303 pp. ISBN 0-517-57427-6.

The many full-color photos and drawings in this reference book make it especially interesting for skimming as well as for studying. It begins in the 1800s with space pioneers from around the world and continues through to spaceships to Mars. A useful time line at the back of the book goes from 1879 to 1989. The whole book shows that Mark Twain was right when he said, "The man with a new idea is a crank—until the idea succeeds."

19.11   Haines, Gail Kay. **Micromysteries: Stories of Scientific Detection.** Dodd, Mead, 1988. 143 pp. ISBN 0-396-09000-1.

You'll feel the excitement of discovery through this author's well-written accounts of such famous scientific discoveries as insulin, radium, and vulcanized rubber. In addition to these older stories, she writes about new discoveries, including Barbara McClintock's work with genetics and Paul Chu's work with superconductors.

19.12   Harrar, George. **Radical Robots: Can You Be Replaced?** Simon and Schuster, 1990. 48 pp. ISBN 0-671-69420-0.

This book assures you that people are not going to be replaced by robots, as you can tell from the three chapter headings, "Why Robots Can't Tie Shoelaces but Can Go to Mars," "Memorizing the Encyclopedia Doesn't Make You Intelligent," and "If Computers Are So Smart, How Come They Didn't Invent Artificial Intelligence?" The book is based on the "Nova" science series on public television.

19.13   Harris, Alan, and Paul Weissman. **The Great Voyager Adventure: A Guided Tour through the Solar System.** Julian Messner, 1990. 80 pp. ISBN 0-671-72538-6.

In the late 1970s, all four of the giant planets, Jupiter, Saturn, Uranus, and Neptune, were aligned as they wouldn't be again for 175 years. Scientists took advantage of this fortunate situation by building and launching the Voyager space probe to photograph these distant planets. This fully illustrated, colorful book tells the story of the hundreds of people who worked together to bring off one of the greatest scientific accomplishments of the twentieth century.

19.14   Jespersen, James, and Jane Fitz-Randolph. **Looking at the Invisible Universe.** Atheneum, 1990. 152 pp. ISBN 0-689-31457-4.

This book talks about whether astronomy is really a science, since astronomers cannot really experiment on the universe. Then it discusses the new tools which allow us to probe the universe, like the radio telescope that has revolutionized the study of outer space and allows us to examine collapsing stars, colliding galaxies, and black holes.

19.15   Kelch, Joseph W. **Small Worlds: Exploring the Sixty Moons of Our Solar System.** Julian Messner, 1990. 160 pp. ISBN 0-671-70013-8.

This book starts with our own moon and then talks about the moons of Mars, Jupiter, Saturn, Uranus, Neptune, and Pluto. The concluding chapter looks at a few billion more "small worlds," that is, asteroids and comets. The book ends with a checklist of moons and an index. Most of these hard-to-get photos are in black and white, but an eight-page color insert adds to the overall appeal of the book.

19.16   Lauber, Patricia. **Seeing Earth from Space.** Orchard Books, 1990. 80 pp. ISBN 0-531-08502-3.

The beautiful pictures in this book are surprisingly varied, ranging from circles of irrigated land in Saudi Arabia and Kansas to lonely sand dunes in southwestern Algeria. The Grand Canyon looks like a scar winding its way across Arizona, while the Mississippi River looks like a squiggle of blue paint squeezed from an artist's tube. The author is a prize-winning science writer, and she does a good job of making complex concepts understandable. ★★★★★

19.17   Lauber, Patricia. **Voyagers from Space: Meteors and Meteorites.** Illustrated by Mike Eagle. Thomas Y. Crowell, 1989. 74 pp. ISBN 0-690-04634-0.

Imagine sitting in your living room watching television when the house suddenly rocks and a loud noise is followed by crashing and splintering sounds and three sharp thumps. You think you have been bombed and dial 911. Police and firefighters arrive and discover a meteorite lying quietly under the dining room table. This is exactly what happened to the Donahue family on November 8, 1982, in Wethersfield, Connecticut. But don't hold your breath waiting for this to happen to you because in all of history, only fifteen houses are known to have been damaged by meteorites. This book, illustrated with photos and drawings, offers many other fascinating facts about meteorites.

19.18   Macaulay, David. **The Way Things Work: From Levers to Lasers, Cars to Computers—a Visual Guide to the World of Machines.** Illustrated by the author. Houghton Mifflin, 1988. 384 pp. ISBN 0-395-42857-2.

Artist and author David Macaulay makes technology less intimidating through his wonderfully illustrated chapters on "The Mechanics of Movement," "Harnessing the Elements," "Working with Waves," and "Electricity and Automation." From a simple explanation of levers, he makes the connection to how pianos and manual typewriters work, using detailed drawings along the way. He takes you from an understanding of thermostats to an understanding of how heat is used to make liquid fuel rockets work, and he even shows how memory in a microcomputer works and how the mouse moves information. ★★★★

19.19   Maurer, Richard. **Airborne: The Search for the Secret of Flight.** Simon and Schuster, 1990. 48 pp. ISBN 0-671-69422-7.

The flights talked about in this book range from something as exciting and dangerous as hang gliding to something as simple and fun as making your own hot air balloon using tissue paper and an ordinary blow-dryer. This history of flight starts way before the Wright brothers, and you'll see that it's not just a coincidence that two bicycle experts became the first ones to build and fly an airplane—and to steer it. The book is based on the "Nova" science series on public television.

19.20 Maurer, Richard. **Junk in Space.** Simon and Schuster, 1989. 48 pp. ISBN 0-671-67768-3.

Thousands of pieces of litter—including a camera, a toothbrush, a spy station, and the bodies of huge rockets—are circling the earth, many of them at speeds seven times faster than a rifle bullet. This book discusses the problem of space junk, showing how a collision in space, even with just a screw or a chip of paint, could be disastrous to one of the 300 working satellites that are presently in orbit. This fact-filled book includes full-color pictures and references to such fanciful books as *The Little Prince* and *Twenty Thousand Leagues under the Sea.* Based on the "Nova" television series.

19.21 Moeschl, Richard. **Exploring the Sky: 100 Projects for Beginning Astronomers.** Chicago Review Press, 1988. 288 pp. ISBN 1-55652-039-5.

Projects, some of them easy and some difficult, are spread throughout this introduction to the universe. You can either browse or read this book, but if you do the projects as you read the book, you will understand the information better and remember it longer. Subjects covered are as easy to understand as sundials and as complicated as the big bang theory.

19.22 Tchudi, Stephen. **Probing the Unknown: From Myth to Science.** Charles Scribner's Sons, 1990. 146 pp. ISBN 0-684-19086-9.

Stephen Tchudi dedicates his book to "noodle users everywhere." It's a book for people who like to use their heads to figure out not only what is happening, but why it's happening. Tchudi praises people who throughout history have created stories to explain natural phenomena, and he ties these historical explanations to modern questions that "noodle users" are interested in. Boxed questions or suggestions under the heading "Probing on Your Own" appear in each section and encourage you to become involved in what the book has to say.

19.23   Walpole, Brenda. **175 Science Experiments to Amuse and Amaze Your Friends.** Illustrated by Kuo Kang Chen and Peter Bull. Random House, 1988. 172 pp. ISBN 0-394-89991-1.

These experiments, which really are amusing and amazing, are divided into four types—those involving water, air, movement, and light. Full-color photos and illustrations help you follow the step-by-step instructions. Most of the experiments can be done with household items, and only a few are dangerous enough that you will need an adult around when you do them. Quizzes at the end of each section and a glossary of scientific terms make this book a good way to learn about science.

19.24   Weiss, Harvey. **Submarines and Other Underwater Craft.** Thomas Y. Crowell, 1990. 64 pp. ISBN 0-690-04761-4.

Among the chapters in this informative book are "How a Submarine Works," "Keeping the Peace," "Hide and Seek," "The Nuclear-Powered Submarine," "Disasters," and "Underwater Treasures." Every page has either a photograph or a drawing to help explain all about submarines, from their beginnings in the American Revolution to today's technologically sophisticated models.

19.25   Whitney, Charles A. **Whitney's Star Finder.** Alfred A. Knopf, 1989. 105 pp. ISBN 0-679-72582-2.

This updated guide for stargazers covers the years 1990 through 1995. It gives such basic information as how to find the North Star, how to tell time by the position of the sun and stars, how to distinguish between a star and a planet, and how to find the constellations of the zodiac. One section tells you how to catch such unusual occurrences as sunspots, aurorae, rainbows, haloes, comets, and meteors. A "Star Finder Wheel" and a "Pop-Up Sky" are extra features.

20 Natural Sciences

20.1   Baldwin, J., editor. **Whole Earth Ecolog: The Best Environmental Tools and Ideas.** Crown/Harmony Books, 1990. 128 pp. ISBN 0-517-57658-9.

This book grew out of *The Whole Earth Catalog*, published twenty years ago, which gave descriptions of nearly everything designed to help people deal with problems of ecology. There are so many things available, however, that they can no longer be gathered together in one book. So instead, this book describes the best and most helpful of them. ★

20.2   Bornstein, Sandy. **What Makes You What You Are: A First Look at Genetics.** Illustrated and edited by Jane Steltenpohl. Julian Messner, 1989. 114 pp. ISBN 0-671-68650-X.

Why are you tall or short? Why do you have curly or straight hair? Why are some people's eyes blue while others are brown? These are the kinds of questions the author discusses in this straightforward explanation of genetics. Charts, illustrations, and do-it-yourself experiments add interest.

20.3   Dowden, Anne Ophelia. **The Clover and the Bee: A Book of Pollination.** Illustrated by the author. Thomas Y. Crowell, 1990. 90 pp. ISBN 0-690-04679-0.

This book offers beautifully drawn and painted illustrations, as well as an informative text. Once you've read this book, you'll look with new appreciation at the flowers and insects that abound in most of our neighborhoods. You'll be aware of the complex, fascinating process of pollination that the author describes in detail. ★

20.4   Downer, John. **Supersense: Perception in the Animal World.** Photographs by the author. Henry Holt, 1989. 160 pp. ISBN 0-8050-1087-4.

This book was created by the producer of the successful nature television series "Supersense." Beautiful pictures add interest, but the book's main value is in its many fascinating facts and theories, which go way beyond what newspapers tell us about animals sensing earthquakes, the purpose of an animal's whiskers, and how lost animals get back home.

20.5   Gay, Kathlyn. **Silent Killers: Radon and Other Hazards.** Franklin Watts, 1988. 128 pp. ISBN 0-531-10598-9.

Here are the stories of the disasters at Bhopal in India, Chernobyl in Russia, and Love Canal in the United States. Along with them, you'll learn about more common hazards, including asbestos, carbon monoxide, radon gas, and other chemical poisoning and contamination. Fortunately, the author includes sound information on prevention and cleanup so that you won't come away afraid to breathe the air or drink the water.

20.6   Hadingham, Evan, and Janet Hadingham. **Garbage! Where It Comes From, Where It Goes.** Simon and Schuster, 1990. 48 pp. ISBN 0-671-69424-3.

Much of the garbage strewn by scientists over a bay at McMurdo Sound, a research base in Antarctica, will last forever because of the extreme cold. This book talks about that problem and many other problems with getting rid of garbage. One note of optimism in this generally depressing book is that in 1988, over half of the aluminum cans sold in America were gathered for recycling. The book is based on the "Nova" television series and is full of informative, high-quality photographs.

20.7   Hecht, Jeff. **Shifting Shores: Rising Seas, Retreating Coastlines.** Charles Scribner's Sons, 1990. 151 pp. ISBN 0-684-19087-7.

When Jeff Hecht was eleven years old, his family moved to Longport, New Jersey, a small beach town near Atlantic City. His house was only a block and a half from the ocean, and he was fascinated when he discovered that the streets in Longport started at Eleventh Street because since the town's founding in the late 1800s, the ocean had claimed First through Tenth Streets. Ever since this discovery, Hecht has watched the interplay between land and water, and this book is the result of his lifetime of study and observations.

20.8   Heinrich, Bernd. **An Owl in the House: A Naturalist's Diary.** Adapted by Alice Calaprice. Little, Brown, 1990. 119 pp. ISBN 0-316-35456-2.

Bernd Heinrich, a professor of zoology at the University of Vermont, found a baby great horned owl buried in the snow. He "felt a moment of kinship with the owlet and instinctively reached out to protect it." Because he is a scientist, he was able to get a permit to raise the owl, a protected species, in his home. He kept a diary, or field notebook, filled with anecdotes, photographs, and incidents from more than two years of daily life. This unusual book is the published version of it.

20.9   Herberman, Ethan. **The Great Butterfly Hunt: The Mystery of the Migrating Monarchs.** Simon and Schuster, 1990. 48 pp. ISBN 0-671-69427-8.

Most of us have seen orange and gold monarch butterflies, but only a few of us have seen them by the hundreds or thousands as they make their annual migration. Where they're going and how they know which direction to go in are among the great mysteries of science. This book, taken from the "Nova" public television series, explores those mysteries and tells about the hundreds of "detectives," including many young people, who have helped to track the butterfly and solve at least part of this fascinating puzzle.

20.10   Jurmain, Suzanne. **Once upon a Horse: A History of Horses and How They Shaped Our History.** Lothrop, Lee and Shepard Books, 1989. 176 pp. ISBN 0-688-05550-8.

As the author says on the first page, "Although most people don't realize it, one of the most important characters in human history had four legs, a mane, and a tail." She goes on to show how for 6,000 years horses have aided humans in changing the world. This book is illustrated with drawings, photos, and etchings. ★

20.11   Lang, Aubrey. **Eagles.** Photographs by Wayne Lynch. Sierra Club Wildlife Library, 1990. 64 pp. ISBN 0-316-51387-3.

The photographs in this book show the many different faces of the "king of birds." Around the world, people have revered various species of eagles—the ancient Assyrians thought the eagle was a god; Persian and Roman armies carried banners with eagles on them; and when our astronauts reached the moon, Neil Armstrong announced, "The eagle has landed." This beautifully illustrated book gives basic information about where and how eagles live, the dangers they now face, and what their future might hold.

20.12 Lasky, Kathryn. **Dinosaur Dig.** Illustrated by Christopher G. Knight. Greenwillow Books, 1990. 65 pp. ISBN 0-688-08575-X.

One summer, Kathryn Lasky's and Christopher Knight's family travelled to the Montana Badlands where they dug for dinosaur bones. If you are ready to go beyond thinking of dinosaurs as cartoon characters, you will be interested in this true account of uncovering bones that have been hidden in the ground for millions of years. ★

20.13 Lasky, Kathryn. **Traces of Life: The Origins of Human Kind.** Illustrated by Whitney Powell. William Morrow, 1990. 144 pp. ISBN 0-688-07237-2.

This book traces the research of six well-known paleoanthropologists—people who dig up fossils and bones in order to try to understand the development of prehistoric people. The questions of how and why the path of human beings became separate from that of the apes about 5 million years ago is the focus of this work, although the book does not present any certain answers. Illustrations show you clearly how the search and recovery process at excavation sites works and also outline the ape-to-human stages of development.

20.14 Lawrence, R. D. **Wolves.** Sierra Club Wildlife Library, 1990. 64 pp. ISBN 0-316-51676-7.

The goal of this Sierra Club book is to engender respect for nature and for the place of the wolf in the overall picture. Every page has a drawing or photograph, making the book more than just an information source.

20.15 Mallory, Kenneth, and Andrea Conley. **Rescue of the Stranded Whales.** Simon and Schuster, 1989. 63 pp. ISBN 0-671-67122-7.

In the winter of 1986, three young whales, affectionately named Baby, Tag, and Notch, stranded themselves on the beach of Cape Cod. In a major scientific undertaking, members of the New England Aquarium's Animal Care Center rescued the beached whales, nursed them back to health, and successfully returned them to the waters of the Atlantic Ocean.

20.16 Oliver, A. P. H. **The Henry Holt Guide to Shells of the World.** Illustrated by James Nicholls. Henry Holt, 1989. 320 pp. ISBN 0-850-1119-6.

Even though *gastropoda*, *bivalvia*, *scaphopoda*, and *monoplaco-phora* sound like diseases, they're not. They are classes of animals with shells, and this book shows that classification is essential for the study of animals and plants. It explains that animals that produce shells belong to the phylum Mollusca and gives subclassifications that further group animals with shells. Maps locate frequent sites where shells are found, and color illustrations show what over 1,000 types look like. Originally published in England in 1975.

20.17   Patent, Dorothy Hinshaw. **How Smart Are Animals?** Harcourt Brace Jovanovich, 1990. 189 pp. ISBN 0-15-236770-5.

This book is dedicated to all the animals that have helped us learn about how their minds work. The opening chapters discuss general concepts about thinking, learning, and intelligence so that you learn about both human and animal thinking processes. Then more specific chapters focus on birds, dogs, monkeys, apes, gorillas, chimpanzees, and finally dolphins and sea lions. The book concludes with a chapter that brings all the information together to help you understand animal intelligence.

20.18   Patent, Dorothy Hinshaw. **Seals, Sea Lions and Walruses.** Holiday House, 1990. 88 pp. ISBN 0-8234-0834-5.

In 1956 the birthrate of northern fur seals fell to only 40 percent of what it had been a few years earlier. This is only one of the mysteries discussed in this book about the relationship between humans and seals, sea lions, and walruses. Excellent black-and-white photographs, a glossary, and a cross listing of scientific and common names add to the usefulness of the book.

20.19   Patent, Dorothy Hinshaw. **The Whooping Crane: A Comeback Story.** Photographs by William Munoz. Clarion Books, 1988. 88 pp. ISBN 0-89919-455-9.

From a population of only twenty-one in the year 1941, the number of whooping cranes has grown to almost 200 in the late 1980s. Both the photos and the writing make this history of the "whooper" interesting reading.

20.20   Pettit, Jayne. **Amazing Lizards.** Scholastic, 1990. 55 pp. ISBN 0-590-43682-1.

An insert of color photographs in the middle of this paperback helps you appreciate the uniqueness of each of the five different types of lizards whose habits, characteristics, and environments are discussed.

20.21   Pringle, Laurence. **Global Warming: Assessing the Greenhouse Threat.** Arcade, 1990. 46 pp. ISBN 1-55970-012-2.

This book's fourteen brief chapters and dozens of full-color pictures treat such topics as the greenhouse effect, what rising seas will do to the world, how weather patterns are likely to change, and what steps we can take to adapt to a warmer world. The book ends with the chapters "Conflict or Cooperation?" and "The Greatest Challenge."

20.22   Reader's Digest Editors. **The Reader's Digest Illustrated Book of Dogs,** revised edition. Reader's Digest Association, 1989. 384 pp. ISBN 0-89577-340-6.

The part of this book that most readers turn to is the "Album of Dogs," which includes a full-color illustration, history, set of characteristics, list of home countries, and any especially interesting information for each of many different kinds of dogs. For instance, it tells why the Neapolitan Mastiff sometimes has cropped ears and how the breed nearly became extinct. Other sections include basic information about dogs in general and about kennel clubs, how to care for dogs, and how to recognize health problems.

20.23   Rifkin, Jeremy, editor. **The Green Lifestyle Handbook: 1001 Ways You Can Heal the Earth.** Henry Holt/Owl Books, 1990. 200 pp. ISBN 0-8050-1369-5.

This book is aimed at adult readers, but it's an interesting resource that you may like to skim through and read parts of. In particular, the notes in the margins offer you little known but fascinating facts, such as the fact that film, records, and even bone china contain gelatins and other slaughterhouse byproducts, and that it takes as much water to produce a pound of steak as a typical household uses in a whole month.

20.24   Sattler, Helen Roney. **The Book of Eagles.** Illustrated by Jean Day Zallinger. Lothrop, Lee and Shepard Books, 1989. 64 pp. ISBN 0-688-07022-1.

The first half of this informative book is divided into five chapters: "Lords of the Skies," "Magnificent Hunters," "Courting and Nesting," "Baby Eagles," and "Humans: Friends or Foes?" The last half is a glossary giving basic information and an illustration for each of sixty-seven species of eagles.

20.25   Sattler, Helen Roney. **Giraffes, the Sentinels of the Savannahs.** Illustrated by Christopher Santoro. Lothrop, Lee and Shepard Books, 1990. 80 pp. ISBN 0-688-08285-8.

Giraffes are the tallest animals in the world, and from their lofty height, they look out on the world that their bodies have adapted to over thousands of years. This book presents scientific information as well as illustrations that give you a feeling of wonder about giraffes. ★★

20.26   Sattler, Helen Roney. **Hominids: A Look Back at Our Ancestors.** Illustrated by Christopher Santoro. Lothrop, Lee and Shepard Books, 1988. 125 pp. ISBN 0-688-06061-7.

If you're fascinated with mysteries, here's a different kind of "mystery story." The author shows how anthropologists take the tiniest clues and use them to piece together information about prehistoric people, including what they ate, what they wore, and what they did. ★

20.27   Savage, Candace. **Wolves.** Sierra Club Books, 1989. 159 pp. ISBN 0-87156-689-3.

David Mech, who writes the foreword to this oversized book, has studied wolves for thirty years. When he first began giving talks about wildlife years ago, he had to explain the word "ecology," but now nearly everyone is familiar with it. This change in education and thinking makes this book praising wolves and seeking to understand them and their place in the world possible. Even if you don't read every page, you'll enjoy the full-color photos, many of which were taken with telescopic lenses so that you can see the animals closer up than you could in real life.

20.28   Stafford-Deitsch, Jeremy. **Shark: A Photographer's Story.** Sierra Club Books, 1988. 200 pp. ISBN 0-87156-733-4.

Author and photographer Jeremy Stafford-Deitsch began learning about sharks when he started scuba diving at age thirteen. But his dream to dive with sharks was not fulfilled until years later. His account of this first, nearly fatal dive makes exciting reading. The author's conversational style brings his adventures to life and allows you to understand the respect and love he feels for sharks and his desire to protect them. The full-color underwater photographs are a bonus in this well-researched and informative book.

20.29 Staple, Michele, and Linda Gamlin. **The Random House Book of 1001 Questions and Answers about Animals.** David McKay, 1990. 159 pp. ISBN 0-679-90731-9.

Sections in this large, fully illustrated book include "The Animal Kingdom," "Soft-bodied Animals," "Insects," "Other Invertebrates," "Fishes," "Reptiles and Amphibians," "Birds," "Mammals," "Where Animals Live," "Animals in Danger," and a chapter for miscellaneous questions called "Who, What, Where, When, Why, How?" Each page has between four and eight boldfaced questions followed by their answers. The book is easy to skim, and the index will help you find information on particular animals.

20.30 Steger, Will, and Jon Bowermaster. **Saving the Earth: A Citizen's Guide to Environmental Action.** Illustrated by Mike Mikos. Alfred A. Knopf, 1990. 306 pp. ISBN 0-679-73026-5.

Will Steger decided to prepare this book of solutions to environmental problems after he saw how much money and effort was spent on the 1988 rescue of two whales trapped in ice in Alaska. If millions of people around the world were that interested and could join hands across countries to save two whales, then maybe there was hope for international cooperation in saving much more of the environment. This oversized book with lots of photos and drawings is divided into sections on the atmosphere, the land, the water, and people. It's an excellent resource for basic information, storyboard illustrations for public presentations, and addresses of environmental organizations.

20.31 Thomas, Peggy. **Keepers and Creatures at the National Zoo.** Photographs by Paul S. Conklin. Thomas Y. Crowell, 1988. 198 pp. ISBN 0-690-04712-6.

It would be impossible to get all the complexities of caring for the hundreds of animals at the National Zoo into a single book. However, this book provides a good sampling. Some chapters focus on particularly interesting animals, such as panda bears or orangutans, while others focus on procedures like starting the day at the zoo.

20.32 Whitfield, Philip. **Can the Whales Be Saved? Questions about the Natural World and the Threats to Its Survival Answered by the**

Natural History Museum. Viking Kestrel, 1989. 96 pp. ISBN 0-670-82753-3.

Illustrations on each page, many in full color, and clear questions make this a good book for either browsing or for reference. The questions range from "How do seashore animals stand being wet then dry?" to "Do the same animals live in the Arctic and the Antarctic?" to "Is the jungle noisy?"

20.33   Zipko, Stephen J. **Toxic Threat: How Hazardous Substances Poison Our Lives,** revised edition. Julian Messner, 1990. 249 pp. ISBN 0-671-69330-1.

The fourteen chapters of this book treat such problems as groundwater contamination, contamination from pesticides, disposal of hazardous substances, and acid rain. The most important chapter is the concluding one, "What You Can Do." It is followed by appendixes showing how to write effective letters, listing and briefly explaining federal laws, and giving names and addresses of environmental and science magazines, organizations, and agencies.

Series

20.34   **The Audubon Society Pocket Guides.** Alfred A. Knopf/Borzoi Sprinters.

These wonderful pocket guides really will fit in your pocket. They are printed on high-quality paper designed to last through real-life encounters with nature. Each double-page spread includes a full-color photo on one page, with basic information about the species pictured on the facing page. North American titles include *Familiar Butterflies, Familiar Marine Mammals, Familiar Mushrooms*, and *Familiar Seashore Creatures.*

20.35   **Earth Alert.** Crestwood House.

These forty-eight-page books are amply illustrated with full-color photos. They introduce you to ecological problems, give suggestions about what you can do, and cite sources for further reading. Titles include *Acid Rain, Drought, Endangered Species, The Ocean, The Ozone Layer, Pesticides*, and *Toxic Waste.*

20.36   **Eyewitness.** Alfred A. Knopf.

Titles in this prize-winning series include *Bird, Butterfly and Moth, Dinosaur, Early Humans, Mammal, Plant, Pond and*

River, *Rocks and Minerals*, *Seashore*, *Shell*, *Skeleton*, and *Tree*. In *Mammal*, it's tempting to reach out and touch the pages to pet the kitten or to see if the hedgehog will move; in *Dinosaur* the large photos are so clear that you can see where a hadrosaur had a cancerous tumor on its backbone and where a sauropod had small scales where its body had to be flexible for moving and larger scales where the skin was more stationary.

20.37   Nature Club. Troll Associates.

The five books in this series are easy to read and are illustrated with full-color drawings on each page. "Nature Club Notes" introduce the topics, which are then divided into short chapters. Titles include *Birds* by Peter Gill, *Insects* by Althea, *Ponds and Streams* by John Stidworthy, *Seashores* by Joyce Pope, and *Trees and Leaves* by Althea.

20.38   Our Planet. Troll Associates.

These thirty-two-page books are easy to read and have large, full-color drawings or photographs on every page. Each one ends with a fact file, giving over a dozen especially interesting pieces of information about its topic. Titles include *Forests* and *Weather* by David Lambert, *Deserts* and *Rivers* by Richard Stephen, and *Mountains* and *Volcanoes and Earthquakes* by Vrobova Zuza.

20.39   Our World. Silver Burdett Press.

Each two-page spread focuses on a single environmental topic, so these amply illustrated books are easy to skim. So far, titles include *Temperate Forests* by Basil Booth and *Pollution and Conservation* by Malcolm Penny.

20.40   Top Dog. Crestwood House.

Each book in this series features a particular breed of dog. Information includes the history of the dog, its unique characteristics, and how it's raised and trained. Nearly every page of these easy-to-read books has a full-color photograph. New titles include *The Beagle*, *The Cocker Spaniel*, *The Dachshund*, *The German Shepherd*, *The Golden Retriever*, *The Labrador Retriever*, *The Poodle*, and *The Siberian Husky*.

21 Social Studies: Contemporary Lives and Issues

21.1   Ammon, Richard. **Growing Up Amish.** Atheneum, 1989. 80 pp. ISBN 0-689-31387-X.

More and more in the United States, we're beginning to realize that not everyone wants to fit into the same mold. Richard Ammon's book shows how the Amish are among those who have chosen to be different, to keep their rural life-style, and to focus their lives around their religion and community. ★

21.2   Anderson, Joan. **The American Family Farm.** Photographs by George Ancona. Harcourt Brace Jovanovich, 1989. 96 pp. ISBN 0-15-203025-5.

The pictures by acclaimed photographer George Ancona tell as much as does the text by Joan Anderson in this book about three farm families. The MacMillans are dairy farmers in Massachusetts, the Adamses are co-op farmers in Georgia, and the Rosmanns are grain and hog farmers in Iowa. Although the three families and their work are all different, they share a dependence on the weather and a commitment to hard work. ★★★

21.3   Ashabranner, Brent. **Always to Remember: The Story of the Vietnam Veterans Memorial.** Photographs by Jennifer Ashabranner. G. P. Putnam's Sons, 1988. 40 pp. ISBN 0-396-09089-3.

This photo essay about the creation of the Vietnam Veterans Memorial illustrates how conflicts can be resolved. You will come away convinced that veteran Jan C. Scruggs's political efforts and architecture student Maya Ying Lin's design efforts were well worth the trouble. ★★★

21.4   Ashabranner, Brent. **Born to the Land: An American Portrait.** Photographs by Paul Conklin. G. P. Putnam's Sons, 1989. 134 pp. ISBN 0-399-21716-9.

Whether you live in the country, in a small town, or in a big city, the interviews in this book and the accompanying photographs will teach you a lot about what it means to belong to a community, to have your dreams and your future tied in with the past and the heritage of the land.

21.5   Ashabranner, Brent. **A Grateful Nation: The Story of Arlington National Cemetery.** Photographs by Jennifer Ashabranner. G. P. Putnam's Sons, 1990. 117 pp. ISBN 0-399-22188-3.

Whether or not you are planning a visit to Arlington Cemetery in Washington DC, this book with its sixty photographs makes interesting reading. Arlington is the world's busiest military cemetery, with 4,000 burials a year. You'll learn its history, what a typical day is like for visitors and workers, and what memorials and events make this such a special place for millions of Americans.

21.6   Bode, Janet. **New Kids on the Block: Oral Histories of Immigrant Teens.** Franklin Watts, 1989. 96 pp. ISBN 0-531-10794-9.

These "new kids on the block" are not the famous singers. They are eleven teenagers who talk about what it is like to have moved from other countries to the United States. An introductory paragraph tells about each kid's home country, but then the teenagers tell their own stories about why their families decided to immigrate and what it has been like trying to fit in as an American teen. ★

21.7   Burstein, Chaya M. **A Kid's Catalog of Israel.** Illustrated by the author. Jewish Publication Society, 1988. 279 pp. ISBN 0-8276-0263-4.

You might start by browsing this book, but you will probably be tempted to read the whole thing. It starts with a "walking tour" of Israel and goes on to give information about Israeli stories, crafts, food, geography, archaeology, and the Hebrew language. Comments from young Israelis bring life in Israel home to you and answer questions about differences from and similarities to your life here.

21.8   Cook, Fred J. **The Ku Klux Klan: America's Recurring Nightmare.** Julian Messner, 1989. 176 pp. ISBN 0-671-68421-3.

This history of prejudice and violence shows that while the old order of the Ku Klux Klan is no longer what it was, racism and bigotry are still very much alive. The concluding chapter, "The

Extremists," focuses on such new groups as neo-Nazis and Skinheads. Mature situations.

21.9   Cytron, Barry D. **Fire! The Library Is Burning.** Lerner, 1988. 56 pp. ISBN 0-8225-0525-8.

The story of the 1966 fire that burned the library of the Jewish Theological Seminary School in New York is a story of community heroism. Hundreds of volunteers removed thousands of books that were damaged by fire, smoke, and water. They placed paper towels between the pages while they laid others out to dry in the sun. Photos of the new library completed in 1983 provide a happy ending to this true account.

21.10   Evans, J. Edward. **Freedom of the Press.** Lerner, 1990. 72 pp. ISBN 0-8225-1752-3.

Both freedom of speech and freedom of the press are discussed in this book, which covers historical as well as current cases. Carol Burnett, for example, won a $1.6 million lawsuit against the *National Enquirer* because it claimed she was drunk in a Washington restaurant. The more than fifty photographs and illustrations add interest.

21.11   Evans, J. Edward. **Freedom of Religion.** Lerner, 1990. 88 pp. ISBN 0-8225-1754-X.

Most of us know that the first amendment to the United States Constitution guarantees religious freedom. But it's not so easy to understand just what that means, as you'll see in some of the cases described in this book. For example, in Wisconsin the Amish people had their own private schools through the eighth grade, but the state of Wisconsin ruled that their children needed to go to school through age 16. It tried to force the Amish children to attend public high schools, which is against their religion. Finally, the Supreme Court ruled in favor of the Amish. One of the other issues discussed is that of religious fraud, which is an especially big problem now that television evangelists and others who want to raise money can speak to millions of people at once. Perhaps the biggest questions of all are how we can define "religion" and how we can measure people's sincerity in their religious beliefs.

21.12   Fisher, Maxine P. **Women in the Third World.** Franklin Watts, 1989. 176 pp. ISBN 0-531-10666-7.

The advent of better medical care and new technologies means that women's lives are changing all around the world. But the changes are different in different countries, and that is the subject of this book. The author has taken studies and statistics and turned them into readable chapters, highlighted by personal accounts of "typical" women in Asian, Middle Eastern, and African countries.

21.13 Fleisher, Paul. **Understanding the Vocabulary of the Nuclear Arms Race.** Dillon Press, 1988. 192 pp. ISBN 0-87518-352-2.

With over 50,000 nuclear weapons in the world today, we hear about them every day on television and in the newspapers. Often the terms are confusing: What is DEFCON? How can a test ban treaty be "partial"? Where can you find the "missile gap"? The more than 300 entries in this book define the most important terms used to describe nuclear arms, the arms race, and arms-limitation agreements.

21.14 Gallant, Roy A. **The Peopling of Planet Earth: Human Population Growth through the Ages.** Macmillan, 1990. 163 pp. ISBN 0-02-735772-4.

That an African Bushman's idea of comfort is nothing like a Texas oil billionaire's is one of the points that Roy Gallant makes in this exploration of human origins, the growth of population centers, and connections between overpopulation and such disasters as famines and plagues. The concluding chapter, "Population and the Quality of Life," brings up many more questions than can presently be answered.

21.15 Gorman, Carol. **Pornography.** Illustrated and edited by Cris Rosoff. Franklin Watts, 1988. 127 pp. ISBN 0-531-10591-1.

The subject of pornography often brings guilty giggles and discomfort, but this author treats the topic straightforwardly, writing about its history, how it's defined, and how it relates to eroticism and obscenity. She discusses legal issues of censorship versus the rights of individuals, child pornography, mass media and big business involvement, and religious and moral views.

21.16 Haban, Rita D. **How Proudly They Wave: Flags of the Fifty States.** Lerner, 1989. 111 pp. ISBN 0-8225-1799-X.

A colorful state flag is the focus of attention in each two-page layout of this book. You'll learn some interesting facts about each of our fifty states and the flag that represents it. For instance,

Utah's first flag was handwoven from silk produced by silkworms raised in the homes of Utah pioneer women, it took Louisiana over 100 years after it became a state to decide on a flag, and only in 1957 did the state of Idaho come to a final agreement on a flag they had been using for fifty years.

21.17   Jacobs, William Jay. **Human Rights.** Charles Scribner's Sons, 1990. 272 pp. ISBN 0-684-19036-2.

The battle for civil rights started long before the 1960s, as this book shows in its thirty biographical articles that include accounts of the work of Jane Addams, Sojourner Truth, Chief Joseph, and Eleanor Roosevelt. The author made a special effort to include accounts of civil rights activities by women and members of minority groups, whose actions aren't always included in textbooks. The book is part of the Great Lives series.

21.18   Landau, Elaine. **Teenage Violence.** Julian Messner, 1990. 113 pp. ISBN 0-671-70153-3.

Are children who play with "action" toys more likely to participate in violence? Do sports such as football encourage spectators to become violent? What effects do drugs and drug dealing have on young people? And what has been the effect of modern systems of punishment and rehabilitation? These are just some of the questions that the author tries to answer in this look at a major problem facing our society: teenage violence.

21.19   Meltzer, Milton, editor. **The American Promise: Voices of a Changing Nation 1945–Present.** Bantam Books, 1990. 192 pp. ISBN 0-553-07020-7.

Many United States history classes begin with a discussion of America before Columbus "discovered" it, and then go on to talk about Plymouth Colony, the American Revolution, the westward expansion, the Civil War, the industrial revolution, and World Wars I and II. Then the end of the school year comes, and the class doesn't look beyond World War II. But this collection of photographs, letters, diaries, interviews, poems, songs, news stories, and excerpts from magazines and books is designed to take up where the history classes leave off. It treats the effects of the atomic bomb, the cold war with Russia, the wars in Korea and Vietnam, civil rights struggles, the youth revolt of the 1960s, the feminist movement, changes in immigration, our declining economy, and environmental concerns.

21.20 Meltzer, Milton. **The Bill of Rights: How We Got It and What It Means.** Thomas Y. Crowell, 1990. 179 pp. ISBN 0-690-04807-6.

Even though most Americans staunchly defend the Bill of Rights and say they believe in these first ten amendments to the Constitution, polls show that most Americans don't really know what is in the Bill of Rights or how its guarantees affect their everyday lives. This book sets out to correct that situation by showing where these rights came from historically and how they have been applied in American life over the past 200 years.

21.21 Meyer, Carolyn. **A Voice from Japan: An Outsider Looks In.** Harcourt Brace Jovanovich/Gulliver Books, 1988. 240 pp. ISBN 0-15-200633-8.

As a visitor to Japan, the author doesn't try to tell you everything there is to know about Japan, but she does talk about her own experiences and what she learned as she interviewed both Japanese and foreign teenagers living in Japan. Because the book focuses on teenagers, it's easy to see beyond some of the stereotypes perpetuated by newspaper articles and television programs featuring more traditional images of Japan and the Japanese.

21.22 Pascoe, Elaine. **Neighbors at Odds: U.S. Policy in Latin America.** Franklin Watts, 1990. 157 pp. ISBN 0-531-10902-8.

Among the many problems that we as a nation need to solve is how to have better relationships with Latin American countries. The author clarifies some of the problems involved and shows how they grow out of both historical and contemporary world conditions. She neither oversimplifies the situation nor takes sides on it, so you can come away with a new appreciation of one of the big challenges that now faces the United States. ★

21.23 Pringle, Laurence. **The Animal Rights Controversy.** Harcourt Brace Jovanovich, 1989. 112 pp. ISBN 0-15-203559-1.

As the author shows, there are no easy answers to such tough questions as whether farmers are being cruel to animals when they deny them exercise and natural food so that their meat will be more tender, or whether scientists are cruel when they use animals to test unknown drugs or when they inflict injuries on them to study healing processes. Is it right to wear a fur coat or to dissect a frog in biology class? How about going hunting or dropping off an unwanted pet in the wild? This book doesn't answer these questions, but it does present lots of different viewpoints to get you thinking about them.

21.24   Strom, Yale. **A Tree Still Stands: Jewish Youth in Eastern Europe Today.** Philomel Books, 1990. 112 pp. ISBN 0-399-22154-9.

It's easy to relate to the young Jewish people interviewed by Sonia Levitin for this book because each interview is accompanied by a couple of clear black-and-white photos. Before World War II, there were 5 million Jews in Eastern Europe. Today there are only 200,000, and one-fifth of these are children. The interviewer talks about history, religion, local attitudes, and lifestyles. The young people are mostly teenagers in East Germany, Czechoslovakia, Poland, Romania, Bulgaria, Yugoslavia, and Hungary.

21.25   Weiss, Ann E. **Prisons: A System in Trouble.** Enslow, 1988. 160 pp. ISBN 0-89490-165-6.

"Out of sight, out of mind" is no way to approach the problem of criminal justice. The author shows why such an attitude is disastrous for society at large as well as for individuals, who often come out of prison with more destructive behavior problems than they had when they went in. Solving this problem is one of the biggest challenges society faces, and this book, especially the sections on experimental programs, is a good source of thought-provoking information.

21.26   Weiss, Harvey. **Shelters: From Teepee to Igloo.** Thomas Y. Crowell, 1988. 76 pp. ISBN 0-690-04533-0.

Besides the shelters mentioned in the title, the author explains and illustrates with drawings the making of Bedouin tents, yurts, log cabins, geodesic domes, Indian pueblos, and oriental houses. He discusses the environmental impact of different kinds of shelters and gives brief histories of them to show a relationship between life-style and home structure.

21.27   Wolfson, Evelyn. **From Abenaki to Zuni: A Dictionary of Native American Tribes.** Illustrated by William Sauts Bock. Walker, 1988. 215 pp. ISBN 0-8027-6790-7.

Abenaki, Havasupi, Pequot, and Yokut are among the sixty-eight Native American tribes described in this dictionary. Each entry contains a brief description of a tribe's life-style: where they live, their villages and houses, food, clothing, means of travel, and religion. Following each listing is a comparison between the historic and contemporary ways of life in these complex societies. The book includes drawings, a glossary, a selected bibliography, maps of language families and cultural areas, and a list of books for further reading.

21.28   Yue, Charlotte, and David Yue. **The Igloo.** Houghton Mifflin, 1988. 107 pp. ISBN 0-395-44613-9.

How *do* people live in those houses of ice called igloos? Why don't the fires built inside melt the ice? The answers to these and many other questions are found in this book about igloos, the Eskimos who live in them, and the harsh life above the Arctic Circle. Pencil drawings on almost every page enhance the clarity of the explanations, and the book is indexed for easy reference.

Series

21.29   **Downtown America Books.** Dillon Press.

Salt Lake City by Becky Ayres and *San Diego* by Karen O'Connor are two of the newest titles in this series that introduces you to nearly thirty of the most interesting cities in the United States. The books all start with chapters called "Fast Facts about . . ." and end with chapters called "Places to Visit in . . . ." They each include time lines of the cities' histories as well. In between these are brief chapters focusing on the unique characteristics of each city. Nearly every page has a full-color photograph.

21.30   **Economics for Today.** Lerner.

Economics and the Consumer by Barbara M. Killen is the first title in this new series which tries to show that economics is not something that, like the weather, just happens. The series also tries to show that economics doesn't only concern faraway politicians. Killen's book brings economic questions close to home and shows how our decisions as buyers and our expectations as citizens affect the economy. An especially interesting chapter is the one on technology, which shows how machines are changing the way we handle money.

21.31   **The Facts About.** Crestwood House.

This easy-to-read series about current issues now has thirty-two titles. The books have forty-eight pages each with a full-color photo on almost every two-page spread. New titles include *The*

*Facts about Animal Rights, The Facts about Leukemia, The
Facts about Rape*, and *The Facts about Transplants.*

21.32   In America. Lerner.

These books give historical information about particular ethnic
groups in America, showing the emerging roles each is playing,
and concluding with sections on their contributions to American
life. Photos appear on every page. More than thirty-two groups
are treated in the series; sample titles include *The Japanese in
America, The Vietnamese in America, The Norwegians in
America*, and *The Puerto Ricans in America.*

21.33   Issues for the 90s. Julian Messner.

Managing Toxic Wastes and *The War on Terrorism*, both by
Michael Kronenwetter, and *The Poor in America* by Suzanne
Coil are among the titles in this series, which does more than just
introduce its topics. *The War on Terrorism*, for example, begins
with the 1972 Olympic Games in Munich, Germany, when the
world watched in horror as a new kind of warfare was played out
before the television cameras that were there to cover the games.
What they filmed instead was young Palestinians killing young
Jews and then the German government killing both in a botched
rescue attempt. Kronenwetter shows how terrorism differs from
conventional warfare, why it is so successful, and what can be
done to control it. New titles in the series include Michael
Kronenwetter's *Drugs in America: The Users, the Suppliers, the
War on Drugs* and Daniel Jussim's *Medical Ethics: Moral and
Legal Conflicts in Health Care.*

21.34   People and Places. Silver Burdett Press.

Full color photos and / or drawings help illustrate each of the two-
page spreads devoted to such topics as government, religion,
foods, history, home life, and predictions for the future of each
country discussed. Titles include *The Caribbean* by Anthony
Mason, *Central America* by Marion Morrison, *Ireland* by Neil
Grant, *Pakistan and Bangladesh* by Susan Brown, and *Spain* by
Marilyn Tolhurst.

21.35   Places in the News. Crestwood House.

These easy-to-read introductions to countries that you see
mentioned in newspaper headlines and featured on television are
fully illustrated with color photographs. Titles include *China,*

Germany, Lebanon, Panama, Northern Ireland, Poland, South Africa, and *The Soviet Union*. Gail B. Stewart is the author.

21.36   Portraits of the Nations. J. B. Lippincott.

High-quality photos and clear writing make these books good sources for getting information about other countries. The books open with a map of the world, showing where the country to be covered is located, and a two-page spread of "Mini Facts" about that country. At the end, helpful bibliographies give sources the authors used and provide suggestions for further reading, both of fiction and nonfiction. Titles include *The Land and People of South Africa* by Alan Paton, *The Land and People of Afghanistan* by Mary Louis Clifford, *The Land and People of Argentina* by Geoffrey Fox, *The Land and People of Finland* by Patricia Lander and Claudette Charbonneau, and *The Land and People of France* by Jonathan Harris.★

21.37   Think. Walker.

Focusing on current events, the authors in this series define the issues and present background information on the problems they examine. They present alternative viewpoints and speculate on the future but steer clear of offering simplistic solutions to these complex problems. Bibliographies and sources of further information are included. Titles so far include *Foreign Policy: The U.S. and the World, Immigration Diversity in the U.S.*, and *Nuclear Arms Control: Understanding the Arms Race*.

21.38   Visual Geography. Lerner.

Every page of the seventy-seven books in this series is illustrated, most of the time with full-color photographs. The books introduce you to the living conditions, natural resources, religions, food, and politics of many countries of the world. Boldface headings and clear-cut organization make the books good for either leisure reading or for finding specific information.

22   History

22.1   Adler, David A. **We Remember the Holocaust.** Henry Holt, 1989. 147 pp. ISBN 0-8050-0434-3.

This book, based on the first-person reports of survivors, is an easy-to-read account of the Holocaust. It gives a real sense of the horror of being a European Jew before, during, and after Hitler's reign. The many photographs add to the book's impact.

22.2   Anderson, David. **The Spanish Armada.** Franklin Watts/Hampstead Press, 1988. 47 pp. ISBN 0-531-19505-8.

This clearly written book sorts facts from myths about the great sea battle between England and Spain that in the year 1588 changed the direction of world history. Author David Anderson cites the findings of underwater archaeologists who have found shipwrecks and other evidence on the ocean floor. Their methods not only provide new information but inspire new interest in sea history.

22.3   Armour, John, and Peter Wright. **Manzanar.** Photographs by Ansel Adams. Random House, 1989. 169 pp. ISBN 679-72275-0.

After the attack on Pearl Harbor in 1941, the United States government began putting Japanese Americans into concentration camps (which it called "relocation centers"). This book describes life in Manzanar, a camp in the California desert. It tells how the people there dealt with their situation by growing crops, sending their children to school, and even publishing a newspaper. Ansel Adams, one of the world's most famous photographers, got there in 1943. The book shows you his photo essay on Manzanar. It also includes commentary by John Hersey.

22.4   The Associated Press. **World War II: A Fiftieth Anniversary History.** Henry Holt, 1989. 320 pp. ISBN 0-8050-1095-5.

The best photos from the Associated Press add to the interest of this comprehensive history of World War II, which is a good source for solid information as well as for browsing and skimming. You'll get a real feel for the impact this war had on the generation that lived through it. Foreword by Harrison Salisbury.

22.5 Ballard, Robert D. **Exploring the Titanic: How the Greatest Ship Ever Lost Was Found.** Scholastic Hardcovers, 1988. 68 pp. ISBN 0-590-41953-6.

Robert Ballard led the French expedition that located the famous *Titanic,* which sank after striking an iceberg in 1912. In this latest book, Ballard returns to the depths with Jason, his tiny swimming robot, to explore and photograph the entire ship in detail. The robot even creeps through the black waters down the Grand Staircase to photograph the chandeliers, which still hang from the ceilings of the once-elegant ship. Artist Ken Marschall studied thousands of photographs before creating the paintings featured in this book. ★★

22.6 Blumberg, Rhoda. **The Great American Gold Rush.** Bradbury Press, 1989. 135 pp. ISBN 0-02-711681-6.

The years 1848–1852 were full of excitement for the thousands of men and hundreds of women who rushed to California in hopes of finding gold. This book tells and shows through photos and drawings, some reproduced from the period, how they came—on horseback, in wagons, in ships, and by foot—and who they were—both Americans and foreigners. Sources are documented and ideas given for further study, so this is a good book either for leisure reading or for doing research. ★★★★

22.7 Cooper, Michael. **Klondike Fever: The Famous Gold Rush of 1898.** Clarion Books, 1989. 80 pp. ISBN 0-89919-803-1.

More than sixty photos from the exciting pioneer times of the Gold Rush show that life before television, automobiles, and movies wasn't as limited as many of us might imagine.

22.8 David, Kati. **A Child's War: World War II through the Eyes of Children.** Avon Books, 1989. 210 pp. ISBN 0-380-71109-5.

The fear, hunger, hardship, and torture of living in war-torn Europe are told through the childhood memories of fifteen survivors of World War II. You get to see what it was like to live through the bombings, the scrounging for food, the separation of families, the hiding, and the ever-present threat of death from a variety of perspectives, including those of Jews, Nazis, resistance fighters, and ordinary families. An epilogue tells you briefly what happened to each person and his or her family after the war.

22.9   Faber, Doris, and Harold Faber. **The Birth of a Nation: The Early Years of the United States.** Charles Scribner's Sons, 1989. 197 pp. ISBN 0-684-19007-9.

This attractive new book covers the history of the United States from the time of George Washington's election as president until his farewell address. It was during this time that the Bill of Rights was adopted, political parties were formed, and departments were created in the executive branch of the government. But the authors don't treat just political developments; they also look at the social life of those who worked together to create the foundation of American democracy.

22.10   Finkelstein, Norman H. **The Other 1492: Jewish Settlement in the New World.** Charles Scribner's Sons, 1989. 100 pp. ISBN 0-684-18913-5.

The author uses the year 1492 (when "Columbus sailed the ocean blue") to help readers grasp the time period that he's writing about. Most of this book is about the persecution of Jews in Spain and Portugal and about their coming to South America and finally to New Amsterdam (now New York) in 1654. ★

22.11   Fisher, Leonard Everett. **Monticello.** Photographs and illustrations by the author and others. Holiday House, 1988. 64 pp. ISBN 0-8234-0688-1.

Thomas Jefferson, the architect, inventor, and statesman, is revealed through the home he designed, built, and named Monticello. This book about Thomas Jefferson's home is illustrated with photographs of the plans drawn by Jefferson in the late 1700s, photographs taken in the 1800s when the house had fallen into disrepair, and photographs showing how it looks today in its refurbished form. Of special interest are Jefferson's designs of dumbwaiters and mechanical doors.

22.12   Fisher, Leonard Everett. **The Oregon Trail.** Holiday House, 1990. 64 pp. ISBN 0-8234-0833-7.

During the 1840s and 1850s, thousands upon thousands of ambitious and brave pioneers crossed the Missouri River and started west along the Platte. After traveling through Nebraska and most of Wyoming, their trail split. While the Mormon pioneers went south to Utah and the gold seekers went southwest to California, most of the settlers stuck to the Oregon Trail and traveled north through Idaho up to the Pacific Northwest. The author uses paintings, photographs, and drawings from the period, along with quotes from diaries and letters, to tell these pioneers' story.

22.13   Fisher, Leonard Everett. **The Wailing Wall.** Illustrated by the author. Macmillan, 1989. 32 pp. ISBN 0-02-735310-9.

Leonard Fisher is an artist who seeks out important places in the world. He tells their stories and then makes them come to life through his drawings. In this book, he explains the importance to the Jews of the first and second temples in Israel and the remnant that now remains and is one of the most sacred spots in Jerusalem. ★

22.14   Fisher, Leonard Everett. **The White House.** Holiday House, 1989. 96 pp. ISBN 0-8234-0774-8.

Many excellent photographs help to bring the history of Washington D. C.'s White House alive, but it's the anecdotes, especially those about presidential children, that will make you want to read this book from cover to cover. ★

22.15   Freedman, Russell. **Buffalo Hunt.** Illustrated by George Catlin, Karl Bodmer, and others. Holiday House, 1988. 50 pp. ISBN 0-8234-0702-0.

The Native Americans of the Great Plains revered the buffalo as a sacred spirit, even while it was their main food source. When they killed a buffalo, every bit of it was used—right down to the tail, which was used as a flyswatter. Unlike the later slaughter by white people's guns, the Native Americans used clever and daring strategies in the hunt. Beautiful reproductions of early paintings allow readers to appreciate the size and magnificence of the vast herds that roamed the plains prior to the 1880s. ★★★

22.16   Hamanaka, Sheila. **The Journey: Japanese Americans, Racism, and Renewal.** Illustrated by the author. Orchard/Richard Jackson Books, 1990. 39 pp. ISBN 0-531-08449-3.

During World War II, many Japanese Americans were taken from their homes and sent to internment camps. This book includes its author's paintings along with her words to present a dramatic and yet simple account of the distressing experiences of those Japanese Americans. ★★★

22.17 Haskins, James, and Kathleen Benson. **The 60s Reader.** Viking, 1988. 244 pp. ISBN 0-670-80674-9.

If you've been wondering what was so different about the 1960s, here's a book of readings to show you just that. The readings are arranged under broad categories with clear introductions that will give you some perspective about this interesting period of American history. You might want to read this nonfiction account alongside such novels as Bruce Brooks's *Midnight Hour Encores*, Norma Fox Mazer's *Downtown*, Katherine Paterson's *Park's Quest*, and Bobbie Ann Mason's *In Country*, all centered around themes of the 1960s.

22.18 Hoffman, Yair. **The World of the Bible for Young Readers.** Edited by Ilana Shamir. Viking Kestrel, 1989. 96 pp. ISBN 0-670-81739-2.

Published first in Israel, each of the ten chapters in this beautiful book introduces and explains a period of ancient Middle Eastern history, beginning with Canaan and the Fertile Crescent and ending with the beginning of Christianity. Full-color pictures on all of the oversize pages make thumbing through the book almost like watching television.

22.19 Hoobler, Dorothy, and Thomas Hoobler. **Vietnam: Why We Fought.** Alfred A. Knopf/Borzoi Sprinters, 1990. 196 pp. ISBN 0-394-91943-2.

America's longest and most unpopular war is the subject of this well-written book for advanced readers. The introduction gives a time line of the war and an emotionally moving statement about the Vietnam Veterans Memorial in Washington, DC. Three parts follow the introduction—Part One gives the history of the war, which started long before most Americans had ever heard of Vietnam; Part Two talks about the United States' role in the war; and Part Three documents how the war ended and how Americans' views on the war have changed. A glossary, index, and suggestions for further reading make the book an even more helpful source of information.

22.20 Katz, William Loren. **Breaking the Chains: African-American Slave Resistance.** Atheneum, 1990. 184 pp. ISBN 0-689-31493-0.

The author shows what life was like for American slaves between the seventeenth century and the Civil War and goes on to answer such questions as: What were the economic and historical reasons behind the development of slavery? What kinds of personal struggles took place? And how did the concept of freedom for slaves change from an idea to a reality? ★★

22.21 Lawson, Dawn. **The Abraham Lincoln Brigade: Americans Fighting Fascism in the Spanish Civil War.** Thomas Y. Crowell, 1989. 149 pp. ISBN 0-690-04699-5.

From 1936 to 1939, the Spanish Civil War was raging. In Spain, thousands of loyalists were fighting against fascism and General Francisco Franco. In an effort to end the threat of a fascist military dictatorship, hundreds of young, brave American people volunteered their services to the International Brigades. These Americans were soon hailed as the Abraham Lincoln Brigade, and they battled for freedom in war-torn Spain against unbelievable obstacles. The story is a tribute to American heroism.

22.22 Marrin, Albert. **The War for Independence: The Story of the American Revolution.** Atheneum, 1988. 288 pp. ISBN 0-689-31390-X.

Albert Marrin retells the story of the American Revolution from its beginnings in the French and Indian War, the famous battle of Bunker Hill, and the Declaration of Independence to its end with the British surrender at Yorktown. In addition to descriptions of the events that are so important to American history, the author recounts the actions and motives of the patriots who carried them out. ★★★

22.23 McKissack, Patricia, and Frederick McKissack. **A Long Hard Journey: The Story of the Pullman Porter.** Walker, 1989. 144 pp. ISBN 0-8027-6885-7.

After the Civil War when the development of the Pullman sleeper car brought a touch of luxury to train travel, George Pullman decided that a good way to enhance the image of luxury was to hire freed slaves to wait on the passengers. This was the beginning of the tradition of having black porters. The authors tell the fascinating story of how this group eventually created the first major black labor union, the Brotherhood of Sleeping Car Porters. It's a story of heroes, including organizer A. Philip

Randolph, and also of ordinary workers and of the roles played
by their wives through the Women's Auxiliaries. ★★

22.24   Meltzer, Milton, editor. **Voices from the Civil War.** Thomas Y.
Crowell, 1989. 203 pp. ISBN 0-690-04802-5.

What was the Civil War really like? This book begins before the
war with photos, letters, diaries, and speeches of people who were
actually there. It includes accounts of blacks who escaped to the
North, eyewitness reports from battlegrounds and battleships,
and even the moving story of Lincoln's final hours, told by
someone who was present at his death. This book portrays the
bright ideals that pulled Americans into the struggle, as well as the
ugliness of the death, disease, prejudice, and destruction that
accompanied the war. ★

22.25   Murphy, Jim. **The Boys' War: Confederate and Union Soldiers
Talk about the Civil War.** Clarion Books, 1990. 110 pp. ISBN 0-
89919-893-7.

The ragtag nature of the Civil War is made vivid by this account,
which focuses on teenagers who were caught up in both Northern
and Southern patriotism and left their farms and homes to join
the army. One observer wrote about them that "the more they
serve, the less they look like soldiers and the more they resemble
day-laborers who have bought second-hand military clothes."
Nearly fifty historical photographs help bring the words to life.

22.26   Rappaport, Doreen. **American Women: Their Lives in Their
Words.** Thomas Y. Crowell, 1990. 317 pp. ISBN 0-690-04817-3.

Perhaps you've noticed that history books tend to focus on the
activities of men as they have led expeditions, explored new lands,
fought wars, and competed in politics. Instead, this book focuses
on women and their roles in American history. The author begins
with a Native American legend of creation in which a woman
plays an important role and then goes on to write about Francisca
Hinestrosa, the first European woman to come to America. She
came to Florida in 1539 with her soldier husband as part of
Hernando de Soto's expedition. Excerpts from diaries, letters,
autobiographies, speeches, resolutions, essays, magazine articles,
and interviews help to trace 350 years of women's history in the
New World. The concluding chapter, "What's Ahead," offers a
challenge as well as a prediction.

22.27 Ray, Delia. **A Nation Torn: The Story of How the Civil War Began.** Lodestar Books, 1990. 102 pp. ISBN 0-525-67308-3.

Once a war is started, might rather than reason seems to take over and push it forward. This book illustrates that tendency much more than most books about the Civil War do. It focuses on the years 1860 and 1861 that led up to the war and uses original sources like newspapers, speeches, diaries, letters, and photographs to illustrate the kinds of personal concerns and feelings that ordinary people as well as political leaders had about the big issues of states' rights and slavery. ★★

22.28 Reader's Digest Editors. **America's Fascinating Indian Heritage.** Reader's Digest Association, 1990. 416 pp. ISBN 0-89577-372-4.

Just skimming through this oversized book will show you what a mistake it is to talk about Native Americans as if they were all in the same group. They may have all come from Siberia to Alaska some 12,000 years ago, but from there they spread over both North and South America, changing and adapting to different geographies and situations. The book begins with a brief general history and then looks specifically at the Native Americans in eight geographical areas of North America. The book concludes with a discussion of contemporary Native Americans. Photographs, paintings, drawings, and charts add interest to every page.

22.29 Reader's Digest Editors. **Great Disasters: Dramatic True Stories of Nature's Awesome Powers.** Reader's Digest Association, 1989. 320 pp. ISBN 0-89577-321-X.

Some of the out-of-the-ordinary events pictured and written about in this book include volcanoes, tornadoes, snow and hailstorms, epidemics, floods, earthquakes, avalanches and landslides, and droughts and famines. It also tells of freak accidents like the carbon dioxide bubble that rose in 1986 from Lake Nyos in Cameroon and killed nearly 2,000 people and the giant tidal wave that in 1970 killed hundreds of thousands of Pakistanis. Full-color news photos add to the impact of these dramatic stories.

22.30 Reedstrom, E. Lisle. **Apache Wars: An Illustrated Battle History.** Sterling, 1990. 272 pp. ISBN 0-8069-7254-8.

This is the story of the Apaches, who resisted the takeover by white civilization longer than any other western Indian tribe. It's fully illustrated with paintings and photographs.

260   *History*

22.31 Reit, Seymour. **Guns for General Washington: The Impossible Journey.** Harcourt Brace Jovanovich, 1990. 144 pp. ISBN 0-15-200466-1.

Today we can move armies halfway around the world, so the story of how hard it was for William and Henry Knox to move guns from Fort Ticonderoga back to Boston for General Washington is all the more striking. Even though it was the middle of winter so they wouldn't be attacked and even though they could cross frozen rivers, the journey was far from easy.

22.32 Rogasky, Barbara. **Smoke and Ashes: The Story of the Holocaust.** Holiday House, 1988. 187 pp. ISBN 0-8234-06970.

Dramatic photographs and clear writing make this account of the Second World War's Holocaust good for either reading in full or for doing research on specific aspects of this dark piece of the world's history. The author makes connections between the Holocaust and the world today by including information on contemporary anti-Semitism. ★★★★★

22.33 St. George, Judith. **Panama Canal: Gateway to the World.** G. P. Putnam's Sons, 1989. 159 pp. ISBN 0-399-21637-5.

The Panama Canal is an area of the world that's likely to remain in the news, especially as the clock ticks away on the United States' lease on it that expires in 1999. This book shows what went into building the canal and why it's such an important part of today's world. ★★

22.34 St. George, Judith. **The White House: Cornerstone of a Nation.** G. P. Putnam's Sons, 1990. 160 pp. ISBN 0-399-22186-7.

Author Judith St. George shows what the White House has meant to America through bad times and good. She has chosen the many photographs and has written her book in order to focus on the White House while letting you learn a great deal about American history at the same time.

22.35 Warren, James A. **Portrait of a Tragedy: America and the Vietnam War.** Lothrop, Lee and Shepard Books, 1990. 196 pp. ISBN 0-688-07454-5.

The author doesn't expect you to have a lot of background information on the Vietnam War, and so he sets out to explain what happened in a straightforward and unbiased tone. Photos, maps, diagrams, and a calendar of events make the book more interesting as well as more informative. ★

22.36 Zeinert, Karen. **The Salem Witchcraft Trials.** Franklin Watts, 1989. 95 pp. ISBN 0-531-10673-X.

Few historical events show us more clearly that we need to learn about history to keep from repeating it than do the Salem witchcraft trials. The author shows the conditions in 1692 that made the people of Salem susceptible to superstition and eventually to mass hysteria. The witch hunt began with accusations against three women, one of whom was a black slave, and it did not end until nineteen people were dead and many lives were shattered. ★

Series

22.37 **The Ancient World.** Silver Burdett Press.

Beautiful full-color photos and drawings, many of them filling the page, add interest to these accounts of life in ancient civilizations. Clearly organized and written, the books treat government, natural resources, literature, legends, daily life, transportation, architecture, clothing, communication, and the political history of each country. Glossaries, indexes, and a "who's who" page make the books good reference sources. Titles include *The Aztecs, The Egyptians, The Greeks, The Incas, The Israelites, The Mayas, The Phoenicians, The Romans, The Sumerians,* and *The Vikings.* Written by Pamela Odjik.

22.38 **Timeline.** Crestwood House.

Gail Stewart wrote the first two titles in this series about the 1920s and 1930s, while Jane Duden wrote about the 1940s, 1950s, 1960s, and 1970s. The books are fun to skim because they summarize each decade's major events along with many minor events, including fads and fashions of each year of each decade. Black-and-white photos add interest and help place famous faces in time. ★

23 Language Arts, Drama, Music, Art, and Architecture

23.1   Andronik, Catherine M. **Quest for a King: Searching for the Real King Arthur.** Atheneum, 1989. 160 pp. ISBN 0-689-31411-6.

Was there a real King Arthur? And how about Merlin, Guenevere, Mordred, and Lancelot? These are the questions that the author tries to answer. She discusses medieval legends, artifacts, recent theories, and archaeology along with beliefs and hopes from popular culture. ★

23.2   Berger, Melvin. **The Science of Music.** Thomas Y. Crowell, 1989. 148 pp. ISBN 0-690-04647-2.

Why is some music loud and some soft? Why is some music jazzy while other music tinkles and other music rocks? *The Science of Music* discusses the reasons behind different sounds and how our ears hear sound. Percussion, keyboards, woodwinds, and brasses, plus electronic technology are all explained.

23.3   Cassedy, Sylvia. **In Your Own Words: A Beginner's Guide to Writing,** revised edition. Thomas Y. Crowell, 1990. 219 pp. ISBN 0-690-04823-8.

The author claims that everybody has something to write about because we all have experiences important enough to put down in words. She says, "Anything that you are aware of is an event in your life. It is yours alone. Private as a daydream or public as a parade, it happens only to you. No one else senses it just as you do. That is why when you write about it, you reveal something new to the whole world." With this in mind, she sets out to help you get the most out of the experience of writing. Ten of the chapters focus on different kinds of prose writing, while eight focus on poetry.

23.4   Degler, Teri. **Straight from the Horse's Mouth . . . and Other Animal Expressions.** Illustrated by Tina Holdcroft. Henry Holt, 1989. 109 pp. ISBN 0-8050-0988-4.

Brief, interesting histories and explanations are given for such animal expressions as "to go whole hog," "to be mad as a March hare," and "to bring home the bacon." The word "chubby" comes from the chub fish, and the word "scapegoat" comes from an ancient religious ceremony in which one goat was sacrificed to God, and the other was allowed to run off carrying away everyone's sins. Cartoon illustrations make reading this book much more fun than reading a dictionary.

23.5 Dufort, Antony. **Ballet Steps: Practice to Performance.** Crown/ Clarkson N. Potter Books, 1990. 160 pp. ISBN 0-517-57770-4.

The drawings in this book, supplemented by photographs, make it almost a picture book, but the wealth of information that accompanies the pictures is intended for serious ballet students, as well as for people who want to get more out of watching ballet. The author's special fondness for ballet is obvious.

23.6 Gallo, Donald R., editor. **Center Stage: One-Act Plays for Teenage Readers and Actors.** Harper and Row, 1990. 361 pp. ISBN 0-06-022171-2.

For a lot of people, the best parts of books are the parts where people talk to each other. Don Gallo, who created this collection of plays, agrees, and so he went out and asked some of the best writers of books for young people to rewrite some of their stories with just the talking parts—that is, as plays. The result is ten plays written by well-known authors about contemporary teenage life. The plays are good for reading alone, for doing readers' theater, or for doing as full-blown productions.

23.7 Giblin, James Cross. **Let There Be Light: A Book about Windows.** Thomas Y. Crowell, 1988. 162 pp. ISBN 0-690-04693-6.

Most of us take windows for granted, but this author doesn't. He begins with the holes—the "wind eyes"—in the shelters constructed by our earliest ancestors and then goes on to trace the important part that windows have played in ordinary homes, as well as in civilization's biggest and best buildings, including its cathedrals and skyscrapers. ★

23.8 Giblin, James Cross. **The Riddle of the Rosetta Stone: Key to Ancient Egypt.** Thomas Y. Crowell, 1990. 85 pp. ISBN 0-690-04799-1.

In 1799 Napoleon's soldiers were tearing down a wall in the town of Rosetta near Alexandria, Egypt, when they found a stone slab with messages carved on it in three different languages. One was in Greek, which French scholars could read; one was in Egyptian hieroglyphs; and the other one was in a mystery language. This book tells how these messages turned out to be only one message written in three different languages and so eventually provided the key that enabled linguists to figure out one of the world's first writing systems. ★

23.9   Greenfield, Howard. **Books: From Writer to Reader,** revised edition. Crown, 1989. 224 pp. ISBN 0-517-568411.

This is a book about books. It shows what is involved in their writing, editing, printing, and binding. The reason that it needed to be revised is that within the last ten years, word processors have dramatically changed the way authors write. Many of them no longer send their editors manuscripts; instead, they send computer disks. The editors work on the disks and then send these disks to the typesetters. Computers also help to create new graphics and allow people to engage in what's called desktop publishing, where people handle everything themselves from their homes or offices, from getting an idea to writing, typesetting, printing, photocopying, and distributing the final product.

23.10   Gregory, Cynthia. **Cynthia Gregory Dances Swan Lake.** Photographs by Martha Swope. Simon and Schuster, 1990. 48 pp. ISBN 0-671-68786-7.

Star ballet dancer Cynthia Gregory narrates this photo essay, which devotes a couple of pages to her childhood training before going on to follow her through the day of a performance of the famous *Swan Lake* ballet. *Swan Lake* was written seventy years before Gregory was born, but it's still used as the standard by which a ballet dancer is judged. She dances her favorite role in her favorite ballet, and she does it beautifully, as is shown in the full-color photographs and in the praise she gets.

23.11   Harrar, George, and Linda Harrar. **Signs of the Apes, Songs of the Whales: Adventures in Human-Animal Communication.** Simon and Schuster, 1989. 48 pp. ISBN 0-671-67748-9.

Full-color photos and illustrations on every page make this book based on the "Nova" public television series visually appealing. The written information about "talking" animals is also presented in an appealing way. The four "stars" of the book are Washoe the chimp and Koko the gorilla, both of whom have learned many of the hand signs used by deaf people, and two dolphins in Hawaii named Phoenix and Akeakamai. These animals have proven themselves capable of responding correctly when words they know are combined in ways they have never seen or heard before.

23.12 Hendrickson, Robert. **The Henry Holt Encyclopedia of Word and Phrase Origins.** Henry Holt/Owl Books, 1990. 581 pp. ISBN 0-8050-1251-6.

This book isn't meant to be read cover to cover, but you'll enjoy skimming through and reading the history of such phrases as "break a leg!" "can't cut the mustard," "I'm from Missouri," and "political plum." Originally titled *The Facts on File Encyclopedia of Word and Phrase Origins*.

23.13 Isaacson, Philip. **Round Buildings, Square Buildings, and Buildings that Wiggle Like a Fish.** Alfred A. Knopf, 1988. 121 pp. ISBN 0-394-99382-9.

Even if you have never thought of becoming an architect, this attractive book with its ninety-three full-color photographs may make you more aware of how buildings influence your mood and inspire certain feelings. Architecture is the one art form that surrounds us all. ★★

23.14 Kenret, Peg. **Encore! More Winning Monologs for Young Actors: Sixty-Three More Honest-to-Life Monologs for Teenage Boys and Girls.** Meriwether, 1988. 176 pp. ISBN 0-916160-54-2.

These up-to-date, often humorous slices of life are good for when you're putting on a program, making a class presentation, needing audition material, or doing readers' theater.

23.15 Klausner, Janet. **Talk about English: How Words Travel and Change.** Thomas Y. Crowell, 1990. 198 pp. ISBN 0-690-04833-5.

If you stop to think about it, you will realize that language is an absolutely amazing thing. This book is about the English language and its relationship to other languages in the world, how people create new words, and how words undergo changes to become more useful. Suggestions for further reading are included.

23.16 Lamb, Wendy, editor. **Sparks in the Park and Other Prize-Winning Plays.** Dell, 1989. 269 pp. ISBN 0-440-20415-1.

A bonus of this paperback collection of short plays is that they were written by teenagers sixteen to eighteen years old. Some are funny and some are sad, but they all treat topics and feelings that are of interest to young readers. They are good for either reading, pondering over, discussing, or producing on stage.

23.17   Lewin, Esther, and Albert E. Lewin. **The Random House Thesaurus of Slang.** Random House, 1988. 435 pp. ISBN 0-679-72700-0.

Over 150,000 uncensored slang terms are included in this collection of informal English words. Twelve thousand standard English words are also listed alphabetically, followed by between 100 and 200 slang terms.

23.18   Manser, Martin. **Melba Toast, Bowie's Knife and Caesar's Wife: A Dictionary of Eponyms.** Avon Books, 1990. 244 pp. ISBN 0-380-70877-9.

Most of us can list five or six eponyms, that is, words that came from someone's name, such as "sandwich" after the Earl of Sandwich, a man who didn't want to stop gambling long enough to have a real meal; "sousaphone" after band director and musical composer John Philip Sousa; and "floral" after Flora, the Roman goddess of flowers. These common words are included in this dictionary, as are some 1,200 others. A paragraph about each word tells its history. Originally published in Great Britain in 1988.

23.19   Mattox, Cheryl Warren, compiler and adaptor. **Shake It to the One That You Love the Best: Play Songs and Lullabies from Black Musical Traditions.** Illustrated by Varnette P. Honeywood and Brenda Joy Smith. Warren-Mattox Productions, 1990. 54 pp. ISBN 0-9623381-0-9.

This lesson in African American history is told through music. Its songs and lullabies are illustrated with eleven full-color paintings. The collector includes historical information about each song and lullaby and tells you about the games that were played along with the music. ★★

23.20   Morris, Christopher. **The Lincoln Writing Dictionary for Children.** Harcourt Brace Jovanovich, 1988. 901 pp. ISBN 0-15-152394-0.

This colorful dictionary is splashed with photographs and illustrations and includes boxed areas with hints on how to be an effective writer. There are also interesting stories about how particular words came into the English language. Most entries are used in sentences, many of which were written by famous American and English writers.

23.21   Sears, Peter. **Gonna Bake Me a Rainbow Poem: A Student Guide to Writing Poetry.** Scholastic, 1990. 143 pp. ISBN 0-590-43085-8.

Whether you want to write poetry or just enjoy reading it, this is a good book for you. It's filled with poems written by young poets who won the Scholastic Writing Awards contest. The author was a judge for one of the contests and was so impressed by the poems that he suggested sharing them with other teenagers. He groups the poems into different types, and in each of the sixteen chapters, he starts out with informal comments and observations that help to make the poems more interesting.

23.22   Silverstein, Alvin, and Virginia Silverstein. **Wonders of Speech.** Morrow Junior Books, 1988. 154 pp. ISBN 0-688-06534-1.

Linguistics is the scientific study of language, and it's usually not taught until college, but the authors take this area of study and make it interesting and understandable for you. An especially interesting chapter, "Are We Alone?" talks about human relationships with "speaking" animals such as dolphins and chimpanzees.

23.23   Weiss, Ann E. **Who's to Know? Information, the Media, and Public Awareness.** Houghton Mifflin, 1990. 160 pp. ISBN 0-395-49702-7.

As Americans, we believe in freedom of the press, but as this author shows, people's right to know is not necessarily guaranteed by the Constitution. Certainly America has a more open information system than many countries do, but that doesn't mean there aren't any secrets. For example, in 1988, the world was shocked to learn that China had suffered a major earthquake nearly twenty years earlier; and we were equally shocked to learn that in 1951, radioactive materials had been released in Ohio, and the matter was kept secret. Both government and industry have reasons for controlling information and now that only a few big corporations own so much of the media, like radio and television stations, newspapers, and magazines, the tendency is for more and more information to be controlled. ★

Series

23.24   **Scholastic's A+ Junior Guides.** Scholastic.

Checklists, examples, and straightforward, well-organized advice take the terror out of testing, the drudgery out of writing papers, and the jitters out of giving a report in front of your classmates. Step-by-step instructions guide you through the most troublesome assignments. Useful titles include *Scholastic's A+ Junior Guide to Taking Tests, Scholastic's A+ Junior Guide to Good Writing, Scholastic's A+ Junior Guide to Studying, Scholastic's A+ Junior Guide to Book Reports,* and *Scholastic's A+ Junior Guide to Giving a Speech.* By Louise Colligan.

VI Books Just for You

Few of the books in this section are likely to be assigned as homework. Instead, these are the books that you'll go looking for on your own. In the first section are the books that will answer your questions about physical and emotional health. Books about such controversial issues as drugs, sex, and steroids are included, along with books on general physical fitness, grooming, and dieting. The "how-to" books give advice on activities you can do right now, as well as on activities that might make up your future career. We chose the title "Fun and Facts" for this section since it includes lots of trivia books, some joke books, and books about sports and entertainment personalities.

24 Managing Your Life: Physical and Emotional Health

24.1 American Medical Association. **The American Medical Association Handbook of First Aid and Emergency Care: A Comprehensive, Step-by-Step Guide to Dealing with Injuries, Illnesses, and Medical Emergencies.** Random House, 1990. 332 pp. ISBN 0-679-72959-3.

This handy book is one you can skim through to learn about the kinds of first aid you are most likely to need to know about. For example, if you're an athlete, you will probably turn first to the back section on sports first aid, but you'll also want to read the first section on being prepared for all kinds of medical emergencies. Lots of sketches, clear organization, boldfaced headings, and a complete index make the book easy to use.

24.2 Blake, Jeanne. **Risky Times: How to Be AIDS-Smart and Stay Healthy.** Workman, 1990. 158 pp. ISBN 0-89480-656-4.

Of course this book includes information on how to have safer sex, but it goes further. There are stories about young people with AIDS (or PWAs), stories about people who have contributed their time and talents to help AIDS sufferers, and scientific information about the latest research on AIDS. ★★

24.3 Bode, Janet. **The Voices of Rape.** Franklin Watts, 1990. 144 pp. ISBN 0-531-15184-0.

This book on rape includes interviews with teenagers who have been raped, with teenagers who have raped someone, and with adult professionals, including a police officer, a judge, a prosecutor, a defense attorney, and a psychologist. By getting each of these perspectives, you will come away better prepared to defend yourself from rape as well as to understand and help those who have been raped. ★★

24.4 Boston Children's Hospital, with Robert P. Masland, Jr., M.D. **What Teenagers Want to Know about Sex: Questions and Answers.** Little, Brown, 1988. 181 pp. ISBN 0-316-25063-5.

The nineteen chapters of this book about sex begin with a discussion of each chapter's general topic, followed by questions that the writers have most often heard from teenagers. Straightforward and concise answers are provided for each question. Because of this format, the book is suitable for quick reference as well as for reading cover to cover.

24.5   Brondino, Jeanne, and others. **Raising Each Other.** Hunter House, 1988. 147 pp. ISBN 0-89793-044-4.

Five students and their teacher wrote this book about teen-parent relationships. Freedom, money, sex, and trust are among the issues brought up for discussion. Communication is shown to be a key to better understanding, and as part of the goal of increasing understanding, the writers also ponder over problems that parents have.

24.6   Clark, Cecil, and Faith Clark. **Hassle Free Homework: A Six Weeks' Plan for Parents and Children to Take the Pain Out of Homework.** Doubleday, 1989. 262 pp. ISBN 0-385-24684-6.

If your parents help you with your homework, or even if they worry about whether or not you're doing it, here's a book to share with them. Together you can figure out how to identify your own learning style, organize homework time, concentrate better, and increase the amount you remember.

24.7   Cohen, Susan, and Daniel Cohen. **What You Can Believe about Drugs: An Honest and Unhysterical Guide for Teens.** M. Evans, 1988. 165 pp. ISBN 0-87131-527-0.

The straightforward and personable approach of the authors makes this a good book to read all the way through or to skim and study parts of when doing research. Narcotics, cocaine, marijuana, cigarettes, caffeine, and steroids are all discussed, along with the political and emotional factors that influence how Americans respond to drugs. ★

24.8   Cohen, Susan, and Daniel Cohen. **When Someone You Know Is Gay.** M. Evans, 1989. 162 pp. ISBN 0-87131-567-X.

The authors discuss the topic of teenage homosexuality in a sensitive and straightforward way. They offer historical and scientific information, including an update on AIDS. Personal commentaries taken from interviews with gay teens illustrate the problems experienced by the teenage homosexual.

24.9　Colman, Warren. **Understanding and Preventing AIDS.** Children's Press, 1988. 123 pp. ISBN 0-516-40592-6.

Addresses and numbers are given for U.S. and Canadian AIDS hotlines along with other sources of help and information. Techniques for avoiding the HIV virus are clearly spelled out. The author explains what the virus does to the immune system and why it's so hard to develop a vaccine against it. ★

24.10　DuPrau, Jeanne. **Adoption: The Facts, Feelings, and Issues of a Double Heritage.** Julian Messner, 1990. 129 pp. ISBN 0-671-69328-X.

Included in the seven informative chapters of this book on adoption are many anecdotes and case histories. A primary focus is on whether or not adopted children should be given access to records of their adoption and helped in finding their biological parents. Originally published in 1981.

24.11　Gardner, Sandra, with Gary Rosenberg, M.D. **Teenage Suicide.** Julian Messner, 1990. 116 pp. ISBN 0-671-70200-9.

This book offers case studies of young people who have attempted suicide and tries to show the causes of suicidal behavior and how some young people have found their way out of their problems. Some unusual chapters in this book include one on the connection between media depictions of suicide and the clusters of suicide that seem to follow them, and one on other kinds of self-destructive behavior, which discusses similarities between suicide and risk taking, drug and alcohol abuse, sexual "acting out," and anorexia. The last third of the book focuses on suicide prevention. The book ends with addresses of sources of help, suggested further readings (including fiction), and a bibliography.

24.12　Gay, Kathlyn. **Changing Families: Meeting Today's Challenges.** Enslow, 1988. 128 pp. ISBN 0-89490-139-7.

The power of the family to love and protect its members is illustrated in this readable book showing the variety in today's family structures. The author does not view all nontraditional families as "broken." Instead, she shows how family needs are being filled by single-parent families, blended families, families with two working parents, older families, and many other combinations. A list of organizations created to help families is included, as is a bibliography of other helpful books.

24.13　　Gilbert, Sara. **Go for It: Get Organized.** Morrow Junior Books, 1990. 144 pp. ISBN 0-688-08852-X.

The conversational style of this book makes it easy to read—plus, the first thing the author does is to give you hints on how to read her book more efficiently. That sets the mood for her tips on getting organized. The book is divided into four sections: "One— Take It Easy," "Two—Get Set," "Three—Action!" and "Four— Go to It." She gives help in establishing priorities, simplifying tasks, setting and reaching goals, and dividing those goals between the "have to's" and the "want to's."

24.14　　Hogshead, Nancy, and Gerald S. Couzens. **Asthma and Exercise.** Henry Holt, 1990. 239 pp. ISBN 0-8050-0878-0.

Although this book by an Olympic swimmer is written for a general adult audience, the focus is on young athletes, and any young person with asthma can probably find both inspiration and important information in it. Chapters give clues on breathing exercises, workouts, swimming, walking, running, bicycling, and aerobics.

24.15　　Hyde, Margaret O. **Teen Sex.** The Westminster Press/John Knox Press, 1988. 115 pp. ISBN 0-664-32726-5.

Social, physical, emotional, and practical aspects of sex are explored in this book. The author is sensitive to the varied attitudes that people have about sex, and she approaches the topic in a straightforward, tactful way. Because of this, her discussions of such controversial topics as AIDS and problems of teenage pregnancy are informative rather than offensive.

24.16　　Isberg, Emily. **Peak Performance: Sports, Science, and the Body in Action.** Simon and Schuster, 1989. 48 pp. ISBN 0-671-67750-0.

How computers help athletes improve their performance, what sports medicine has done to help bodies heal, and how research on the limits of human endurance helped a team fly the *Daedalus 88* glider for three hours and fifty-four minutes, powered only by the strong legs of bicyclist Kanellos Kanellopoulos, are three of the many stories told in this book based on the "Nova" public television program. Although most science and sports news is good, the author also includes a section on the controversial problem of athletes and steroids.

24.17   Johanson, Sue. **Talk Sex.** Viking Penguin, 1989. 215 pp. ISBN 0-14-010377-5.

Sue Johanson, a trained nurse and well-respected sex educator, has spent nearly twenty years answering teenagers' questions about sex, both in person and on weekly radio and television shows. She uses a question-and-answer format for this book but prefaces each chapter with her own short, straightforward introduction. The book covers a wide range of topics, including the body, sexual fantasies, love, safer sex, orgasms, breaking up, having babies, homosexuality, and talking with parents. The book is concise yet thorough and clearly shows the author's respect and concern for young people. ★

24.18   Johnson, Julie Tallard. **Understanding Mental Illness.** Lerner, 1989. 68 pp. ISBN 0-8225-0042-6.

Three types of mental illness—depression, manic depression, and schizophrenia—are introduced with real-life scenarios from teenagers who have a mentally ill person in their family. The author discusses ways of coping with fear, stress, and embarrassment and illustrates solutions to difficult situations. A "Where to Look for Help" section is especially useful.

24.19   Krementz, Jill. **How It Feels to Be Adopted.** Photographs by the author. Alfred A. Knopf, 1988. 107 pp. ISBN 0-394-75853-6.

Being adopted is different from not being adopted—just ask any adopted person. Author Jill Krementz interviews nineteen young people in her book, most of whom were adopted into traditional families. All of them address the issue of biological parents, and most have come to terms with whether they wish to pursue that issue, while a few have met and built relationships with their biological mothers. Krementz's photos and her direct writing style make reading the book seem almost like listening to interviews on a television talk show. Originally published in 1982.

24.20   Krementz, Jill. **How It Feels to Fight for Your Life.** Little, Brown, 1989. 132 pp. ISBN 0-316-50364-9.

How do fourteen young people who deal with pain and other adversity brought on by serious illness or disability live their lives in ways that can inspire others facing similar challenges? Personal accounts allow the reader into the private worlds of children and young adults who share an explanation of their afflictions, fears, dreams, struggles, and triumphs. Photos of each speaker make the stories more personal. ★

24.21 Krementz, Jill. **How It Feels When a Parent Dies.** Photographs by the author. Alfred A. Knopf, 1988. 110 pp. ISBN 0-394-75854-4.

Eighteen young people describe the feelings they experienced upon the death of one of their parents. Some have only recently experienced their loss and are in the first stages of grieving. Others are distanced from the experience by several years and are able to put things in perspective. Some of the parents died after long illnesses, others by unexpected accidents, and two by suicide. Even though each experience is different, together the interviews show that grieving takes time, space, and understanding from the surviving parent. Originally published in 1981.

24.22 Krementz, Jill. **How It Feels When Parents Divorce.** Alfred A. Knopf, 1988. 115 pp. ISBN 0-394-75855-2.

These interviews with young people whose parents have divorced show there is no single way of dealing with the matter. All of the children describe the hurt they feel and then proceed to tell how they have come to terms with their own frustrations. Some, but certainly not all, have managed to build a closer relationship with each parent. In contrast, not all of the young people have succeeded in going on, and some may never get over the unrealistic belief that their mom and dad will get back together. Originally published in 1984.

24.23 Landau, Elaine. **Child Abuse: An American Epidemic.** Julian Messner, 1990. 138 pp. ISBN 0-671-68874-X.

Although the stories of child abuse in this book are no worse than those that you can read in the newspaper nearly every day, when they are put together, they present a frightening and depressing picture. Cases from real life are used as the center of chapters on physical, emotional, and sexual abuse. The concluding chapters are a little more optimistic, as they present possible solutions and show what is being done to solve a horrifying problem. Originally published in 1984.

24.24 Landau, Elaine. **Teenagers Talk about School—and Open Their Hearts about Their Closest Concerns.** Julian Messner, 1988. 106 pp. ISBN 0-671-65668-4.

The author interviewed twenty-three teenagers and recorded their impressions of and reactions to different aspects of school life. She picked out a key quote to use as the title for each of the brief chapters, such as "Kids don't have any rights," "To them we're all alike," "He tried to make me into a miniature of himself," and "Every so often you come across a gem."

24.25   Landau, Elaine. **We Have AIDS.** Franklin Watts, 1990. 126 pp. ISBN 0-531-10898-8.

Nine teenage victims of AIDS tell their stories—how they got AIDS, what it feels like, what they hope and fear, and how their families and friends treat them. Facts about AIDS are presented in between these stories. References to recent magazine articles may be helpful for you if you're doing a research paper on AIDS. ★

24.26   Lee, Essie. **Breaking the Connection: How Young People Achieve Drug-free Lives.** Julian Messner, 1988. 191 pp. ISBN 0-671-63637-5.

These eight case studies of teenagers whose lives have been disrupted by drug and/or alcohol addiction will give readers a better understanding of some of the reasons that adolescents turn to drugs. The focus is on urban environments, and treatment programs are listed.

24.27   Madaras, Lynda. **Lynda Madaras Talks to Teens about AIDS: An Essential Guide for Parents, Teachers, and Young People.** Newcastle, 1988. 128 pp. ISBN 1-55704-010-9.

The goal of this straightforward book is to help teenagers protect themselves from AIDS and to understand what it does to those who have it. Separating truth from rumor, the author talks openly about the sexual transmission of AIDS, offering practical advice on not having sex and on having "safer" sex. The book also discusses other forms of AIDS transmission and prevention and tells you how you can get more information on the fight against AIDS. ★★★★★

24.28   Madison, Arnold. **Drugs and You,** revised edition. Julian Messner, 1990. 128 pp. ISBN 0-671-69147-3.

This easy-to-read book discusses major drugs and their effects on the human body. It also talks about medicinal drugs and the addictive effects of alcohol, caffeine, and nicotine. The last chapter, "Drugs and You," lays out the individual's responsibilities in relation to drugs.

24.29   Miller, Judi. **How to Be Friends with a Boy—How to Be Friends with a Girl.** Scholastic, 1990. 116 pp. ISBN 0-590-42806-3.

The emphasis in this book is as much on friendship as it is on romance, since you might have either relationship with a member of the opposite sex. The author talked to lots of kids in junior high school and then used what they said to make up fictional characters for the book. Throughout the easy-to-read chapters, these characters are frequently quoted as they make their points about the pleasures and problems of developing new friends.

24.30   Rench, Janice E. **Teen Sexuality: Decisions and Choices.** Lerner, 1988. 72 pp. ISBN 0-8225-0041-8.

Unlike many books that simply discuss the physical changes that young people experience, this one is based on the idea that feelings and emotions, and not just your body, are central to sexuality. But at the same time, this book does not ignore the physical aspects of sexuality as it answers some tough questions about sexually transmitted diseases. The book also addresses difficult questions about date rape.

24.31   Rench, Janice E. **Understanding Sexual Identity: A Book for Gay Teens and Their Friends.** Lerner, 1990. 56 pp. ISBN 0-8225-0044-2.

In fifty easy-to-read pages, the author presents six chapters beginning with "Facts about Homosexuality" and continuing with "Friends," "Families," "Religion," "Coming Out," and "Healthy Sexuality." The author's goal is to dispel some of the myths about gay and lesbian people and to help all readers, regardless of their sexual orientation, become more comfortable with differences and more able to work against violence, hatred, and ignorance.

24.32   Rosenberg, Maxine B. **Talking about Stepfamilies.** Bradbury Press, 1990. 144 pp. ISBN 0-02-777913-0.

In a typical group of young people, one out of five lives in a stepfamily, and each day 1,300 new stepfamilies are formed. When you become part of a stepfamily, more than your relationships change—there is a new house, a new school, and perhaps even a new town, and it usually takes at least two years for you to get to know the personalities of your new family members. The author hopes to make such adjustments a little easier by sharing the stories of sixteen different young people and what they went through in learning to live in a new family.

24.33 Schmitt, Lois. **Smart Spending: A Young Consumer's Guide.** Charles Scribner's Sons, 1989. 102 pp. ISBN 0-684-19035-4.

If you've felt cheated or even disappointed after making a purchase, here's a book for you. The author shows what to look for in the fine print, how to be efficient in comparison shopping, and what to do if you have a justified complaint. She also includes a discussion of tricks and scams that you need to watch out for.

24.34 Seixas, Judith S. **Living with a Parent Who Takes Drugs.** Greenwillow Books, 1989. 102 pp. ISBN 0-688-08627-6.

Jason shares his concerns about drug-abusive parents with his school counselor. As his story unfolds, you learn the danger signs, facts, and legal implications of drug abuse. As Jason's family begins to cross the line into child abuse and neglect, you labor with Jason over what to do while he worries about revealing his family secret to outsiders. Jason's story is factual, easy to read, and understandable.

24.35 Shuker, Nancy. **Everything You Need to Know about an Alcoholic Parent.** Rosen, 1989. 64 pp. ISBN 0-8239-1076-8.

Twenty million young people in the United States have a parent who is alcoholic, and this book is meant to help them cope with the situation. It's a readable book with photos and straightforward advice on do's and don'ts. The main focus is on feelings and the point of view of the young person rather than on alcoholism and its causes. Part of the Need to Know Library series.

24.36 Shuker-Haines, Frances. **Everything You Need to Know about Date Rape.** Rosen, 1989. 64 pp. ISBN 0-8239-1075-X.

This book is designed to help young women cope with the difficult situation of date rape—of being assaulted by someone they know. It's mainly made up of stories about date rape put in fictional form. The stories are accompanied by discussions of the situations described. Part of the Need to Know Library series. ★

24.37 Silverstein, Alvin, and Virginia Silverstein. **Glasses and Contact Lenses.** J. B. Lippincott, 1989. 135 pp. ISBN 0-397-32184-8.

The authors show not only how glasses have changed in the last six hundred years, but they also explain the technical aspects of glasses and contact lenses and what wearers need to know to care for their eyes, their glasses, and their contact lenses.

24.38   Silverstein, Alvin, Virginia Silverstein, and Robert Silverstein. **Overcoming Acne: The How and Why of Healthy Skin Care.** Morrow Junior Books, 1990. 93 pp. ISBN 0-688-08344-7.

Close to 90 percent of teenagers between the ages of twelve and seventeen are bothered by acne, and this is a book for all those teenagers who ask, "Why me?" Besides giving helpful hints for good skin care and general health, the authors show the underlying causes of acne and what medicine and science are doing for the problem. Preface by Dr. Christopher M. Papa.

24.39   Simon, Nissa. **Good Sports: Plain Talk about Health and Fitness for Teens.** Thomas Y. Crowell, 1990. 118 pp. ISBN 0-690-04904-8.

This book is organized so that it leads you from preparation for healthy competition to dealing with risks and injuries. The first part explains basic concepts of fitness and training, while the concluding sections discuss specific physical problems, how to avoid them, and how to treat them in case they do occur. A bibliography of terms and sketches illustrating the exercises are helpful additions.

24.40   Weiss, Ann E. **Lies, Deception and Truth.** Houghton Mifflin, 1988. 143 pp. ISBN 0-395-40486-X.

Haven't we all been taught that honesty is the best policy and that the lie comes back to haunt the liar? But is lying acceptable if the intent is to do good? Must some lies be told so that important truths can survive? Is the result of the lie the only way to judge whether the act was good or bad? While reading this book, you will examine historical and contemporary fibs, lies, outrageous deceptions—and your own conscience.

24.41   Wirths, Claudine G., and Mary Bowman-Kruhm. **Where's My Other Sock? How to Get Organized and Drive Your Parents and Teachers Crazy.** Illustrated by Molly Coxe. Thomas Y. Crowell, 1989. 128 pp. ISBN 0-690-04667-7.

You'll learn three secrets in this book designed to help readers become better managers of time, work, and money: (1) how to break large problems into smaller ones, (2) how to take charge of your life, and (3) how to find an organizational plan that fits your personality and your goals. Along with "Super Slob Tips," there are forms for making lists and hints for saving money, arranging your room, taking tests, completing homework, and using leisure time wisely.

Series

24.42   Smart Talk. Troll Associates.

Eating Pretty by Elizabeth Karlsberg, *Looking Good* by Susan Sloate, and *Skin Deep* by Susan Wallach are easy-to-read guides to personal care and health in this series. Attractive photos on the covers and line drawings inside add appeal.

25 How-to Books: Crafts, Hobbies, and Future Careers

25.1   Allison, Linda. **The Sierra Club Summer Book.** Illustrated by author. Little, Brown, 1989. 169 pp. ISBN 0-316-03433-9.

Do you know how to make your own rainbows? How about a solar cooker? (You really can fry eggs on the sidewalk!) If that doesn't appeal to you, how about creating a peanut farm? By using sun power, you can even make pictures without a camera. Building a bird feeder, growing plants, or making an insect zoo might be for you. Whatever your interests, you'll find a bundle of new ideas with clear illustrations that can help to make a summer vacation both interesting and fun. Originally published in 1977.

25.2   Arnosky, Jim. **Sketching Outdoors in Autumn.** Lothrop, Lee and Shepard Books, 1988. 46 pp. ISBN 0-688-06288-1.

Artist and naturalist Jim Arnosky uses his own sketches and finished drawings to illustrate both his techniques and the pleasure he gets from transferring nature's work to his sketchpad. Here he tells you how to draw fall time subjects. ★★

25.3   Arnosky, Jim. **Sketching Outdoors in Winter.** Lothrop, Lee and Shepard Books, 1988. 48 pp. ISBN 0-688-06290-3.

Jim Arnosky is an artist and naturalist. In this book, he shares with you his techniques for drawing wintertime subjects. There are plenty of sketches and finished drawings to demonstrate the techniques.

25.4   Barkin, Carol, and Elizabeth James. **Jobs for Kids: The Guide to Having Fun and Making Money.** Illustrated by Roy Doty. Lothrop, Lee and Shepard Books, 1990. 113 pp. ISBN 0-688-09324-8.

Even if you're not sixteen, it doesn't mean that you can't earn money. This upbeat and easy-to-read book gives guidance and ideas on how to be your own company in such businesses as caring for children and pets; caring for yards, houses, and cars; teaching and tutoring children; running errands and helping with parties; doing paper-related work, such as stuffing envelopes or delivering advertising flyers; and selling things you make. It also has a good chapter on the pros and cons of working for your parents.

25.5   Berliner, Don. **The World Aerobatics Championships.** Lerner, 1989. 63 pp. ISBN 0-8225-0531-2.

The 1986 World Aerobatics Championship in England and pilot Debby Rihn are the focus of this book, but it also gives general information about the sport of flying and doing stunts in lightweight airplanes. Many color and black-and-white photos and a glossary are included.

25.6   Bierne, Barbara. **Under the Lights: A Child Model at Work.** Carolrhoda Books, 1988. 55 pp. ISBN 0-87614-316-8.

Through the story of junior high school student Michelle Bush, readers learn what it is like to be a child model. At the time of the telling, Michelle is no longer modeling because she is too old to be a child model. Perhaps she will try again as an adult or teenage model, but for now she's just a student who enjoys sharing both the experience she had and several photos.

25.7   Coombs, Charles. **Soaring: Where Hawks and Eagles Fly.** Henry Holt, 1988. 118 pp. ISBN 0-8050-0496-3.

The author's step-by-step explanation will get you as close to the experience of gliding as you can get without leaving the ground. Photos and diagrams help maintain interest, while a glossary of terms provides sound technical information. Sources of further information are provided for those seriously interested in becoming glider pilots.

25.8   Cushman, Kathleen, and Montana Miller. **Circus Dreams: The Making of a Circus Artist.** Photographs by Michael Carroll. Little, Brown/Joy Street Books, 1990. 90 pp. ISBN 0-316-16561-1.

In 1988, after graduating from high school, Montana Miller left her Massachusetts home to enroll as the first American in the National Center for Circus Arts in France. This special school trains circus performers, and this book is a record in pictures of Montana's first year in circus college. ★

25.9 Dunnahoo, Terry. **How to Win a School Election.** Franklin Watts, 1989. 92 pp. ISBN 0-531-10695-0.

Here's help with everything from planning a school election platform to giving a campaign speech and making your supporters feel good about helping you. Line drawings add interest and humor.

25.10 Haskins, James. **Black Dance in America: A History through Its People.** Thomas Y. Crowell, 1990. 232 pp. ISBN 0-690-04659-6.

Haskins starts his book with the story of how Africans were made to dance for exercise as they were brought to the United States to be slaves. Then he goes on to talk about minstrel shows, jazz dancing in Harlem during the 1920s, tap dancing and concert dancing in the 1930s, modern dancing in the 1940s, rock 'n' roll and ballet in the 1950s, and integration and innovation in the 1960s. The concluding chapter shows the variety that characterizes today's black dancers, both professionals and amateurs. ★

25.11 James, Elizabeth, and Carol Barkin. **How to Be School Smart: Secrets of Successful Schoolwork.** Illustrated by Roy Doty. Lothrop, Lee and Shepard Books, 1988. 94 pp. ISBN 0-688-06798-0.

Roy Doty's drawings give an upbeat tone to the eight chapters in this book that deal with everything from organizing study space to tackling tests. Readers will have heard much of this advice before, but it's convenient to have it gathered together and presented in a small, useful, and appealing package.

25.12 Kogan, Judith. **Nothing but the Best: The Struggle for Perfection at the Julliard School.** Random House, 1987. 239 pp. ISBN 0-394-55514-7.

Nothing but the Best shatters the myth that it is truly wonderful to be "the best." Most of the stories about students at the Julliard School of Music reveal lives that have been put on hold or denied so that the art of music can be perfected. Short glimpses of student life center around the grueling rounds of practice and competition that each student endures to be "the best."

25.13 O'Connell, Dorothy R. **Baby-Sitting Safe and Sound.** Fawcett Books, 1990. 115 pp. ISBN 0-449-14650-2.

This is a small enough book that you could tuck it in your pocket and take it with you when you go babysitting, but you'll be safer and you'll enjoy your job more if you read it ahead of time. Besides safety tips, there are ideas for entertaining children, tips on getting children of different ages to respect and mind you, and advice on dealing with your employers.

25.14   Pellowski, Anne. **Hidden Stories in Plants: Unusual and Easy-to-Tell Stories from around the World Together with Creative Things to Do While Telling Them.** Illustrated by Lynn Sweat. Macmillan, 1990. 93 pp. ISBN 0-02-770611-7.

This book includes more than a hundred simple stories and legends, all involving plants. Each story is accompanied by instructions for toys or crafts to make while you tell the story. The stories should continue to be told, as they have been for centuries. The crafts include the making of ornaments, disguises, toys, dolls, and musical instruments and complement the stories.

25.15   Perl, Lila. **The Great Ancestor Hunt: The Fun of Finding Out Who You Are.** Clarion Books, 1989. 104 pp. ISBN 0-89919-745-0.

In the opening chapter, "Who Cares About Great-Uncle Edgar?" readers are shown both the practical and the fun reasons for finding out about their ancestors. Reasons for migrations, naming practices, census taking, and government and personal record keeping are other subjects treated in this book, which includes directions for making rubbings from gravestones. As the author explains, "Family history isn't all *past* history. It's history in the making as well. And every time we 'talk family' with our relatives, we are strengthening our sense of 'belonging'."

25.16   Rosenberg, Maxine B. **Artists of Handcrafted Furniture at Work.** Photographs by George Ancona. Lothrop, Lee and Shepard Books, 1988. 61 pp. ISBN 0-688-06875-8.

Four artists reveal how they got interested in working with wood, where their ideas come from, and how they feel about their creations. Woods and woodworking tools are also photographed and described. As one artist explains, "Furniture that is used has more life. I want my furniture to be part of people's lives." ★

25.17   Shachtman, Tom, and Harriet Shelare. **Video Power: A Complete Guide to Writing, Planning, and Shooting Videos.** Henry Holt, 1988. 102 pp. ISBN 0-8050-0414-9.

This is the book to help you make professional-looking videos. The authors describe both documentary and fictional videos, show script formats, and give suggestions on how to narrow the subject of your video and outline an idea for it. They also give hints on technical aspects, such as lighting and sound.

25.18 Sills, Leslie. **Inspirations: Stories about Women Artists.** Illustrated by Ann Fay. Albert Whitman, 1989. 56 pp. ISBN 0-8075-3649-0.

It's easy to find books about men who are artists, but it's not so easy to learn what it's like for a woman to earn her living doing art. Leslie Sills's book is meant to counterbalance this lack of information by telling the stories of four women artists—what they do and what they aspire to do. ★★

25.19 Simon, Seymour. **How to Be an Ocean Scientist in Your Own Home.** Illustrated by David A. Carter. J. B. Lippincott, 1988. 136 pp. ISBN 0-397-32292-5.

Although this book cannot provide you with a mysterious, beautiful ocean, it does provide twenty-six experiments that will help you learn about oceans and ocean life. You'll find answers to questions like, "When does seawater freeze?" and "How does salinity affect ocean currents?" There's also information on how to set up a saltwater aquarium, as well as suggestions for further reading.

25.20 Smith, Lucinda Irwin. **Women Who Write.** Julian Messner, 1989. 165 pp. ISBN 0-671-65668-6.

After a brief overview of the history of women's literature, author Lucinda Irwin Smith provides a glimpse into the lives and characters of several successful women writers from the past. She also includes enlightening interviews with such modern women writers as Beth Henley, Nikki Giovanni, and Joyce Carol Oates. In these interviews, the older writers offer advice to young writers and explain why they write, how they write, and what they do about problems like writer's block. Smith concludes with a section on what it takes to become a writer and gives advice on how to get started.

25.21 Smith, Norman F. **How to Do Successful Science Projects,** revised edition. Julian Messner, 1990. 111 pp. ISBN 0-671-70685-3.

This helpful guidebook will take you from deciding what kind of experiment you want to do to deciding how to do it and then finally to drawing your conclusions and reporting your results. In the appendix you'll find a section on making charts and graphs that is especially helpful.

25.22   Stine, Megan. **Wheels! The Kids' Bike Book.** Little, Brown/ Sports Illustrated for Kids Books, 1990. 83 pp. ISBN 0-316-81625-6.

You'll want to skim or read this book with its attractive photos even if you're not into biking as a sport. But you'll find it very useful if you are a cyclist—it tells you how to find the right bike and understand its mechanics; it offers tips and techniques for riding, touring, and racing; it teaches you to tell the difference between necessary and fun gear; and it talks about tune-ups, repairs, the history of bicycles, and the sport of cycling.

25.23   Weiss, Harvey. **Cartoons and Cartooning.** Houghton Mifflin, 1990. 64 pp. ISBN 0-395-49217-3.

Weiss's book is fun to read whether you want to be a cartoonist or just get more enjoyment out of the cartoons that we see all around us. Only a couple of pages are devoted to teaching you how to draw because, as Weiss says, "Drawing skill is, of course, something that would be nice to have, but it isn't absolutely essential." More important, he says, are "a few bright ideas, a little imagination, and a sense of humor."

25.24   Yepsen, Roger. **Smarten Up! How to Increase Your Brain Power.** Little, Brown, 1990. 117 pp. ISBN 0-316-96864-1.

The brainteasers in this book are fun to work out, but there's also a lot of solid information on how our brains are structured, how they are affected by what we eat and what we do, how emotions affect our brain, and how we can improve our memories and our creativity.

25.25   Zubrowski, Bernie. **Tops: Building and Experimenting with Spinning Toys.** Illustrated by Roy Doty. Morrow Junior Books, 1989. 96 pp. ISBN 0-688-07561-4.

This Boston Children's Museum Activity Book not only provides directions for building and having fun with tops, yo-yos, and rotating toys, but also for doing experiments and science projects. You can make fascinating tops from materials you find around the house, like paper plates, spools, and margarine tubs. You'll find the variety of visual effects you can create by applying stickers and strips of colored tape to the surface of these toys especially fun.

Series

25.26   Be the Best. Troll Associates.

These easy-to-read sports guides have full-color action photos on the covers and many line drawings inside. They come in both paperback and library editions. Each one has a different author, and the individual titles include *Baseball, Basketball, BMX Racing, Football, Freshwater Fishing, Fun and Fitness, Gymnastics, Nature Explorer, Soccer, Softball, Swimming, Tennis, Track and Field*, and *Volleyball*.

25.27   Draw Fifty. Doubleday.

Whether you are serious in wanting to learn to draw, or you just want to have fun or create a special project, you will enjoy these Draw Fifty books. Recent titles include *Draw Fifty Beasties and Yugglies and Turnover Uglies and Things That Go Bump in the Night* by Lee J. Ames and *Draw Fifty Sharks, Whales, and Other Sea Creatures* by Lee J. Ames with Warren Budd.

25.28   Easy Menu Ethnic Cookbooks. Lerner.

Cooking is a pleasant way to learn about different countries, as well as the heritages of ethnic groups in the United States. The recipes in this book are easy to follow, and photos show how the food is supposed to look. Twenty-four books are in the series, including *Holiday Cooking around the World, Cooking the Australian Way, Cooking the Mexican Way*, and *Cooking the Vietnamese Way*.

25.29   The Inside Track Library. Silver Burdett Press.

Nancy Dunnan is the author of both *The Stock Market* and *Entrepreneurship* in this new series about money management. *The Stock Market* starts out with some basic explanations and works up to the final chapter on how to get a job working on Wall Street. *Entrepreneurship* is focused closer to home, showing how even high school students can identify a need in the marketplace and then set out to fill it. Dunnan is also the author of *Collectibles*, which tells you how to find, buy, and sell baseball cards, greeting cards, campaign buttons, dolls, movie posters, or just about anything else you'd like to collect.

26 Fun and Facts: Entertainment, Jokes, and Interesting Information

26.1 Adamson, Joe. **Bugs Bunny: Fifty Years and Only One Grey Hare.** Henry Holt/Donald Hutter Books, 1990. 192 pp. ISBN 0-8050-1190-0.

This book is as much fun as going to the movies—it lets you sit and enjoy your favorite pictures and cartoons as long as you like. It was published in honor of Bugs Bunny's fiftieth anniversary (he was created in 1940). Browsing through the book will help you learn about Bugs—and about American attitudes and ideas as well as careers in cinematography and animation. There are more than 400 pictures, most in full color.

26.2 Bush, Mildred Kerr. **Millie's Book: As Dictated to Barbara Bush.** William Morrow, 1990. 141 pp. ISBN 0-688-04033-0.

This dog's eye view of life at the White House—complete with more than a hundred full-color photos—is fun to read not only for animal lovers but for anyone who wants a painless introduction to the softer side of the American presidency. The book begins when Millie comes to live with the Bush family in February 1987, and it ends with her telling about where each of her famous White House puppies now lives. Proceeds from the book go to help the Barbara Bush Foundation for Family Literacy.

26.3 Catalano, Grace. **Alyssa Milano: She's the Boss.** Bantam/Starfire Books, 1989. 112 pp. ISBN 0-553-28158-5.

In 1980, eight-year-old Alyssa Milano was taken to an audition for the touring production of *Annie* by her babysitter. Without ever having had an acting lesson, and to her family's amazement, she was one of four "Annies" chosen from the 1,500 children who auditioned for the part. She's gone on to star as Samantha Micelli in TV's "Who's the Boss?" This book explores the young actress's life and personality through her ideas on dating, fitness, style, success, and her future.

26.4   Catalano, Grace. **New Kids on the Block.** Bantam Books, 1989. 128 pp. ISBN 0-553-28587-4.

This is a backstage, inside look at the five members of the rock group, New Kids on the Block. In addition to biographical information about group members, you'll learn about how the group was formed and how it's managed. Photos from work and leisure are also included.

26.5   Catalano, Grace. **Richard Grieco: Hot 'n' Cool.** Bantam/Starfire Books, 1990. 99 pp. ISBN 0-553-28804-0.

This biography of Richard Grieco, superstar of TV's *Booker*, tells you how he got where he is and what he plans for the future. He was born in Watertown, New York, in 1965 and now lives in one condo in Vancouver, Canada, and another in Hollywood Hills—and he's searching for yet a new house. Grieco is a writer as well as an actor; he has written 450 poems, several short stories, and two screenplays.

26.6   Cohen, Daniel, and Susan Cohen. **Zoo Superstars.** Simon and Schuster/Minstrel Books, 1989. 85 pp. ISBN 0-671-66709-2.

You might see an animal from your own city's zoo in this book. Among the featured "stars" are the elephants at Portland, Oregon's zoo; the pandas, Hsing-Hsing and Ling-Ling, at the National Zoo in Washington; the snow leopards at the Bronx Zoo; and the white alligators at New Orleans's Audubon Park Zoo. The authors treat the animals the way they would treat human superstars, telling you interesting facts and anecdotes about the animals and what they have done to draw people to the zoos.

26.7   Deem, James M. **How to Find a Ghost.** Houghton Mifflin, 1988. 138 pp. ISBN 0-395-46846-9.

Where is the best place to look for ghosts? Not at a cemetery, says James Deem, a professor of communication, who hopes to correct the media's sometimes misleading information about ghosts. He offers "authentic" records of ghost sightings to help you learn about the several types of ghosts. Also included are tips for finding ghosts, useful charts, forms for reports, and an index to aid the person who wishes to become a ghost detective.

26.8   Drimmer, Frederick. **Born Different: The Amazing Stories of Some Very Special People.** Atheneum, 1988. 182 pp. ISBN 0-689-31360-8.

Here's a book that gives insights not only into what it's like for someone whose body is very different, but also into the morbid fascination that people have with deformities. The subjects include Siamese twins Chang and Eng, "elephant man" Joseph Merrick, and Charles "Tom Thumb" Stratton.

26.9   Heller, David. **Dear God: What Religion Were the Dinosaurs?** Illustrated by John Alcorn. Doubleday, 1990. 158 pp. ISBN 0-385-26127-6.

In this collection of children's letters to God, we get a glimpse into the private thoughts of children. They seek answers to the mysteries of life; for example, "Was Samson and the haircut thing a big disappointment to you?" And they express their views on social issues—one girl wrote that the Bakkers "should no better. The PTA scandal is disgusting." Another wrote that she hoped God was a woman because "men are such dorks."

26.10   Ingram, Jay. **Amazing Investigations: Twins.** Illustrated by Harvey Chan. Simon and Schuster, 1989. 96 pp. ISBN 0-671-66263-5.

Identical twins, fraternal twins, mirror twins, super twins, vanishing twins, twin superstitions, twin telepathy, twin savants, and twin language are all discussed in this well-documented, factual book. Harvey Chan's amusing illustrations add to the light touch and the fascination with such issues as the influence of heredity versus that of environment and why identical twins get the same cavities in their teeth.

26.11   Jack, Adrienne. **Pocket Encyclopedia: The Handy Reference for Young People.** Random House, 1989. 186 pp. ISBN 0-394-89993-8.

The more-than-600 alphabetically arranged entries are concise and illustrated by many full-color photographs and drawings. Cross-referencing makes for easy access. In addition, special tables list everything from major wars to inventors and their inventions.

26.12   Perl, Lila. **Don't Sing before Breakfast, Don't Sleep in the Moonlight: Everyday Superstitions and How They Began.** Illustrated by Erika Weihs. Clarion Books, 1988. 90 pp. ISBN 0-89919-504-0.

Most of us know more superstitions than we realize. For example, do you remember when you and your friends used to chant things like, "Step on a crack, break your mother's back"? Although we don't really believe such things, we usually help to pass them on. In this book, you will learn how some of these superstitions started and other trivia about them. A bibliography provides sources for further reading.

26.13 Perl, Lila. **From Top Hats to Baseball Caps, from Bustles to Blue Jeans: Why We Dress the Way We Do.** Illustrated by Leslie Evans. Clarion Books, 1990. 128 pp. ISBN 0-90010-972-4.

One of the points this author makes is that clothes are a kind of language. By "reading" people's clothing, we can tell such things as their occupation, the kind of event they're going to, and whether they are rich or poor. Besides the opening chapter, "The Secret Language of Clothes," there are chapters on pants, skirts, shoes, hats, and why people dress the way they do.

26.14 Powers, Tom. **Horror Movies.** Lerner, 1989. 80 pp. ISBN 0-8225-1636-5.

These six summaries of popular horror films released between the early 1930s and 1984 include explanations of production and special effects as well as quotes from actors, directors, and producers. The book contains more than forty photographs, some from the movies themselves. It may be useful for research on horror movies.

26.15 Powers, Tom. **Movie Monsters.** Lerner, 1989. 80 pp. ISBN 0-8225-1637-3.

The author gives summaries of seven monster movies released between 1931 and 1984, together with background information on some of them. Explanations of viewers' enjoyment and why viewers side with the monster are offered. More than fifty photographs are included, some from the movies themselves and others of actors behind the scenes without their makeup or costumes. There are also discussions of special effects, makeup, the directors, and other details related to the making of the movies.

26.16 Quackenbush, Robert. **Treasury of Humor.** Doubleday, 1990. 96 pp. ISBN 0-385-26654-5.

This author and collector of humor brings you a colorful book of nonsense, stories, songs, jokes, limericks, and riddles. He's organized his collection by the month, but you won't want to wait until November to read about "Sheriff Sally Gopher and the Thanksgiving Caper," or until March to sing "There was a young man named Michael Finnegan,/ He went fishing with a pin again . . . ." The cartoon-like drawings fill at least half of the pages, so the book is fun to browse as well as to read.

26.17   Reader's Digest Editors. **How in the World? A Fascinating Journey through the World of Human Ingenuity.** The Reader's Digest Association, 1990. 448 pp. ISBN 0-89577-353-8.

This book's 448 pages are full of interesting information about all kinds of things. Some of the questions that are answered include, "How will they build the wonder planes of tomorrow?" "How do they build up a prehistoric animal from a few bones?" and "How do they make cloth out of chemicals?" Full-color pictures add interest to every page.

26.18   Reed, Don C. **The Dolphins and Me.** Illustrated by Pamela and Walter Carroll. Little, Brown, 1989. 135 pp. ISBN 0-316-73659-7.

The author of this book worked for fifteen years at Marine World in California, where one of his jobs was to scrape the algae from the inside of the dolphins' tanks. Over the years, he got to know each dolphin and its individual characteristics. His interactions with the dolphins ranged from riding around the tanks on their backs to being attacked by some of the more aggressive dolphins.

26.19   Reisfeld, Randi. **So You Want to Be a Star! A Teenager's Guide to Breaking into Show Business.** Archway Paperbacks, 1990. 208 pp. ISBN 0-671-70192-4.

The author is editor of *16 Magazine* and uses the same style in this book as she does in the magazine. General advice on how to get into show business alternates with success stories of such stars as Paula Abdul, the New Kids on the Block, Tiffany, and Jason Hervey.

26.20   Rosenbloom, Joseph. **Perfect Put-Downs and Instant Insults.** Illustrated by Sanford Hoffman. Sterling, 1988. 128 pp. ISBN 0-8069-6866-4.

This book gathers together all kinds of insults and put-downs in an easy-to-read paperback. Even if you've heard some of them before, you'll find this book fun to read.

26.21 Rosenbloom, Joseph. **School's Out! Great Vacation Riddles and Jokes.** Illustrated by Sanford Hoffman. Sterling, 1990. 128 pp. ISBN 0-8069-5760-3.

You don't need to wait for summer vacation to enjoy these jokes that make fun of the frustrating parts of school and teachers.

26.22 Schwartz, Perry. **Making Movies.** Lerner, 1989. 72 pp. ISBN 0-8225-1635-7.

Many photos, both from behind the scenes and in front of the cameras, add interest to the six chapters of *Making Movies* that show what happens between the time a movie is first thought of and when you see it. There's a helpful glossary of terms and addresses to write to for more information.

26.23 Scott, Elaine. **Ramona: Behind the Scenes of a Television Show.** Photographs by Margaret Miller. William Morrow, 1988. 88 pp. ISBN 688-06819-7.

This exploration of what is involved in producing a television show has the added bonus of focusing on the successful television production of Beverly Cleary's "Ramona Quimby."

26.24 Sennett, Ted. **The Art of Hanna Barbera: Fifty Years of Creativity.** Viking Penguin, 1989. 270 pp. ISBN 0-670-82978-1.

Browsing through this book with its full-color reproductions on every page is like sitting in front of the television set and seeing such old friends as Tom and Jerry, the Flintstones, Yogi Bear, Scooby-Doo, Quick Draw McGraw, Huckleberry Hound, the Jetsons, and the Smurfs. The book opens with a couple of fully illustrated biographical chapters about Joe Barbera and Bill Hanna.

26.25 Seuling, Barbara. **It Is Illegal to Quack Like a Duck: And Other Freaky Laws.** Illustrated by Gwenn Seuling. Lodestar Books, 1988. 128 pp. ISBN 0-525-67257-5.

Does your state have any ridiculous laws on the books? It probably does, and perhaps one of them will be included in this collection. In North Carolina, for example, farmers can't use elephants to plow their cotton fields, and in Kansas it's illegal to eat rattlesnake meat on the Sabbath.

26.26 Sullivan, George. **Any Number Can Play.** Illustrated by John Caldwell. Thomas Y. Crowell, 1990. 126 pp. ISBN 0-690-04814-9.

This is a fun-to-read trivia book all about numbers. Most of the one-and two-page stories are sports related, but there's also the story of how on July 7, 1977 (7/7/77) so many people in the Maryland lottery wanted to play No. 777 that officials quit selling it—if they hadn't and the number had won, the lottery would have gone out of business!

Series

26.27   Gulliver Travels. Harcourt Brace Jovanovich/Gulliver Books.

These large, illustrated travel books give you ideas for activities and places to go, along with snippets of history. They include travel diary entries, crossword puzzles, games, and activity calendars. And Peter Lerangis's *A Kid's Guide to New York City* also cautions you about dangers there.

26.28   Peanuts Classics. Henry Holt/Owl Books.

Each of these Charles M. Schulz books is like getting a whole year of Sunday funnies all in one day. They are reprints of favorite "Peanuts" cartoon strips. Titles include *Dr. Beagle and Mr. Hyde*; *Fly, You Stupid Kite, Fly!*; *Kiss Her, You Blockhead!*; and *There Goes the Shutout*.

26.29   The Simon and Schuster Color Illustrated Question and Answer Books. Simon and Schuster.

When Did It Happen? Placing Important Events, People, Inventions—and More—in Time and *Who Were They? A Guide to Who Made Things Happen throughout History* are among the books in this series. The books present two or three questions with succinct answers on each page. A drawing or photograph accompanies each answer, and an index helps you use the books for reference. Available in paperback.

26.30   Wild Wings. Julian Messner.

Phyllis Emert is the author of these informative, easy-to-read books of about sixty pages each. Full-color photos add interest. Titles include *Fighter Planes, Helicopters, Special Task Aircraft*, and *Transports and Bombers*.

Appendix for Teachers and Librarians

Although we've organized *Your Reading* and written the annotations to speak directly to young people, we know that teachers and librarians have come to depend on it as a help in making purchasing decisions, finding books to fit curricular needs, and, most important of all, helping to match the right book with the right reader. In hopes of making this edition just as useful to you as the previous ones have been, we have taken the issues that follow into account in adapting this eighth edition of *Your Reading* to the changes occurring in the publishing world.

Timeliness: We are publishing the eighth edition only three years after the seventh edition in hopes of lessening the chances that recommended books will already be out of print by the time you read this. The marketing of books to young readers has changed considerably over the last decade. More books are published, but because of expenses connected with storage and inventory taxes, publishers do not keep books in print as long as they used to. Many paperback originals—particularly the series books—are sold in the same way that magazines are distributed through outlets in shopping mall bookstores and in grocery and drug stores. The paperback that may be a winner in March will be gone from the shelves by June, but five years later it may be issued again under a new cover—and sometimes a new title—to be marketed to a new generation of middle school and junior high readers.

Completeness: Over the past few years, books have become more expensive, and more evaluation sources have come into existence, so it has become difficult for publishers to provide free copies of books to all those who ask for and need them. We appreciate the generosity of the many publishers who contributed books to us. We also reviewed books from our local libraries and bookstores. Nevertheless, so many new books for children and young adults were published during the last three years that we make no claim that *Your Reading* is a comprehensive list.

Books That Have Lasted: To supplement the relatively brief period covered in the main sections of the book, we have prepared lists of

"Recommended Books Published before 1988" and appended these to each of the chapters, except for the nonfiction chapters, "Books to Help with Schoolwork" and "Books Just for You." We didn't prepare pre-1988 recommendations for these sections because information books become dated so quickly that it's usually better to guide students to recent titles. The pre-1988 lists are made up of committee members' favorite books and books selected from such lists as *School Library Journal*'s annual "Editors' Choices."

Incorporating the Work of Other Reviewers: If we noticed favorable reviews of books we didn't have copies of or found those books listed on a "best book" list, we searched out other reviews and went looking for copies in libraries and bookstores. We hope that we have included most of the books that we, as well as other nationally recognized evaluators, consider the best of the books published in 1988, 1989, and 1990.

We also took advantage of the fact that our list is cumulative, and we therefore had the luxury of looking at several yearly "best book" lists. As explained in the "Introduction for Young Readers," one star at the end of an annotation means that the book appeared on one nationally recognized "best book" list, two stars means that it appeared on two lists, three stars that it appeared on three lists, and so on. A summary of the books we chose from these lists appears after this appendix, but it includes only those books appearing on more than one "best book" list. We thought it would be helpful to you to see in one place the books that critics judged as outstanding in each of the three years we cover here. And although it seemed too cumbersome to include such details in the annotations themselves, we thought you would like to know which groups chose to honor which books, since each group has its own criteria for the books it selects. For example, those books on the American Library Association's list of "Notable Children's Books" and those chosen by the editors of *School Library Journal* are likely to be more appropriate for younger readers than are those chosen by the Young Adult Services Division (YASD) of the American Library Association. And the books on the YASD "Quick Picks" list, which used to be called "Recommended Books for the Reluctant Young Adult Reader," are likely to be fairly easy to read and possibly of lesser literary quality than are those cited as winners of miscellaneous prizes. In addition to the specific evaluation sources shown in our summary lists, we consulted the "Children's Choices" lists prepared by the International Reading Association in cooperation with the Children's Book Council. However, we did not include their listing in the final summary because of our publishing deadline.

Series Books: Rather than trying to write individual annotations for series books, which in most cases would have been unavoidably repetitious, we have written general annotations for the series and mentioned only sample titles. These annotations are necessarily less complete, especially in that we could not include the number of pages or International Standard Book Numbers (ISBNs), which you usually need for purchasing, because the annotation refers to a whole set of books, some of which may not have been published yet and others of which are already out of print. In both the index and the annotations, the books are alphabetized under the series title rather than the authors' last names because it's common for several authors to write different titles in a series. You'll find series titles at the ends of chapters, just after the annotations for individual books.

The Question of Paperback versus Hardback: The question of paperback versus hardback is another changing area of publishing, and over the last few years, some very good books (and also some very bad ones) have come out as original paperbacks, while others have been simultaneously published in both formats. From reading our annotations, you won't be able to tell whether a book is in paperback or hardback. Because our assignment was to review books newly published during the years 1988, 1989, and 1990, we reviewed books that came out as original paperbacks, but not paperback books that were reprints of hardbacks. By the time you read this, many of the books that are cited here in their hardback editions will also be available in paperback. Please consult the most recent edition of *Paperbound Books in Print*, published annually by R. R. Bowker Company, which is available in most libraries.

Encouraging Students to Use This Book: We have written these annotations in the form of miniature book talks aimed at junior high and middle school readers, so please do what you can to bring *Your Reading* to the attention of your students. If you're a teacher, keep it on your desk and encourage students to refer to it. When you are focusing on free reading or on a particular theme or topic, photocopy and distribute lists of recommended books so students can take them along to the library. If you are a librarian, keep a copy of *Your Reading* out where students can easily use it. Highlighting or putting a check mark by the annotations of the books that you have in your library will save time for you and your students.

We hope this book proves itself useful. It was a labor of love by the committee and by our friends, students, relatives, neighbors, colleagues, and anyone else we could get to read and write about the thousands of books that came our way. Happy Reading!

Alleen Pace Nilsen
Tempe, Arizona

Best Books for Young Teens 1990, 1989, and 1988

The books listed below appear on two or more "best-books-of-the-year" lists. The initials following the titles identify which standard reviewing sources judged the books as exceptional. Only those titles judged appropriate for young teens were gleaned from these lists.

Key to Reviewing Sources

ALSC: Association of Library Service to Children "Notable Children's Books."

BKLT: *Booklist* Editors' Choices.

MISC: Newbery Awards, *Boston Globe-Hornbook* Awards, *New York Times,* and other miscellaneous lists, such as cumulative lists of the "best of the 1980s."

SLJ: *School Library Journal* Editors' Choices.

YASD-B: Young Adult Services Division of the American Library Association annual "Best Books for Young Adults" list.

YASD-Q: Young Adult Services Division of the American Library Association annual "Recommended Books for the Reluctant Young Adult Reader" published under the title of "Quick Picks."

1990 Best Books

Aamundsen, N. R. *Two Short and One Long.* ALSC, MISC.

Agard, J., compiler. *Life Doesn't Frighten Me at All.* YASD-B, YASD-Q.

Avi. *The True Confessions of Charlotte Doyle.* ALSC, BKLT, MISC, SLJ, YASD-B.

Blake, J. *Risky Times: How to Be AIDS-Smart and Stay Healthy.* YASD-B, YASD-Q.

Bode, J. *The Voices of Rape.* BKLT, YASD-B.

Brooks, B. *Everywhere.* ALSC, BKLT, SLJ.

Byars, B. *Bingo Brown, Gypsy Lover.* ALSC, SLJ.

Clarke, J. *The Heroic Life of Al Capsella.* BKLT, YASD-B.

Defelice, C. *Weasel.* ALSC, SLJ.

Doherty, B. *White Peak Farm.* ALSC, BKLT, SLJ, YASD-B.

Fleischman, P. *Saturnalia.* BKLT, MISC, SLJ.

Freedman, R. *Franklin Delano Roosevelt.* ALSC, BKLT, SLJ, YASD-B.

Gilmore, K. *Enter Three Witches*. BKLT, YASD-B.

Hall, B. *Dixie Storms*. ALSC, BKLT, SLJ, YASD-B.

Hamanaka, S. *The Journey: Japanese Americans, Racism, and Renewal*. SLJ, YASD-B, YASD-Q.

Hamilton, V. *Cousins*. ALSC, BKLT, YASD-B.

Hendry, F. M. *Quest for a Maid*. ALSC, YASD-B.

Ho, M. *Rice without Rain*. BKLT, YASD-B.

Katz, W. L. *Breaking the Chains: African-American Slave Resistance*. SLJ, YASD-B.

Klause, A. C. *The Silver Kiss*. BKLT, SLJ, YASD-B, YASD-Q.

Korman, G. *Losing Joe's Place*. YASD-B, YASD-Q.

Lauber, P. *Seeing Earth from Space*. ALSC, BKLT, SLJ, YASD-B, YASD-Q.

Mattox, C. W., compiler and adaptor. *Shake It to the One That You Love the Best: Play Songs and Lullabies from Black Musical Traditions*. ALSC, BKLT.

Meltzer, M. *Columbus and the World around Him*. ALSC, BKLT, SLJ, YASD-B.

Paulsen, G. *Woodsong*. ALSC, BKLT, SLJ, YASD-B, YASD-Q.

Price, L. *Aida*. ALSC, BKLT.

Ray, D. *A Nation Torn: The Story of How the Civil War Began*. SLJ, YASD-B.

Sattler, H. R. *Giraffes, the Sentinels of the Savannahs*. ALSC, SLJ.

Schami, R. *A Hand Full of Stars*. ALSC, MISC, YASD-B.

Sleator, W. *Strange Attractors*. BKLT, YASD-B.

Snyder, Z. K. *Libby on Wednesday*. SLJ, YASD-B.

Soto, G. *Baseball in April: And Other Stories*. MISC, YASD-B.

Spinelli, J. *Maniac Magee*. ALSC, MISC, YASD-B.

Stanley, D., and P. Vennema. *Good Queen Bess: The Story of Elizabeth I of England* . ALSC, BKLT.

Sutcliff, R. *The Shining Company*. ALSC, BKLT, SLJ.

Wrede, P. C. *Dealing with Dragons*. BKLT, SLJ, YASD-B.

1989 Best Books

Anderson, J. *The American Family Farm*. ALSC, SLJ, YASD-B.

Bawden, N. *The Outside Child*. ALSC, MISC.

Blumberg, R. *The Great American Gold Rush*. ALSC, BKLT, MISC, SLJ.

Brooks, B. *No Kidding*. BKLT, SLJ, YASD-B.

Byars, B. *Bingo Brown and the Language of Love*. MISC, SLJ.

Carter, A. R. *Up Country*. BKLT, YASD-B.

Cole, B. *Celine*. BKLT, MISC (3), YASD-B.

Conrad, P. *My Daniel*. BKLT, YASD-B.

Dickinson, P. *Eva*. ALSC, BKLT, MISC (2), SLJ, YASD-B.

Duder, T. *In Lane Three, Alex Archer*. BKLT, SLJ, YASD-B.

Duncan, L. *Don't Look behind You*. YASD-B, YASD-Q.

Facklam, M. *The Trouble with Mothers.* YASD-B, YASD-Q.

Fritz, J. *The Great Little Madison.* ALSC, BKLT, MISC (2), SLJ.

Grant, C. D. *Phoenix Rising: or How to Survive Your Life.* SLJ, YASD-B, YASD-Q.

Hudson, J. *Sweetgrass.* ALSC, BKLT, MISC, SLJ, YASD-B.

Janeczko, P. B. *Brickyard Summer.* YASD-B, YASD-Q.

Laird, E. *Loving Ben.* SLJ, YASD-B.

Little, J. *Hey World, Here I Am!* ALSC, SLJ.

Lowry, L. *Number the Stars.* ALSC, BKLT, MISC, SLJ.

McKissack, P., and F. McKissack. *A Long Hard Journey: The Story of the Pullman Porter.* ALSC, MISC.

Nelson, T. *And One for All.* ALSC, BKLT, MISC, SLJ, YASD-B.

Newth, M. *The Abduction.* SLJ, YASD-B.

Paulsen, G. *The Voyage of the Frog.* ALSC, SLJ, YASD-B, YASD-Q.

Paulsen, G. *The Winter Room.* ALSC, MISC.

Peet, B. *Bill Peet, an Autobiography.* ALSC, MISC (2), SLJ.

Pevsner, S. *How Could You Do It, Diane?* BKLT, YASD-B, YASD-Q.

Pinkwater, J. *Buffalo Brenda.* ALSC, YASD-B.

Rodowsky, C. *Sydney, Herself.* BKLT, YASD-B.

Sacks, M. *Beyond Safe Boundaries.* MISC, SLJ.

Sieruta, P. *Heartbeats.* BKLT, MISC, SLJ, YASD-B, YASD-Q.

Sills, L. *Inspirations: Stories about Women Artists.* ALSC, BKLT.

Slepian, J. *The Broccoli Tapes.* ALSC, BKLT, SLJ.

St. George, J. *Panama Canal: Gateway to the World.* ALSC, SLJ.

Staples, S. F. *Shabanu, Daughter of the Wind.* ALSC, MISC (3), YASD-B.

Voigt, C. *Seventeen against the Dealer.* BKLT, SLJ.

Yep, L. *The Rainbow People.* ALSC, BKLT, MISC.

1988 Best Books

Arnosky, J. *Sketching Outdoors in Autumn.* ALSC, BKLT.

Ashabranner, B. *Always to Remember: The Story of the Vietnam Veterans Memorial.* ALSC, BKLT, YASD-B.

Ballard, R. D. *Exploring the Titanic: How the Greatest Ship Ever Lost Was Found.* SLJ, YASD-Q.

Bawden, N. *Henry.* ALSC, BKLT.

Byars, B. *The Burning Questions of Bingo Brown.* BKLT, SLJ.

Chaucer, G. *Canterbury Tales.* BKLT, SLJ.

Cleary, B. *A Girl from Yamhill: A Memoir.* ALSC, MISC, YASD-B.

Davis, J. *Sex Education.* BKLT, SLJ, YASD-Q.

Deaver, J. R. *Say Goodnight, Gracie.* BKLT, YASD-B, YASD-Q.

Ehrlich, A. *Where It Stops, Nobody Knows.* BKLT, MISC.

Ellis, S. *A Family Project.* ALSC, MISC.

Fleischman, P. *Joyful Noise: Poems for Two Voices.* ALSC, MISC (2), YASD-B.

Fox, P. *The Village by the Sea.* BKLT, MISC, SLJ.

Freedman, R. *Buffalo Hunt.* BKLT, MISC, SLJ.

Fritz, J. *China's Long March: 6,000 Miles of Danger.* ALSC, BKLT.

Garfield, L. *The Empty Sleeve.* BKLT, SLJ.

Hamilton, V. *Anthony Burns: The Defeat and Triumph of a Fugitive Slave.* ALSC, MISC, SLJ, YASD-B.

Hamilton, V. *In the Beginning: Creation Stories from around the World.* ALSC, BKLT, MISC (2), YASD-B.

Hartling, P. *Crutches.* ALSC, MISC.

Hinton, S. E. *Taming the Star Runner.* YASD-B, YASD-Q.

Isaacson, P. *Round Buildings, Square Buildings, and Buildings that Wiggle Like a Fish.* MISC (2).

Janezcko, P., compiler. *The Music of What Happens: Poems That Tell Stories.* BKLT, SLJ, YASD-B.

Jones, D. W. *The Lives of Christopher Chant.* ALSC, BKLT.

Little, J. *Little by Little: A Writer's Education.* ALSC, MISC.

Lyon, G. E. *Borrowed Children.* BKLT, SLJ.

Macaulay, D. *The Way Things Work: From Levers to Lasers, Cars to Computers—a Visual Guide to the World of Machines.* ALSC, MISC (2), SLJ.

MacLachlan, P. *The Facts and Fictions of Minna Pratt.* ALSC, MISC.

Madaras, L. *Lynda Madaras Talks to Teens about AIDS: An Essential Guide for Parents, Teachers, and Young People.* BKLT, MISC (2), SLJ, YASD-B.

Mahy, M. *Memory.* BKLT, MISC, SLJ, YASD-B.

Marrin, A. *The War for Independence: The Story of the American Revolution.* BKLT, MISC, SLJ.

McKinley, R. *The Outlaws of Sherwood.* ALSC, MISC, YASD-B.

Meltzer, M. *Rescue: The Story of How Gentiles Saved Jews in the Holocaust.* ALSC, MISC, SLJ, YASD-B.

Morrison, L., compiler. *Rhythm Road: Poems to Move To.* ALSC, YASD-B.

Myers, W. D. *Fallen Angels.* BKLT, MISC (2), SLJ, YASD-B, YASD-Q.

Myers, W. D. *Scorpions.* ALSC, MISC.

Pullman, P. *Shadow in the North.* BKLT, YASD-B.

Rogasky, B. *Smoke and Ashes: The Story of the Holocaust.* ALSC, BKLT, MISC, SLJ, YASD-B.

Rylant, C. *A Kindness.* SLJ, YASD-B.

Sleator, W. *The Duplicate.* SLJ, YASD-B, YASD-Q.

Wolff, V. E. *Probably Still Nick Swanson.* BKLT, MISC, SLJ, YASD-B.

Wyss, T. H. *Here at the Scenic-Vu Motel.* YASD-B, YASD-Q.

Directory of Publishers

Algonquin Books. Division of Workman Publishing Company, Inc. Orders to: 708 Broadway, New York, NY 10003. 800-722-7202.

Apple Paperbacks. Imprint of Scholastic, Inc. Orders to: 2931 East McCarty Street, Jefferson City, MO 65102. 800-325-6149.

Arcade Publishing, Inc. Imprint of Little, Brown and Company. Orders to: Order Department, 200 West Street, Waltham, MA 02154. 800-759-0190.

Archway Paperbacks. Imprint of Simon and Schuster. Orders to: 200 Old Tappan Road, Old Tappan, NJ 07675. 800-223-2336.

Arte Público. University of Houston, M. D. Anderson Library, Room 2, 4800 Calhoun, Houston, TX 77204-2090. 713-749-4768.

Atheneum Publishers. Imprint of Charles Scribner's Sons. Orders to: Riverside Distribution Center, 100 Front Street, Riverside, NJ 08075. 800-257-5755.

Avon Books. Orders to: P.O. Box 767 Dresden, TN 38225. 800-223-0690 (for customers with accounts at Avon Books) or 800-238-0658 (for individual orders and customer service).

Ballantine Books. Division of Random House. Orders to: Order Department, Westminster Distribution Center, 400 Hahn Road, Westminster, MD 21157. 800-726-0600 (customer service); 800-733-3000 (orders).

Bantam Books. Division of Bantam Doubleday Dell Publishing Group, 666 Fifth Avenue, New York, NY 10103. 800-223-6834 ext. 9236.

Borzoi Sprinters. Imprint of Alfred A. Knopf. Orders to: Order Department, Westminster Distribution Center, 400 Hahn Road, Westminster, MD 21157. 800-726-0600 (customer service); 800-733-3000 (orders).

Bradbury Press. Imprint of Macmillan Publishing Company, Inc. Orders to: Riverside Distribution Center, 100 Front Street, Riverside, NJ 08075. 800-257-5755.

Bullseye Books. Imprint of Alfred A. Knopf. Orders to: Order Department, Westminster Distribution Center, 400 Hahn Road, Westminster, MD 21157. 800-726-0600 (customer service); 800-733-3000 (orders).

Camelot Books. Imprint of Avon Books. Orders to: P.O. Box 767, Dresden, TN 38225. 800-223-0690 (for customers with accounts at Avon Books) or 800-238-0658 (for individual orders and customer service).

Carolrhoda Books, Inc. 241 First Avenue North, Minneapolis, MN 55401. 800-328-4929.

Chelsea House Publishers. Division of Main Line Book Company. Administrative Office, 1974 Sproul Road, Suite 400, Broomall, PA 19008. 800-848-2665.

Chicago Review Press, Inc. 814 North Franklin Street, Chicago, IL 60610. 800-888-4741.

Children's Press. Division of Grolier, Inc. 5440 North Cumberland Avenue, Chicago, IL 60656. 800-621-1115.

Chronicle Books. Division of Chronicle Publishing Company. 275 Fifth Street, San Francisco, CA 94103. 800-722-6657; 800-445-7577 in California.

Clarion Books. Subsidiary of Houghton Mifflin. Orders to: Wayside Road, Burlington, MA 01803. 800-225-3362.

Columbine. Imprint of Fawcett Books. Orders to: Order Department, Westminster Distribution Center, 400 Hahn Road, Westminster, MD 21157. 800-726-0600 (customer service); 800-733-3000 (orders).

Crestwood House, Inc. Distributed by Macmillan Publishing Company, Inc. Orders to: Riverside Distribution Center, 100 Front Street, Riverside, NJ 08075. 800-257-5755.

Thomas Y. Crowell. Distributed by HarperCollins. Thomas Y. Crowell has been phased out, so some titles may have gone out of print; call ahead to find out whether the title you want is available. Orders to: 1000 Keystone Industrial Park, Scranton, PA 18512. 800-331-3761. (See HarperCollins.)

Crown Publishers, Inc. Division of Random House. Orders to: Order Department, Westminster Distribution Center, 400 Hahn Road, Westminster, MD 21157. 800-726-0600 (customer service); 800-733-3000 (orders).

Delacorte Press. Imprint of Dell Publishing Company, Inc. 666 Fifth Avenue, New York, NY 10103. 800-223-6834 ext. 9236.

Dell Publishing Company, Inc. Division of Bantam Doubleday Dell Publishing Group. 666 Fifth Avenue, New York, NY 10103. 800-223-6834 ext. 9236.

Michael di Capua Books. Imprint of Farrar, Straus and Giroux. Distributed by The Putnam Berkley Group, Inc., 390 Murray Hill Parkway, East Rutherford, NJ 07073, ATTN: Mail Order Department (for individual orders) or ATTN: Order Editing (for school or library orders). 800-847-5515; 607-775-1740 in New York.

Dial Books for Young Readers. Division of E. P. Dutton. Orders to: Penguin USA, P.O. Box 999, Bergenfield, NJ 07621. 201-387-0600.

Dial Press. Imprint of Doubleday and Company, Inc. 666 Fifth Avenue, New York, NY 10103. 800-223-6834 ext. 9236.

Dillon Press, Inc. 242 Portland Avenue South, Minneapolis, MN 55415. 800-962-0437.

Dodd, Mead and Company has gone out of business. Some of their titles are being distributed by Siena Publishers' Associates, 45 West 36th Street, New York, NY 10018. Call first at 800-223-0282 to see if the title you are interested in is available. Some other titles are also available through The Putnam Berkley Group, Inc., 390 Murray Hill Parkway, East Rutherford, NJ 07073, ATTN: Mail Order Department (for individual orders) or ATTN: Order Editing (for school or library orders). 800-847-5515; 607-775-1740 in New York.

Doubleday and Company, Inc. Division of Bantam Doubleday Dell Publishing Group. 666 Fifth Avenue, New York, NY 10103. 800-223-6834 ext. 9236.

E. P. Dutton. Division of Penguin USA. Orders to: Penguin USA, P.O. Box 999, Bergenfield, NJ 07621. 201-387-0600.

Enslow Publishers, Inc. Box 777, Bloy Street and Ramsey Avenue, Hillside, NJ 07205. 201-964-4116.

M. Evans and Company, Inc. Distributed by National Book Network, 4720 Boston Way, Lanham, MD 20706. 800-462-6420.

Facts on File Inc. Subsidiary of Commerce Clearing House. 460 Park Avenue South, New York, NY 10016. 800-322-8755.

Farrar, Straus and Giroux. Distributed by The Putnam Berkley Group, Inc., 390 Murray Hill Parkway, East Rutherford, NJ 07073, ATTN: Mail Order Department (for individual orders) or ATTN: Order Editing (for school or library orders). 800-847-5515; 607-775-1740 in New York.

Fawcett Books. Division of Ballantine Books. Orders to: Order Department, Westminster Distribution Center, 400 Hahn Road, Westminster, MD 21157. 800-726-0600 (customer service); 800-733-3000 (orders).

Fawcett Junior Books. Imprint of Fawcett Books. Orders to: Order Department, Westminster Distribution Center, 400 Hahn Road, Westminster, MD 21157. 800-726-0600 (customer service); 800-733-3000 (orders).

Flare Books. Imprint of Avon Books. Orders to: P.O. Box 767, Dresden, TN 38225. 800-223-0690 (for customers with accounts at Avon Books) or 800-238-0658 (for individual orders and customer service).

Four Winds Press. Imprint of Macmillan Publishing Company, Inc. Orders to: Riverside Distribution Center, 100 Front Street, Riverside, NJ 08075. 800-257-5755.

David R. Godine Publisher, Inc. Distributed by American International Distribution Corp., 64 Depot Road, Colchester, VT 05446. 800-445-6638.

Stephen Greene Press. Division of Penguin USA. Orders to: Penguin USA, P.O. Box 999, Bergenfield, NJ 07621. 201-387-0600.

Greenwillow Books. Division of William Morrow and Company, Inc. Orders to: Wilmor Inc., Order Department, 39 Plymouth Street, Fairfield, NJ 07004. 800-237-0657 (customer service); 800-843-9389 (orders).

Grosset and Dunlap, Inc. Imprint of The Putnam Berkley Group, Inc. 390 Murray Hill Parkway, East Rutherford, NJ 07073. ATTN: Mail Order Department (for individual orders) or ATTN: Order Editing (for school or library orders). 800-847-5515; 607-775-1740 in New York.

Gulliver Books. Imprint of Harcourt Brace Jovanovich, Inc. Orders to: 465 South Lincoln Drive, Troy, MO 63379. 800-225-5425.

Hampstead Press. Formerly an imprint of Franklin Watts. Hampstead Press has been phased out, but some titles are still available. Call ahead to find out if the one you want is still in print. Orders to: P.O. Box 1741 Sherman Turnpike, Danbury, CT 06816, ATTN: New Orders. 800-843-3749.

Harcourt Brace Jovanovich, Inc. Orders to: 465 South Lincoln Drive, Troy, MO 63379. 800-225-5425.

Harmony Books. Imprint of Crown Publishers, Inc. Orders to: Order Department, Westminster Distribution Center, 400 Hahn Road, Westminster, MD 21157. 800-726-0600 (customer service); 800-733-3000 (orders).

Harper and Row Junior Books Group. Division of Harper and Row, Publishers, Inc. (Now HarperCollins). Orders to: 1000 Keystone Industrial Park, Scranton, PA 18512. 800-331-3761. (See HarperCollins.)

Harper and Row, Publishers, Inc. (Now HarperCollins). Orders to: 1000 Keystone Industrial Park, Scranton, PA 18512. 800-331-3761. (See HarperCollins.)

Harper Keypoint Books. Formerly an imprint of Harper and Row Junior Books Group. Titles are now available as HarperCollins titles. Orders to: 1000 Keystone Industrial Park, Scranton, PA 18512. 800-331-3761.

HarperCollins was formed in July of 1990 when Harper and Row, Publishers, Inc. reorganized and changed their name. Most titles in this edition of *Your Reading* came out before the change, but we listed HarperCollins to avoid any confusion about where to order Harper and Row books. You can order them through HarperCollins, which has kept the same ordering address as Harper and Row had before the change: 1000 Keystone Industrial Park, Scranton, PA 18512. 800-331-3761.

HarperCollins/Trade Division. Orders to: 1000 Keystone Industrial Park, Scranton, PA 18512. 800-331-3761.

Harpercrest. Division of HarperCollins. Orders to: 1000 Keystone Industrial Park, Scranton, PA 18512. 800-331-3761.

Holiday House. 425 Madison Avenue, New York, NY 10017. 212-688-0085.

Henry Holt and Company. Orders to: Order Department, P.O. Box 30135, Salt Lake City, UT 84130. 800-488-5233.

Houghton Mifflin Company. Orders to: Wayside Road, Burlington, MA 01803. 800-225-3362.

Hunter House, Inc. Publishers. Distributed by Publisher's Services, Box 2510, Novato, CA 94948. 415-883-3140.

Donald Hutter Books. Imprint of Henry Holt and Company. Orders to: Order Department, P.O. Box 30135, Salt Lake City, UT 84130. 800-488-5233.

Ivy Books. Division of Ballantine Books. Orders to: Order Department, Westminster Distribution Center, 400 Hahn Road, Westminster, MD 21157. 800-726-0600 (customer service); 800-733-3000 (orders).

Richard Jackson Books. Orders to: Orchard Books. P.O. Box 1741 Sherman Turnpike, Danbury, CT 06816, ATTN: New Orders. 800-843-3749.

Jewish Publication Society. 60 E. 42nd Street, Suite 1339, New York, NY 10165. 212-687-0809.

Joy Street Books. Imprint of Little, Brown and Company. Orders to: Order Department, 200 West Street, Waltham, MA 02154. 800-759-0190.

Juniper Books. Imprint of Fawcett Books. Orders to: Order Department, Westminster Distribution Center, 400 Hahn Road, Westminster, MD 21157. 800-726-0600 (customer service); 800-733-3000 (orders).

Alfred A. Knopf. Subsidiary of Random House. Orders to: Order Department, Westminster Distribution Center, 400 Hahn Road, Westminster, MD 21157. 800-726-0600 (customer service); 800-733-3000 (orders).

Lerner Publications Company. 241 First Avenue North, Minneapolis, MN 55401. 800-328-4929.

J. B. Lippincott Company. Subsidiary of Wolters Kluwer U.S. Corp. Orders to: P.O. Box 1580, Hagerstown, MD 21741. 800-638-3030.

Little, Brown and Company. Division of Time, Inc. Orders to: Order Department, 200 West Street, Waltham, MA 02154. 800-759-0190.

Lodestar Books. Imprint of E. P. Dutton. Orders to: Penguin USA, P.O. Box 999, Bergenfield, NJ 07621. 201-387-0600.

Lothrop, Lee and Shepard Books. Division of William Morrow and Company, Inc. Orders to: Wilmor Inc., Order Department, 39 Plymouth Street, Fairfield, NJ 07004. 800-237-0657 (customer service); 800-843-9389 (orders).

Macmillan Publishing Company, Inc. Orders to: Riverside Distribution Center, 100 Front Street, Riverside, NJ 08075. 800-257-5755.

Margaret K. McElderry Books. Imprint of Charles Scribner's Sons. Orders to: Riverside Distribution Center, 100 Front Street, Riverside, NJ 08075. 800-257-5755.

David McKay Company, Inc. Subsidiary of Random House. Orders to: Order Department, Westminster Distribution Center, 400 Hahn Road, Westminster, MD 21157. 800-726-0600 (customer service); 800-733-3000 (orders).

Meriwether Publishing, Ltd. Box 7710 Colorado Springs, CO 80933. 800-937-5297. 719-594-4422.

Julian Messner. Division of Silver Burdett Press. Orders to: 200 Old Tappan Road, Old Tappan, NJ 07675. 800-223-2336.

Minstrel Books. Imprint of Simon and Schuster. Orders to: 200 Old Tappan Road, Old Tappan, NJ 07675. 800-223-2336.

Morrow Junior Books. Division of William Morrow and Company, Inc. Orders to: Wilmor Inc., Order Department, 39 Plymouth Street, Fairfield, NJ 07004. 800-237-0657 (customer service); 800-843-9389 (orders).

William Morrow and Company, Inc. Orders to: Wilmor Inc., Order Department, 39 Plymouth Street, Fairfield, NJ 07004. 800-237-0657 (customer service); 800-843-9389 (orders).

National Council of Teachers of English. 1111 Kenyon Road, Urbana, IL 61801. 800-369-6283.

New American Library. Division of Penguin USA. Orders to: Penguin USA, P.O. Box 999, Bergenfield, NJ 07621. 201-387-0600.

Newcastle Publishing Company, Inc. P.O. Box 7589, Van Nuys, CA 91409. 213-873-3191.

Orchard Books. Division of Franklin Watts. Orders to: P.O. Box 1741 Sherman Turnpike, Danbury, CT 06816, ATTN: New Orders. 800-843-3749.

Orion Books. Imprint of Crown Publishers, Inc. Orders to: Order Department, Westminster Distribution Center, 400 Hahn Road, Westminster, MD 21157. 800-726-0600 (customer service); 800-733-3000 (orders).

Owl Books. Imprint of Henry Holt and Company. Orders to: Order Department, P.O. Box 30135, Salt Lake City, UT 84130. 800-488-5233.

Pantheon Books. Division of Random House. Orders to: Order Department, Westminster Distribution Center, 400 Hahn Road, Westminster, MD 21157. 800-726-0600 (customer service); 800-733-3000 (orders).

Penguin USA. P.O. Box 999, Bergenfield, NJ 07621. 201-387-0600.

Philomel Books. Imprint of The Putnam Berkley Group, Inc. 390 Murray Hill Parkway, East Rutherford, NJ 07073, ATTN: Mail Order Department (for individual orders) or ATTN: Order Editing (for school or library orders). 800-847-5515; 607-775-1740 in New York.

Pocket Books. Imprint of Simon and Schuster. Orders to: 200 Old Tappan Road, Old Tappan, NJ 07675. 800-223-2336.

Clarkson N. Potter Books. Imprint of Crown Publishers, Inc. Orders to: Order Department, Westminster Distribution Center, 400 Hahn Road, Westminster, MD 21157. 800-726-0600 (customer service); 800-733-3000 (orders).

G. P. Putnam's Sons. Division of The Putnam Berkley Group, Inc. 390 Murray Hill Parkway, East Rutherford, NJ 07073, ATTN: Mail Order Department (for individual orders) or ATTN: Order Editing (for school or library orders). 800-847-5515; 607-775-1740 in New York.

Random House. Orders to: Order Department, Westminster Distribution Center, 400 Hahn Road, Westminster, MD 21157. 800-726-0600 (customer service); 800-733-3000 (orders).

Reader's Digest Association, Inc. Distributed by Random House. Orders to: Order Department, Westminster Distribution Center, 400 Hahn Road, Westminster, MD 21157. 800-726-0600 (customer service); 800-733-3000 (orders).

Rosen Publishing Group Inc. 29 East 21st Street, New York, NY 10010. 800-237-9932; 212-777-3017 in New York.

Scholastic Hardcovers. Imprint of Scholastic, Inc. Orders to: 2931 East McCarty Street, Jefferson City, MO 65102. 800-325-6149.

Scholastic, Inc. Orders to: 2931 East McCarty Street, Jefferson City, MO 65102. 800-325-6149.

Charles Scribner's Sons. Distributed by Macmillan Publishing Company, Inc. Orders to: Riverside Distribution Center, 100 Front Street, Riverside, NJ 08075. 800-257-5755.

Sierra Club Books. Distributed by Random House. Orders to: Order Department, Westminster Distribution Center, 400 Hahn Road, Westminster, MD 21157. 800-726-0600 (customer service); 800-733-3000 (orders).

Sierra Club Wildlife Library. Distributed by Little, Brown and Company. Orders to: Order Department, 200 West Street, Waltham, MA 02154. 800-759-0190.

Silver Burdett Press. Division of Simon and Schuster. Orders to: 200 Old Tappan Road, Old Tappan, NJ 07675. 800-223-2336.

Simon and Schuster. Orders to: 200 Old Tappan Road, Old Tappan, NJ 07675. 800-223-2336.

Skylark Books. Imprint of Bantam Books. 666 Fifth Avenue, New York, NY 10103. 800-223-6834 ext. 9236.

Sports Illustrated for Kids Books. Distributed by Little, Brown and Company. Orders to: Order Department, 200 West Street, Waltham, MA 02154. 800-759-0190.

Starfire Books. Imprint of Bantam Books. 666 Fifth Avenue, New York, NY 10103. 800-223-6834 ext. 9236.

Sterling Publishing Company, Inc. 387 Park Avenue South, Fifth Floor, New York, NY 10016-8810. 800-367-9692.

Ellen C. Temple Publishing Inc. Distributed by Texas Monthly Press, P.O. Box 1569, Austin, TX 78767. 512-476-7085; 800-252-4437 in Texas.

Troll Associates. Subsidiary of Educational Reading Services. 100 Corporate Drive, Mahwah, NJ 07430. 800-526-5289.

Trophy. Imprint of Harper and Row Junior Books Group. Orders to: 1000 Keystone Industrial Park, Scranton, PA 18512. 800-331-3761. (See HarperCollins.)

Viking. Division of Penguin USA. Orders to: Penguin USA, P.O. Box 999, Bergenfield, NJ 07621. 201-387-0600.

Viking Kestrel. Imprint of Viking Penguin. Orders to: Penguin USA, P.O. Box 999, Bergenfield, NJ 07621. 201-387-0600.

Viking Penguin. Division of Penguin USA. Orders to: Penguin USA, P.O. Box 999, Bergenfield, NJ 07621. 201-387-0600.

Walker and Company. Division of Walker Publishing Company, Inc. 720 Fifth Avenue, New York, NY 10019. 800-289-25537. (This number looks nonstandard, but it does work.)

Warner Books, Inc. Distributed by Little, Brown and Company. Orders to: Order Department, 200 West Street, Waltham, MA 02154. 800-759-0190.

Warren-Mattox Productions. Distributed by Lancaster Productions, P.O. Box 7820, Berkeley, CA 94707. 415-549-7110.

Franklin Watts. Subsidiary of Grolier, Inc. Orders to: P.O. Box 1741 Sherman Turnpike, Danbury, CT 06816, ATTN: New Orders. 800-843-3749.

The Westminster Press/John Knox Press. 100 Witherspoon Street, Louisville, KY 40202-1396. 800-523-1631.

Albert Whitman and Company. 5747 West Howard Street, Niles, IL 60648. 800-255-7675.

Workman Publishing Company, Inc. 708 Broadway, New York, NY 10003. 800-722-7202.

Yearling Books. Imprint of Dell Publishing Company, Inc. 666 Fifth Avenue, New York, NY 10103. 800-223-6834 ext. 9236.

Floyd Yearout Books. Orders to: Farrar, Straus and Giroux, The Putnam Berkley Group, Inc., Distributors, 390 Murray Hill Parkway, East Rutherford, NJ 07073, ATTN: Mail Order Department (for individual orders) or ATTN: Order Editing (for school or library orders). 800-847-5515; 607-775-1740 in New York.

Jane Yolen Books. Imprint of Harcourt Brace Jovanovich, Inc. Orders to: 465 South Lincoln Drive, Troy, MO 63379. 800-225-5425.

Charlotte Zolotow Books. Imprint of Harper and Row Junior Books Group. Orders to: 1000 Keystone Industrial Park, Scranton, PA 18512. 800-331-3761. (See HarperCollins.)

Author Index

Aamundsen, Nina Ring, 8.1
Aaseng, Nathan, 11.1, 11.2
Abt, Samuel, 9.9
Adamson, Joe, 26.1
Adler, C. S., 2.1, 2.2, 2.3, 5.1
Adler, David A., 22.1
Agard, John, 17.1
Aiken, Joan, 13.1, 18.1, 18.2
Aisenberg, Nadya, 17.2
Alcock, Vivien, 3.1
Aleksin, Anatoly, 18.3
Alexander, Lloyd, 13.2, 13.3
Allen, Richard E., 5.2
Allison, Linda, 25.1
American Medical Association, 24.1
Ames, Mildred, 1.1
Ammon, Richard, 21.1
Anderson, Dave, 9.10
Anderson, David, 22.2
Anderson, Joan, 21.2
Andronik, Catherine M., 23.1
Angell, Judie, 1.2, 15.1
Appel, Mary, 9.11
Armour, John, 22.3
Arnosky, Jim, 25.2, 25.3
Asch, Frank, 14.1
Ash, Russell, 16.1
Ashabranner, Brent, 21.3, 21.4, 21.5
Asimov, Isaac, 14.2, 18.4
Asimov, Janet, 14.2
Aska, Warabe, 17.3
Associated Press, The, 22.4
Auch, Mary Jane, 1.3, 2.4, 2.5
Avi, 13.4

Bach, Alice, 16.2
Baczewski, Paul, 9.1
Baehr, Patricia, 2.6
Baird, Thomas, 14.3, 14.4
Baklanov, Grigory, 10.1
Baldwin, J., 20.1
Ballard, Robert D., 22.5
Banks, Lynne Reid, 14.5, 15.2
Barkin, Carol, 25.4, 25.11
Barrie, Barbara, 6.1

Barron, Thomas A., 14.6
Bauer, Marion Dane, 13.5
Baum, L. Frank, 16.3
Bawden, Nina, 2.7, 10.2
Beatty, Patricia, 10.3
Bell, Clare, 14.7
Bellairs, John, 14.8
Bennett, James, 5.3
Bennett, Jay, 15.3
Benson, Kathleen, 22.17
Bentley, Judith, 11.3
Berger, Melvin, 19.1, 23.2
Bergman, Tamar, 8.2
Berliner, Don, 19.2, 25.5
Berry, James, 16.4
Betancourt, Jeanne, 1.4
Bierne, Barbara, 25.6
Bird, E. J., 18.5
Birdseye, Tom, 2.8
Blair, Cynthia, 3.2
Blake, Jeanne, 24.2
Blassingame, Wyatt, 11.4
Blue, Rose, 3.3
Blumberg, Rhoda, 22.6
Bober, Natalie S., 11.5
Bode, Janet, 21.6, 24.3
Booth, Nicholas, 19.3
Bornstein, Sandy, 20.2
Boss, David, 9.25
Boston Children's Hospital, 24.4
Bowermaster, Jon, 20.30
Bowman-Kruhm, Mary, 24.41
Boyd, Brendan, 9.12
Bradbury, Ray, 15.4
Brandel, Marc, 15.5
Branley, Franklyn M., 19.4
Branscum, Robbie, 1.5
Brennan, J. H., 13.6
Brenner, Richard J., 9.13, 9.14
Briggs, Carole S., 11.6, 19.5
Brittain, Bill, 3.4, 14.9
Brondino, Jeanne, 24.5
Brooke, William J., 18.6
Brooks, Bruce, 2.9, 14.10
Brooks, Martha, 18.7

Title Index

Subject Index

Paleontology, 7.3, 7.17, 20.12
Panama Canal, 22.33
Parents and children, 1.31, 2.66, 2.70, 3.26,
  3.34, 4.25, 5.15, 5.29, 8.2, 8.3, 8.25,
  14.70, 24.5, 24.6, 24.10, 24.19, 24.22,
  24.23, 24.34, 24.35
Pets, 2.44
Photography, 22.3
Physical fitness, 24.39
Poetry, 3.31, 17.1–22, 23.21
Poets, 17.9
Poland, 10.11
Political change, 8.16
Political freedoms, 21.10
Politics, 11.20
Pollution, 19.8, 20.5, 20.33
Popularity, 1.9, 1.19, 2.10, 3.1, 3.12, 3.38,
  3.41, 3.45, 5.51, 15.29
Population growth, 21.14
Pornography, 21.15
Poverty, 5.26, 7.24, 7.36, 7.37
Practical jokes, 5.50
Preachers, 7.32
Pregnancy, 2.61, 4.7, 5.17, 5.18
Prehistoric humans, 13.6, 20.13
Prejudice, 3.24
Presidents, U.S., 11.4, 11.5, 11.12, 11.13,
  11.32, 11.42, 22.9, 22.11
Prisons and prison life, 11.29, 21.25
Protest, 1.1, 1.11, 2.22, 3.34, 4.10, 8.22,
  8.29, 8.37, 10.18, 10.20, 11.3
Publishing, 23.9

Race relations, 6.13–16, 7.6, 7.11, 7.13,
  7.19, 8.1, 21.8, 21.17
Racing, 9.28
Ranches, 2.62, 15.5
Rape, 24.3
Relationships, 18.21
Relatives, 1.13, 2.15
Religions and religious beliefs, 2.36, 2.42,
  2.71, 6.1, 6.11, 14.68, 16.23, 21.1, 21.11,
  26.9
Repression, 8.25
Responsibility, 1.21
Revenge, 3.7, 3.28, 7.4
Revolution, 11.34
Robots, 19.12
Rock groups, 26.4
Romance, 1.32, 2.2, 2.60, 3.2, 3.3, 3.22,
  3.35, 3.59, 3.63, 4.1, 4.2, 4.4–20, 4.22–
  29, 4.31, 4.32, 5.31, 5.34, 5.56, 5.57, 6.3,
  6.12, 7.1, 8.27, 10.12, 13.19, 14.54,
  15.24, 15.33, 15.56, 15.59, 15.70, 15.73,
  16.24, 16.28, 16.29, 24.29

Running away, 1.8, 2.63, 5.2, 5.20, 5.28,
  5.47, 6.17, 7.9, 8.4, 8.20, 15.53, 15.62
Rural life, 1.5, 1.24, 2.13, 2.31, 2.32, 2.37,
  2.41, 2.47, 3.53, 7.24, 7.25, 7.29, 7.35,
  8.7, 14.46, 18.5, 21.1, 21.2
Russia, 10.1, 11.25

Scavenger hunts, 13.13
School, 3.25, 3.37, 15.37, 15.70, 17.6,
  18.18, 23.24, 24.24
Science experiments, 19.1, 19.6, 19.7,
  19.23, 20.2, 23.11, 25.19, 25.21, 25.25
Science fiction, 14.1–4, 14.6, 14.8, 14.10,
  14.11, 14.14, 14.15, 14.17, 14.22, 14.24,
  14.26, 14.27, 14.30, 14.32, 14.38, 14.45,
  14.48, 14.54, 14.55, 14.57, 14.59, 14.61,
  14.63, 14.64, 14.66, 14.69–72, 14.76–78
Scientific classification, 20.16
Scientific discoveries, 19.4, 19.11
Scientists, 20.15
Scuba diving, 20.28
Sea mammals, 14.60, 20.18
Secrets, 3.41, 3.44
Self-discovery, 1.1, 1.4, 1.7, 1.9, 1.10, 1.12,
  1.20, 1.26, 1.28, 1.31, 2.10, 2.30, 2.32,
  2.49, 2.70, 3.13, 3.52, 4.1, 4.3, 4.13,
  4.20, 5.1, 5.15, 5.23, 5.30, 5.45, 5.48,
  6.10, 6.18, 8.28, 9.5, 13.14
Self-help, 24.6, 24.13, 24.33, 24.41, 25.11,
  25.24
Self-image, 1.28, 2.67, 3.4, 3.6, 3.45, 4.16,
  4.20, 4.21, 5.7, 5.9, 8.3, 13.18, 15.48
Sex education, 24.2, 24.4, 24.8, 24.9, 24.15,
  24.17, 24.27, 24.30, 24.31
Sex roles, 1.5, 1.12, 1.25, 2.13, 2.16, 3.6,
  3.29, 3.30, 7.14, 7.31, 7.38, 9.3, 12.4,
  24.42
Sexual assault, 5.41, 24.3, 24.36
Shark hunting, 13.17, 20.29
Sharks, 20.28
Shells, 20.16
Ships and sailors, 10.3, 13.4, 16.20, 22.2,
  22.5
Shopping, 24.33
Shorelines, 20.7
Short stories, 18.1–29
Show business, 26.19
Single-parent families, 2.73, 11.19
Sisters, 2.3, 2.75, 2.76, 3.16, 3.64, 4.14,
  4.30, 4.32, 5.51, 8.34, 15.14
Sisters and brothers, 2.12, 2.17, 2.18, 2.25
Sixteenth century, 8.35
Skating, 3.62, 15.40
Slavery, 7.8, 7.10, 8.23, 11.29, 11.30, 16.31,
  22.20

Contributors

Standing, from left: Susan Rakow, Anne Sherrill, Maryann Eeds, C. Anne Webb. Seated, from left: June Harris, Alleen Pace Nilsen, Mary-Lynn Thomas, Carole A. Williams. Not pictured: Marie Donelson, Diane Freeman, Beverly Merrill. *Photo by Anna Meacham.*

Marie Donelson teaches English and journalism at Horizon High School in Paradise Valley, Arizona.

Maryann Eeds teaches courses in children's literature and reading at Arizona State University. Many of her students contributed annotations to this booklist.

Diane Freeman is a reading teacher at Barry Goldwater High School in Phoenix, Arizona.

June Harris is a reading specialist in the Department of English at East Texas State University in Commerce. She mostly read books in science fiction and fantasy.

Beverly Merrill is a language arts supervisor for the Mesa, Arizona, Public Schools.

Committee chair **Alleen Pace Nilsen** is a professor of English education and is Assistant Vice President for Academic Affairs at Arizona State University. She was the founding editor of *News from ALAN*, now *The ALAN Review*.

Susan Rakow is a seventh-grade language arts teacher at Beachwood Middle School in Beachwood, Ohio, as well as a doctoral student at Kent State University.

Anne Sherrill is a professor of English at East Tennessee State University, where she teaches children's and adolescent literature. She is coauthor of *Voices of Readers: How We Came to Love Books* with G. Robert Carlson.

Mary-Lynn Thomas is currently a reading specialist at Waukesha North High School in Wisconsin. In addition to teaching, she is enrolled in a doctoral program in curriculum and instruction at Marquette University.

C. Anne Webb is a seventh- and eighth-grade language arts teacher at Buerkle Junior High School in St. Louis. She is former president of the Assembly on Literature for Adolescents of the National Council of Teachers of English.

Carole A. Williams is a teacher and language arts coordinator for the Mehlville School District in suburban St. Louis. She has used books from the booklist with all levels of students.